D0717039

Torey Hayden

One Child
The Tiger's Child

HARPER
element

Excerpts from *The Little Prince* by Antoine de Saint-Exupéry, copyright 1943 and renewed 1971 by Harcourt Brace & Company, reprinted by permission of the publisher. Lines from "The Stolen Child" by W. B. Yeats are from *The Poems of W. B. Yeats: A New Editing*, edited by Richard J. Finneran (New York: Macmillan, 1983).

HarperElement
An Imprint of HarperCollins*Publishers*
77–85 Fulham Palace Road,
Hammersmith, London W6 8JB

The website address is: www.thorsonselement.com

and *HarperElement* are trademarks of
HarperCollins*Publishers* Ltd

This omnibus edition published by Harper Element 2008
Reprinted 2008

One Child © Torey Hayden 1980
Tiger's Child © Torey Hayden 1995

Torey Hayden asserts the moral right to
be identified as the author of this work.

A catalogue record of this book is
available from the British Library

ISBN 978 0 00 783493 8

Printed and bound in Great Britain by
Clays Ltd, St Ives plc

One Child

To Sheila R., of course.

I am asked repeatedly about
the poem on my office wall.
It seems only right that
they should know the child
who wrote it. And I
only hope I have been
half as good a writer.

Prologue

For the better part of my adult life I have been working with emotionally disturbed children. The autumn of my freshman year in college I took a volunteer position in a day program for disturbed and disadvantaged preschoolers. From that season I have remained captivated by the perplexing aspects of mental illness in childhood. Since that time I have acquired three degrees; devoted several years as a teacher's aide, a teacher, a university instructor and a psychiatric researcher; lived in five states; and worked in private day-care centers, public schools, locked psychiatric wards and state institutions, all the while pursuing the elusive answers to these children, the magic keys that will finally open them to my understanding. Yet, within me, I have long known there are no keys, and that for some children, even love will never be enough. But belief in the human soul escapes all reason and flies beyond the frail fingers of our knowledge.

I am often asked about my work. Perhaps the commonest question is Isn't it frustrating? Isn't it frustrating, the college student asks, to live day to day with violence, poverty, drug and alcohol addiction, sexual and physical abuse, neglect and apathy? Isn't it frustrating, the regular classroom teacher asks, to work so hard for so little in return? Isn't it frustrating, they all ask, to know your greatest success will probably never have more than an approximation of normalcy; to know that these very little children have been sentenced to live a life which, by our standards, will never be productive, contributing, or normal? Isn't it frustrating?

No. No, it isn't really. They are simply children, frustrating at times as all children are. But they are also gratifyingly compassionate and hauntingly perceptive. Madness alone seems to allow the whole truth to be spoken.

But these children are more. They are courageous. While we turn on the evening news to hear of new excitements and conquests on some distant front, we miss the very real dramas that play themselves out among us. This is unfortunate, because there is a bravery here unsurpassed by any outside event. Some of these children live with such haunted nightmares in their heads that every move is fraught with unknown terror. Some live with such violence and perversity that it cannot be captured in words. Some live without the dignity accorded animals. Some live without love. Some live without hope. Yet they endure. And for the most part they accept, not knowing any other way.

This book tells of only one child. It was not written to evoke pity. Nor was it intended to bring praise on one teacher. Nor to depress those who have found peace in not knowing. Instead, it is an answer to the question of frustration in working with the mentally ill. It is a song to the human soul, because this little girl is like all my children. Like all of us. She is a survivor.

Chapter One

I should have known.

The article was a small one, just a few paragraphs stuck on page six under the comics. It told of a six-year-old girl who had abducted a neighborhood child. On that cold November evening, she had taken the three-year-old boy, tied him to a tree in a nearby woodlot and burned him. The boy was currently in a local hospital in critical condition. The girl had been taken into custody.

I read the article in the same casual manner that I read the rest of the newspaper and felt an offhand what-is-this-world-coming-to revulsion. Then later in the day it came back to me while I was washing the dishes. I wondered what the police had done with the girl. Could you put a six-year-old in jail? I had random Kafkaesque visions of the child knocking about in our old, drafty city jail. I thought about it only in a faceless, impersonal manner. But I should have known.

I should have known that no teacher would want a six-year-old with that background in his or her classroom. No parent would want a child like that attending school with his or her child. No one would want that kid loose. I should have known she would end up in my program.

I taught what was affectionately referred to in our school district as the "garbage class." It was the last year before the effort to mainstream special children would begin; it was the last year to pigeonhole all the odd children into special classes. There were classes for the emotionally disturbed, classes for the physically handicapped, classes for the behaviorally disordered, classes for the learning disabled, and then there was my class. I had the eight who were left over, the eight who defied classification. I was the last stop before the institution. It was the class for young human refuse.

The spring before I had been teaching as a resource person, supplying help to emotionally disturbed and learning disabled children who attended regular classrooms part of the day. I had been in the district for some time in a variety of capacities; so I had not been surprised when Ed Somers, the Director of Special Education, had approached me in May and had asked if I would be interested in teaching the garbage class the next fall. He knew I had had experience with severely disturbed children and that I liked small children.

And that I liked a challenge. He chuckled self-consciously after saying that, aware of how contrived the flattery sounded, but he was desperate enough to try it anyway.

I had said yes, but not without reservations. However, I longed for my own classroom again with my own set of kids. I also wanted to be free of an unintentionally oppressive principal. He was a good-hearted man, but we did not see things in the same way. He objected to my casual dress, to my disorderly classroom, and to my children addressing me by my first name. These were minor issues, but like all small things, they became the major sore spots. I knew that by doing Ed the favor of taking this class, allowances would be made for my jeans and my sloppiness and my familiarity with the kids. So I accepted the job, confident that I could overcome any of the obstacles it presented.

My confidence flagged considerably between the signing of the contract and the end of the first day of school. The first blow came when I learned I was to be placed back into the same school I had been in and under the same principal. Now not only did he have to worry about me but also about eight very peculiar children. Immediately we were all placed in a room in the annex which we shared with the gymnasium and nothing else. We were totally isolated from the rest of the school. My room would have been large enough if the children had been older and more self-contained. But for eight small children and two adults, plus ten desks, three tables, four bookcases and countless chairs that seemed to mate and multiply in the night, the room was hopelessly crowded. So out went the teacher's desk, two bookshelves, a file cabinet, all but nine little chairs and eventually all the student desks. Moreover, the room was long and narrow with only one window at the far end. It had originally been designed as a testing and counseling space, so it was wood-paneled and carpeted. I would have gladly traded all that grandeur for a room that did not need lights on all day or for a linoleum floor more impervious to spills and stains.

The state law required that I have a full-time aide because I was carrying the maximum load of severely disturbed children. I had been hoping for one of the two competent women I had worked with the year before, but no, I received a newly hired one. In our community, which had in close proximity a state hospital, a state prison and a huge migrant workers' camp, there was a staggering welfare list. Consequently, unskilled jobs were usually reserved for the unemployed listed with Social Services. Although I did not consider my aide position an unskilled one, Welfare did, and the first day of school I was confronted with a tall, gangly Mexican-American who spoke more Spanish than English. Anton was twenty-nine and had never graduated from high school. Well, no, he admitted, he had never worked with children. Well, no, he never especially wanted to. But you see, he explained, you had to take the job they gave you or you lost benefits. He dropped his gargantuan frame onto one of the kindergarten-sized chairs, mentioning that if this job worked out, it would be the first time he had ever stayed north all winter instead of following the other migrant workers back to California. So then we were two. Later, after the school year started, I acquired a fourteen-year-old junior high school student who devoted her two hours of study hall to coming over and working with my class each day. Thus armed, I met the children.

I had no unusual expectations for these eight. I had been in the business long enough to have lost my naiveté. Besides, I had learned long before that even when I was shocked or surprised, my best defense was to never show it. It was safer that way.

The first to arrive that morning in August had been Peter. Eight years old and a husky black with a scraggly Afro, Peter had a robust body that belied the deteriorating neurological condition that caused severe seizures and increasingly violent behavior. Peter burst into the room in anger, cursing and shouting. He hated school, he hated me, he hated this class and he wasn't going to stay in this shitty room and I couldn't make him.

Next was Tyler, who startled me by being a girl. She slunk in behind her mother, her dark curly head down. Tyler was also eight and had already tried to kill herself twice. The last time the drain cleaner she had drunk had eaten away part of her esophagus. Now her throat bore an artificial tube and numerous red-rimmed surgical scars in ghoulish testimony to her skill.

Max and Freddie were both hauled in screaming.

Max, who was a big, strapping, blond six-year-old, carried the label of infantile autism. He cried and squawked and twirled around the room flapping his hands. His mother apologized because he always acted so unpredictably to change. She looked at me wearily and let the relief to be free of him for a few hours show too plainly in her eyes. Freddie was seven and weighed 94 pounds. The fat rolled over the edges of his clothing and squeezed out between the buttons on his shirt. Once allowed to flop on the floor, he ceased crying, ceased everything, in fact, to lie lifelessly in a heap. One report said that he, too, was autistic. One stated that he was profoundly retarded. One admitted not knowing.

I had known Sarah, age seven, for three years. I had worked with her when she was in preschool. A victim of physical and sexual abuse, Sarah was an angry, defiant child. She had been electively mute throughout the previous year when she had been in a special first grade class at another school. She had refused to talk to anyone except her mother and sister. We smiled upon seeing each other, both of us thankful for a familiar face.

A smartly dressed, middle-aged woman carried in a beautiful, doll-like child. The little girl looked like a picture from a children's fashion magazine, her soft blond hair carefully styled, her crisp dress spotless. Her name was Susannah Joy, she was six, and this was her first time in school. My heart winced. To be placed in my class upon entrance to school was not a hopeful sign. The doctors had told the parents that Susannah would never be normal; she was a childhood schizophrenic. She apparently hallucinated both visually and auditorily, and spent most of her days weeping and rocking her body back and forth. She rarely spoke and even when she did, seldom meaningfully. The mother's eyes implored me to perform the magic ritual necessary to turn her fairy child back to normal. My heart ached seeing those pleading eyes, because they signified nonacceptance. I knew the pain and agony that lay ahead for those parents as they learned that none of us would ever have the type of magic they needed for Susannah Joy.

Last to come were William and Guillermo. Both were nine. William was a lanky, pasty-faced boy haunted by fears of water and darkness and cars and vacuum cleaners and the dust under his bed. To protect himself, William engaged in elaborate rituals, compulsively touching himself or chanting little spells under his breath. Guillermo was one of the countless Mexican-American migrants who came to work in the fields each year. He was an angry boy but not uncontrollable. Unfortunately, he was also blind. At first I was stymied that he had been placed in my class, but was informed that the classes for the blind and partially sighted did not feel equipped to deal with his aggressive behaviors. Well, I thought, that made us even. I did not feel equipped to deal with his blindness.

So, then we were ten, and with Whitney, the junior high student, we were in all eleven. When first I surveyed this motley bunch of children and my

11

equally motley staff, I felt a wave of despair. How would we ever be a class? How could I ever get them doing math or all the other miracles that needed accomplishing in nine months? Three were not toilet trained, two more had accidents. Three could not talk, one wouldn't. Two would not shut up. One could not see. Certainly it was more of a challenge than I had bargained for.

But we managed. Anton learned to change diapers. Whitney learned to get urine out of the carpet. And I learned Braille. The principal, Mr. Collins, learned not to come over to the annex. Ed Somers learned to hide. And so we became a class.

By Christmas vacation we belonged to one another and I was beginning to look forward to each new day. Sarah had begun to talk regularly again; Max was learning his letters; Tyler was smiling occasionally; Peter didn't fly into rages quite so often; William could pass all the light switches in the hallway to the lunchroom and not say one charm to protect himself; Guillermo was begrudgingly learning Braille. And Susannah Joy and Freddie? Well, we were still trying with them.

I had read the newspaper article in late November and had forgotten it. But I shouldn't have. I should have known that sooner or later we would be twelve.

Ed Somers appeared in my room the day after school resumed following Christmas vacation. He came early, his kind face swathed in that apologetic expression that I was beginning to realize meant trouble for me. It was the expression attached to things like not getting a special tutor for Guillermo, or yet another hopeless report from the newest doctor Susannah's parents had found. Ed wanted things to be different; I believe he genuinely did, which made it impossible for me to be angry with him.

"There's going to be a new child in your class," he said, his face mirroring his hesitance to tell me.

I stared at him a long moment, not comprehending. I already had the state-allowed maximum and had never anticipated having another child. "I have eight now, Ed."

"I know, Torey. But this is a special case. We don't have any place to put her. Your class is the only option we have."

"But I've got eight kids already," I repeated dumbly. "That is all I can have."

Ed looked pained. He was a big bear of a man, tall and muscular like a football player but padded with the extra softness of middle age. His hair was nearly gone and what was left he had carefully combed across the shiny dome. But above all, Ed was gentle and I was amazed that he had ever made it to such a high position in education, a profession not known for its kind treatment of gentle people. But perhaps that was his secret, because I never failed to soften when he looked so hurt by what he was having to do to me.

"What's so special about this kid?" I asked tentatively.

"This is that girl who burned the little boy in

November. They took her out of school and made arrangements to send her to the state hospital. But there hasn't been an opening in the children's unit yet. So the kid's been home a month and getting into all sorts of trouble. Now the social worker is beginning to ask why we aren't doing anything for her."

"Can't they put her on homebound?" I asked. A number of my children had been taught by home-bound, a term referring to the practice of sending a teacher into the home to teach a child when for some reason he could not attend school. Often, severely disturbed children were handled in this manner until appropriate placement could be found.

Ed frowned at the floor. "No one is willing to work with her."

"The kid's six years old," I said in surprise. "They're scared of a six-year-old?"

He shrugged, his silence telling me more about this child than words could have.

"But I already have all the children I can handle."

"Choose a child to be transferred. We have to put this child in here, Torey. It will just be tempo-rary. Until a place opens up at the state hospital. But we have to put her in here. This is the only place equipped to handle her. This is the only place she'll fit."

"You mean I'm the only one idiotic enough to take her."

"You can pick whom you want transferred."

14

"When is she coming?"

"The eighth."

By that point the children were beginning to arrive and I had to prepare for our first day back from vacation. Sensing my need to get to work, Ed nodded and left. He knew that, if given time, I would do it. Ed knew that, for all my bravado, I was a pushover.

After telling Anton the news, I looked over the children. As we went through the day I kept asking myself who should go. Guillermo was the obvious choice, simply because I was least equipped to teach him. But what about Freddie or Susannah Joy? Neither was making progress of much note. Anyone could lug them around and change their pants. Or maybe Tyler. She wasn't so suicidal now; she hardly ever spoke of killing herself anymore; she no longer drew those black-crayoned pictures. A resource teacher could probably handle her. I looked at each one of them, wondering where they would go and how they would make it. And how our room would be without them. I knew in my heart none of them would survive the rigors of a less-sheltered class. None of them was ready. Nor was I ready to give them up, nor give up on them.

"Ed?" I clutched the receiver tightly because it kept slipping in my sweating hand. "I don't want to transfer any of my kids. We're doing so well together. I can't choose any one of them."

"Torey, I told you we have to put that girl in

there. I'm really sorry. I hate to do it to you, but there isn't any other place."

I stared morosely at the bulletin board beside the phone with all its proclamations of events my children never could attend. I was feeling used. "Can I have nine?"

"Will you take nine?"

"It's against the law. Do I get another aide?"

"We'll see."

"Does that mean yes?"

"I hope so," Ed replied. "But we'll just have to see. Will you need another desk?"

"What I need is another teacher. Or another room."

"Will you settle for another desk?"

"No. I don't have any desks. There wasn't room for the first eight. So we just sit on the carpet or at the tables. No, I don't need another desk. Just send me the kid."

Chapter Two

She arrived January eighth. Between the time I had agreed to accept her and the morning she arrived, I had heard nothing, received no files, learned no background. All I knew was what I had read in a two-paragraph article under the comics on page six a month and a half earlier. But I suppose it did not matter. Nothing could have prepared me adequately for what I got.

Ed Somers brought her, holding tightly on to her wrist and dragging her behind him. Mr. Collins also came out to the annex with Ed. "This is going to be your new teacher," Ed explained. "And this will be your new room."

We looked at one another. Her name was Sheila. She was six and a half, almost; a tiny little mite of a thing with matted hair, hostile eyes and a very bad smell. I was surprised she was so small. I had expected something bigger. The three-year-old must have been nearly as tall as she was. Clad in worn denim overalls and a well-faded boy's striped T-shirt, she looked like one of those kids in the Save the Children ads.

"Hi, my name's Torey," I said in my friendliest teacher's voice while reaching for her hand. But she did not respond. I ended up taking the limp wrist from Ed. "This is Sarah. She's our welcome person. She'll show you around."

Sarah extended a hand but Sheila remained impassive, her eyes darting from face to face. "Come on, kid." Sarah grabbed her wrist.

"Her name is Sheila," I said. But Sheila bristled at these acts of familiarity and yanked her hand away, retreating backwards. She turned to run, but Mr. Collins was fortunately standing in the doorway and Sheila ran right into him. I captured one arm and dragged her back into the classroom.

"We'll leave you," Ed said, that apologetic look creeping across his face. "I left her cumulative folder in the office for you."

Anton slipped the bolt lock into place after closing the door behind Ed and Mr. Collins as they left. I dragged Sheila across the room to my chair where we always held morning discussion and set her on the floor in front of me. The other children cautiously gathered around us. Now we were twelve.

We always began each morning with "discussion." Ours was a school that enjoyed saying the pledge to the flag and singing patriotic songs before starting classes. I felt patriotism was not an appropriate topic for children who could not even communicate basic needs; however, the school board took a dim view of anyone who refused this display of nationalism. There were too many other issues I had to fight that were more important to me than the pledge of allegiance. So I compromised and created discussion. The children all came from such chaotic and disrupted homes that we needed something to reunite us each morning after being apart. And I had wanted something which would stimulate communication and develop verbal understanding. The first thing we did was the pledge, and I put it to good use by having one child lead it, which meant he had to learn it. Even this process was valuable because it presented words in an organized sense that implied meaning. Afterwards I started discussion with a "topic." Usually topic explored feelings, such as talking about things that made one happy; or topic was a roundtable for solving problems, such as what would one do if he saw someone else hurt himself. We went from there as a jumping-off point, making sure that everyone had a chance to participate. In the beginning I had brought all the topics in, but after the first month or two the children had their own suggestions and I had not started the discussion in ages.

After topic, I let each child have a few moments to tell what had happened to him since the release of school the previous day or Friday. These two aspects of morning discussion had gotten increasingly livelier, and even Susannah participated meaningfully on occasion. The kids all had a lot to say and I was hard put some days to terminate the activity. Afterwards, I outlined a schedule of the day and then we closed with a song. I had a repertoire of action songs that I could sing with more gusto than tune, usually pulling one of the kids through the actions puppetlike. The children loved that and we always ended laughing, even on those days when we had not come in merry.

So this morning I gathered the children around me. "Kids, this is Sheila, and she's going to join our class."

"How come?" Peter asked suspiciously. "You never told us we was getting a new girl."

"Yes, I did, Peter. Remember how we rehearsed last Friday things to show Sheila that we're glad she's with us? Remember what we did?"

"Well, I'm not glad she's with us," he replied. "I liked us just the way we was." He placed his hands over his ears to shut me out and began rocking.

"It'll take some getting used to, I imagine. But we will." I patted Sheila's shoulder and she pulled away. "Now, who's got a topic?"

Everyone sat around me on the floor. No one spoke.

"No one has a topic? Well then, I've got one: what do you suppose it feels like when you're new and don't know anyone, or maybe you want to be part of a group and no one wants you to? How's that feel inside?"

"Bad," Guillermo said. "That happened to me once and I felt bad."

"Can you tell us about it?" I asked.

Suddenly Peter leaped to his feet. "She stinks, teacher." He backed away from Sheila. "She stinks terrible and I don't want her sitting with us. She'll stink me up."

Sheila regarded him blackly but did not speak or move. She had folded herself up into a little lump, her arms wrapped tightly around her knees.

Sarah stood up and moved around to where Peter had reseated himself. "She does stink, Torey. She smells like pee."

Good manners were certainly not our forte. I was not surprised by the lack of tact, but as always I was dismayed. Silencing their clear-eyed perceptions of the world was an impossibility. For every step forward I made in teaching good manners, I took two back and six to the side. "How do you suppose that feels, Peter, to have someone say you stink?"

"Well, she does stink terrible," Peter retorted.

"That's not what I asked. I asked how you'd feel if someone said that to you?"

"I wouldn't want to stink everybody out of the class, that's for sure."

"That's not what I asked."

"It'd hurt my feelings," Tyler volunteered, bouncing up on her knees. Any displays of anger or disagreement frightened Tyler tremendously and sent her into rounds of appeasement, acting overly mature for her eight years and motherly toward those who disagreed.

"How about you, Sarah?" I asked. "How would you feel?"

Sarah stared at her fingers, reluctant to look at me. "I wouldn't like it too good."

"No, I don't think any of us would. What might be a better way of handling the problem?"

"You could learn her in private that she stinked," William offered. "Then she wouldn't get embarrassed."

"You could learn her not to," Guillermo added.

"We could all plug our noses," Peter said. He wasn't quite willing to admit yet that he had been inappropriate in his remarks.

"That wouldn't help any, Peter," William said. "Then you couldn't breathe."

"You could too. You could breathe through your mouth."

I laughed. "Everybody, try Peter's suggestion. Peter, you too." All the children except Sheila plugged their noses and breathed through their mouths. I urged her to try too, but she steadfastly refused to unfold. In a few moments we were all laughing, even Freddie and Max, at the funny faces we made. All of us, except Sheila. I was beginning to fear that she saw this as a joke at her expense and I hastened to explain it wasn't. She ignored me, not even looking at me. This was the way we solved our problems, I told her.

"How's this make you feel?" I asked her at last. There was a long silence, pregnant with our waiting. The other children became impatient.

"Don't she talk?" Guillermo asked.

"I used to not talk either, remember that?" Sarah offered. "Back when I was mad, I used to

22

never talk to nobody." She looked over at Sheila. "I used to never talk, Sheila. So I know how it feels."

"Well, I think we've put Sheila in the hot seat enough for now. Let's give her some time to get used to us, okay?"

We went on with the rest of morning discussion and finished with a rousing chorus of "You Are My Sunshine." Freddie clapped gleefully; Guillermo directed with his hands; Peter sang at the top of his lungs; and I manipulated Tyler like a rag doll. But Sheila sat, her face stormy, her little body a solid lump in the way of the dancers.

After discussion we dispersed for math activities. Anton began orienting the others while I showed Sheila around the room. Actually, I did not show her. I had to pick her up and carry her around from place to place because she would not move. I was thankful I was not teaching adolescents. Then when I got her where I wanted her, she refused to look, covering her face with her hands. But I hauled her around anyway, determined she become part of us. I showed her her cubby and her coat hook. I introduced her to Charles, the iguana, and Benny, the snake, and Onions, the rabbit who bit if you bothered him too much. I pointed out the plants we had started before Christmas that I had had to come in on vacation to water; and the stories we read before lunch every day; and the dishes we cooked with on Wednesday afternoons. I showed her our aquarium and our toys. I lifted her up to view the scene from our lone window. All this was accomplished by lugging her from place to place and chattering as if she were very interested in what I had to say. But if she was, she did not let me know. She remained a dead weight in my arms, rigid and tense against my body. And she stank like an outhouse on a muggy July afternoon.

Finally I deposited Sheila on a chair at the table and got out a math paper. This evoked her first response. She grabbed the paper, wadded it up and threw it at me. I took another. She repeated the action. I took another. Again it was flung in my face. I knew I would run out of papers before she would run out of energy. So I took her on my lap, wrapping an arm around her wiry body so she could not get her hands free. I set another math paper down. It was simple addition; two plus one, one plus four, nothing fancy. I pulled a tray of blocks toward me with my free arm and spilled them on the table.

"Okay, now we do math," I stated. "First problem, two plus one." I showed her two blocks and added a third. "How much is that? Let's count them." She averted her head, straining her stiff body against me. "Can you count, Sheila?" No response. "Come on, I'll help. One, two, three. Two plus one is three." I picked up a pencil. "Here, we'll write it down."

Everything was a battle. I had to pry a hand free from her body, then uncurl her fingers, then place the pencil in it. Suddenly those tightly clenched fingers lost their strength and the pencil slid effortlessly out of them and onto the floor. In the moment I bent to pick up the pencil she had grabbed two blocks with her free hand and flung them across the room. I clutched at the hand, shoved the pencil back into it and tried to recurl her fingers around it and grip it with my own hand before she could let the pencil drop again. But she had me at a disadvantage; I was left-handed and forced to use that arm to subdue her in my lap. Having to use my right to perform all these dexterous movements, I was just not fast enough. Perhaps I would not have been even with my left. She was skilled at this little bit of guerilla warfare and the pencil fell again. After another struggle I gave up.

"Evidently you don't want to do math just yet. Okay, you may sit. I will say to you that everyone in here does his work and tries his best. But we're not going to fight about it. You want to sit, you sit." I lugged her over to the corner where I isolated the children when they became too overstimulated and needed to regain control, or when they acted miserably, trying to command attention. I pulled the chair out and sat Sheila in it. Then I returned to the other children.

In a few moments I looked up. "Sheila, if you're ready to join us, you may come over."

She sat, her face to the wall and did not move. I let her sit. In another few minutes, I reissued the conditions. And again a little later. It was obvious that she was not going to do anything I wanted. I went over and pulled the chair away from the corner and into the room. Then I went back to the others. If she wanted to sit, she could. However, I was not going to let her isolate herself from us. If she sat, it would be right out in the middle of us.

Our morning routine went as usual. Sheila participated in nothing. Once ensconced upon that small wooden chair, she would not move, but instead drew in upon herself, folding knees up under her chin and wrapping her arms around them. She got off the chair one time to use the bathroom but returned to her seat to resume her contorted position. Even during recess she sat, only this time on the freezing cement. I had never seen such a motionless child. But her eyes followed me continuously everywhere I went. Brooding, angry, bitter eyes never left my face.

When lunch came, Anton helped the children prepare for their trek from the annex over to the cafeteria. Sheila had been lugged into line but I came and got her, taking her skinny wrist and pulling her out of the line. We waited until the others had gone. I looked down at her and she up at me. I thought that for a brief moment I saw an emotion other than hate flicker through those eyes, something other than anger. Fear?

"Come over here." I tugged her to the table and set her down in a chair opposite me. "You and I have something to get straight."

She glowered at me, her tiny shoulders humping up under the worn shirt.

"There aren't a lot of rules in this room. There are just two really, unless we need to make special rules for special times. But generally there are just two. One is that you can't hurt anybody in here. Not anybody else. And not yourself. The second is that you always try to do your best job. That's the rule I don't think you have straight yet."

She lowered her head slightly but kept her eyes on me. The legs came up and once again she began to fold in upon herself.

"You see, one of the things you have to do in here is talk. I know that's hard when you're not used to doing it. But in here you talk, that's part of your best job. The first time is always the hardest, and sometimes it kind of makes you cry. Well, that's okay to do in here. But you have to talk. And sooner or later you will. It'll be a lot better if you do it sooner." I looked at her, trying to match her unflinching stare. "Is that clear to you?"

Her face blackened with anger. I was fearful of what might happen if all that hate got loose, but I tried to squash the fear, not letting it show in my eyes. She was a good reader of eyes.

I had always felt strongly about setting expectations for my kids. Some of my colleagues had been skeptical of my directness with the children, pleading the frailty of their egos. I disagreed. While certainly all of them had sad, well-trampled little selves, none of them was frail. Much to the contrary. The fact that they had survived long enough to be where they were after what most of them had been through was testimony to their strength. However, all of them lived chaotic lives and brought chaos on others by the nature of their disturbance. I did not feel it was my right to add to the chaos by leaving them to guess what I expected of them. I found establishing a structure a useful and productive method with all the children because it erased the fuzziness of our relationship. Obviously, they had already shown they could not handle their own limits without help, or they never would have arrived in my class to begin with. As soon as the time came that they could, I began the process of transferring the power to them. But in the beginning I wanted there to be no doubt about what I expected from them.

So Sheila and I sat in icy silence while she digested this bit of information. I did not have the endurance to stare her down, nor did I feel the need to do so. After a few moments I rose from my chair and went to collect the math papers from the correction basket.

"You can't make me talk," she said.

I continued shuffling through the papers trying to find the marking pen. Three-fourths of being a good teacher is timing.

"I said you can't make me talk. There don't be no way you can do that."

I looked over at her.

"You can't make me."

"No, I can't." I smiled. "But you will. That's part of your job in here."

"I don't like you."

"You don't have to."

"I hate you."

I did not respond. That was one of those statements that I find is often best left unanswered. So

I continued my search for the pen, wondering who had walked off with it this time.

"You can't make me do nothing in here. You can't make me talk."

"Maybe not." I dropped the papers back into the basket and came over to her. "Shall we go to lunch?" I extended a hand to her. Some of the anger had dissipated to be replaced by a less readable emotion. Then without further urging she got off the chair and came with me, careful not to touch me.

Chapter Three

After escorting Sheila to the lunchroom I retired to the office to have a look at her file. I wanted to know what others had done with this perplexing child. From watching her, it was apparent that she did not suffer from the crippling, unexplainable disturbances such as Max and Susannah displayed. Instead, she was in surprisingly good control of her behavior, more so than most of the children coming into my class. Behind those hate-filled eyes I saw a perceptive and most likely intelligent little girl. She had to be in order to manipulate her world with such conscious effort. But I wanted to know what had been tried before.

The file was surprisingly thin for one that had worked its way to me. Most of my children had thick, paper-bloated folders, glutted with verbose opinions of dozens of doctors and therapists and judges and social workers. It was plain to me every time I read one of those files that the people filling them never had to work with the child day in and day out for hours at a time. The words on the papers were erudite discourses, but they did not tell a desperate teacher or frightened parent how to help. I doubt anyone could write such words. In reality, each of the children was so different and grew in such unpredictable ways that one day's experience was the only framework for planning the next. There were no textbooks or university courses specializing in Max or William or Peter.

But Sheila's file was thin, only a few bits of paper: a family history, test results and a standard data form from Special Services. I paged through the social worker's report of the family. Like so many others in my room, it was filled with lurid details that, despite my experience, my middle-class mind could not fully comprehend. Sheila lived alone with her father in a one-room shack in the migrant camp. The house had no heat, no plumbing, and no electricity. Her mother had abandoned Sheila two years earlier but had taken a younger son. She now lived in California, the form stated, although no one actually knew her whereabouts. The mother had been only fourteen when Sheila was born, two months after a forced wedding, while her father was thirty. I shook my head in grim amazement. The mother would only be twenty years old now, barely more than a child herself.

The father had spent most of Sheila's early years

in prison on assault-and-battery charges. Since his release two-and-a-half years before, he had also had stays at the state hospital for alcoholism and drug dependency. Sheila had been shifted around among relatives and friends of the family, mostly on the mother's side, before finally being abandoned on a roadside, where she was found clinging to a chain-link fence that separated the freeway lanes. Taken to the juvenile center, Sheila, then four, was discovered to have numerous abrasions and healed multiple fractures, all the results of abuse. She was released to her father's custody and a child-protection worker was assigned to the case.

A court statement appended to the file said that the judge felt it was best to leave the child in her natural home. A county-appointed physician had scrawled across the bottom that her small size probably resulted from malnutrition, but otherwise she was a healthy Caucasian female with well-healed scars and fractures. Loose behind these two assessments was a memo from the county's consulting psychiatrist with the single statement: Chronic Maladjustment to Childhood. I smiled at it in spite of myself; what an astute conclusion this man had drawn. How helpful to us all. The only normal reaction to a childhood like Sheila's would be chronic maladjustment. If one did adjust to such pornography of life, it would surely be a testimony to one's insanity.

The test results were even more obscure. Beside each title on the battery, written in tight, frustrated printing: Refused. The bottom summary simply stated she was untestable and underlined the fact twice.

The Special Services questionnaire contained only demographics. The father had filled out the form and he had been in prison all those crucial years. She had been born with no apparent complications in a local hospital. Nothing was known of her early developmental history. She had attended three schools in her short education history, not including the one she was in now. All the moves had resulted from her uncontrollable behavior. At home she was reported to eat and sleep within the normal limits. But she wet the bed every night and she sucked her thumb. She had no friends among the migrant workers' children at the camp; nor did she appear to have any solid relationships with adults. The father wrote that she was a loner, hostile and unfriendly even to him. She spoke erratically at home, usually only when she was angry. She never cried. I stopped and reread that statement. She never cried? I could not conceive of a six-year-old who did not cry. He must have meant she seldom cried. That must have been a mistake.

I continued reading. Her father saw her as a wayward child and disciplined her frequently, mostly by spanking or taking away privileges. I wondered what sort of privileges there were in her life to be taken away. In addition to the burning incident, she had been reprimanded for setting fires in the migrant camp and for smearing feces in the restroom of a bus station. By six-and-a-half,

Sheila had encountered the police three times.

I stared at the file and its bits of random information. She was not going to be an easy child to love, because she worked at being unlovable. Nor was she going to be an easy child to teach. But she was not unreachable. Despite her exterior, Sheila was indeed probably more reachable than Susannah Joy or Freddie, because there was no indication that her functioning was garbled with retardation, or neurological impairments or other mysteries of the brain. From what I could glean, Sheila was a normally functioning child in that respect. Which made the battle ahead for me even harder because I knew it rested solely with us on the outside. We had no cute phrases, no curtains like autism or brain damage to hide behind when we failed with the Sheilas. We had only ourselves. Deep down behind those hostile eyes was a very little girl who had already learned that life really isn't much fun for anybody; and the best way to avoid further rejection was to make herself as objectionable as possible. Then it would never come as a surprise to find herself unloved. Only a simple fact.

Anton came in while I was paging through the file. He pulled up a chair beside me and took the forms as I finished them. Despite our clumsy beginning, Anton and I had become a fully functioning team. He was an adroit worker with these children. Having spent all his life prior to this year in the fields, and still living in the migrant camp in a small hut with his wife and two sons, Anton knew much more intimately than I the world my kids came from. I had the training and the experience and the knowledge, but Anton had the instinct and the wisdom. Certain aspects of their lives I never would understand because in my existence warm houses and freedom from violence and hunger and cockroaches was my due. I had never had reason to expect otherwise. Now as an adult, I had learned that others lived differently and that this different way of life, to them, was also normal. I could accept the fact, but I could not understand it. I do not believe that anyone for whom it is not a living reality can; anyone claiming that extra measure of understanding either lies to himself or is a deluded braggart. But Anton compensated for my lack and together we had managed to build a supportive relationship. He had come to know without being told when and how and whom to help. An additional benefit was that Anton spoke Spanish, which I did not. Thus, he saved me innumerable times when Guillermo went beyond his limit of English. Now Anton sat beside me, quietly reading Sheila's folder.

"How did she do at lunch?"

He nodded without looking up from the papers. "Okay. She eats like she never sees food. But she probably doesn't. And, oh, so bad on the manners. But she sat with the children and did not fuss."

"Do you know her father out at the camp?"

"No. That's the other side of the camp, where the whites live. The junkies are all over there. We never go over."

Whitney came in and leaned over the counter. She was a pretty girl in a nondescript way: tall, slender, with hazel eyes and long, straight, dishwater-blond hair. Although Whitney was an honors student at her junior high and came from one of the community's most prominent families, she was a painfully shy girl. When she had come in the fall she had carried out all her tasks in great silence, never looking me in the eye, always smiling nervously, even when things were going wrong. The only time she did talk was to criticize her work, to put herself down or to apologize for doing everything wrong. Unfortunately, in the beginning that seemed all too true. Whitney made every mistake in the book. She dropped half a gallon of freshly mixed green tempera paint on the gym floor. She forgot Freddie in the men's room at the fairgrounds. She left the door to our room ajar one afternoon after school and Benny, the class boa constrictor, escaped and went to visit Mrs. Anderson, the first grade teacher. For me, Whitney was like having another child. If I had not been so desperate in those early months for a third set of hands to help, I might not have had the patience for her. Those first weeks I was always re-explaining, always cleaning something up, always saying, "Don't worry about it," when I did not mean it. Whitney was always crying.

But like Anton, Whitney had been worth the trouble, because she cared so much about the kids. Whitney was hopelessly devoted to us. I knew she skipped classes occasionally to stay longer with us, and she often came over in her lunch hour or after school to help me. From home she brought her own outgrown toys to give the children. She came with ideas for me that she had found in teaching magazines she read in her spare time. And always that hungry, pleading look to be appreciated. Whitney very seldom talked about the rest of her life outside my classroom. Yet, despite her affluence and the prominent name of her family, Whitney, I suspected, was no better off in some ways than the kids in the class. So I remained tolerant of her clumsiness and ineptitude and tried to make her feel a valued part of our team. Because she was.

"Did you get your new girl?" Whitney asked, stretching over the counter and causing her hair to tumble onto the papers I was reading.

"Yes, we did," I said and mentioned briefly what had transpired during the morning. That was when I heard the screaming.

I knew it was one of my children. None of the regular kids seemed to have that high vibrant note of desperation in their voices when they yelled. I looked at Anton, asking him wordlessly what was going on. Whitney went to look out the door of the office.

Tyler came careening in, wailing. She motioned out the door but her explanation was strangled in her sobs. Then she turned and ran.

All three of us sprinted after her toward the door that led to the annex. Normally over the lunch hour, lunch aides were in charge of the children. In the cold months, the kids all played inside in their rooms and the aides patrolled up and down the halls keeping order. I kept telling them that my children could not be left unattended at any time, but the aides hated supervising my room and avoided it by congregating outside the annex door and keeping an ear cocked for disaster. My children had the latest lunch hour, which meant the aides only had about twenty minutes of actual supervision. But they still protested and still refused to stay in the room with the kids. I usually ignored the aides, because I had worked hard to instill in my kids the independence to function without my physical presence. Lunch hour was a daily test of this skill. Moreover, both Anton and I desperately needed that half-hour break. Still things occasionally got out of hand.

Tyler was sobbing something out to us as we ran, something about eyes and the new girl. I came storming into a room in chaos.

Sheila stood defiantly on a chair by the aquarium. She had apparently caught the goldfish one by one and poked their eyes out with a pencil. Seven or eight of the fish lay flopping desperately on the floor around the chair, their eyes destroyed. Sheila clutched one tightly in her right fist and stood poised threateningly with the pencil in the other. A lunch aide was near her, dancing nervously about, but too frightened to attempt disarming Sheila. Sarah was wailing, Max was flying about the room flapping his arms wildly and screeching.

"Drop that!" I shouted in my most authoritative voice. Sheila glared at me and shook the pencil meaningfully. I had no doubt she would attack if at all provoked. Her eyes had the glazed wildness of a threatened animal. The fish flopped hopelessly about, leaving little bloody spots on the floor where their empty eye sockets hit. Max crunched through one on his flight around the room.

Suddenly a high-pierced shriek knifed the air. Behind us Susannah had entered the room. She has a psychotic fear of blood, of any red liquid, and would go into a frenzy of crazed screaming while darting senselessly about when she thought she saw blood or even hallucinated it. Now, seeing the fish, she bolted off across the room. Anton moved after her and I took that moment of surprise to disarm Sheila who was not so off-guard as I had suspected. She slammed the pencil into my arm with such vehemence that for a moment it stuck, waving uncertainly before falling to the ground. My mind was filled with too much confusion to feel any real pain. Freddie had joined Max in circling the room. Tyler was wailing; Guillermo hid under the table; William stood in one corner and cried. Whitney was off trying to capture Max and Freddie as they reeled around the perimeter of the room screaming. The decibel level was unbearable.

"Torey!" came William's cry. "Peter's having a seizure!" I turned to see Peter collapse to the floor. Passing Sheila to Whitney, I ran for Peter to remove the chairs among which he had fallen.

Sheila gave Whitney an audible crack in the shins and won her freedom. Within seconds she was out the door. I fell onto the floor beside Peter, still writhing in his seizure, and felt the pressure of what was happening lie upon me. It had all happened within minutes. Everyone had lost the tenuous control we fought so hard to keep. All the children except Peter were crying. Sarah, Tyler and William wailed on the sidelines, their bodies huddled together against catastrophe. Guillermo sobbed from his retreat under the table. He kept his hands protectively over his head and pleaded in Spanish for his mother. Susannah struggled frantically in Anton's arms. Max and Freddie still flew deliriously around the room, colliding with furniture and other children only to rise and resume their flight. Peter lay incoherent in my arms. I looked around. Whitney had disappeared after Sheila. The lunch aide had left long ago. We were in shambles. After months and months of careful effort, everything had fallen around our ears.

Mr. Collins and the school secretary appeared in the doorway. Normally I would have been horrified to have him see my classroom in such distress. But things had gotten completely out of control and I needed help. I had to admit that. After all the years he and I had worked together, I had managed my crazy children and we had never had a major slip. But now I had failed. Just like he always predicted. My crazies had gotten loose at last. I knew he must be thanking God he had put us in the annex where no one could see.

The secretary took Peter to the nurse's office to be sent home because he always needed to sleep after a major seizure. Mr. Collins helped me round up Freddie and Max and get them to sit in chairs. I dragged poor Guillermo out from under the table and hugged him. What this must have sounded like to him, who could not see . . . Anton was still trying to soothe Susannah Joy. Once we seemed to recapture some semblance of control, Tyler and Sarah were willing to sit down in the discussion corner and comfort each other. But William remained glued to the spot, quaking and sobbing. Mr. Collins made an effort to calm him, but he could not bring himself close enough to hug the child. We kept crunching and sliding on the dead goldfish, grinding gold scales into the carpet, the sound our shoes made stepping on them a muffled squeak. At last I had all the kids herded together and the crying had diminished. Whitney and Sheila were still gone but I couldn't let myself think of that at that particular moment.

Mr. Collins had the decency not to ask what had happened. He had simply done as I asked, his face unreadable. When I got all the children settled down, I thanked him at the door for his help and asked if he could send me Mary, one of the regular school aides, who had been such a competent helper of mine the year before. I still had one on the loose, I explained, and the afternoon would be difficult. With one extra adult, I could get around to more of the children individually and try to set things straight.

When Mary arrived, the kids helped her choose a story they liked and I went in search of Sheila. Evidently when she had bolted, she was confused by the maze of doors and hallways connecting us to the main building. Whitney had been able to secure the outside doors before Sheila found them and she had been trapped into going into the gym, more by accident than design. Whitney stood in the doorway of the huge cavernous room and Sheila was on the far side.

Tears streamed over Whitney's cheeks as she held her post. My heart ached when I saw her. This was too much to expect of a fourteen-year-old. I should never have put her in this spot. Yet, my string of miracles had run out. Two adults alone could not manage that many disturbed children. I had been surviving on good luck, and now it had finally expired.

I entered the gym, gave Whitney a pat on the shoulder, and approached Sheila. She clearly had no intention of being caught. Her eyes were wild, her face flushed with terror. Each time I moved closer, she tore off in another direction. I spoke softly, my tone gentle and coaxing. But it quivered with my own frenzy. Slowly I edged closer. It did not matter. She could elude me forever in the huge gymnasium.

Pausing, I looked around, my mind racing for ideas. I had to catch her. Her eyes mirrored her uncontrolled panic. She had gone beyond the limits she could comprehend in the situation and was reacting from animal instinct alone now. At this point she was far more dangerous to herself and to others than back in the classroom with the fish.

I could not think what to do. My head pulsed. My arm throbbed where the pencil had sunk in. Blood had soaked through my shirt sleeve. If a number of us approached her, that would undoubtedly terrify her even more. If I boxed her in, that too would heighten her irrationality. She had to relax and regain some control of herself. She was too dangerous this way. Despite her size and her age, I had the experience to know that in this condition she posed a very real threat, if not to me, then to herself.

I went back to Whitney and told her to return to the classroom and tell Anton to manage as best he could with Mary. Then I closed the door to the gym. I pulled closed the heavy divider that separated the room into two parts, because I remembered it having a door in it that locked. I could not afford to let Sheila escape again. Then, together in the far half of the gym, I came as close to her as I dared and sat down.

We regarded each other. Frantic terror gleamed in her eyes. I could see her trembling.

"I'm not going to hurt you, Sheila. I'm not going to hurt you. I'm just going to wait until you're not so scared anymore and then we'll go back to class. I'm not angry. And I'm not going to hurt you."

Minutes passed. I scooted forward on my seat. She stared at me. The tremors had taken over her entire body and I could see her scrawny shoulders shake. But she did not budge.

I had been angry with her. God Almighty, I had been angry. Seeing our beloved fish on the floor, their eyes gouged out, I had been livid. I had an intolerance of cruelty to animals. But now the anger had faded and as I watched her, I was awash with pity. She was being so brave. Frightened and tired and uncomfortable, she refused to give in. Her world had been a very untrustworthy one and she was confronting it in the only way she knew how. We did not know each other; there was no way of determining that I would not hurt her. There was no reason why she should trust me and she was not going to. Such a courageous little being to face up to all of us, who were so much bigger and stronger and more powerful, to face us unflinchingly, without words or tears.

I inched closer. We had been there waiting at least a half hour. I was within ten feet of her now and she was beginning to view my approach with suspicion. I stopped moving. All the while I spoke in gentle tones, reassuring her that I meant her no harm, that we would go back to the classroom together, that nothing would happen. I spoke of other things too; things the children liked to do in our room; things we enjoyed doing together; things she would do with us.

Endless minutes passed. I was getting sore from not moving. Her legs were shaking from standing so long without shifting position. This had become a test of endurance. An eternity was strung out over the ten feet separating us.

We waited. The frenzy was fading from her eyes. Tiredness was taking over. I wondered what the time was but was afraid to move my arm to see my watch. Still we waited.

The front of her overalls darkened and a puddle of urine formed around her feet. She looked down at it, taking her eyes from me for the first time. She caught her lower lip in her teeth. When she looked up, the horror of what had just happened showed plainly.

"Accidents happen. You haven't had a chance to go to the bathroom, so it really isn't your fault," I said. It amazed me that after the havoc she had wreaked in the classroom, this was the act that caused her regret.

"We can clean it up," I suggested. "I've got some rags back in the room for when this sort of thing happens."

She looked down again and then back at me. I remained silent. She took a cautious step backwards to better survey the situation. "You gonna whip me?" she asked hoarsely.

"No. I don't whip kids."

Her brow furrowed.

"I'll help you clean it up. We won't have to tell anybody. It can be our secret, because I know it was an accident."

"I didn't mean to."

"I know it."

"You gonna whip me?"

My shoulders dropped in exasperation. "No, Sheila, I don't whip kids. I said that to you once."

She looked at her overalls. "My Pa, he gonna whip me fierce when he sees I do this."

Throughout our exchange I had remained motionless in my spot, fearful of breaking this tenuous relationship. "We'll take care of that, don't worry. We've still got a while before school is over. It'll dry by then."

She rubbed her nose and looked at the puddle and then at me. For the first time since she'd arrived, she seemed uncertain. Very slowly I rose to my feet. She took a step backwards. I extended an arm to her. "Come on, we'll go get something to clean it up. Don't worry about it."

For a long moment she regarded me. Then cautiously she came toward me. She refused my hand but walked back to the classroom at my side.

Things had quieted in the room. Anton and the children were singing songs. Whitney was holding Susannah and Mary was rocking Max. The dead fish were all gone. Heads turned toward us but I motioned to Anton to keep them busy. Sheila accepted the rags and bucket from me and we went back to the gym and cleaned the floor without speaking. Then she followed me back to the room.

Surprisingly the remainder of the afternoon went quietly. The children were all subdued, fearful of toppling their frail control again. Sheila retreated to the chair she had occupied all morning, folded herself up in it and sucked her thumb. She did not move for the rest of the afternoon. Yet she continued to watch us. Her eyes were unreadable. I went around to each of the children and cuddled them and talked with them trying to soothe their unworded feelings. Finally I came to Sheila.

Sitting down on the floor beside her chair, I looked up at her. She regarded me seriously, thumb still in her mouth. The toll of the afternoon showed on her. I made no attempt to touch her. Anton was conducting the closing exercises and no one was watching us. I did not want to spook her by being too intimate, but I did want her to know I cared.

"It's been kind of a hard afternoon, hasn't it?" I said. She did not respond other than staring at me. I got the full benefit of her odor from this position. "Tomorrow will be better, I think. First days are always hard." I tried to read her eyes, to glean some understanding of what was going on in her head. The open hostility was gone, momentarily at least. But I could see nothing beyond that. "Are your pants dry?"

She unfolded and stood up, inspecting them. They were passably dry, the damp outline barely distinguishable from the other filth. She nodded slightly.

"Is that going to be good enough so you don't get in trouble?"

Again an almost imperceptible nod.

"I hope so. Everybody has accidents. And this wasn't really your fault. You didn't have a chance to use the bathroom." I kept some spare clothes around because this sort of thing happened all too frequently in our room. I hadn't mentioned it, being afraid of frightening her with too much familiarity. But I wanted her to know that such problems were acceptable in here.

The thumb rotated in her mouth and she turned away from me to watch Anton. I remained near her until dismissal.

After the children were gone, Anton and I cleaned up the room in silence. Neither of us mentioned what had happened. Neither of us said much of anything. This certainly had not been one of our better days. When I got home after work, I washed out my pencil wound and put a Band-Aid on it. Then I lay down on my bed and wept.

Chapter Four

Life in my classroom was a constant battle whether I wanted to acknowledge it or not. Not only with the children but with myself. To cope with these youngsters from day to day I locked up my own emotions in many ways because I found that when I didn't I became too discouraged, too shocked, too disillusioned to function effectively. My days were a constant shooing of my own fears back into the little corners where they dwelled. The method worked for me but every once in a while a child came along who could really rock my bulwark. Out came tumbling all the uncertainties, the frustrations, and the misgivings I had so carefully tried to ignore and I became overwhelmed with defeat.

Basically, though, I was a dreamer. Beyond the children's incomprehensible behavior and my own vulnerability, beyond the discouragement, the self-doubts, soared a dream which admittedly was seldom realized, a dream that things could change. And being a dreamer, my dream died hard.

This time was no exception. The tears were short-lived and instead, I fell asleep. Later, I settled down with a tuna fish sandwich to watch "Star Trek." I had never watched much television and had never seen "Star Trek" when it had been a prime-time program. But now, years later, it was shown in syndication each evening at six. At the beginning of the school year when our classroom adjustment had been slow to come and my disillusionments had been many, I had started watching the program while I ate dinner and it had become a ritual. It divided my day into the work part and the rest part; that hour being the recuperative time when I put away all the problems and frustrations that had occurred at school. Marvelously emotionless Mr. Spock became my after-work martini.

So by the time Chad arrived at seven, I had recovered. Chad and I had been seeing each other regularly over the previous eighteen months. At first it had been the typical courting relationship: the endless rounds of dinner, movies, dances and mindless conversation. However, neither of us was suited for that sort of affair. So we drifted into a warm, comfortable alliance. Chad was a junior partner in a law firm downtown and spent most of his time as a court-appointed attorney for the drifters and ne'er-do-wells who found themselves in jail. Consequently he did not have a good track record of winning cases. So we would spend our evenings together commiserating good-naturedly over my kids and his clients. We had talked once or twice about marriage, but that had been the extent of it. Both of us were sociable loners, satisfied with the status quo.

When Chad came over, bringing a quart of Baskin-Robbins chocolate fudge ice cream, I told him about Sheila as we fixed sundaes. I had met my match, I stated firmly. The kid was a savage and I did not think I was the one to civilize her. The sooner the opening at the hospital came up, the better.

Chad laughed amiably and suggested I call her former teacher. After our ice cream orgy when I was feeling comfortably full and a little more mellow about things, I looked in the telephone book for Mrs. Barthuly.

"Oh my gosh," Mrs. Barthuly said when I told her who I was and why I had called. "I thought they had put her away for good."

I explained that there had been no openings yet at the state hospital and asked her what she had done while Sheila was in her class. I could hear her making little clucking sounds, those indescribable little noises of defeat.

"I've never seen such a child. Destructive, oh my gosh, every time I took my eyes off her she destroyed something. Her work, the other children's work, bulletin boards, art displays, anything. One time she took all the other kids' coats and stuffed them down the toilets in the girls' lavatory. Flooded the entire basement." She sighed. "I tried everything to stop her. She always destroyed her work before you could get a look at it. I started laminating the work-sheets so she couldn't tear them up. You know what she did? She shoved them into the cooling system and jammed the air conditioner. We went three days with no ventilation when it was ninety-four degrees."

Mrs. Barthuly went on to describe event after event. Her voice was rapid at first as if she had never had an adequate opportunity to tell about the chaos visited on her the first three months of the school year. But then it began to take on a weary note. Despite everything, she had liked Sheila, drawn by the same enigmatic force that had attracted me. The child seemed so vulnerable and still so brave. She had wanted to do right by Sheila. But nothing she did helped. Sheila refused to speak to her. She refused to be touched, to be helped, to be liked. In the beginning Mrs. Barthuly had tried to be kind. She attempted to show affection to this unlovable child, to include her in special activities, to give her extra attention. The school psychologist had set up behavior-management programs to reward Sheila's good behavior. But Sheila appeared to delight in never doing whatever it was they decided to reward. Mrs. Barthuly was convinced that Sheila purposely set out to ruin the programs, going so far as to stop doing some things she had previously been doing well when those things were included on the program.

Next, Mrs. Barthuly tried controlling her outlandish behavior negatively. She took away privileges, confined her to a time-out corner, and at last ended up sending Sheila to the principal for paddling. Still Sheila continued to terrorize the class, attacking other children, destroying things and refusing to work. At last, Mrs. Barthuly gave up. This child took too much time away from the other children. So Sheila was left on her own and the first semblance of peace settled in the room. Allowed to do as she pleased, Sheila spent most of the day wandering around the classroom or paging through magazines. If countered, Sheila would scream and tear about in revenge, destroying whatever was in her path. However, left entirely alone, she was tolerable and would ignore the others if they ignored her. She still never spoke, never did any work, nor participated in any classroom activities. Then the event in November occurred and she was removed immediately from school in response to fears expressed by other children's parents.

The voice on the other end of the phone was sad and pessimistic. Mrs. Barthuly regretted that so little had been done. No one knew if Sheila had even the most basic command of letters or numbers. Nothing about the child's learning or feelings was known at all. She was, Mrs. Barthuly admitted, the closest thing to an unteachable child she had ever encountered. Whatever could be done for Sheila was beyond her patience, ability and time. She wished me luck, amending it to say she hoped the state hospital placement came through soon. Then she hung up.

The news filled me with renewed depression

because I did not know what I could do that had not been tried. With my group of children, I did not have much more of a chance to give her one-to-one attention than Mrs. Barthuly. I discussed the matter with Chad and decided there was nothing I could do other than wait and see.

The next morning before school, Anton and I sat down to plan our course of action. Clearly the occurrence which had happened the day before could not be repeated. The other children could not afford to go through that sort of experience. Some disruption was healthy in the classroom because it taught them how to respond in a supportive environment when things went wrong; but we could not afford chaos for days on end.

The social worker came in dragging Sheila about fifteen minutes before class started. She explained that the only bus they could get to connect with Sheila's home was the high school bus. Therefore, Sheila would be arriving each day a half hour early and would not be able to catch the bus home in the evening until two hours after class had finished. I was horrified. First of all, I did not feel Sheila was in any shape to be riding a bus with a bunch of high school kids; I doubted seriously that she could be trusted on any bus. Second, what was I supposed to do with her for two hours after school? The mere thought had frozen my stomach into a cold, iron-heavy lump.

The social worker smiled blankly. We would have to go along with the idea because the school district would not pay for special transportation when existing buses could be used. Arrangements would simply have to be made for her to stay at school. Other buses out to the country came almost as late and other children had to be waiting somewhere in the school. Sheila could wait with them. Transferring Sheila's limp wrist to me, she turned and left.

I looked down at Sheila and felt all my anxiety from the day before flood over me. She was regarding me, her eyes round and guarded, the hostility more hidden than the day before. I smiled weakly. "Good morning, Sheila. I'm glad you're with us again today."

In the few moments we had before the other children all arrived, I brought Sheila over to one of the tables and pulled a chair out for her. She had come with me from the door without protest and sat in the chair. "Listen," I said, sitting down next to her, "let's get an idea about what's going to happen in here today so we won't have another one like yesterday. That wasn't very much fun for me, and I don't suppose it was for you either."

Her brow wrinkled in a questioning expression as if she did not understand what I was doing.

"I don't know how it was for you at your other school, but I want you to know how it's going to be in here. Yesterday, I think we may have scared you a little bit, because you didn't know any of us and it might not have been clear what we expected. So, I'm going to tell you."

She began hunching herself up into the chair,

drawing her knees up and folding in upon herself again. I noticed that she was still wearing the same worn denim overalls and T-shirt. Neither had been washed since yesterday and she smelled very strongly.

"I'm not going to hurt you. I don't hurt kids in here. Neither does Anton or Whitney or anyone else. You don't have to be frightened of us."

The thumb was in her mouth. She seemed scared of me and looked so little and vulnerable, making it difficult for me to remember her as she had been yesterday. The bravado was gone, at least temporarily. But her gaze remained unflinching as she watched me.

"Would you like to sit in my lap while I talk to you?"

She shook her head almost imperceptibly.

"Okay, well, here's the plan. I want you to join us when we do things. All you have to do is sit with us. Anton or Whitney or I will help you find out what is happening until you get used to it." I went ahead to explain the day's schedule. I told her she did not have to participate if she did not want to, just yet. But she did have to join us and there was no choice on that. Either she came of her own accord or one of us would help her.

"And," I concluded, "sometimes when things get out of control, the place I will have you go is over to the quiet corner." I indicated our chair in the corner. "You go and you sit there until both of us think you have things under control again. You just sit, that's all. Is that clear?"

If it was, she did not let me know. By that point the others were arriving. I rose and patted her on the back before going to greet the other children. She did not pull away from my touch but then she did not acknowledge it either.

When morning discussion came, Sheila was still sitting in the chair. I pointed to the floor beside me. "Sheila, over here, please, so we can start discussion."

She did not move. I repeated myself. Still she remained folded up in the chair. I could feel my stomach tighten in anticipation. She regarded me, her thumb in her mouth, her eyes wide. I looked to Anton, who was settling Freddie into place. "Anton, would you help Sheila join us?"

When Anton turned to approach her, Sheila came to life and bolted off the chair. She made a mad dash for the door, falling hard against it when the latch did not respond.

"Torey, make her stop," Peter said worriedly. The other children were watching Anton as he circled to catch her. She had that trapped-animal stare again and was dashing recklessly about trying to avoid capture. But the room was so small it was a futile flight. She attempted to deter him by knocking books off the counters but within a minute Anton had her cornered on the far side of one of the tables. Briefly, they danced back and forth, but Anton unexpectedly shoved the table toward her pinning her against the wall just long enough to reach and catch hold of her arm.

For the first time she made a sound. She let loose

with a scream that startled all of us. Susannah began to cry, but the others sat in fearful silence while Anton wrestled Sheila over to the group. I remained sitting and pointed to the spot I had indicated earlier. Taking her by the arm from Anton I pushed her into a sitting position. She continued to scream, a throaty, tearless yell, but she sat without struggling.

"Okay," I said with fake brightness. "Who has a topic?"

"I do," said William, straining to be heard over Sheila's screams. "Is it always going to be like this in here?" His dark eyes were fearful. "Is she always going to be like this?"

The other children were watching me anxiously, and I realized, not for the first time, what a con job my position was, because I was honestly as frightened as they were. We had been together four months and had learned each other's differences and problems. I knew Sheila would have been hard on us even if she had been quiet and cooperative, simply because she was new, testing our tenuous hold on order. But she was in no way easy to accept and she shook us all to our foundation.

So the topic that day was Sheila. I tried to explain as best I could that Sheila was adjusting and like all the rest of us was having a hard time. She simply needed our patience and understanding.

Sheila was not entirely ignoring us as we discussed her. Her screaming had diminished to sporadic squawks, inserted when there was too great a gap in our conversation or when one of us looked at her and she caught us at it. Otherwise, she was quiet. I let the children ask questions and express their fears and unhappiness. And I attempted to answer them honestly. All except Peter had the sensitivity not to be too critical in front of Sheila. Peter did not. Like the day before when he had complained of her smell, he angrily stated that he wanted this girl out of his room. She was ruining everything. I did not attempt to protect Sheila from his comments because I knew he would make them to her later anyway. That was all part of Peter's own problems and I preferred to be present when he talked.

So instead we discussed alternate ways of dealing with the inconveniences put upon us while Sheila adjusted. Tyler suggested sending her to the quiet corner to save our ears. Sarah opted to get freetime every time Sheila started a ruckus. And Guillermo, who seemed to be feeling particularly magnanimous, thought the children might take turns sitting with Sheila and keeping her company while she hollered so she wouldn't get lonely. I suspected he was reflecting more on his own feelings than on Sheila's.

In the end we decided that when Sheila yelled or in other ways demanded Anton's or my attention and disrupted the class, the other kids were to get busy at their own work and the more responsible ones were to keep an eye on Max and Freddie and Susannah. I told them that at the end of the week we would have a treat if everyone cooperated. After a short discussion we decided that we would make ice cream on Friday if everything worked out. The children were full of ideas.

"If you get busy with Sheila and Freddie starts crying, I can read him a story," Tyler suggested.

"We could sing a song by ourselves," Guillermo added.

"I'll hold Susannah Joy's hand so she won't run and hurt herself."

I smiled. "Everybody's got good ideas. This is going to work out real well, I can tell. So you just think what kind of ice cream topping you want on Friday." I looked down at Sheila, who was still making angry grunts. I continued hanging on to one overall strap, but she was sitting peacefully. "Do you like ice cream?"

She narrowed her eyes.

"I expect you'll want some, won't you? Do you like ice cream?"

Cautiously she nodded.

Sheila was more cooperative about moving to a chair while we had math. She climbed on one and folded herself up, watching me suspiciously as I went from child to child. The rest of the morning passed uneventfully.

I did not dare let lunch follow as it had the previous day, not only because I did not want a replay of the disastrous afternoon, but because the lunch aides had stated that they unequivocally refused to supervise her until she was more predictable. So I took my lunch and ate with the children.

I sat next to Sheila, who inched away from me on the cafeteria bench. Anton came and sat down on the other side of her and she inched back in my direction. She bolted her lunch down in minutes by cramming it into her mouth as fast as she could chew. Her manners were atrocious, but she could maneuver a fork, which was more than some of the others could manage.

After lunch I escorted her back to the room, sat down at one of the tables and graded papers while the children played. Sheila resumed her seat on the chair, put her thumb in her mouth and stared at me.

All afternoon she moved as requested, although when given a choice she always returned to the same chair at the table and hunched up on it. She appeared considerably subdued from the day before, almost depressed, but I made no attempt to question her. She seemed unduly frightened of me, which I did not understand, so I did not want to intensify her concerns by forcing myself upon her. The other children seemed disappointed that nothing happened and Peter came up to me after closing exercises to ask if we would still have ice cream if Sheila never misbehaved again. With a grin I assured him that if we went all the way to Friday with no problems, there would certainly be ice cream.

After the other children left, we were alone, Sheila, Anton and I. Those two hours after school were normally my preparation time for the next day, but I thought that perhaps for the first few days at least, I might use them to get better acquainted with Sheila. She still sat in her chair, having not even gotten up when the other children put on their snowsuits and prepared to go home.

I came over to the table and sat down across from her. She regarded me, her eyes wary. "You did a nice job today, scout. I really liked that."

She averted her face.

I looked at her. Under the dirt and tangles was a handsome child. Her limbs were straight and well-formed. I longed to hold her, to take her in my lap and hug away some of that pain so obvious in her eyes. But we remained a table apart, which might as well have been a universe. With me so close, she would not even meet my eyes.

"Have I frightened you, Sheila?" I asked softly. "I didn't mean to, if I did. It must be very scary for you, having to come to a new school and be with all of us when you don't know us. I know that's scary. It scares me too."

She put her hand up to the side of her face to block me entirely from view.

"Would you like me to read you a story or something while we wait for your bus?"

She shook her head.

"All right. Well, I'm going to go over to the other table and make plans for tomorrow. If you change your mind, I'll be glad to read to you. Or you play with the toys or whatever you like." I rose from the table.

As soon as I had settled at my work she put her hand down and turned to me, studying me as I wrote. I looked up a few times but there was no response from that steady gaze.

Chapter Five

The next day I decided it was time for Sheila to participate. The bus which brought her dropped her off at the high school two blocks away, so Anton had gone to get her and walk her to our school. When they arrived, Sheila pulled off her jacket and went straight to her chair. I came over and sat down, explaining that today she was going to be asked to do some things. I went over the schedule of the day with her and told her I expected her to join us for everything just like the day before, and that I also expected her to work some math problems for me at math time. Also on Wednesday afternoons we always cooked, I said, so I wanted her to help us make chocolate bananas. Those two things she was expected to do.

She watched me as I spoke, her eyes clouded with the same distrust they had shown the day before. I asked if she understood what I wanted. She did not respond.

During morning discussion Sheila joined us when requested after I gave her the evil eye. She sat at my feet and did nothing. Math was a different story. I had planned to do some simple counting exercises using manipulatives. So I got out the blocks and called her to come over to me. She remained sitting in the spot where she had been for morning discussion.

"Sheila, come over here, please." I indicated a chair. It was the one she was so fond of. "Come on."

She did not move. Anton began to move cautiously to catch her if she bolted when I approached. Instantly she perceived our plan and panicked. This child was phobic about being chased. Shrieking wildly, she darted off, knocking children and their work over as she fled. But Anton was too close and snagged her almost immediately. I came and took her from him.

"Honey, we're not going to do anything to you when we come to get you. Don't you know that?" I sat down with her, holding her tightly as she struggled and listening to her breathing, raspy with fear. "Take it easy, kitten."

"Hey, everybody," Peter hollered delightedly, "everybody be good now." Little heads bent eagerly over their work and Tyler rose solicitously to check on Susannah and Max.

Sheila resumed screaming, her face reddening. But she did not cry. Holding her in my lap, I spilled out the counting blocks. I lined them up evenly while waiting for her to calm down. "Here, I want you to count some blocks for me."

She yelled louder.

"Here, count three out for me." She struggled to break my hold. "I'll help you." I manipulated a writhing hand toward the blocks. "One, two, three. There. Now you try."

Unexpectedly she grabbed a block and hurled it across the room. Within a split second she had another which hit Tyler squarely in the forehead. Tyler let out a wail.

I pinned Sheila's arm to her side and stood up, lugging her over to the quiet corner. "We don't do that in here. Nobody is hurt in here. I want you to sit in the chair until you quiet down and can come back and work." I motioned Anton over. "Help her stay in the chair if she needs it."

I returned to the other children, rubbed Tyler's sore spot and praised everybody for keeping busy. Putting a check on the board to indicate our approach toward Friday's ice cream, I then settled in next to Freddie to help him stack blocks. Over in the corner all hell had broken loose. Sheila shrieked wildly, kicking the wall with her tennis shoes and bouncing the chair. Anton was grimly silent, holding her firmly in place.

Throughout math period Sheila continued the ruckus. By the time free play had started half an hour later, she was tiring of kicking and fighting. I came over.

"Are you ready to come do your math with me?" I asked. She looked up at me and screamed wordlessly in anger. Anton was no longer holding on to her, just to the chair, and I motioned him away to keep an eye on the others. "When you are ready for math, you may come over. Until then I want you in the chair." Then I turned and left.

Leaving her entirely alone startled her momentarily and she stopped yelling. When she became fully aware that neither Anton nor I was standing over her to keep her in the chair, she stood up.

"Are you ready to do math?" I asked from across the room where I was helping Peter build a highway out of blocks.

Her face blackened with my question. "No! No! No! No!"

"Then sit back down."

She screeched in rage, her sudden change in volume causing everyone to pause. But she remained beside the chair.

"I said sit down, Sheila. You may not get up until you're ready to do math."

For an eternal moment she stormed with so much loudness I felt my head pulse. Then suddenly, startlingly, everything was quiet and she glowered at me. Such obvious hate withered what little self-confidence I had about what I was doing.

"Sit down in that chair, Sheila."

She sat. She turned the chair around so she could watch me, but she sat. Then she resumed screaming. I sighed a deep, private sigh of relief.

Peter looked at me. "You know, Torey, I think we ought to get two marks for good behavior on this one. She's pretty hard to ignore."

I grinned. "Yeah, Peter, I think you're right. This is worth two."

Sheila screamed and yelled all through playtime. The ruckus had been going over an hour and a half by then. She stomped her feet and bounced and rocked the chair. She pulled at her clothes and shook her fists. But she remained in the chair.

By snacktime she was hoarse and all that came from the corner was little strangled croaks. But her rage had not diminished and the croaks continued furiously. I stayed inside while Anton took the others out for recess. This increased Sheila's agitation for a few moments and she gasped out a few more shouts and rattled the chair around. But she was tiring. By the end of recess there were no sounds at all coming from the corner. My head was throbbing.

I did not restate the conditions for leaving the corner. I believed she was bright enough to know by that time and I did not want to give her added attention. The other children came in, frosty and red-cheeked from recess, full of tales about playing fox-and-geese in the snow with Anton, who got caught every time. Reading period started without event, all of us settling down to our tasks as if the little lump on the chair in the corner did not exist.

Toward the close of the period I felt a feather-light touch on my shoulder as I worked with Max. I turned to see Sheila standing behind me, her skin mottled with her anxiety, her face puckered with that cautious expression so frequently reflected in her eyes.

"You ready to do math?"

She pursed her lips a moment and then nodded slowly.

"Okay. Let me get Sarah to help Max. You go over and pick up the blocks you threw and get the others out of the cupboard by the sink." I spoke in a casual, offhanded manner as if it were normal to expect her to comply, my tight chest belying the degree of the con. She looked at me carefully but then went and did as I had asked.

Together we sat down on the floor and I spilled out the blocks. "Show me three blocks."

Cautiously she picked out three.

"Show me ten." Again, ten cubes were lined up on the rug before me. "Good girl. You know your numbers well, don't you?"

She looked up anxiously.

"I'm going to make it harder. Count me out twenty-seven." Within seconds twenty-seven blocks appeared.

"Can you add?"

She did not respond.

"Show me how many blocks are two plus two." Four blocks appeared without hesitation. I studied her a moment. "How about three plus five?" She laid out eight cubes.

I could not tell if she actually knew the answers or was solving them as she went along. Yet she clearly understood the mechanics behind adding. I was reluctant to get out pencil and paper, knowing her tendency to destroy paper. I did not want to ruin our fragile, newly won relationship. But I did want to know how she was working the problems.

70

So I decided to switch to subtraction, which would tell me more. "Show me three take away one."

Sheila flipped two blocks out. I smiled. That problem she obviously knew without having to place three blocks out and remove one.

"Do six take away four."

Again two cubes.

"Hey, you're pretty smart. But I've got one for you. I'll get you this time. Show me twelve take away seven."

She looked up at me and the very smallest hint of a smile colored her eyes although it did not touch her lips. She stacked one, two, three, four, five blocks on top of one another. She did it without even looking down at the cubes. The little devil, I thought. Wherever she had been these past few years and whatever she had been doing, she was also learning. Her abilities were better than the average child her age. She gave no indication of even hesitating before laying the blocks out. My heart leaped at the possibility of having a bright child under all that protest and grime.

She did a few more problems for me before I said enough and she could put the blocks away. It was reading period now and I had told her in the morning that she did not have to participate in this activity. I rose to check on the other kids and Sheila rose with me. Still clutching the box of blocks she wandered after me.

"Honey," I said turning to her, "you can put those away, if you want. You don't have to carry them around."

Sheila had other ideas. The next time I looked up, she was in her favorite chair at the other end of the table with the blocks spilled before her. Busily she was manipulating them, doing something, but I could not tell what.

Lunch subdued her again and she retreated to hunching up in the chair. But when it came time to cook, I coaxed her off quite easily with a banana on a Popsicle stick.

Every Wednesday we made something to eat. I had done it for a variety of reasons. For the more controlled kids, it was a good exercise in math and reading. For everyone it encouraged social activity, sharing, conversation and mutual work. Moreover, cooking was fun. Once a month we repeated a favorite recipe that the kids had chosen and this afternoon it was chocolate bananas, a messy affair involving a banana stuck on a stick that was dipped into chocolate and rolled in topping and then frozen. I had decided not to tackle a new recipe on Sheila's first day out to simplify things, and chocolate bananas were a popular standby. Almost all the kids could manage all the parts by themselves. Even Susannah could do most of it, leaving only Max and Freddie to supervise carefully. Naturally, there was chocolate everywhere and a good share of the toppings were eaten before they found a banana to adhere to, but we all had a marvelous time.

Sheila hesitated to join in, clutching her banana tightly and watching from the sidelines as the others babbled gaily. Yet, she was not resistant and

Whitney lured her over to the chocolate sauce when everyone else had finished. Once Sheila started, she became fully absorbed and began trying to roll all four different toppings onto her sticky banana. I watched from the far side of the table. She never spoke but it became apparent she had some definite ideas about how to get the toppings to stick by redipping the banana in the chocolate after each roll in a topping. One by one the other children began pausing to watch her as she experimented with her idea. Voices became hushed as curiosity got the better of them. Rolling the huge, sticky mass in the last dish of topping, she lifted it up carefully. Her eyes rose to meet mine and slowly a smile spread across her face until it was broad and open, showing the gaps where her bottom teeth were missing.

At the end of each day we had closing exercises which, like morning topic were designed to unite us and prepare us for our time apart. One of the activities was the Kobold's Box. I loved to make up stories to tell the children and had once told them back at the beginning of the year that kobolds were like fairies, but that they lived in people's houses and watched over them to keep things safe while people slept. Peter had suggested that there might be a kobold in our room who took care of all our things and kept Benny, Charles and Onions, the bad-tempered rabbit, company during the night. This spawned a number of tales about our kobold. So one day I brought a large wooden box and told the kids that this was where the kobold was going to leave messages. I said he had watched all of us at work and had been extremely pleased with how kind and thoughtful everyone in the room was becoming. Therefore, every time he saw a kind deed done, he would leave a message in the box. So during closing exercises each day, I read the notes from the Kobold's Box. After a few days I told them the kobold was getting writers' cramp and needed a helping hand because so many people were being kind. I asked the children to be on the lookout for others doing kind things and to write a note and put it in the box, or if they could not write, to come to me and I would write it for them. Thus, one of our most popular and effective exercises occurred. Every night there were about thirty notes from the kids to each other over perceived kindnesses. This not only encouraged the children to observe positive behaviors in others, but they also knocked each other over being kind in hopes that their names would appear in the box at the end of the day. Some notes were traditional but others showed particular insight praising a child for small but significant steps, sometimes for things I myself had missed. For instance, Sarah was complimented for not using a particularly favorite vulgar phrase during an argument one day, and Freddie was praised for finding a Kleenex instead of blowing his nose on his shirt. I loved opening that box every night because I seldom contributed to it myself except to make sure everybody had at least one note. The thrill of seeing what the children had perceived was so exciting to me. And admittedly, I also enjoyed finding a note for myself in there.

So closing exercises after cooking on Wednesday were particularly fun because for the first time Sheila's name appeared in handwriting other than my own. Sheila who still sat apart from us kept her head down when the kids clapped over her notes. But she accepted the notes readily when I gave them to her.

Anton walked the other children out to their buses after school ended. I settled down at the table to grade papers and to bring some behavioral charts I was keeping on a couple of the kids up to date. Sheila had gone into the bathroom to clean the final dregs of the chocolate banana from her face. She had been in there some time and I had become involved in my work. I heard the toilet flush and she came out. I did not look up because I was completing a graph with marking pen and did not want to make an error. Sheila came over to the table and watched me a moment. Then she came closer, putting her elbows on the table and leaning way over so that we were only inches apart. I raised my eyes to look at her. She examined my face thoughtfully.

"How come them other kids don't go to the bathroom in the toilet?"

"Huh?" I sat back in surprise.

"I say, how come them other kids, them big kids, go in their pants and not in the toilet?"

"Well, that's something they haven't learned yet."

"How come? They do be big kids. Bigger than me."

"Well, they just haven't learned it yet. But we're working on it. Everyone's trying."

She looked down at the graph I was drawing. "They oughta know that by now. My Pa, he'd whip me fierce bad if I do that."

"Everybody's different and nobody gets a whipping in here."

She was pensive a long moment. She traced a little circle on the table with her finger. "This here be a crazy class, don't it?"

"Not really, Sheila."

"My Pa, he say so. He say I be crazy and they put me in a class for crazy kids. He says this here be a crazy kidses class."

"Not really."

She frowned a moment. "I don't care much. This here do be as good as that other place I be before. It be as good as anyplace. I don't care if it be a crazy class."

I was at a loss for words, not knowing how to deny the obvious. I had not expected to be involved with one of my children in this sort of discussion. Most were either not coherent enough to be that perceptive or not brash enough to say it.

Sheila scratched her head and regarded me thoughtfully. "Do you be crazy?"

I laughed. "I hope not."

"How come you do this?"

"What? Work here? Because I like boys and girls a lot and I think that teaching is fun."

"How come you be with crazy kids?"

"I like it. Being crazy isn't bad. It's just different, that's all."

She shook her head without smiling and straightened up. "I think you do be a crazy person too."

Chapter Six

"Sheila, come over here, please," I motioned to a chair near where I was sitting. "I have something for you to do." Sheila sat across the room in her favorite chair. Thus far, the morning had gone smoothly. Like the previous two days, I had used the time before school to tell her what would happen that day. She had been cooperative, joining us for morning discussion without being reminded, and then for math. Although she still did not speak, she appeared considerably more relaxed in the classroom. Now she watched me from her chair.

"Come here, hon. I want you to do something with me." I beckoned to her. She unfolded from her post hesitantly. I had borrowed a test from the school psychologist called a Peabody Picture Vocabulary Test or more affectionately the PPVT.

Although I never cared much for the test, it gave a general idea of a child's functioning verbal IQ quickly and without the child needing to talk. After the previous day's encounter with the math cubes, I was intensely interested to know the level at which the girl was functioning. With such a severe disturbance as Sheila displayed, it was typical for her to be academically behind. Most seriously disturbed children simply do not have the extra energy available to learn. So when she evidenced normal math skill, I became alive with curiosity. I was also excited to think she might have above-average intelligence. I was already beginning to mellow about her placement in my room and wondering about keeping her out of the state hospital. Of all the things she needed right now, I realized that was not one of them.

"You and I are going to do something together." I had had to get up and bring her over to my table. "Here, sit down. Now, I'm going to show you some pictures and say a word. Then I want you to point to the picture that best shows what that word means, okay? Do you understand that?"

She nodded. I showed the first set of four pictures and asked her to point to "whip." What a picture to have to start with, I thought ruefully. She studied the four line drawings, looked up at me, then cautiously pointed to one.

"Good girl," I smiled at her. "That's just exactly right. Point to 'net.' "

As I read each word, Sheila would point to a picture, hesitantly at first, studying each of the four

80

choices carefully, then more freely. After six or seven plates a small smile slipped across her face and she raised her eyes, "This be easy," she whispered hoarsely so the others could not hear.

She missed one, "thermos," a word she had probably not encountered in her short, destitute life. But the next one she did correctly. A child had to miss six out of eight to stop the test, and she gave no indication of reaching that level. We continued. The words were beginning to get harder and she was taking more time to consider the pictures. Occasionally she would miss one, sometimes two. I could see the concern in her eyes; she knew when she missed them, even if I made no comments.

I had stopped making comments some time back. I had suspected she was above average in intelligence, maybe even bright, but she had long since passed my expectations. We were moving into a part of the test I had never given before because none of my kids had ever gone that high. We were working with words like "illumination" and "concentric." Sheila was missing words regularly, but never six out of eight. Tension mounted around us. She was obviously trying very hard not to make mistakes and I was touched by her concentration. But we were up into the adolescent end of the test; there were words no normal six-year-old would know. Biting her lips between her teeth, she kept trying. In her lap, I could see her wringing her hands.

"Sweetheart, you're doing a nice job," I said. I hadn't expected her to take the test so seriously and become so involved, to try so hard and to last so long. I really could not believe she knew these words.

She looked up at me. Her eyes were dilated, the soft skin at her throat mottled with nervousness. "I ain't getting them all right."

"Oh, that's okay, honey. You aren't supposed to get them all right. These are words for great big kids and you're not expected to know them all. This is just to see which ones you do know. But it doesn't matter if you get some wrong. I'm proud of you for trying so hard."

Her face puckered and she looked on the verge of tears. "These be fierce hard words now." She looked down at her hands. "First they be easy, but these do be terrible hard for me. I don't know them all."

Her tiny voice, her slipping hold on her composure, her small shoulders hunched up under the worn shirt all combined to rip at my heart. Such innocence, even in the worst of these kids. They were all simply little children.

I reached an arm out. "Come here, Sheila." She looked up at me and I leaned over and pulled her up into my lap. Under my hands her little body was tense, the omnipresent odor of old urine floating around us. "Kitten, I know you're trying your best. That's all that counts. I don't really care which ones you get right or wrong, that doesn't matter. Why, these are really hard words. I bet there isn't another boy or girl in here who could do better."

I held her, smoothing back the tangled hair from her face. Waiting for her to relax I looked over the test score sheet, mentally subtracting out the errors. I suspected she was very close to reaching the ceiling of her ability on the test. She was missing three and four at a time. But even so, she had surpassed any other child I had ever tested.

"How do you know all these words?" I asked, my curiosity getting the better of me.

She shrugged. "I dunno."

"Some of these are big kids' words. I just wondered where you heard them."

"My other teacher, she let me have magazines. Sometimes I read the words in there."

I looked down at her. Her body was still rigid against mine and light as that of a little bird. "Can you read, Sheila?"

She nodded.

"Where'd you learn to do that?"

"I dunno. I always read."

I shook my head in amazement. What sort of changeling did we have here? At first I had been titillated by the thought of a bright child, because as dear as the others were, most were slow learners and it was always hard to know where the disturbance left off and the retardation began. Some, like Sarah and Peter, were average, but I had seldom had an above-average child. At first, the thought had excited me. But clearly Sheila was not simply above average. She was way beyond the comfortableness that came with easy learning and mastery. Instead, she had been catapulted into that little-known realm of true giftedness. I feared that fact would not ease my job at all.

There was no scale to measure Sheila's score on the PPVT. For her age group the scale stopped at 99, which translated into a 170 IQ. Sheila had a score of 102. I stared at the test sheet. We don't have a concept for that kind of brilliance. Statistics tell us that less than 1 in 10,000 has that high a level of functioning. But what does it mean? It is a deviant score, an abnormality in a society that worships sameness. It would set her apart as surely as her disturbance could.

I looked across the room to where Sheila sat. It was playtime now and Sheila had resumed her favorite chair. I looked at her as she sat, thumb in mouth, limbs wrapped around herself protectively. She was watching Tyler and Sarah, who were playing with dolls in the housekeeping corner. I wondered. Under that long matted hair, behind those wary eyes, what kind of child was there? I now felt more concerned than ever before, because if anything, the situation had become more complicated.

After lunch I showed Anton the test. He shook his head in disbelief. "That can't be right," he muttered. "Where would she learn those words? She just had to guess lucky, Torey. No kid in the migrant camp is going to know those kinds of words."

I could not believe it myself. So I put in a call to Allan, our school psychologist. He was out of the office but I left a message with his secretary saying

I had a child that I wanted tested.

One thing from the testing situation puzzled me. As Sheila spoke to me more, it became increasingly apparent that she used a highly idiosyncratic dialect. I hadn't heard her enough to pick out the unusual features precisely, but the grammar was bizarre. Most of the migrant camp children came from Spanish-speaking homes and often their command of English vocabulary was below age-level but within normal limits grammatically. There was no other major speech variation in the locality. Sheila was not from a Spanish-speaking home; the IQ test substantiated that there was nothing wrong at all with her vocabulary. I could not fathom why she spoke so oddly. To me her dialect almost sounded like the inner-city blacks I had worked with in Cleveland. But Sheila was not black and our small Iowa farming community was far from inner-city Cleveland. Perhaps it was a family speech pattern. I decided I would have to investigate because the phenomenon left me so perplexed.

The remainder of the day went uneventfully. I still made minimal requirements of Sheila. I wanted to give her ample time to adjust to us without taxing the other kids too much. After the first tumultuous days, this was a welcome relief. She moved willingly with us, but participated infrequently and only when coaxed. She would not talk to the other children or to Whitney. In most instances she would not speak to Anton or me unless we were quite isolated. Yet, she was peaceful, sitting in her chair when given the opportunity and watching us with guarded interest.

The next major step that had to be taken with Sheila concerned her hygiene. Every day she arrived in the same denim overalls and boy's T-shirt. Apparently, the clothes had never been washed from the first day she wore them and she reeked of urine. I suspected she wet the bed and dressed each morning without washing. Consequently, she was extremely unpleasant to be near for any length of time. Both Anton and I were used to the strong odors of unchanged pants, since Max, Freddie, and Susannah were all not reliably toilet trained. But Sheila was even stronger than we were accustomed to. Moreover, the plain everyday grime was crusted over her face and arms. When I had sent her in to wash off the chocolate from cooking the day before, there were lines on her forearms indicating how high she had washed. Those same lines were visible today. She had long hair that went halfway down her back in tangled strands. I had checked the first day for lice or mites. We had struggled twice with lice already and I was not game for another encounter. The second time I had ended up catching them myself and had been furious. Sheila did not appear to have any, although she did have impetigo around her mouth, which I hoped none of the other children would catch.

A school nurse came once a week for an afternoon. I had tried to send my children down. Most of them had had impetigo or rat bites or other evils of poverty. But I ended up getting the salve and

Kwell shampoo from the nurse and taking care of the kids myself, simply because once a week on Thursday afternoons was not often enough to tend to all the problems.

I waited until all the children had left at the end of the day to tackle Sheila's hygienic needs. She had remained sitting in her chair while the others had gotten ready to go home. She was still sitting when I went to the cupboard and got out the combs and brushes I kept there. The night before I had stopped at the drugstore and bought a little package of hair clips.

"Sheila, come here," I said. "I got something for you."

She rose and came over. Her brow was furrowed with wary interest. I handed her the sack. For a moment she just held it, looking at me quizzically. But I urged her to open it and she did. Taking the clips out she looked at them and then at me. Her forehead was still wrinkled in puzzlement.

"They're for you, sweetheart. I thought we could comb your hair out nice and put clips in it. Like I've got in mine." I showed her my hair.

She fingered the clips carefully through the plastic wrapping. With a frown she regarded me. "How come you do this?"

"Do what?"

"Be nice to me?"

I looked at her in disbelief. "Because I like you."

"Why? I be a crazy kid; I hurt your fishes. Why do you be nice to me?"

I smiled through my own perplexity. "I just

wanted to, Sheila. That's all. I thought you might like something nice for your hair."

She continued to rub the clips through the wrapping, feeling the plastic shapes with her fingertips. "Ain't nobody give me nothing before. Ain't nobody be nice to me on purpose."

I stood watching her in bewilderment. There was nothing in my experience to relate to that. "Well, things are different in here, kiddo," was all I could reply.

I brushed the tangles out of her hair carefully. It took much longer than I had anticipated it would because I did not want to hurt her in any way. I was fearful of this fragile relationship we were forming, of accidentally harming it because we were from such different worlds. She sat very patiently clutching the clips in her hands but never taking them out of the wrapping. Over and over again she fingered them, but she would not open the package. Her hair was that fine, soft, impossibly straight hair that fortunately never tangles too badly. When brushed out, it hung down below her shoulder blades in a thick curtain. In front I combed her bangs. They were too long, falling into her eyes. She was a pretty girl with bold, well-formed features. With soap and water she would be even lovelier.

"There you are. Here, give me the clips and I'll put them in your hair."

She squashed the clips to her breast.

"Here, let's put them in your hair."

She shook her head.

"Don't you want them there?"

"Pa, he take them away from me."

"He wouldn't do that, would he? Just tell him that I gave them to you."

"He say I steal them. Nobody give me nothing before." She held on to the clips tightly, looking at the plastic bluebirds and ducks through the wrapping.

"Maybe for now, you can leave them at school until I get hold of your dad and tell him I gave them to you. How's that sound?"

"You fix my hair nice again?"

I nodded. "I'll fix it tomorrow morning when you come."

She looked at the clips a long moment and then hesitantly handed them to me. "Here. You keep them for me."

My heart thumped within my chest as I took the clips. It was so obvious how hard she was finding giving them back. At that moment Anton came into the room with an armload of dittos he had been running off. He reminded me that it was almost time for him to walk Sheila over to the high school to catch her bus. I was surprised that so much time had slipped by. We hadn't even gotten around to washing up and she did smell so terrible.

"Sheila," I asked, "do you get a chance to wash yourself at home?"

She shook her head. "We ain't got no bathtub."

"Can you use the sink?"

"Ain't got no sink either. My Pa, he brings us

down water in a bucket from the gas station." She paused staring at the floor. "It just be to drink out of. He'd be fierce awful mad at me if I get it dirty."

"Do you have any other clothes?"

She shook her head.

"Well, I'll tell you what. We'll see what we can do about that tomorrow, okay?"

Nodding she went to the coat hook to find her thin cotton jacket. I sighed as I watched her. So much to do, I thought. So much to change. "Goodbye, Sheila. Have a nice evening. I'll see you tomorrow."

Anton took her hand and opened the door into the blowy January darkness. Just as he was shutting the door behind him, Sheila paused, peering under his arm and toward me. She smiled slightly. "Bye, teacher."

Chapter Seven

The next afternoon I came ready for action. Armed with three bath towels, a bar of soap, shampoo and a bottle of baby lotion, I arrived at school. First I went down to check the church box in the office. Although the school I was in was in one of the upper-income areas, enough children like those in my room were bussed in to warrant a box of spare clothes that could be given away. I kept my own box in my room, but primarily it contained underwear. What was in there was far too large for little Sheila. Having found a pair of corduroy pants and another T-shirt, I went back to my room.

Thus when Sheila arrived, I was running water into the sink in the back of the classroom. The sink was a large, roomy, kitchen-sized sink and I figured I would get a good share of her into it, since we lacked shower facilities. The moment she saw me, Sheila yanked off her jacket and came trotting over. That was the fastest I had seen her move toward me since she had come. Her eyes were wide with interest as she leaned over to see what I was doing. "You gonna put clips in my hair now?"

"You bet. But first we're going to give you the full beauty-shop routine. We're going to wash you top to bottom. How does that sound?"

"It gonna hurt?"

I laughed. "No, silly. I don't think so."

She had pulled the bottle of baby lotion out of the bucket I had it in and she removed the top. "What do this be for? Do you eat it?"

I looked at her in surprise. "No, it's lotion. You put it on your body."

A sudden look of pleasure rippled across her face. "It do smell good, teacher. Smell it. It smell good and you put it on to be pretty smelling." Her eyes were animated. "Now that kid, he ain't gonna say I stink no more, huh?"

I smiled at her. "No, I guess he won't. Look here, I found some clothes for you to wear. Then Whitney can take your overalls over to the Laundromat when she comes this afternoon."

Sheila surveyed the corduroy pants, picking them up gingerly. "My Pa, he ain't gonna let me keep them. We don't take no charity things."

"Yes, I understand that. You just wear them until the others get dry. Okay?"

I lifted Sheila up onto the counter beside the sink and took off her shoes and socks. She watched

me carefully as I eased off her clothes but she made
no attempt to help. I felt pressed for time because
the other children would be arriving in less than a
half hour, and although they were used to washing
and seeing others washed in the sink, I was afraid
Sheila might feel too vulnerable at this point to
have an audience. I asked her about it and she said
she did not mind, but I still felt it would be better
to finish before the others came.

She was a scrawny little whip of a child with all
her ribs showing. I noticed the many scars on her
body. "What happened here?" I asked as I washed
one arm. A scar two inches long ran up the inside
of it.

"That be where I brokeded my arm at, once."

"How'd you do that?"

"Falling down playing. The doctor putsa cast on
it."

"You fell down playing?"

She nodded matter-of-factly, inspecting the scar.
"I fall on the sidewalk. My Pa, he says I do be a
godawful clumsy child. I hurt myself a lot."

In my mind was forming the question I had
learned to ask of my kids; a question I dreaded.
"Does your Pa ever do anything that leaves scars
like these? Like spank you hard or something?" I
asked.

She looked at me, her eyes clouding over. She regarded me so long in silence that I wished I had not
asked. It was a personal question and perhaps I
had not laid a firm enough foundation in our relationship to be so intimate. "My Pa, he wouldn't do

that. He wouldn't hurt me bad. He loves me. He just hits me a little bit to make me good. You gotta do that to kids sometimes. But my Pa, he loves me. I just be a clumsy child to get so many scars." Her voice was tinged with defiance.

I nodded and lifted her out of the sink to dry her off. For several moments she did not speak to me. I had her on my lap and was drying her legs when she twisted around to look me in the eye. "You know what my Mama done though?"

"No."

"Here, I'll show you." She lifted the other leg up and pointed to a scar. "My Mama she take me out on the road and leave me there. She push me out of the car and I fall down so's a rock cutted up my leg right here. See." She fingered a white line. "My Pa, he loves me. He don't go leaving me on no roads. You ain't supposed to do that with little kids."

"No, you're not."

"My Mama, she don't love me so good."

In silence I began combing out her hair. I did not really want to hear any more because it hurt to listen to her; her voice was so calm and matter-of-fact that I felt that I shouldn't be listening to what she was saying. It was like reading someone's diary, the very calmness of the print making the words more pathetic.

"My Mama, she take Jimmie and go to California. That be where they live right now. Jimmie, he be my brother and he be four years old, 'cept that he only be two when my Mama, she leave. I ain't seen Jimmie in two whole years." She paused thoughtfully. "I miss Jimmie sort of. I wish I could see him again. He be a real nice boy." Again she turned around in my lap so she could see me. "You'd like Jimmie. He be a nice boy and don't yell or be bad or anything. He be a nice boy to have in this here crazy kidses class. 'Cept I don't think he be crazy like me. You like Jimmie. My Mama do. She like Jimmie better'n me, that's why she tooked him and leaved me behind. You ought to have Jimmie in this here class. He don't do bad things like I do."

I hugged her to me. "Kitten, you're the one I'd want. Not Jimmie. He'll have his own teacher some day. I don't care what kids do, I just like them. That's all."

She sat back and looked at me, a bemused look falling across her face. "You do be a funny lady for a teacher. I think you be as crazy as us kidses be."

That fifth day, Friday, she still did not talk to the other kids although when asked a direct question she would answer any of the adults. At the end of the day after everyone had had ice cream and we had finished closing exercises, we were standing in line waiting for the buses to arrive to take the other children home. We had finished up a bit early and everyone was standing around in their snowsuits getting hot, so I suggested a song. Max shouted out that he wanted "If You're Happy and You Know It, Clap Your Hands," one of the few songs he would sing with the rest of us. It was a simple action song that required the children to clap, then stomp, then nod their heads. I looked over to see Sheila standing on the edge of the group not singing but paying close attention. When we had finished all the actions, the buses still had not arrived so I asked for suggestions for new actions. Tyler said, "If you're happy and you know it, jump up and down." So we sang a verse using Tyler's action. Again I asked for new actions. From her corner Sheila shyly raised her hand. With all our other problems and with so few children I just never got around to requesting that they do that unless we were having a moment of mass confusion. To see this little kid—who thus far had never spoken to the other children, who came in with a history of uncooperativeness—standing there with her hand up was a heart stopper.

"Sheila, do you have an idea?"

"Turn around?" she said diffidently.

And so we sang our song turning around. The first week had ended in the heat of success.

Sheila came alive in our room during the next weeks. She began speaking, first with reserve, and then with none. Sheila had thoughts on everything and was most articulate when given the chance. I was delighted to have a verbal child in the room. The other children enjoyed her company and I was tickled that she could tell me about so many things.

Sheila never brought up the burning incident, not during the early stages of our relationship, not later, not ever. Most of the more coherent kids in my class were aware of some of the reasons why they had been placed in there. We talked about those reasons regularly, during the times we set weekly and long-term goals for change, occasionally during morning topic and at other less formal times: out on the playground while we all stood shivering in the lee of the building too engrossed in conversation to go in, over lunch or art or cooking, alone together on the pillows in the secluded animal-cage corner. There seemed to be a pressing need in most of the kids to talk about these things.

The conversations were low-keyed and often casual, much experience having gone into my ability to discuss such topics as committing suicide or burning cats alive with the same casualness with which I had made out my laundry list or asked about baseball scores. The kids did not need to know the behaviors were wrong or that they frightened or repelled others—they already knew that. Otherwise they would not have been in my room in the first place. Instead they needed to explore the width and breadth and depth of those acts, how they felt when they did them, how they had expected they would feel and the seemingly meaningless myriad of details surrounding the episodes. Mostly I listened, asked a question or two if things were not clear, mmmm-hmmmed a lot to let them know I heard. And I kept us busy at dozens of mindless tasks like coloring or making papier mâché projects so that we could talk without having to look at one another, without having to acknowledge we were talking.

Sheila knew why she was there. From the second

day on she continued to refer to us affectionately as a "crazy class." And she was a crazy kid who did bad things. Often she would join the conversations. Yet not once was the abuse incident brought up. Not with the kids. Not with me or the other adults. Never. I did not suggest the topic either. Although I seldom avoided issues, this one I felt instinctively I should leave alone, for no other reason than what my gut told me. So we never discussed it. I never found out what had been going through Sheila's mind that cold November evening.

I remained perplexed about her speech patterns. The more she talked, the more obvious the discrepancy was between the way Sheila spoke and the way the rest of us did. There were no reports of her father speaking any sort of dialect. He was a native of the area and should have spoken in the same manner as the rest of us. The major variations were word insertions, especially "do" and "be," and the absence of a past tense. The word "do" was used as an auxiliary verb, inserted at will throughout Sheila's conversations. "Be" took the place of "am," "is" and "are." For Sheila, the past tense simply did not exist with very few exceptions. Everything was spoken as if it were in the present or future. This mystified me because she had a good command of very difficult tenses such as conditionals like "should" and "would," and was capable of putting together complex sentences far beyond the grasp of most six-year-olds. Repeatedly, I taped samples of her speech and sent them off to experts to be analyzed. In the meantime, I let her speak as she chose.

Allan, the school psychologist, gave Sheila an IQ and reading test. The IQ test Sheila topped out, earning the highest possible score. Allan was astonished, coming out of his little room shaking his head. He had never had a child do that on the test he was using, and certainly had never expected it from a child they would place in a class like mine. Sheila read and comprehended on a fifth grade level, despite the fact that no one had ever taught her to read. Allan left that day, vowing to find a test that could measure her IQ.

Each morning before school Sheila and I worked on hygiene. I bought a plastic bucket at the discount store and put a comb, brush, washcloth, towel, soap, lotion and toothbrush in it. Most days Sheila was willing to wash and brush her teeth, if I would fix her hair. She delighted in the hair clips. I bought another package like the kind that I wore and Sheila guarded them all like a king's treasure. Each morning she went through them, counting them and deciding which ones she would wear. Each evening she took them out of her hair, laying them carefully in the folds of the towel. Again she counted them to make sure no one had taken any. Her clothes were a bit more of a problem. I kept clean underpants at school and insisted she change every morning. We never discussed the problem because I deduced that after the first day, it was a sensitive area. I did, however, make sure she changed, regardless of what subjects we mentioned. On Mondays Whitney trotted Sheila's overalls and shirt down to the Laundromat around the corner from the school. It was hardly a foolproof solution but at least Sheila did not stink so much anymore. All in all, she was a handsome child cleaned up. She had thick, long blond hair and much to the pleasure of all of us she had sparkly eyes and a ready smile that showed three gaps on the bottom awaiting new teeth.

To my relief one problem which I had anticipated but which never materialized was Sheila's bus ride to and from the migrant camp. With such a terrible history of uncontrollable behavior, Sheila, unsupervised on a bus, was something I could not imagine working out well. However, my fears proved to be unfounded. Perhaps putting her with forty high school students was enough to intimidate even Sheila.

Anton or I walked her to and from the bus, but once on it, she settled down in a seat toward the back. The only incident that ever occurred was in late January after she had been on the route for some time. We had walked her to the bus in the evening and put her on. However, by the time the bus had arrived at the migrant camp and the high school students had climbed off, Sheila was not there. The bus driver stood up from his seat and looked back, but the bus was empty. Alarmed because the bus only made two stops before the camp and he had not seen her disembark at either of them, the driver called me at home to make sure she had gotten on. I told him she had. There were more than a few panicky moments before the bus driver called back. Apparently, Sheila had gotten down on the floor by the rear tire where the heat came in and she fell asleep. After she discovered that warm, vibrating spot, she regularly curled up on the floor under the seat and slept during the hour ride both in and out. The driver always checked after that, to make sure she awakened and got off. The high school students, at first only tolerant of her presence, began to save that seat near the heater for her, began also to give her book bags or extra sweaters for a pillow and to see she was walked home on those nights she was too sleepy to be reliable.

A problem that was not solving itself was Sheila's father. I had tried relentlessly to get hold of him for a conference. He had no phone so I sent a note home with Sheila asking him to come to school. No response. I sent a second note. Again no response. I sent a third note saying I was coming to visit him at his home. When the evening came that Anton and I went out, the house was empty. I was getting the distinct impression he did not want to see me. Finally I contacted Sheila's social worker. Together we went out only to be greeted at the door by Sheila. Her father was gone.

I wanted to see him very badly. First I wanted to make some arrangements for Sheila to get proper clothing. I had mentioned this to the social worker. Although Sheila had only one outfit, my main concern was her outerwear. She owned only a boy's thin cotton jacket, something like a baseball Windbreaker. She had no gloves, no hat, no boots. And it was, after all, January. The temperature hovered around 20 degrees most days and had even been below zero on occasion. Sheila would arrive at school almost blue some mornings after her walk from the high school two blocks away. In desperation I had taken my car to get her on the worst days. I gave her more to wear at recess, but the one time I sent things home, they came back the next day in a paper bag. Sheila remarked with embarrassment that she had gotten a spanking for accepting "charity." The social worker explained that they had repeatedly gotten on the father for this and had even taken him downtown once to buy clothes for Sheila from his welfare check. But apparently he had returned the clothes later. You couldn't force the man, she said, shrugging. She did not want to endanger Sheila by forcing the issue because it was a known fact that he took his anger out on the child. Wasn't that child abuse? I had asked. Not technically. There were not any marks on her. I had slammed the door in frustration after the social worker left. Not any marks on her, huh? Then what the hell was she doing in my class? If that wasn't a mark, I didn't know what was.

During the hours that school was in session, I tried to provide her with all the experiences that her disturbance or circumstances had robbed her of. She came alive. Every moment of her day was filled with exploring and chattering. The first weeks she followed me around all day long. Every-where I went, when I turned around there she would be, clutching a book to her chest or a box of math cubes. A silly smile would spill over her lips when she caught my eye, and she'd scuttle up ready to share. I had to divide my time equally with the other children, of course, but this did not deter her. She would stand patiently behind me waiting until I had finished. Sometimes I would feel a hand ten-tatively take hold of my belt as she got braver and longed for more physical contact. Anton would laugh and kid me in the teacher's lounge about looking like a subway, because as I walked around the room helping the other children, Sheila would go with me, one hand locked into my belt like a seasoned straphanger.

During those first weeks of intense devotion, I was both thankful and dismayed for the two hours we had alone after school. My planning time was shot. Much to Chad's displeasure I was having to haul my work home and do it in the evenings. Anton groused about never getting to talk over matters anymore unless we both came in at seven thirty in the morning. But for Sheila it was ideal. She needed undivided attention.

For all of her six years she had been unwanted, ignored, rejected. Pushed out of cars, pushed out of people's lives. Now there was someone to hold her and talk to her and cuddle her. Sheila soaked up every little bit of intimacy I could spare. Despite the inconvenience of losing those two hours of planning time, I felt less anxious about dragging her around all day hanging on my belt and ignoring her while I worked with the other children, because after school she had me all to herself.

The other children were as delighted as Anton and I were to see Sheila blossom. Notes filled the Kobold's Box scribbled in childish hand. Most of the children were relieved that she did not smell so often or so badly and were quick to comment on that. But they also perceived her budding attempts at kindness.

Sheila had evidently not had much of an opportunity to learn how to be considerate of others or how to be kind. She had been busy surviving and altruism had little place in survival. Consequently, she was used to having to fight for what she wanted. When someone got the place in line she had chosen, she socked that person hard enough to win it back. If another child had a toy she wanted, she grabbed it, wrestled it out of the child's hands and scuttled off to safety with it to hiss angrily at anyone who tried to take it away. In many ways she was much cruder and more obnoxious in her directness than even Peter, but hers was an animal-like aggressiveness, without malice.

I knew that, after six years, it was not going to be a simple matter to convince her that there was another way to do things. My reprimands and cautions and forced marches to the quiet corner did not noticeably dent her behavior. But the Kobold's Box did.

Each night Sheila listened carefully as I read the notes and complimented the children who earned them. Greedily she would count hers after each session and, if given the opportunity, she would count other children's also to see if they got more or less than she did. I tried to discourage that activity. The other kids were not competitive and did not feel the need to measure their worth by the number of notes they received. I did not want them to start. But Sheila could not resist. Her meager portion of self-confidence would not let her rest. Over and over again she wanted to prove that she was the best child in the class, the smartest, the hardest-working, my favorite. When I steadfastly refused to confirm that, she set out to prove it to herself with notes in the Kobold's Box. But that eluded her. She could show me how well she read. That was simple; it only entailed getting out a book. She could show me how well she did math. That, too, was simple. But she could not figure out how to be kind or polite or considerate in order to earn herself more notes.

One afternoon after school she had stayed by the table where I was taking apart a science experiment. "How come Tyler gets so many notes?" she asked. "She gets more than anybody else does. Do you give them to her?"

"No, you know that. Everybody writes out notes."

"How come she gets more?" She cocked her head. "What she do? How come everybody likes her so good?"

"Well," I considered the matter a moment. "For one thing, she's polite. When she wants something

105

she asks, and almost always says please. And thank you too. That makes a person feel more like helping her or being with her, because she makes you feel good for it."

Sheila frowned, looking down at her hands. After a long pause she looked accusingly at me. "How come you never tell me you want me to say please and thank you? I don't know you want that. How come you tell Tyler and you don't tell me?"

I looked at her in disbelief. "I didn't tell Tyler, Sheila. It's just something people do. Everybody likes other people to be polite."

"I don't know that. Nobody ever told me," she said reproachfully. "I never know you want me to do that."

In considering the matter, I knew she was right. I probably never had told her. It was one of those things I took for granted a child would know, especially a bright child like her. I had just assumed she knew. But the unfairness of the assumption was dawning on me. Sheila might never had heard those words in her environment. Or perhaps they had never been meaningful to her before.

"I'm sorry, Sheila. I thought you knew."

"I don't. I can say them if I know you want me to."

I nodded. "I do. They're good words to use, because they make other people feel good. That's important. People like you better for it."

"Will they tell me I'm a nice girl?"

"It'll help them see that you are."

And so, little by little she began to attend to

what others were doing to be kind and considerate. When she did not understand, she asked. At other times when it occurred to me that she did not know, I would tell her during one of our quiet moments.

Chapter Eight

Unfortunately, as in all Gardens of Eden, there were a few snakes. During that first month there were two problems that we did not seem able to lick.

The first problem was perhaps not as major as it felt. Despite all her progress, Sheila steadfastly refused to do paperwork. The instant a piece of paper was given to her, she destroyed it. Occasionally under dire threat from Anton or me, she would not tear it up immediately but actually appear to be working on it. However, it never reached the correction basket. Partway through she would rip it to shreds or scribble over it or crumple it into a tight little wad, stuffing it under the radiator or into the rabbit's cage to be eaten.

I tried any number of methods to stop her. I taped the work to the table so that she could not get it up. Then she simply scribbled over it until it tore. I put it into plastic folders. She would sit before it and refuse to pick up her crayon. On one occasion, she even ate the crayon. I tried using workbooks. But they were more expensive and I got angrier when they were ruined in one sitting. I tried Mrs. Barthuly's technique of laminating, since we had no air conditioner. It was a costly, time-consuming alternative and when presented with one, Sheila would just sit, refusing to do anything. I put the work on the chalkboard. She would erase it when I wasn't looking. There was not a method I could think of that she could not foil.

Sheila was not selective. If it required a written answer, she would not touch it. This included all the academics, coloring sheets and even art projects. She had no objection to oral work or even letting Anton or Whitney or me fill out a paper for her. But she would not do it herself.

Needless to say, this caused considerable friction between us. I tried all my tricks. I sent her to the quiet corner. But she would sit motionless and soundless for such a long time that I felt that was not solving the problem. I did not want her to miss too much of the program simply sitting in a chair. Unlike the first week when the quiet corner provided a means of getting control of her behavior, this did not. The quiet corner was not intended as punishment. So I was not concerned when the children sat there crying or struggling. They were out of control and trying to regain it. But when the child simply went there and sat, it became punishment. Occasionally a few minutes of punishment were warranted, but not long stretches at a time. So if I sent her to the corner and she went and was still not willing to do paperwork after twenty minutes of sitting, I let it drop. My winning the power struggle was not so important as keeping her active and participating in class. Moreover, I was concerned that something else lay behind her refusal to do paperwork. Unless she were angry, there was little else Sheila refused to do outrightly. We had long ago settled who was boss in the classroom and I did not feel she was testing. She went to ridiculous heights to please me in other ways, so it did not make sense to me that she was holding out on this one thing simply to irk me.

But admittedly the behavior did. And not just a little. I became obsessed with it after the third week, storming into the teachers' lounge and raging at the other teachers after school. At night Chad bore the brunt of my frustrations. Finally, one day, in desperation, I dittoed one worksheet off on a whole ream of paper. I maneuvered Sheila over to a table and sat her down at math. I decided that if we had to sit there until Valentine's Day and go through all 500 copies, we would.

"We're going to do this math worksheet today, Sheila. All I want is this one sheet and it's got easy problems on it."

She looked at me distrustfully. "I don't wanna do that."

"Well, it isn't your choice today." I tapped the paper on the table agitatedly with one finger.

"Come on, let's get started."

She sat staring at me. I could tell she was leery of the situation. I had never forced her in such a direct confrontation and she did not seem to be able to tell what to expect from me. Inside myself my own irritation was clenching my organs. My stomach was tight and knotted, my heart beating rapidly. For a split second I wanted to retreat, but my anger over all these weeks of refusal overwhelmed me.

"Do it." I could hear my voice louder and sharper in my ears than I wanted it to be. I reached over and grabbed a pencil, shoving it into her hand. "I said do the paper. Now do it, Sheila."

She wadded up the first paper. I carefully straightened it out and taped it down to the table. Sheila gouged it out with the pencil. Grimly we struggled, me putting out new copies, Sheila ripping at them. Math period passed and the litter of destroyed dittos deepened around our chairs. The others rose for freetime. Sheila glanced around in concern. Freetime was her favorite period and already she noticed Tyler was getting out the little toy people she liked to play with.

"Finish this paper and you can go," I stated, taping a new one down. I had swallowed my anger but a subdued sort of frenzy remained, causing my pulse to continue to run faster.

Sheila was losing patience with me. Angry little grunts were coming out with her heavy breaths. We went through another half-dozen copies of the worksheet. Moving my chair close to hers I pinned her in her chair against the table. Then I taped down a new sheet. Holding down her free hand, I took her other in mine. "I'll help you, Sheila, if you can't do it by yourself," I said doggedly. I could feel perspiration soaking my shirt.

Sheila began to scream, cutting loose with an earsplitting yell. Thankfully she was left-handed as I was, so I could move her hand. I asked her the answer to the first problem. At first she refused to say but then angrily shouted it out. I pushed her hand along the paper, writing a 3. Sheila struggled violently, trying to knock loose my hold of her chair, trying to bite me. Second problem now. Again I dragged the answer out of her and forced her to write it.

We struggled the rest of freetime and finished the paper with her screaming protests and me forcing her hand. The second I let go, she scrabbled the paper up from the tape and shredded it before I could catch her hands. Angrily she threw the paper in my face and broke away from my hold, knocking over the chair. Running to the other side of the classroom she turned to glower at me.

"I HATE YOU!" she screamed as loudly as possible. The other children were finishing their snacks and getting ready for recess, but they paused, watching us. "I hate you! I hate you! I hate you!" Then her frustration with me overpowered her and she stood shrieking wordlessly from her corner behind the animal cages.

Anton cleared the other kids out to recess, but I remained sitting at the table. Expecting her to go

113

off into one of her destructive rages, I was poised to catch her. But she didn't. After a few moments she regained her composure and stopped screaming. However, she remained across the room, staring at me reproachfully. She seemed on the verge of tears, her mouth turned down, her chin quivering. I was beginning to feel like a first-class heel. Her disappointment in me for behaving so antagonistically was bright in her eyes. As I watched her, I knew I had done the wrong thing. I had been desperate, my teacher's instinct to get work accomplished on paper having overcome my better sense. But I shouldn't have let that happen. It had been wrong. I hated myself for allowing such an unimportant thing rule me.

I regarded her. Bad feelings rippled through me, recriminations, self-doubt. Had I destroyed our relationship? We had been doing so well in the three weeks since she had come. Had I screwed it all up in one morning? She watched me. For long, eternal moments we looked at each other in silence.

Slowly Sheila came toward me. Her eyes were still on me all the time, big, wary, accusing eyes. She came over to the far edge of the table. Tracing an invisible design on the smooth top, she studied it before looking back up at me. "You not be very nice to me." Her voice was heavy with feeling.

"No, I guess I wasn't, was I?" I felt the silence again. "I'm sorry, Sheila. I shouldn't have done that."

"You shouldn't oughta be mean to me. I be one of your kids."

"I'm sorry. I just got upset because you never do papers. I just wanted you to do papers like everyone else does. It makes me mad that you won't ever do them because it is important to me that you do. I got angry."

She studied me carefully. Her lower lip was shoved out and her eyes were hurt-looking, but she sidled closer. "Do you still like me?"

"Of course I still like you."

"But you be mad at me and yell."

"Sometimes people get mad. Even at people they like a lot. It doesn't mean they stop liking them. They're just mad. And after a while the anger goes away and they still like each other. I like you as much as ever."

She pressed her lips together. "I don't really hate you."

"I know that. You were just angry like I was."

"You yell at me. I don't like you to yell at me like that. It hurts my ears."

"Look, kitten, I was wrong. I'm sorry. But I can't make it not happen because it already did. I'm sorry. For right now we won't worry about paperwork. We'll do it some other time when you feel like it."

"I ain't never going to feel like it."

My shoulders sagged with discouragement. "Well, then maybe we'll never do any."

She looked at me quizzically. "There gotta be paperwork."

I sighed tiredly. "Not really, I suppose. There are things more important. Besides, maybe someday you will feel like it. We'll do it then."

And so I gave up the paperwork war. Or at least the battle.

I can never understand what it is about being human that allows one to become fixed on small matters and think the world will collapse if things don't go just the way one wants them. Once I got that struggle out of my system, I could never understand why it had been so important to me. But for those first few weeks, it had.

The second problem Sheila presented was much more serious and much less easily resolved. She had a keenly developed sense of revenge that knew no limits. When crossed or taken advantage of, Sheila retaliated with devastating force. Her intelligence made it all the more frightening because she could perceive quickly what was valuable to a person and that was what she abused to get back for being wronged. When Sarah kicked snow on her at recess, Sheila systematically destroyed all of Sarah's artwork around the room. For art-loving Sarah this was crushing. Anton got angry with Sheila running in the halls to lunch one day and she returned afterwards and throttled all the baby gerbils Anton had brought to school that morning on loan from his son. Her cold, clear-eyed appraisal of everyone's sensitivities left me chilled.

But it went beyond destroying papers or even baby gerbils. It was calculated and long-abiding, and often over events which were not intentional. Sheila had to be watched every second. Even when we did think we were watching her carefully, she managed to get away from us.

Lunch hour was the most dangerous time of day. Neither Anton nor I wanted to give up our only break to police Sheila constantly. The lunch aides were clearly still frightened of her, although they did supervise her once more.

One day while Anton and I were in the teachers' lounge finishing up our sandwiches, one of the aides came shrieking in to us, Sheila's name spilling out incoherently. Having nightmares of a repeat of the first day, we dashed out after her as she left.

Sheila had gotten into one of the other teachers' rooms. In a short period of time, only ten or fifteen minutes, she destroyed the room completely. All the student desks were awry or knocked over, personal belongings strewn about. The window blinds were pulled down, books were out of the bookcase, the screen of one of the teaching machines was shattered. I could not have dreamed of further destruction in such a short time.

I yanked open the door. "Sheila!" She whirled around, her eyes dark and forbidding. A pointer was clutched in one hand. "Drop that!"

She stared at me for a long moment but let the pointer drop. She had been with us three weeks. By now she knew when I meant business. If I could get her to drop what she was doing and come over to me, I could take her out calmly. I knew better than to spook her so that she would flee. She would do more damage if she bolted and would become so frightened that she could not be reasoned with. She already had that wild-animal, frenzied look in her eye and I realized how tenuous her hold on control was.

However, as I looked around the room at the disaster, I could not imagine what we were going to do. I was flooded with discouragement at the fact that she would do this kind of thing, that I had let it happen. Sitting in the quiet corner hardly seemed adequate to cover hundreds of dollars' damage. This was also not my room. It was somebody else's. So I knew the matter was out of my hands.

By the time I had coaxed Sheila over to the door, Mr. Collins and the teacher, Mrs. Holmes, whose room this was, were behind me. When I finally got hold of Sheila's hand, Mr. Collins began to roar.

I suppose he roared with very good reason. But I knew what his solution to the problem was going to include. Mr. Collins was of the old school where most infractions were cured, or at least helped, by the paddle. He took hold of Sheila's arm. I already had her by the overall strap and did not let go.

We eyed each other, neither of us speaking. Sheila was stretched out between us.

I could not let him take her. Not after all this time of reassuring her that she could never be hurt here. There had been too many spankings in her past already. And too many people who had broken their promises. I could not let this happen.

Still the principal and I did not speak. However, that did not diminish the strength of the challenge. Under my fingers on her shoulder, I could feel the tenseness of Sheila's muscles.

When he finally did speak, Mr. Collins' voice came out in a hoarse whisper pushed between gritted teeth. He made it clear that not only was Sheila going down to the office for a paddling but I was coming along as witness.

Oh cripes, I was thinking. All I wanted to do was argue with him while Sheila was strung out between us, like two dogs fighting over a bone. But there wasn't much choice. I could not agree with him. Certainly I did not want Sheila to think I did.

We were hissing back and forth, one-or two-word responses mostly. He was losing patience with me.

"So help me God, Miss Hayden, you come with me right now or you're not going to have a job by the time this day is out. I don't care what I have to do. Is that clear?"

I stared at him. All sorts of things came into my head then. I had tenure. I belonged to the union. He had no power to fire me. Those things all came to me, but on a very academic level. What came at gut level was fear. What would happen to me if I got fired? Could I ever find another teaching job in town? Who would take care of my class? I had a history of rash and impulsive actions. Was this going to be one more? And what for? A kid bound for the state hospital? Here I was about to lose my job over a kid I'd barely known three weeks, who sooner or later would be elsewhere anyway, and who by all accounts wasn't very important to anybody anyhow. What would everyone think if I lost my job? Would Chad still want me? How would I explain it to my mom? What would people think? For the worst excuse of all, I let go of that overall strap.

Mr. Collins turned and took Sheila down the hall. I followed at a distance and felt like Benedict Arnold. Yet maybe they were right. I had lost control in a major way twice in three weeks with this kid. Maybe she did need a state hospital placement. I did not know. This had gotten to be more than I could manage.

I flopped into a chair in Mr. Collins' office. Sheila was calm. Far calmer than I. She came in beside Mr. Collins and stood complacently, not looking at me and not making any sound. Mr. Collins shut the door. From his desk drawer he took out a long paddle. Sheila did not flinch as he sized it up next to her.

I was bitter. Why did he have to have such neolithic methods of education? What kind of man was he? A lusty, full-bodied hate rose in me. How could he do this to me? How could I let him? After all my reassurances to her that I did not whip kids, what would she think of me now? What would I think of myself, now that I knew when the going got rough I would opt for my own skin?

Through the chaos in my own head, I was suddenly and deeply touched by Sheila's innocent courage. She glanced at me briefly and then looked back at Mr. Collins. She looked very much like any other six-year-old just then. Her lips were parted to reveal the gaps where teeth had fallen out. Her eyes were wide and round, the fear in them disguised enough so that if one had not known her, one would not have recognized it for what it was. I saw the little white and orange duck barrettes in her hair and thought how much she liked them. Those were her favorites, her lucky clips, she told me one day. *Well, your luck's run out this time, kid,* I thought. Like so many other times before. The duck clips seemed obscene in this place.

She stood so staunchly; no six-year-old should be able to do that. I wondered how often a board had been shown to her. Yet about her persisted such a little child's innocence; the duck barrettes, the long, impossibly straight hair not quite captured in pigtails, the worn overalls. I felt like crying. But the tears would be for myself for finding out I did not have the kind of strength that she had.

My viscera crinkled. This should not be happening.

But it was. Mr. Collins stated flatly that he had had it. Did she know what she had done? No response. She might even be suspended from school, he said. I knew the lecture was as much for my benefit as Sheila's. We were both being put in our places. He told her she was getting three whacks of the board. She had sucked her lips between her teeth. She watched him without blinking.

"Lean over and grab your ankles."

She stared without moving.

"Lean over and take hold of your ankles, Sheila."

She did not move.

"If I have to tell you one more time, I'll add an-other whack. Now bend over."

"Sheila, please," I said. "Please do as he says."

Still no response. Her eyes flickered toward mine a moment.

Mr. Collins yanked her down roughly and with a whoosh the board hit her. She fell on her knees on that first whack, but her face remained un-changed. Mr. Collins lifted her back to her feet. Again came the whack. Again she fell to her knees. The last two whacks she stood up and did not fall. But not a sound came out of her, not a tear came to her eyes. I could tell this had infuriated Mr. Collins.

I sat watching, numbed. After all my reassur-ance to her, it had come to this. I had worked so hard, so damned hard on this kid. I normally never let myself fully realize how much I invested in the children. Like the little fears and discouragements that I kept shooing out of consciousness during day-to-day living. I also spooked away into hiding how much the kids really meant to me. Because I knew that if I was aware, I would feel even more disheartened when my kids failed. Or when I did. That was what burned so many people out in this business: knowing they cared too much. So I tried not to see it. I was a dreamer. But my dream was a very expensive one. For all of us.

Mr. Collins had me sign a witness form that I had been present when he had paddled her. Then wearily I took Sheila's hand and we went down the hall.

I did not know what to do next. My head was spinning. When I got to the classroom door, I peered through the window. Anton had started afternoon activities and Whitney was there. Things seemed peaceful enough. I looked down at Sheila. "We need to talk, kiddo."

Knocking on the door, I waited for Anton to answer. When he arrived, I explained that I wanted to be alone with Sheila a little while, that too much had happened and I needed to get some things straightened out. I asked if he thought he and Whitney could manage while we were gone. He nodded with a smile. So I left them, one uneducated migrant worker and a fourteen-year-old kid, in charge of eight crazy children. The ludicrousness of the situation struck me and I almost laughed. But I could find no laughter in me just then.

I ended up taking Sheila into a book closet because I could not find anywhere else we could be alone undisturbed. I hauled in two teensy chairs, turned on the light and sat down, shutting the door behind me. For a long moment we stared at each other.

"Why on earth do you do those things?" I asked, my discouragement ringing clearly in my voice.

"You ain't gonna make me talk."

"Oh geez, Sheila, come off it. I can't play games with you. Now don't do that to me." I could not tell if she were angry or what. Inwardly, I wanted to apologize to her for having given in and letting Mr. Collins take her. But I did not do it. The need

123

was more mine. I wanted to be forgiven.

We regarded each other without talking and the silence seemed to draw into eternity. Finally I shook my head and sighed wearily. "Look, that whole thing didn't turn out so well. I'm sorry."

Still silence. She would not talk to me. Her gaze was unwavering and I had to look away. Outside the door of the book closet I could hear classes getting ready for recess, noisy and rambunctious, such that they thudded against the door. Inside it was so quiet no one would ever know we were in there.

I looked at her. Looked away. Looked back. She stared. "Good God, Sheila, what *is* it you want out of me?"

The pupils in her eyes dilated. "Are you mad at me?"

"You could say that, yes. I'm just a little mad at everybody right now."

"You gonna whip me?"

My shoulders sagged. "No, I'm not. Like I told you a million times now, I don't whip kids."

"Why not?"

I looked at her in dismal disbelief. "Why should I? It doesn't help any, does it?"

"It helps me."

"Does it? Does it really, Sheila? Did what Mr. Collins just do to you help you?"

"My Pa," she said softly, "he says it be the only way to make me decent. He whips me and I must be betterer, 'cause he ain't never leaved me on no highway like my Mama done."

My heart melted. I certainly hadn't intended it

to. I had been so angry at her for all this trouble she had caused. But my heart melted when she spoke. Jesus, I thought, what did this kid expect out of people. I reached an arm out to her. "Come here, Sheila, and let me hold you."

Willingly she came, climbing up into my lap clumsily like a toddler. She wrapped her arms around my ribs and clutched me tightly. I pressed her close. I was doing it as much for myself as I was for her because I didn't know what to do. God Almighty, I hurt inside.

What were we going to do? She had to stop this destructiveness, that went without saying. But how? What were a bunch of tipped-over desks and broken window shades against a little girl? Even if she had done a million dollars' worth of damage, what was that against a life? If they sent her out of the school, suspended her, she wouldn't come back. I had been in the business long enough to know that. Sooner or later, it would be off to the state hospital as planned. What then? What chance did a six-year-old have of coming out of a state hospital to live a normal life? I doubted it had ever happened. We'd lose her, without most of us even realizing she had been there at all. This bright, creative little girl who had never had a chance at life, would never get one. Were a bunch of lousy desks worth that much?

"What're we gonna do, Sheila?" I asked, rocking her in my arms. "You just can't keep doing these sorts of things and I don't know how to stop you."

"I won't do it again."

"I wish you wouldn't. But let's not make any promises we can't keep just now, okay? I just want you to tell me why you did it to begin with. I want to understand that."

"I dunno. I do be awful mad at her. She yell at me at lunch and it not be my fault. It be Susannah's fault but she yell at me. I be mad." Her voice quivered. "Do they gonna make me go away?"

"I don't know, honey."

"I don't want them to." Her voice rose suddenly to a little squeak, betraying her nearness to tears. "I won't never ever do that again. I wanna stay. I wanna stay in this here school. I won't never do it again, I promise." She pressed her face against me.

I stroked her hair, feeling the duck clips under my fingers. "Sheila," I asked, "I never see you cry. Don't you ever feel like it?"

"I don't never cry."

"Why not?"

"Ain't nobody can hurt me that ways."

I looked down at her. The cold perception in her statement was fearsome. "What do you mean?"

"Ain't nobody can hurt me. They don't know I hurt if I don't cry. So they can't hurt me. Ain't nobody can make me cry neither. Not even my Pa when he whips me. Not even Mr. Collins. You seen that. I don't cry even when he hits me with the stick. You seen that, didn't you?"

"Yes, I saw it. But don't you want to cry? Didn't it hurt?"

For a very long moment she did not respond.

126

She took hold of one of my hands in both of hers. "It sort of hurts." She looked up, her eyes unreadable. "Sometimes I do cry a little, at night sometimes. My Pa, he don't come home 'til it be real late sometimes and I have to be by myself and I get scared. Sometimes I cry a little bit; it get wet right here on my eyes. But I make it go away. Crying don't do no good, and it makes me think of Jimmie and my Mama if I cry. It makes me miss them."

"Sometimes it does help."

"It don't never help me. I ain't never gonna cry. Never."

She had turned around so that she straddled my legs and was facing me. I had my arms around her back. She fingered my shirt buttons while she talked.

"Do you ever cry?" she asked

I nodded. "Sometimes. Mostly when I feel bad, I cry. I can't help it much. I just do. But it makes me feel better. Crying is a good thing in a way. It washes out the hurt, if you give it a chance."

She shrugged. "I don't do it."

"Sheila, what're we gonna do to fix up what you did in Mrs. Holmes' room?"

Again she shrugged. She feigned involvement in twisting one of my buttons.

"I want your ideas. I'm not going to whip you and I don't think suspending you is a good idea either. But we've got to do something. I want your ideas."

"You could make me sit in the quiet corner the rest of the day and you could take away the housekeeping corner for a week or something. You could take away the dolls from me."

"I don't want to punish you. Mr. Collins did that already. I want a way to make it better for Mrs. Holmes. I want to fix up what happened in there."

A pause ensued. "Maybe I could pick it up."

"I think that's a good idea. But what about being sorry? Could you apologize?"

She tugged at the button. "I don't know."

"Are you sorry?"

She nodded slowly. "I be sorry this here happened."

"Apologizing is a good thing to learn to do. It makes people feel better about you. Shall we practice together saying you're sorry and offering to pick up, so it'll be easier to do? I can be Mrs. Holmes and we'll practice."

Sheila fell against me heavily, pressing her face into my breasts. "I just want you to hold me for a little bit first. My butt do be fierce sore and I wanna wait 'til it feels better. I don't wanna think now."

With a smile I clutched her to me and we sat together in the dim light of the book closet, waiting—she for relief for her bottom and the courage for what lay ahead; I for the world to change.

Chapter Nine

Resolving that situation did not turn out to be simple. Sheila and I did go to Mrs. Holmes' room and Sheila apologized and offered to pick up. As I had hoped, Sheila's childlike innocence, her small size, her natural beauty all brought out the motherliness in Mrs. Holmes. She was willing to accept Sheila's attempts to make amends.

On the other hand, it was not so easy with Mr. Collins. This had been the last straw for him, not only for Sheila, but for my class. Everything came to a head—including things not even related to Sheila's destructiveness. The two of us simply had different value systems, each of which seemed better in our own eyes. It all came out in a full-scale war after Sheila's incident and finally Ed Somers had to come and mediate. In no uncertain terms Mr. Collins wanted Sheila out of the school. The child was violent, uncontrolled, dangerous and destructive. She frightened the other children with her behavior, as well as the other teachers and the staff. She had caused $700 worth of damage in Mrs. Holmes' room alone. There was a point, he said, when society had the right to protect itself from harm. An identified threat such as this child should not be allowed to run loose in a public school. She belonged in the state hospital. Why wasn't she there?

I tried to explain Sheila's progress in my room. I explained how it had only taken three days to crack through this child and get her to work productively in the classroom. I spoke of her IQ, of her history of abuse and abandonment. I implored Ed to let me keep her. This was just one incident, I said. I'd watch her better after this. I'd give up my own lunch hour if I had to. But give me another chance, I asked. Let me try again. I wouldn't be so careless.

The mood was grim. Ed explained to me that they had the very real pressure from parents to consider. When word got out from the children in Mrs. Holmes' class, parents would call. And the court had arranged for her commitment before I had ever entered the picture. My room was the holding tank. I shouldn't get so involved, Ed said politely, but firmly. It was affecting my better judgment. He smiled sadly. It was nice she was making progress, but that was not why she had been placed with me. She was there to wait until a space came open at the hospital. That was all.

As I listened to him I could feel the lump in my throat and the stinging in my eyes. I did not want to cry in front of them. I did not want them to know they were getting to me that much. But I could feel the tears starting. My rational side kept urging calmness. They were not being intentionally cruel; indeed, they probably were not being cruel at all. But it felt that way to me. Goddamn them, what were they doing to me? I was a teacher. My job was to teach. I wasn't a jailer. Or was that all Ed had wanted when he had established my class? I was full of recriminations. What had they thought they had given me but a little girl—a scared, hurt, mistreated six-year-old. What was it that was so frightening about her? Now they told me that I didn't have to worry about her; she was only with me to wait. She could have sat in that chair of hers for however many months it took for the space in the state hospital to come through, and then she could leave. I had obviously misunderstood the matter. I had thought I was supposed to be her teacher.

Ed leaned forward resting his elbows on the table and blowing into his hands. He tried to reassure me, telling me not to get upset. He was embarrassed that the situation was making me cry and for a moment I was pleased he was. I wanted everyone as unhappy as I. But the moment passed and the gloom settled over all of us.

I left the room still tearful, went directly to my car and drove home. Feeling bitter and resentful, I feared I would need more than "Star Trek" to calm me that evening. My idealism had taken a mighty blow. I had learned some people were not even worth $700.

As always, Chad proved the calm center in my storm. Listening to me rage, he shook his head good-naturedly. Go to bed, he advised, it wasn't so bad as it seemed. Despite my feelings, it wasn't me against the world. It'd come out in the end, everything always does. Not in a mood to be placated, I shut myself in the bathroom and sobbed through a forty-five-minute shower. Chad was still sitting in the living room pulling a string for the cat when I emerged. Chad smiled. And then I smiled. I wasn't happy, but I was resigned.

It did not turn out so badly as I had anticipated. An education had to be provided for every child and I was at that moment Sheila's only source of education. In compromise, Ed told Mr. Collins that he could have an extra lunch aide solely to supervise my room and that Sheila was never under any circumstances to leave my room except under my direct supervision. The matter was at least temporarily settled.

Despite the furor over Sheila's placement, things were going smoothly in class. We were becoming a group again, adjusting to Sheila's being with us. February had dawned cold and crisp with a groundhog's promise of six more weeks of winter. Sheila was fitting in and we were quite happily twelve. I appreciated those unexpected days of peace because they were rare in our class.

Academically, Sheila was plunging ahead. I could hardly find enough to keep her agile mind busy. I had dropped the paperwork altogether, conceding her the victory, although I had to admit still thinking about it. Whitney, Anton and I tested her orally and had discussions with her over what she was doing. She was an avid reader, consuming books faster than I could find them. I was thankful for this new interest because without the paperwork, which makes up a good share of each child's academic day, she finished her assignments rapidly.

Socially Sheila was making slower progress, but it was steady. She and Sarah had become friends and were beginning to share the typical pleasures of small girls' friendships. I also assigned Sheila to help Susannah Joy to learn her colors. This had a multiple effect: it gave me a much-needed helper; it occupied Sheila's extra time; it gave her responsibility; and it helped Sheila learn the finer points of an interpersonal relationship. An added benefit was the boost to Sheila's self-confidence. She was elated to be on the giving end for once and have someone need her. Some evenings after school she would busily make materials and carry on long earnest discussions with Anton or me about things she could do with Susannah to help Susie learn. Watching her, I always wanted to laugh, wondering if I looked like that to someone watching me. But she took the job with such innocent seriousness that I contained myself.

Sheila was beginning to grow away from needing to follow me around all day long. She still watched me often and would sit nearby if given a choice, but she did not need physical contact all the time. On bad days when things had gone wrong before she came to school, or even the other kids gave her a hard time, or even when I reprimanded her, it was not unusual to feel her hand go through my belt and for a while once more, she would move around the room with me while I worked. I did not discourage it; I felt she needed the security of knowing I was not going to leave her. The line was fine between dependence and overdependence, but I had noticed that most of my kids went through a period of intense involvement and attachment in the beginning. It seemed to be a natural phase and if things progressed right, the child outgrew the behavior, becoming secure enough in his relationships that he no longer needed such tangible evidence of caring. So it was with Sheila.

One good thing came out of the incident with Mrs. Holmes' room. I tracked down Sheila's father. After school one evening in early February Anton and I piled into the car and drove out to the migrant camp. Sheila and her father lived in a small, tarpaper shack beside the railroad tracks.

He was a big man, over six feet tall, heavy-set with a huge belly that slopped over his belt, only one tooth on the bottom and very evil-smelling breath. When we arrived he was carrying a can of beer and was already quite drunk.

Anton forged ahead into the tiny house. It was only one room really, divided by a curtain. A lumpy brown couch was at one end and a bed was at the other. Otherwise there was no furniture. The place reeked of stale urine.

Sheila's father came into the house behind us and motioned us to sit on the couch. Sheila was crouched in a far corner by the bed, her eyes round and wild. She had failed to acknowledge either Anton or me, but sat folded in upon herself as she had in the first days of school. I mentioned that perhaps it would be best if Sheila were not present, as I needed to discuss some things with her father that might be painful for her to listen to.

He shook his head and flapped a hand in Sheila's direction. "She's gotta stay in that corner. You can't trust that kid out of your sight for five minutes. She tried to set fire to a place down the road the other night. If I don't keep her in, the police will be here again." He went on to give us the details.

"She ain't really my child," he explained, offering Anton a beer. "That bitch of a woman who's her mother, that's her bastard. She ain't my child and you can tell it. Just look at her. And the kid don't have a decent bone in her body. I haven't in all my born days seen a child like that one for causing trouble."

Anton and I listened speechlessly. I was mortified for her sake that Sheila was in the room. If he told her these things every day, no wonder she had such a low opinion of herself. At least, though, it was private. To tell it to us in front of her—I was horrified even to be there. It was like some scene out of a poorly written novel. Anton made an effort to refute the man's view but that only made him angry with us. So we let him talk, fearful of bringing repercussions on Sheila if we upset him.

"Now Jimmie, he was my boy. Better little boy you never seen than my Jimmie. And that bitch, she took him. Just upped and took him right out from under my nose, she did. And what did she do? She leaves this little bastard." He sighed. "I told her if one more school person came out here about her, I wouldn't forget it."

"I didn't come to say anything bad," I said quickly. "She's doing a nice job in our room."

He snorted. "She should. With a class full of crazies, she should know how to act. Jesus Christ, woman, I'm at my wit's end with that child."

The conversation never improved. My blood was icy with horror and I wished I could shrink up and fall through a crack in the floor to save Sheila from the humiliation of having people she cared about hear his words. But I couldn't, nor could I stop him. Her father went on and on. I tried to tell him that Sheila was a gifted child with marvelous intelligence. That was not in his world. What did she need with that, he asked, it'd only give her more of a chance to think up trouble. Finally the conversation turned back to his beloved, lost Jimmie. He began to cry, big tears rolling over his fat cheeks. Where, oh where, had Jimmie been taken, and why had he been left with this little bogie that he did not even believe was his child?

In a detached way I felt sorry for the man. I think he did love the boy and the loss must have been difficult. In his tangled, immature way he seemed to see Sheila as somehow to blame for losing Jimmie. If she hadn't been so impossible perhaps his woman would have stayed. He did not know what to do with Sheila or himself. So he lost himself in a couple of six-packs of beer and wept to two complete strangers about a life thirty years out of control.

As wretched as Sheila's life looked, I knew we would have a difficult time getting her removed from her father's care. This was a community with a huge population of losers. The migrants, the penitentiary, the state hospital, all combined to make a town within a town, one that was so large that the parent community could not meet its needs. There were not enough social workers and foster homes and welfare checks to sort out the disasters and repair the damage. Only the most severely abused children were removed from their homes because there was no place to put the others. Yet I felt compelled to ask her father if he had considered voluntary foster placement since he was having such a hard time.

My question was a mistake. From tears, he exploded into a rage, leaping up and waving his hands at me. Who was I to suggest he give his child up? What kind of person was I? He had never accepted help from anyone before; he was man enough to solve his own problems without any help from me, thank you. With that he demanded that Anton and I leave his house immediately. Filled with frustration and angry sorrow, we left hoping we had not endangered Sheila. It was a grim visit and I wished I had never gone.

Afterwards, I rode across the migrant camp to Anton's. He too lived in little more than a hut. There were three rooms which he shared with his wife and two young sons. It seemed pitifully inadequate to someone with my middle-class upbringing, but it was clean and well-kept. The Spartan furniture was offset by handmade rugs and needlepoint pillows. A large crucifix adorned a wall in the main room. Anton's wife was cheerful and welcoming, even though she spoke no English and I spoke no Spanish. Hs boys were eager, chattery little fellows who climbed all over me asking about the classroom their daddy had told them of. They were so verbal and spirited despite their youth that they seemed to be geniuses in my eyes. I had grown so used to viewing my kids as normal. The five of us shared three Cokes and a bowl of corn chips while Anton diffidently asked about the possibilities of his going back to school and earning a teaching degree. He did not even have a high school diploma yet, although he eagerly told me that he was studying for his General Equivalency Diploma. I had not previously heard about these secret dreams he had been nursing. He had grown to love the children in our class, in spite of his initial reluctance, and someday he hoped he might teach in a class of his own. I was touched by his dreams, because that indeed was what I feared they were. I doubted he was aware of all the time and money involved in attaining that level of education. But watching his wife beam as her husband talked of such great plans and seeing the little boys dance at the thought that their daddy was going to be a real teacher and someday they might live in a real house and have bicycles, I did not mention the drawbacks. Besides, my emotions had not fully recovered and my mind still wandered across to the other side of the camp, wondering what was happening in the shack by the railroad tracks.

Chapter Ten

During the two hours that Sheila and I had alone together, after school, I had begun reading aloud to her. Although she was perfectly capable of reading most of the books herself, I wanted to provide her with some extra closeness as well as share some of my favorite books with her. We also needed to talk about some of the things in the books, I found out, because Sheila had had such a deprived childhood that she did not understand many things. This was not because she did not know what the words meant, but because she had no idea how they applied to real life.

For instance, in *Charlotte's Web* Sheila puzzled the longest time over why the little girl wanted to keep the runt pig, Wilbur, in the first place. He was a runt after all, the poorest of the litter. In Sheila's mind it was perfectly understandable that

141

the father did not want to keep him. I explained that Fern loved him because he was tiny and could not help being a runt. But Sheila could not conceptualize that. She lived strictly by the law of survival of the fittest.

So I read to her, holding her on my lap as we sat in the reading corner surrounded by pillows. When she did not understand a word or a passage, we talked about it, often wandering off into long discussions about the way things were. I was fascinated by this girl who possessed a child's innocence in reasoning and a child's directness, but an adult's comprehension. Her clear-eyed perception of things was in many ways frightening because it was so often nakedly right. But the child's way she put some things together made me laugh.

One night I brought in a copy of *The Little Prince*. "Hey, Sheil," I called to her. "I've got a book to share with you."

She came running across the room, leaping squarely onto my stomach and snatching the book from my hands. Carefully she inspected all the pictures before we settled down to read. Once started, she sat motionless, her fingers gripping the cloth of my jeans.

The Little Prince is a short book and within half an hour I was almost halfway through it. When we came to the part about the fox she became even more intent. I could feel her bony little hips in my lap as she wiggled to become more comfortable.

"Come and play with me," proposed the little

prince. "I am so unhappy."

"I cannot play with you," the fox said. "I am not tamed."

"Ah! Please excuse me," said the little prince. But, after some thought, he added:

"What does that mean—'tame'?"

"It is an act too often neglected," said the fox. "It means to establish ties."

" 'To establish ties'?"

"Just that," said the fox. "To me, you are still nothing more than a little boy who is just like a hundred thousand other little boys. And I have no need of you. And you, on your part, have no need of me. To you, I am nothing more than a fox like a hundred thousand other foxes. But if you tame me, then we shall need each other. To me, you will be unique in all the world. To you, I shall be unique in all the world . . ."

"My life is very monotonous," he said. "I hunt chickens; men hunt me. All the chickens are just alike, and all the men are just alike. And, in consequence, I am a little bored. But if you tame me, it will be as if the sun came to shine on my life. I shall know the sound of a step that will be different from all the others. Other steps send me hurrying back underneath the ground. Yours will call me, like music, out of my burrow. And then look: You see the grain-fields down yonder? I do not eat bread. Wheat is of no use to me. The wheat fields have nothing to say to me. And that is sad. But you have hair that is the color of gold. Think how wonderful that will be when you have tamed me! The grain, which is also golden, will bring me back the thought of you. And I shall love to listen to the wind in the wheat . . ."

The fox gazed at the little prince, for a long time.

"Please—tame me!" he said.

"I want to, very much," the little prince replied. "But I have not much time. I have friends to discover, and a great many things to understand."

"One only understands the things that one tames," said the fox. "Men have no more time to understand anything. They buy things all ready made at the shops. But there is no shop anywhere where one can buy friendship, and so men have no friends any more. If you want a friend, tame me . . ."

"What must I do, to tame you?" asked the little prince.

"You must be very patient," replied the fox. "First you will sit down at a little distance from me—like that—in the grass. I shall look at you out of the corner of my eye, and you will say nothing. Words are the source of misunderstandings. But you will sit a little closer to me every day . . ."

Sheila put her hand on the page. "Read that again, okay?"

I reread the section. She twisted around in my lap to look at me and for a long time locked me in her gaze. "That be what you do, huh?"

"What do you mean?"

"That's what you done with me, huh? Tamed me."

I smiled.

"It be just like this book says, remember? I do be so scared and I run in the gym and then you come in and you sit on the floor. Remember that? And I peed my pants, remember? I be so scared. I think you gonna whip me fierce bad 'cause I done so much wrong that day. But you sit on the floor. And you come a little closer and a little closer. You was taming me, huh?"

I smiled in disbelief. "Yeah, I guess maybe I was."

"You tame me. Just like the little prince tames the fox. Just like you tamed me. And now I be special to you, huh? Just like the fox."

"Yeah, you're special all right, Sheil."

She turned back around, settling into my lap again. "Read the rest of it."

So the little prince tamed the fox. And when the hour of his departure drew near—

"Ah," said the fox, "I shall cry."

"It is your own fault," said the little prince. "I never wished you any sort of harm; but you wanted me to tame you . . ."

"Yes, that is so," said the fox.

"But now you are going to cry!" said the little prince.

"Yes, that is so," said the fox.

"Then it has done you no good at all!"

145

"It has done me good," said the fox, "because of the color of the wheat fields." And then he added:

"Go and look again at the roses. You will understand now that yours is unique in all the world. Then come back to say goodbye to me, and I will make you a present of a secret."

The little prince went away, to look again at the roses.

"You are not at all like my rose," he said. "As yet you are nothing. No one has tamed you, and you have tamed no one. You are like my fox when first I knew him. He was only a fox like a hundred thousand other foxes. But I have made him my friend, and now he is unique in all the world."

And the roses were very much embarrassed.

"You are beautiful, but you are empty," he went on. "One could not die for you. To be sure, an ordinary passerby would think that my rose looked just like you—the rose that belongs to me. But in herself alone she is more important than all the hundreds of you other roses: because it is she that I have sheltered behind the screen; because it is for her that I have killed the caterpillars (except the two or three that we saved to become butterflies); because it is she that I have listened to, when she grumbled, or boasted, or even sometimes when she said nothing. Because she is *my* rose."

And he went back to meet the fox.

"Goodbye," he said.

"Goodbye," said the fox. "And now here is my secret, a very simple secret: It is only with the heart that one can see rightly; what is essential is invisible to the eye."

"What is essential is invisible to the eye," the little prince repeated, so that he would be sure to remember.

"It is the time you have wasted for your rose that makes your rose so important."

"It is the time I have wasted for my rose—" said the little prince, so that he would be sure to remember.

"Men have forgotten this truth," said the fox. "But you must not forget it. You become responsible, forever, for what you have tamed. You are responsible for your rose . . ."

Sheila slid off my lap and turned around, getting on her knees so that she could look directly into my eyes. "You be 'sponsible for me. You tame me, so now you be 'sponsible for me?"

For several moments I looked into her fathomless eyes. I was not certain what she was asking me. She reached up and put her arms around my neck, not releasing me from her gaze.

"I tame you a little bit too, huh? You tame me and I tame you. And now I do be 'sponsible for you too, huh?"

I nodded. She let go of me and sat down. For a moment she lost herself, tracing a design on the rug with her finger.

"Why you do this?" she asked.

"Do what, Sheil?"

"Tame me."

I did not know what to say.

Her water blue eyes rose to me. "Why you care? I can't never figure that out. Why you *want* to tame me?"

My mind raced. They had never told me in my education classes or my child-psych classes that there would be children like this one. I was unprepared. This seemed like one of those moments when if I could only say the right thing . . .

"Well, kiddo, I don't have a good reason, I guess. It just seemed like the thing to do."

"Do it be like the fox? Do I be special now 'cause you tame me? Do I be a special girl?"

I smiled. "Yeah, you're my special girl. It's like the fox says, now that I made you my friend, you're unique in all the world. I guess I always wanted you for my special girl. I guess that's why I tamed you to begin with."

"Do you love me?"

I nodded.

"I love you too. You be my special best person in the whole world."

Sheila scrunched herself down and around, lying on the carpet with her head resting on my thigh. She fiddled with a piece of lint she had found on the floor. I prepared to read again.

"Torey?"

"Yes?"

"You ain't never gonna leave me?"

I touched her bangs brushing them back. "Well, someday, I reckon. When the school year is over and you go on to another class and another teacher. But not before then and that's a long time away."

She shot up. "You be my teacher. I ain't never gonna have another teacher."

"I'm your teacher now. But someday we'll be finished."

She shook her head; her eyes had clouded. "This here be my room. And I do be gonna be in here forever."

"It won't be for a long time yet. When the time comes, you'll be ready."

"No sir. You tame me; you be 'sponsible for me. You can't never leave me cause you be 'sponsible for me forever. It says so right there, and that's what you done to me, so it's your fault that I got tame."

"Hey honey," I pulled her into my lap. "Don't worry about it."

"But you gonna leave me," she said accusingly, pulling out of my hold. "Just like my Mama done. And Jimmie. And everybody. My Pa, he would if they wouldn't put him in jail for it. He telled me that. You do be just like everybody else. You leave me too. Even after you tame me and I not ask you to."

"It won't be that way, Sheila. I'm not leaving you. I'm staying right here. When the year is over things will change, but I won't leave you. Just like it says in the story, the little prince tamed the fox and now he's gone, but really he's always going to

149

be with the fox because every time the fox sees the wheat fields he thinks of the little prince. He remembers how much the little prince loved him. That's how it'll be with us. We'll always love each other. Going away is easier then, because every time you remember someone who loves you, you feel a little bit of their love."

"No you don't. You just miss them."

I reached an arm out to her, bringing her close once again. She wasn't going to be convinced. "Well, it's a little too hard to think about right now. You're not ready to leave and I won't leave you. Someday you will be ready and it'll be easier."

"No, I won't. I won't never be ready."

I was rocking her in my arms, holding her very tightly. This was too scary a thing for her right now. I did not know how to treat the issue because the time would come when she would have to leave, either when the state hospital had an opening or at the end of the school year in June. I already suspected my class would not exist the next year for a number of reasons. There was no use hoping that I would have her beyond the end of the year. So the time was coming and I did not know if in four short months she would feel much differently than she did right now.

Sheila let me rock her. She was studying my face. "Will you cry?"

"When?"

"When you leave?"

"Remember what the fox said? 'One runs the risk of weeping, if one lets himself be tamed.' He's right. One cries a little. Every time someone goes away, you cry a little. Love hurts sometimes. Sometimes it makes you cry."

"I cry about Jimmie and my Mama. But my Mama, she don't love me none."

"I don't know about that. That happened before I knew you and I never met your Mama. But I can't imagine that she didn't love you some. It's very hard not to love your kids."

"But she leaved me on the highway. You don't do that to your kids if you love them. Pa, he tell me that."

"Like I said, Sheila, I don't know. I don't know who's right. But it isn't always that way. I'm never going to leave you in that way. When school is over and you go somewhere else, we'll still be together, even if we don't see each other. Because like the fox said, every time he saw a wheat field he thought of the little prince. So in a special way the little prince was with him. That's the way it'll be with us."

"I don't want no wheat fields. I want you."

"But that's special too, Sheil. At first we'll be a little sad, but it'll get better and then it'll be good. Every time we think of the other, we will feel nice inside. You see, there won't ever be enough miles to make us forget how happy we've been. Nothing can take away your memories."

She pushed her face into me. "I don't want to think about it."

"No, you're right. This isn't the time to worry about it. It's a long ways away. In the meantime, we'll think of other things."

Chapter Eleven

Although I had ceased to be obsessed with our paperwork war, it was never completely out of my mind. First, I had a hard time keeping Sheila busy without needing one of the adults with her constantly. I also worried that she would not be acceptable to a regular class teacher if she would never do any worksheets or workbooks. While in my class we could get away with it, a regular teacher with twenty-five other children and an academic schedule to keep would never be able to afford such frivolity. Finally, I worried that she was finding out that her current method kept a lot of adult attention focused on her. She was perfectly capable of answering any question we thought up for her, but she thrived on capturing Anton, Whitney or me and reciting her answers. This was not particularly acceptable behavior even in my room.

I still had no firm idea why she was so negative about paperwork. I suspect that it had something to do with failure. If she never committed anything to paper, it was impossible to prove that she ever made a mistake. And Sheila fell apart when she did make an error and was corrected, regardless of how gentle the correction was. I had an awful suspicion from random comments she made that once she had taken a paper home and had had a bad encounter with her father regarding it. But she had a large number of bad encounters with him, so I doubted that that alone accounted for her phobia. Perhaps she simply was bright enough to figure out that this method saved her a lot of work and got her the attention she craved. I did not usually think that, because there were a lot of easier ways for a bright child to achieve the same end. After a particularly hectic day, though, Anton expressed those sentiments.

However, there was one thing Sheila seemed to be finding more and more irresistible. I encouraged a great amount of creative writing in class. The children kept journals in which they recorded what they felt, things that happened to them and other important events in their lives. Often when I tangled with a child and one or both of us got angry, the child had learned that one place for expression was in the journal. Thus, kids were scribbling in their journals on and off all day. Each night I went through and left notes or comments to the children about what they had written. It was a personal communication and we each valued the opportunity to find out how the other felt. In a similar manner I had formal writing assignments almost daily in which the children wrote on an assigned topic. I had found that after the children learned to write easily and to associate words with the feelings they could evoke, all of them, even Susannah, could express themselves in some instances better on paper than face-to-face. So in our room a great amount of written correspondence took place.

Needless to say, Sheila, with her distaste for paper, did not write. This seemed to bother her a bit. She would crane her neck to see what the other kids were writing, or wander close to them during creative writing time, instead of going over to the reading corner or somewhere to play as she was supposed to. Finally, a day came in mid-February where her curiosity got the better of her.

She came over to me after I had handed out the sheets for writing. "I might write something, if you give me a piece of paper."

I looked down at her. It occurred to me that I might be able to swing the whole paperwork issue around to my side with a little reverse psychology. So I shook my head. "No, this is paperwork. You don't do paperwork, remember?"

"I might do this."

"No, I don't think so. I can't risk wasting any more paper on you. You wouldn't like it anyway. You go play. That's more fun."

She wandered away for a few moments. Then she came back. I was leaning over William helping him spell a word. Sheila tugged on my belt. "I wanna do it, Torey."

I shook my head. "No, you don't. Not really."

"Yes, I do."

Ignoring her, I went back to William.

"I won't waste no paper."

"Sheila, writing is for kids who do paperwork. Now you don't do it, so writing isn't for you."

"I could do some paperwork. A little bit, maybe, if I could have a piece of paper to write on."

I shook my head. "No, you don't like it. You've told me that yourself. You don't have to do it. Go play now, so I can help William."

She remained standing beside me. After a few moments of not getting results, she went and asked Anton. "Torey's got the paper," he said, pointing in my direction. "You'll have to ask her."

"She won't give me none."

He shrugged and rolled his big brown eyes. "Well, then I'm sorry for you. I don't have any paper you can use."

Sheila came back to me. She was getting angry with me and trying not to show it. "I want you to give me a piece of paper, Torey. Now, gimme it."

I raised an eyebrow in warning.

She gave a frustrated stomp with one foot and shoved out her lower lip. I bent back over William.

She changed tactics. "Please? Please? I won't wreck it. I won't tear it up. Cross my heart and hope to die. Please?"

I regarded her. "I can't believe you. Maybe if you do some papers for me tomorrow and I see you don't tear them up, then I'll give you writing paper during creative writing tomorrow afternoon."

"I want it now, Torey."

"I know you do. But you show me I can trust you and you can have some tomorrow. We're almost out of time today anyhow."

She eyed me carefully, trying to determine a way to make me give in. "If you give me paper I'll write something you don't know about me. I'll write you something secret."

"You write me something secret tomorrow."

At that she gave a grunt of anger and stalked off across the room to the other table. She pulled out a chair very loudly and sat down with great emphasis. Little snorts punctuated the air. I smiled inwardly. She was cute when she was mad, now that she was learning to handle it more appropriately. Giving me absolutely black stares, she remained at the other table.

After a few moments I wandered over in her direction. "I suppose, if you write fast, I could give you a piece of paper today."

She looked up expectantly.

"Except you can't tear it up."

"I won't."

"What will we do if you do tear it up?"

"I won't. I said I won't. I promise."

"Are you going to do other papers for me, if I give you this one?"

She nodded emphatically.

"You'll do your math paper?"

She frowned in exasperation. "I ain't gonna have no time left if you keep talking to me all day."

I grinned and handed her a piece of paper. "This better be a good secret."

Clutching the paper in both hands she scurried over to the other table to grab a felt-tipped pen. She had been eyeing the pens for some time and now with both the pen and the hard-earned paper she darted off to the far side of the room. Scrambling under the rabbit's cage, she began to write.

She *was* fast. Somehow I had expected her to have difficulty since she had not written in so long. But as in so many other ways, Sheila surprised me. Within minutes she was back, the piece of paper folded into a tiny square. She sidled up next to me when I wasn't looking and pressed it into my hand.

"This here be a secret now. You don't go showing it to nobody. It do be just for you."

"Okay." I began unfolding it.

"No, don't read it now. Save it."

Nodding, I slipped the little square of paper into my pocket.

I forgot about it until that night when I was changing for bed. Then the folded square fell out onto the floor. Carefully I picked it up and straightened it out. Inside, written in blue felt-tip, I found what must have been for Sheila, with all her dignity, a very personal note.

A special thing I want you to know but not tell Nobody
You know sometimes the kids make Fun of me and call me names and befor I used not to put on clene Close. But sometimes I dont cos

you know what I do but please dont tell I wet the bed. I dont mean to Pa he wips me for it if he knows but He dont mostly. I just dont know why Torey I try real hard to Stop. You wouldnt be mad at me would you. My pa he is but I dont mean to Honest. it bothers me alot but it Make me ashamed of myself. Pa he says Im a baby but I be 7 soon when I do then there aint no clene underpanz and the kids make fun of me. Please dont tell no kids about this ok. Or dont tell Mr Colinz. or Anton or Whiteney or anybody ok. I just want you to know.

I read the note through, touched by her openness and amazed by her writing ability. By and large the note was well-written, punctuated and spelled correctly. It puzzled me that she used "I'm," since I did not ever remember hearing her say it. I smiled to myself and sat down and wrote her a note back.

So the first break in the paperwork war had been made. The next day with help she managed to do a math paper. It was carefully done and I suggested it go up on the bulletin board where I displayed all the children's good work. This was too much for Sheila and I later found the math paper shredded in the trash can. I was more careful after that. She became able to do two or three written assignments without supervision. Occasionally she would slip back and destroy the paper partway through the assignment or after completing it, especially those that were difficult for her. But if

I gave her a second sheet, she would try again. I never marked anything wrong because Sheila had such a tenuous hold on herself in committing her work to paper. It was far too fragile at that point to take any criticism, however well-meaning the critic's intentions. Instead, Anton or I always checked on her while she did the papers and discussed some alternatives to questions she was answering incorrectly. Otherwise I kept a low profile on her increasing ability to do this task. It was not that important a matter, despite what my teacher's instinct told me, and I never wanted her to feel that I measured her worth by how many papers she did. Obviously someone had already communicated that to her and I wanted it clear that that was not true in our classroom. Regardless of how inconvenient her distrust of paperwork had been, she needed to know that nobody would be valued less than a stack of school papers.

Interestingly enough, Sheila found great outlet in creative writing. In this area the old fears seemed to drop away, and she wrote spontaneously and copiously. Line after line of her loose, rather sloppy writing would hurry across the page telling about things that often seemed too personal to say face-to-face. I could usually count on five or six extra pages in the correction basket each night.

I never learned whatever it was that motivated Sheila toward her paper phobia. Later interactions with her over it and later comments that she made reaffirmed my belief that it was related to a fear of failure. But I never really knew. Nor did I feel a pressing need to know, only because so few human behaviors can be reduced to such simple cause-effect terms. There were more important things to worry about, things more important than ferreting out a mysterious and ultimately academic "why."

Allan, the school psychologist, returned shortly after Valentine's Day with a whole battery of tests for Sheila, including a Stanford-Binet IQ test. I balked a bit when I met him and his armload in the office that morning. I knew to my satisfaction that Sheila was a gifted child; she proved it daily. What difference did it make if her IQ were 170 or 175 or 180? It was all so far beyond normal that the numbers were meaningless. Even a variation of thirty points did not matter much. I would not know how to handle her any differently if she had an IQ of 150 or 180; she was too discrepant. But I suspect Allan was excited over finding such an interesting specimen and wanted to test her more for his own education than for any added benefit to Sheila. I relented because I knew the time was coming when we would have to face the authorities who had committed her to the state hospital. She certainly did not belong there; I could see that beyond a doubt now. I was hoping all the illustrious IQ scores would serve us in the end.

She topped out the Stanford-Binet as she had done on the other tests. An extrapolated score gave her an IQ of 182. As I looked at it, I was affected in a mystical way; 182 is beyond anyone's comprehension. That is as far in the direction of genius as an IQ of 18 is in the direction of retardation. And everyone knows how very different from the normal population a child with an 18 IQ is. What people generally fail to realize is that a child with a 182 is just as different.

What moved me most was considering how she ever came to possess that kind of knowledge. It almost seemed to me as if it were some sort of anomaly like brain damage in reverse. Her father—if he was, indeed, her father—was of normal intelligence and from what I could make out, so was her mother. Where in Sheila's abused, deprived six years had she learned what words like "chattel" meant? How had that happened? It seemed as nearly impossible to me as anything I had ever encountered. I was flooded with thoughts that she must be proof of reincarnation. I could see no other explanation for this extraordinary child.

Almost before I realized what I was thinking, a second emotion entered into the mystery. In the back of my head I heard the chant of a TV commercial I had seen once; "A mind is a terrible thing to waste." My gut tightened. There was so much to do with this child, and so little time. I did not know if it would be nearly enough.

Chapter Twelve

The last week in February I was speaking at a conference out of state. I had known about the engagement since before school had started in the fall and had reminded Ed Somers periodically that I was still planning to attend. Now as the time grew near, I once again called Ed to make arrangements for my replacement.

The children had been with a substitute earlier in the year in November when I had gone to a workshop. It was only one day and I had prepared the kids, so things had gone well. I felt it was very important that they have these little tests of independence. Regardless of how much progress they had made during their year with me, it would be futile if they only performed reliably in my presence. I had seen more good teachers fail because of this problem than any other and was haunted by the thought that I might fall prey to that difficulty. I suppose what worried me was that I tended to form a closer, more intense relationship with my kids than did a number of teachers in the same general area as I. When I saw them breeding dependency in their more detached manners, I feared I was in trouble. Thus far, I hadn't been, but I took every opportunity to let my children cope without me.

Sheila worried me though. She had not been with us very long yet and was still quite dependent. I saw this as a natural stage for her at the time, but I worried that my leaving, even for a short period of time, might frighten her.

On the Monday before my absence, which would be Thursday and Friday of that week, I mentioned casually to the children that I would be gone. Again on Tuesday, I mentioned it. On neither occasion did Sheila appear to attend to the comment. But on Wednesday after lunch I sat the kids down for a discussion. I explained I would be gone the next two days and not in the room. Anton would be there and so would Whitney and there would be a substitute teacher. Things would go just as always and there was no need to worry. I would be back on the next Monday when we were all going on a field trip to the fire station. We discussed ways of behaving properly around a substitute teacher; things that would make the job easier for her and things that should not be done. We role-played how to talk to her and how to deal with the minor crises that always seemed to crop up with subs. Everyone participated actively in the discussion. Everyone but Sheila. As the reality of what I was saying dawned on her, she regarded me anxiously. Her hand went up.

"Yes, Sheila?"

"You gonna be gone?"

"Yes, I am. That's what this is all about. I won't be here tomorrow or Friday, but I'll be back on Monday. That's what we're talking about."

"You gonna be gone?"

"Jeepers, Sheila," Peter said, "you deaf or something? What you think we been doing all this time?"

"You gonna be gone?"

I nodded. The other kids were looking at her strangely.

"You ain't gonna be here?"

"I'll be back on Monday. Just two days and then I'll be back."

Her face clouded over, her eyes filling with wary concern. She rose to her feet and retreated backwards toward the housekeeping corner, watching me the entire time.

I went on to answer other questions and finally broke up the group when it seemed everyone was satisfied. It was almost time for recess and then cooking.

Sheila remained in the housekeeping corner fiddling aimlessly with toy pots and pans. Anton called her to get her coat on for recess but she refused to come, popping her thumb into her mouth and looking defiantly at him. I motioned to Anton

165

to go out with the others and went over to her. Turning a chair around backwards, I straddled it, resting my chin on the back.

"You're upset with me, aren't you?"

"You never tell me you go away."

"Yes, I did, Sheil. Both Monday and yesterday in morning discussion."

"But you didn't tell me."

"I told everybody."

She threw a tin pan down so that it clattered. "It ain't fair you go leave me. I don't want you to."

"I know you don't and I'm sorry for your sake that I have to. But I am coming back, Sheila. I'll only be gone for two days."

"I ain't never, never gonna like you again. I ain't never gonna do anything you ask. You do be so mean to me. You tame me so's I like you and then you leave. You ain't supposed to do that, don't you know? That be what my Mama done and that ain't a good thing to do to little kids. They put you in jail for leaving little kids. My Pa, he says so."

"Sheila, it's different from that."

"I ain't gonna listen to you. I ain't never gonna listen to you again. I liked you and you be mean to me. You are gonna go away and leave me and you said you wouldn't. That be a fierce awful thing to do to a kid you tame. Don't you know that?"

"Sheila, listen to me . . ."

"I ain't never gonna listen to you. Don't you hear me say that?" Her voice was almost inaudible, but pregnant with feeling. "I hate you."

I looked at her. She kept her face averted. For

the first time since she had come I saw her bring a finger up to one eye to stop an unfallen tear. In panic she pressed her fingers tight against her temples, willing the tears back. "Look what you make me do," she muttered accusingly. "You make me cry and I don't want to. You know I don't like to cry. I hate you more than anybody and I ain't never gonna be nice in here again. No matter what."

For a single moment the tears glistened in her eyes. They never fell. She darted past me, grabbed her jacket and ran out the door to the playground.

I got my own jacket and joined the children. Sheila sat by herself in the very farthest corner. Hunched up against the chilly February wind, she sat with her face hidden in her arms.

"Not taking it so well, eh?" Anton said.

"Nope, she's not taking it so well."

After recess when the other children readied for cooking, Sheila remained in the housekeeping corner idly clattering toys around. I let her be. She was upset and had reason to be. Despite her isolation from us, she was handling her distress quite well. No tantrums, no destruction, no bolting. I was surprised and pleased with the manner in which she was coping. Sheila had come a long way in two months.

The other kids tried to coax Sheila into joining them. Tyler, ever the class mother, fussed over Sheila until Whitney told her to get back to the cookies. Peter kept asking why she was standing there and not joining us. I explained that Sheila was feeling a little angry just then and was keeping herself in control by not being with us.

After the cookies were done and everyone sat around eating, I joined William and Guillermo. Tyler had taken some cookies over to Sheila, who was still in retreat midst the dolls and dishes of the housekeeping corner. Guillermo was showing me a new Braille watch his grandfather had given him and he and William were testing me to see if I could read it with my eyes closed.

"Torey," Sarah shouted from the other side of the room, "come here. Sheila's throwing up."

Peter bounced over in delighted glee. "Sheila just puked all over everything." Peter loved gruesome catastrophes.

Anton went for the janitor and I went back to see what had happened. The other kids gathered around like we had a three-ring circus.

I lifted Sheila out of the area and set her down beside me. Pushing back her bangs, I felt her forehead. She wasn't hot.

"Maybe she's got a virus," Peter said. "Last year I puked about a million times one night and all over my bed and stuff, and my mom said I had a virus."

"No," I replied. "I don't think Sheila's sick. I think she's just a little nervous about things today and it got to her tummy."

"That happened to me once. My uncle was coming and I got really excited," William said. "And I got sick because of it. He was going to take me fishing."

Peter snorted. "I bet it was Tyler's cookies."

"I think it would help if everybody would clear out of here and go sit down someplace," I said.

When Anton returned, I took Sheila into the bathroom to clean her up. She was compliant but refused to look at me or to speak. So in silence I washed off her face and clothes.

"Do you think you might throw up again?" I asked.

No response.

"Sheil, cut that out. Now answer me. I asked how you were feeling. Are you going to be sick again?"

"I didn't mean to."

"I know you didn't. But I wanted to know if you thought you were still feeling sick, so we could be prepared if we needed to be. It's almost time to go home."

"My bus don't come 'til five."

"I think it would be better if you went home when school's out. They sort of have a rule about throwing up at school. They wouldn't want you on the bus. And I just think it'd be better for you to go home. Anton can take you after school."

"But I didn't mean to. I won't do it again."

"Honey, that's not the point."

"You hate me. You hate me and won't even be nice to me when I be sick. You do be such a mean person."

I rolled my eyes in exasperation. "Sheila, I do not hate you. Honestly, what can I do to get through to you that I am coming back? I will only be gone tomorrow and Friday. Just two short days. Then I'll be back. Don't you understand that?"

I was frustrated. She was a bright child, she knew how long two days were. Yet she stood there uncomprehending. I doubted her vomiting was any more than a physical reaction to emotional distress, but I did not know what to do with her. She would not hear what I was saying.

Rising from where I had been washing her off, I shook my head. Then I shrugged. "Do you want me to rock you a little while until school gets out? Maybe that will help settle your tummy some."

She shook her head.

The janitor was just leaving and the children were starting to get ready to go home. Anton looked questioningly in my direction. I spread my hands in a gesture of bewilderment.

The other kids were getting their coats on, and Sheila stood in the bathroom doorway and watched. When I looked at her, she seemed a little pale. Perhaps I had been too hasty in judging, perhaps it was a virus. But I didn't think so. There had been too many nervous stomachs in my experience. She was, after all, struggling with a hard thing.

I sat down in the rocking chair and turned in her direction. She remained in the doorway. The distance seemed so far between us. How fragile the bond was that held us. Uppermost in my mind was the frustration of being unable to convince her that I, unlike all the others, was not abandoning her. However, underneath the frustration blossomed such admiration for this child. She was so strong and courageous. There was no reason why she should suspect I was being honest with her. Nothing in her past gave her grounds to think that I would return, and she was doing the only sensible thing. Yet as she stood in the doorway watching me, a pantomime of self-doubt and fear and sorrow played across her face. She was trying so hard to believe me, the war between her experience and her dreams vivid in her eyes. I was filled with respect for her, such heart-grinding, unspeakable respect, because she was trying so hard. This was one of those moments that made all the others worthwhile. We were touching each other's souls.

I reached a hand out. "Come here, kitten. Let me rock you."

She hesitated, then slowly approached. Without a word she climbed into my lap.

"This has been a hard day, hasn't it?"

She pressed her fingers to her temples.

"I know you don't understand what's happening, Sheila. You don't understand how I can do this to you and still like you." I rocked her, pushing back her bangs and feeling the silky softness of her hair. "You're just going to have to trust me."

Her body was rigid against mine, like it had been in the beginning. She did not relax. "You tamed me. I didn't ask you to, but you did. Now you leave. It ain't fair. You be 'sponsible for me. You said so yourself."

I puzzled over her sudden change to the past tense. I had never heard it except in rare, random instances. "Kitten, please trust me. I'll be back. It won't be so bad as you think. Anton will still be here, and Whitney. And the substitute will be real nice, I just know it. You'll have fun if you just give yourself the chance."

She did not answer, but simply sat, her fingers white against her temples. There wasn't any more to say. She did not believe me or else she could not bring herself to admit she did. I was too used to her verbal ability. I sometimes forgot she was a six-year-old child. I forgot how many problems she had and how short a time she had been with us. I was expecting too much in wanting her to understand.

The conference was in a West Coast state which had a milder February climate. Chad went with me and we spent most of the time on the beach walking in the surf. It was a marvelous change. I seldom realized how tied up with the children I was until a moment like this occurred and I got away. My interactions were intense and all-consuming for me. When I was working, I could never perceive how tense the involvement left me. Now, on the sunny beach, I felt the weariness drain away.

It was a good conference and an even better vacation. I never thought of the children at all except in bed at night. Even then it was a hazy recollection. I knew they would take care of themselves in my absence. For Chad and me it was a spiritual rebirth. Since Sheila had come, proving such a challenge and forcing me to take my planning home at night, Chad had been slighted. He understood my fascination with the kids, but he still resented the fact that they absorbed every moment. Four days alone together left us happy and relaxed.

On Monday morning I returned, anxious to get back to work. We had the field trip to the fire station planned in the afternoon and I had to make last-minute calls on arrangements and check with all the parents who had promised to help.

Anton met me in the hallway as I was returning from the phone. He bulged his eyes. "We had quite a time in your absence," he said.

I could tell from his tone of voice that the "time" had not been a good one and I feared to ask. "What happencd?"

"Sheila went absolutely berserk. She refused to talk. She pulled all the stuff off the walls, all the books out of the bookcases. She gave Peter a bloody nose on Friday. She wouldn't do any work at all. I couldn't even get her to sit in her chair. On Thursday she broke the record player. And on Friday afternoon she tried to break the glass out of the door with her shoe."

"You're kidding!"

"Uh-uh. Jesus, Torey, I wish I was. She was a holy terror."

"Cripes," I muttered, "I thought she was getting over doing that kind of junk."

"She was worse than I've seen her in ages. She spent the whole time in the quiet corner, ha___ be held in the chair every moment worse than she ever was when she came."

My heart sank. A vast cesspool of emotions gurgled unhappily within me. I had honestly believed I could trust her to behave while I was gone. It hurt to realize I had misguessed so badly. I felt like I had been personally insulted. I had trusted her; I had depended on her good behavior and she had let me down.

I planned to discuss the matter with her but her bus was late. The other kids began to arrive, all bearing tales. "You ought to have seen what Sheila done," Sarah said excitedly. "She wrecked the whole room."

"Yeah!" Guillermo chirped. "That substitute, Mrs. Markham, she spanked Sheila and made her sit in the quiet corner and Whitney had to hold her all afternoon, 'cause she wouldn't.'"

Peter bounced around me, his dark eyes blazing with delight. "And she was real mean to Whitney and Whitney cried and then guess what? Even Mrs. Markham cried. And Sarah cried and Tyler cried. All the girls cried because Sheila was so naughty. But I didn't. I socked her. I hit her good for being so bad."

"Her bad," Max confirmed, twirling around me.

My dismal discouragement turned to anger. How could she have done this to me? She had apparently behaved worse than she ever had when I was there. I thought she should have had good enough control to make it for two days without my lurking about every minute. I was deeply disappointed; my confidence about handling her had reached an all-time low. She was getting back at me; she had behaved that way on purpose and all the time and effort I had given her had been to no avail.

Sheila arrived after we had started morning discussion. She regarded me suspiciously as she sat down. The familiar musty odor of stale urine wafted up. She hadn't even bothered to wash since I had left.

My own displeasure did not lessen when I saw her. I was feeling very defensive, believing that her behavior had been a direct assault on my credibility as a teacher. As with all the others with whom she had come into contact, she had figured out what was most important to me and had used it as revenge. The more I thought about it, the worse I felt. This was far harder for me to accept than the incident of the first day or even Mrs. Holmes' room, because it had been so directly aimed at me.

After discussion I called her over. We sat in chairs away from the others. "I hear you didn't handle yourself very well."

She stared at me, her feelings unreadable.

"I came back and all I heard was about the bad things you did. I want you to explain that to me."

She said nothing but met me with unwavering eyes.

"I'm mad at you, Sheila. I'm the maddest I've been in a long time. Now I want to hear why you did that."

Still no response.

Rage rose within me as I saw those cold, distant eyes. In sudden desperation I grabbed her shoulders and shook her roughly. "Speak to me, dammit! Speak to me!" But what emotion was there closed, and she gritted her teeth. Horrified at losing control of myself, I let go of her shoulders. God, this job was getting to be too much for me.

She remained in stony silence, glaring at me. My aggressiveness had brought up her own anger and she was an equal match for me, if not better. This was her world, this realm of physical force. She was more a master of it than I and I could tell I had made a mistake in touching her that way. I imagined that she could outlast any sort of physical devastation I was capable of and still not speak. But I was so full of disappointment. My shoulders sagged.

"I trusted you," I said, my voice soft, the discouragement undisguised. "I trusted you for two lousy days, Sheila. I trusted you, can't you see that? And you want to know how it makes me feel to come back and hear you behaved like that?"

Sheila exploded with a fury I had been unprepared for. "I never told you to trust me! I never said that; you did! I never said you could trust me. You can't! Nobody can trust me! I never said you could!" She tore off, careening frantically around the perimeter of the room before scuttling under the table the animal cages were on. Her distress was so great that she sat under the table emitting little strangled noises that were not exactly sobs or screams or words. But their emotion was clear enough.

Her response had surprised me and I sat in the chair without moving. The other children had paused to look at us, their concern mirrored in one another's eyes. I just sat and looked at her in her hiding place under the table. I did not know what to do.

"Well, then you're not going anywhere with us this afternoon, Sheila," I said at last. "I'm not taking anyone I can't trust. You can stay with Anton."

She crawled out from under the table. "I can too go."

"No, I'm afraid not. I can't trust you."

She looked horror stricken. I knew that the field trip meant a great deal to her. She loved going places with us. "I can too go."

I shook my head. "No, you can't."

Sheila screamed, letting loose high-pitched ear-splitting shrieks. She still stood over by the animal cages and began leaping up and down, beating the air with her hands.

"Sheila cut it out or over to the quiet corner. Right now."

She was clearly out of control. Flinging herself on the floor she banged her head violently on the ground. Anton made a flying leap toward her to intercept the self-destruction. Never before had she done such a thing; I had expected her to go off into one of her destructive rages and evidently so had the children who were covertly putting their valuables out of the way. But she had never attempted to hurt herself before. Some of the other kids, particularly Max and Susannah, would do that, but never Sheila.

177

Anton had her tight in his arms. She struggled savagely, all the while screaming. I couldn't hear myself think. Then as suddenly as it started, it stopped, the room falling into unearthly silence. I dashed over fearing that she had hurt herself to stop so abruptly. Anton released his grip on her and she melted through his arms like warm butter, slithering into a little lump on the carpet. Her arms were over her head, her face into the tweed of the rug.

"Are you all right, Sheila?" I asked.

She turned her head. "Please let me go," she whispered.

After that terrible show of emotion I was alarmed. "I don't think you'd better." If she were behaving like this I was fearful of controlling her outside the room.

"I do be sorry for what I done. Let me go. You can trust me. Please?" Her voice was very small. "Gimme a chance. I'll show you how good I can be. Please? I wanna go."

I looked down at her. My own feelings were returning and I was beginning to think all that violent behavior was a con because she had stopped it so fast. That renewed some of my anger. "I don't think so, Sheila. Maybe next time."

She began screaming again, covering her face with her hands but remaining on the floor. She looked like a rag doll in the contorted position she lay in. I turned and walked away to work with the other children.

All morning she lay in a lump on the floor. She screamed for a while longer and then fell into silence, not moving, not looking up from her huddle. At first I was tempted to move her to the quiet corner, but I changed my mind. I was feeling defeated; I did not want to tangle with her.

By lunch my spirits had flagged completely. I was beginning to realize that I had been angry with her for exposing what I perceived as a teaching deficit in myself. I was mad because I was not able to leave her successfully. I was angry because she had done to me what I had watched her do to so many others. Somehow, I had honestly believed she would never take revenge against me. She had not until then and I had enough of an inflated ego to believe she never would. Now that I had been put on an equal footing with everyone else, my feelings had been hurt. With great embarrassment, I realized I had done back to her the same thing by taking away the field trip. She had hurt me and I had wanted to show her that she'd be sorry. I had chosen the one thing within my power that I knew would hurt her back.

Realizing this made me feel worse than ever. What a crass, egotistical boor. I hated myself, hated the world. Feeling absolutely bleak, I could not decide how to recover the situation.

Over our sandwiches at lunch, I unloaded my guilt onto Anton. "Boy. I blew it this time," I mumbled into my peanut butter. Why had I ever become a teacher if I had such lousy control over my own feelings? Anton tried to reassure me. She had behaved very badly, he reminded me. She deserved to know that it was unacceptable.

But I felt like a zero. The poor kid. Here this day should have been a happy reunion for everyone. And I came back a shrew. What she had done was not so unpredictable. The kid was upset and was showing it the best way she knew how. Hell, that was why she was in this room to begin with. But what about me? Was that my reason for being there too? This day should have been a joyous affirmation that she could trust me; I returned like I had promised. Instead I yelled at her. And I took away a privilege she didn't even know was in jeopardy. God, how had I ever gotten into teaching?

I spent the entire lunch hour feeling like a monster and not knowing how to fix things. Even if I apologized, I could not undo becoming so mad at her in the morning. I choked unhappily through the last of my sandwich. She had been right. She had never said I could trust her.

Back in the classroom, I sat down next to her. The other kids were getting ready to go and parents milled around. Sheila sat alone over in the corner.

"Honey, I have to talk to you. I did something wrong this morning. I got mad at you when I was really mad at myself. I told you that you couldn't go on the field trip, but I've changed my mind. You can go. I'm sorry I was angry with you."

Without responding, without even looking at me, Sheila rose and got her coat.

After school, when the other children had gone home, the strained silence between us lingered. I had tried to break it all afternoon, outdoing myself to be funny and make everyone laugh. But Sheila remained apart, holding on to Whitney's hand. I gave up. As in all things, the best healer, I decided, would be time. I was recovering, knowing that I had acted inappropriately, but also knowing, as Anton had pointed out, that I was human.

I took the papers from the basket and sat down to grade them. I had offered to read but Sheila declined and busied herself playing cars on the floor across the room. The first hour passed and Sheila got up to stand by the window and watch the shadows lengthen across the snow. When next I looked up, she was still by the window but she was watching me.

"How come you come back?" she asked softly.

"I just went away to give a speech. I never intended to stay away. This is my job here with you kids."

"But how come you come back?"

"Because I said I would. I like it here."

Slowly she approached the table where I was sitting. The hurt was clear in her eyes now.

"You really didn't think I was coming back, did you?"

She shook her head.

Across a tremendous gulf of silence we looked at each other. I could hear the clock jumping the minutes. Onions, the rabbit, rustled in his cage. I was looking at her eyes, wide and fluid and the color of the water where I used to go diving off the coast. I wondered what she was thinking. And I realized sadly, that we never do understand what it is like to be someone else. Nor do we ever seem to be quite able to accept that truth, feeling glibly omniscient despite the limitations of flesh and bone. Especially with children. But we really never know.

She stood twisting an overall strap. "Would you read that book again?"

"Which book is that?"

"The one about the little boy who tamed the fox."

I smiled. "Yeah, I'll read it."

Chapter 13

March came in breezy and warm, a welcome relief for the winter-weary North. The snow finally melted, and cool, brown mud rose through the grass from all the water. We were all anxious for spring that year. It had been a hard winter with more snow and cold than we usually received.

March was also peaceful as far as school went; as peaceful as one got in a class like mine. There were no vacations, no disruptions to cause friction, no unexpected changes. The migrant population was coming up from the South, the camp swelling to meet their influx. Teachers in the lounge groused because migrant kids were finding their way into their classes, but I had nothing to worry about in that way. The return of the workers, however, had a strange sad-sweet effect on Anton. When the first few trucks filled with migrants began arriving,

Anton did not mention it but he became quieter and more distracted. I finally asked him about it. I was wondering if he were nostalgic for that less encumbered life-style.

He had smiled when I asked. Smiled and looked at me in the compassionate way one does when an issue is completely beyond the other's comprehension. Then he drew up one of the tiny chairs and dropped his huge frame in it. No, he explained to me, he did not miss the migrant life-style. There was nothing about living that way for a man to miss. He smiled again, more to himself than to me. What was affecting him, he said, was realizing how much he had changed since the trucks had rumbled out in the autumn. How different from them he had become. How he had never noticed the changing until now. Like Rip van Winkle must have felt upon awaking, he said, then gave a laugh of disbelief. He hadn't even known who Rip van Winkle was last year and now had more in common with Rip than with his own people.

I watched him as he talked. I studied the dark Latin features, the angular bones, the physical stigmata of a hard life too early. We both had changed, in ways I could not quite give words to, but which were no less immense for lack of expression. I was awed that we could have such vast effect on each other's lives and for the most part never realize it, certainly not while it was happening. For several minutes we sat looking at one another, openly, admiringly, the taboo on staring temporarily suspended. So many differences: our backgrounds, our sex, our education, so much. Yet somehow, in some way, we had managed to touch each other. That flicker of understanding silenced the two of us as we sat at the table. There was no need for words.

Like the daffodils, Sheila bloomed in spite of the harsh winter. Each day she was back showing more and more improvement. Within the limits of her situation she was now always quite clean. She would come bounding in each morning, wash her face and brush her teeth. She paid close attention to how she looked, inspecting her image carefully in the mirror. We experimented with new hairstyles. After school some days we played beauty shop. I let her work with my long hair and in turn I was allowed to play with hers, devising new ways to braid or style it. She had become a truly handsome child, evoking comment from the other teachers.

Sarah and Sheila had become fast friends and I caught them sending notes during class occasionally. Sheila had gone home with Sarah to play on several occasions after school before her bus came. And Sheila and Guillermo played together at the migrant camp. Tyler was a bit too much of a priss for Sheila's taste, and she would rebuff Tyler's motherly attentions. I was pleased to see that she generally attracted the favor of the children in the class.

Academically Sheila sailed. She willingly did almost anything I gave her to do. A paper was occasionally destroyed, but only very occasionally. If it happened twice a week, that was the exception. Even at that she had learned to come up and ask for another one. I had her working on third grade reading material and fourth grade math. Both were considerably below her ability level, but because of her deprived background and her fear of failure, I felt it was better to keep her in work which could cement her knowledge and confidence more solidly.

She was still overly sensitive about correction, going off into great sulks or heartrending sighs if she made a mistake. Some days seemed worse than others in that respect and she would spend the whole day with her head buried in her arms in dismal despair over missing one math problem. But as a rule there were not many disasters. With a bit of extra cuddling and reassurance she would usually try again.

Oddly enough in my mind, our falling out over my two days' absence did not appear to have adverse effects on Sheila's emotional stability. For a few days after my return she resorted to hanging on to me again, but soon after, abandoned that behavior. Never again did she do it. We talked a lot about that incident. She seemed to need to rehash the event over and over and over. I had left her. I had come back. She had gotten angry and destructive. I had gotten angry and lost my temper. I had told her I was wrong and I was sorry. Each little piece of the drama she wanted to discuss again and again, telling me how she'd felt, what had made her throw up that day, how she'd been scared. The saga was repeated over and over and over until I thought I would never hear the end of it. It held some secret significance that I did not fully understand and the ritualistic retelling seemed to reassure her. Certainly the fact that I had come back was important, but that was not the only facet she dwelled upon. That we had been angry with each other and weathered that appeared equally significant in her mind. Perhaps she felt assured to have seen me at my worst. She could trust me now, knowing what I was like even when I was upset with her. Whatever it was, she was learning to solve her problems verbally. No longer did she need physical contact; words were enough.

Oddly, the destructiveness all but disappeared after the event of my absence and return. When she became angry, which she still did with great regularity, she did not fly into a rage, throwing things to the floor and rampaging about. Revenge was becoming less important. When I thought about it, I wished I could have fully understood the importance of that incident because in many ways it greatly altered Sheila's behavior. But the full picture always remained a mystery. Sheila still had a lot of problems, but they were becoming more readily solved and much more manageable.

One of the things which still puzzled me was her language. Visiting her father had substantiated that her peculiar speech patterns with the lack of past tense and overuse of "be" did not come from home. As bright as she was, I could not fathom why she persisted in speaking so oddly, although as time passed she did appear to be using more normal speech. During March I decided to finally ask her about it, pointing out that some words were said differently if you were talking about something that happened yesterday. She was surprisingly antagonistic toward my comments, saying that I understood her, didn't I? When I said yes, I did, she asked me what did it matter how she talked if I understood her? That took me off-guard because it made me feel that the behavior was more premeditated than I had previously thought.

No one had any suggestions on the matter. All the speech experts to whom I sent tapes answered saying it was a dialect and often asking if she were black. When I replied that no, she wasn't, and no, it wasn't a family dialect, they had no other ideas. One night Chad and I were discussing it and he suggested that perhaps by not using the past tense, she was trying to keep everything anchored in the present where she could keep better control of things. The more I pondered that, the more possible it seemed. In the end, I concluded it was a psychologically based problem and let it go at that. We did understand what she was saying and perhaps someday she would feel comfortable enough to want to change. Right now, though, she did not.

The issue still uppermost in Sheila's mind was abandonment. She was preoccupied with her mother and her brother, where they were and what they were doing. Often her conversations were punctuated with comments to the effect that if she could have done this thing or that thing better, maybe her family would still be intact. In my mind this was all directly tied to her intense fear of failure.

One night after school Sheila had busied herself doing math problems. She loved math and excelled in it beyond all other areas. From the time she had arrived, she could do basic multiplication and division problems. Together we had worked out the more complicated techniques. She had discovered a dittoed exam from one of the fifth grade classes in a trash can at recess and brought it in to do after school.

When she had finished it, Sheila came over to show it to me. The problems were in division of fractions. This was not an area we had ever covered. Consequently all the problems were wrong because she had not inverted the divisor.

"Here's this. Is it done good?" she asked, handing it to me to look at.

Regarding the paper, I wondered whether or not I should point out the error. "Sheil, I want to show you something." On the back of the paper I drew a circle and divided it into four parts. "Now, if I wanted to know how many eighths were in it . . ." She immediately perceived that the way she was solving the problem would not give the correct answer.

"I done them wrong, didn't I?"

"You didn't know, kiddo. No one showed you."

She flopped down beside me and put her face in her hands. "I wanted to do them right and show you I could do them without help."

"Sheil, it's nothing to get upset about."

She sat for a few moments covering her face. Then slowly her hands slid away and she uncrumpled the paper which she had mashed. "I bet if I could have done math problems good, my Mama, she wouldn't leave me on no highway like she done. If I could have done fifth grade math problems, she'd be proud of me."

"I don't think math problems have anything to do with it, Sheila. We really don't know why your Mama left. She probably had all sorts of troubles of her own."

"She left because she don't love me no more. You don't go leaving kids you love on the highway. And I cut my leg. See?" For the hundredth time the scar was displayed to me. "If I'd been a gooder girl, she wouldn't have done that. She might still love me even now, if I could have been gooder."

"Sheil, we don't really know that. It was a bad thing, but it's over. I don't think your being good or bad had anything to do with it. Your Mama had her own problems to straighten out. I think she loved you a lot; mamas generally do. I think she just couldn't cope with having a little girl right then."

"But she copeded with Jimmie. How come she tooked Jimmie and left me?"

"I don't know, love."

Sheila looked over at me. That haunted, hurt expression was in her eyes. God, I thought, would I never fill that emptiness? Absently she twisted one pigtail. "I miss Jimmie."

"I know you do."

"His birthday's gonna be next week. He be five years old then and I never seen him since he be two. That do be an awful long time." She turned away from me and went to the window, staring out at the winter-wet March afternoon. "I miss Jimmie almost more than anything. I can't forget him."

"I can tell that."

She turned to look at me. "Could we have a birthday party for him? On March twelfth, that be his birthday. Could we have a party like we have for Tyler when it be her birthday in February?"

"I don't think so, kitten."

Her face fell and she shuffled back over to me. "Why not?"

"Because Jimmie isn't here, Sheil. Jimmie lives clear out in California and not here with us."

"It could be just a little birthday party. Maybe just you and me and Anton. Just after school maybe."

I shook my head.

"But I want to."

"I know you do."

"Then why not? Just a little, little party? Please?" Her face had puckered, her voice pleaded. "I'll be your goodest girl. I won't mess up any other math papers."

"That's not the point, Sheila. I'm saying no

because Jimmie isn't here anymore. Jimmie's gone. As much as it hurts to think about, Jimmie may not be coming back. I know you miss him a terribly lot, kitten, but I don't think it's a good idea to keep remembering him the way you are. All it does is hurt you."

She covered her face with her hands.

"Sheil, come here and let me hold you." Without removing her hands she came and I lifted her into my lap. "I know you feel awful about this. I can just feel you hurt from sitting here. It's a very hard thing you have to do."

"I miss him." Her voice broke with a dry sob and she clutched at my shirt, shoving her face into my breasts. "I just want him to be here."

"I know you do, love."

"Why did it happen, Torey? Why did she tooked him and leaved me behind? What made me such a bad girl?" The tears shimmered momentarily in her eyes. But as always they never escaped.

"Oh lovey, it wasn't you. Believe me on this. It wasn't your fault. She didn't leave you because you were bad. She just had too many of her own problems. It wasn't your fault."

"My Pa, he says so. He says if I be a gooder girl she'd a never done that."

My heart sank. There was so much to fight and so little to fight with. Why should she believe me and not her father? What could I do to show her he was wrong in that respect? I felt discouraged. "Your Pa made a mistake on this one, Sheil. He doesn't know what happened either and he doesn't know what it's like to be a little girl. He's wrong on this one. Believe me, please, because it's true."

We sat in silence several minutes. I held her close, feeling her warm unsteady breath against my skin. My heart hurt. I could feel it in my chest and it hurt. Her pain soaked through my shirt and my skin and my bones to be absorbed into my heart. God, it hurt.

At last she looked up. "Sometimes, I'm real lonely."

I nodded.

"Will it ever stop?"

Again I nodded, slowly. "Yes. Someday I think it will."

Sheila sighed and pulled away from me, standing up. "Someday never really ever comes, does it?"

Despite our sad moments, Sheila surprised me by being filled with joy. She had a tremendous capacity for joy. Working with these kids whose entire lives were chaotic tragedies affirmed my faith on a daily basis that humans are by nature joyous creatures. Sheila's moods fluctuated a great deal and she was never able entirely to escape the emotional devastation she had suffered. But by the same course, she was never far from happiness.

The smallest thing would ignite a merry sparkle in her eyes and not a day went by now that we did not hear her skitterish laughter. This was heightened by the fact that she had been deprived for so long that everything was new to her. She could not get her fill of the wonders that the world held.

Perhaps her greatest discovery in March was the flowers.

Our part of the state comes alive in March with crocuses and daffodils waving from every patch of ground. Sheila was fascinated by the flowers. None had ever grown in the migrant camp and, as unbelievable as it seemed to me, she had never before seen a daffodil up close. One morning I brought a huge bouquet from my landlady's garden into class.

Sheila came squealing over, toothpaste still in her mouth. She was just in her T-shirt and underpants, her bare feet slapping the floor as she ran. "What them things be?" she gurgled through the toothpaste.

"They're daffodils, silly. You've seen them before, haven't you?"

Peering at them she shook her head. "Uh-uh. Just in books, that's all. Them be real flowers?"

"Sure they're real. Touch them."

Putting down her toothbrush, she cautiously reached out, touching the edge of one flower with her fingertip. "Oooooh!" she squealed with delight, spraying toothpaste all around. Jumping up and down, she clutched herself with pleasure. Then stopping suddenly, she hesitantly touched another. Again the little dance of joy.

"Go finish brushing your teeth and get your clothes on, then you can help me put them in a vase."

Dashing back, she spat out the rest of the toothpaste, but was unable to contain her glee long enough to put on the overalls. She came running back. "They do be so soft. Let me touch them."

"Smell them. Daffodils don't smell as good as some flowers, like roses, for instance. But they have a special odor all their own."

She sniffed deeply. "I wanna hug them."

I chuckled. "Flowers don't especially like being hugged."

"But they smell that good and they do be so pretty. They make me feel like hugging them."

"Yes, they do, don't they?" I had gotten out one of the vases a child had made for me years earlier. There were too many flowers to fit in it. Beside me Sheila bounced in delight, first on one foot and then on the other. Her whole body reflected her joy.

"Sheil, would you like a flower of your own?"

She looked up at me, her eyes widening to what seemed to be the very perimeters of her face. "I can have one?"

"Yes, there's too many to fit in my vase. We could put it in a milk carton over by where you always sit at the table."

"Could it really be mine?"

I nodded.

"For me?"

"Yes, silly, for you. Your own flower."

Her face fell suddenly. "My Pa, he wouldn't let me keep it."

I smiled. "Flowers are different than that. They don't last very long, hardly even a day. Your Pa wouldn't care about something like a flower."

Tenderly she reached out and caressed one of the daffodils. "Remember in that book about the fox and the little prince? Remember, the prince had a flower and he tamed it. Remember that?" Her eyes were full of wonder as she looked up at me. "Do you suppose I could tame one? It would be my very own special flower and I could be 'sponsible for it and everything. I could tame it for my very own."

"Well, you'll have to remember flowers don't last too long. But they tame easily. I think you could do it. Which one would you like?" I pointed to the ones left over from the vase.

Considering them all carefully she chose one that looked no different to me from all the others, but it must have said something special. Perhaps the taming had already begun, because like the little prince and his rose, this daffodil was Sheila's and to her it was like no other flower in the world.

Holding the flower gently and stroking its golden cup, she smiled. I had gone over and gotten her overalls and came back, leaning over her, urging her to put her legs in. The other children were arriving, noisy and curious about what was happening. But Sheila stood oblivious, letting me dress her and not looking at the other children. Her lips were pressed tight between her teeth to keep a smile in check.

"My heart do be so big," she whispered, "it be so big and I do reckon I be about the happiest kid for it."

I kissed her soft temple and smiled. Then I picked up the vase of yellow daffodils and took them to the table.

Chapter 14

We laughed a lot.

Things were not always very funny in our room. Often the things I did find myself laughing about were matters that, if I had stopped and really thought about them, were only tragic. Perhaps the greatest magic of the human spirit is the ability to laugh. At ourselves, at each other, at our sometimes hopeless situation. Laughter normalized our lives.

Whitney, more than anyone else, kept us in line with what was normal. I loved her wholeheartedly for that quality, for never letting me or Anton or the kids ever quite convince her that this room was different.

Despite her shyness, Whitney had a sense of humor that sometimes did not know limits. Her wit could be dry and shockingly adult on occasion, especially when she was alone with Anton and me. However, Whitney was at her best when practical joking. Perhaps I would have been better prepared for that side of her if it had seemed more in keeping with her meek, bumbling exterior. Or maybe if our room had seemed a likelier place for playing practical jokes. Whatever it was, Whitney consistently took me by surprise. I never failed to be genuinely startled by the spring snakes that jumped out of Susannah's crayon box or the fake vomit sitting on the table while Peter and William and Guillermo feigned sudden stomachaches.

When Sheila arrived, that side of Whitney hit its zenith. The other kids loved Whitney's jokes and readily participated in them. Sheila, however, was bright enough to catch on to what Whitney was planning ahead of time, to make creative suggestions of her own, to see the inherent humor in a given situation. And Sheila was naive enough to do some of the crazier things Whitney suggested.

Much of March had passed and nothing happened. That made me suspicious. Each morning I began checking my drawers and my ceramic mug and other things that regularly fell prey to jokes. Usually I could count on Sheila to tip me off, primarily because she could not keep secrets well. Even when she was trying, she was not too sophisticated about hiding the evidence. However, nothing was happening. I did catch the two of them giggling together frequently enough to continue to be on-guard, but as the days went by, nothing occurred. Perhaps this was because Whitney had caught a bad cold and was absent almost a week.

Toward the latter half of the month Mrs. Crum, Freddie's mother, came to visit me after school. A small woman, sparrow-brown and mouse-scared, she slipped inside the door and apologized for bothering me. I had been playing cars on the floor with Sheila and assured her I did not mind being interrupted. Could I help her? Head down, she wrung her hands. So sorry to bother me with her problems. I asked Sheila to trot down to the office and help Anton who was there cutting mimeo stencils. Once we were alone, I invited Mrs. Crum to sit down.

She had come to ask me if the children had been eating anything at school lately. I thought. It was Wednesday, so we had just had cooking. We'd made egg foo young, I told her. Other than that, they hadn't eaten anything. Except lunch, of course. She wrinkled her brow. Freddie had come home three times in the last week and vomited. That would not have surprised her so much, she said, if she could have figured out what it was he was vomiting up. Little bright red, green, blue and yellow balls about a quarter inch in diameter. A couple dozen of them every time.

I was genuinely perplexed. Nothing I could think of fit that description. Not only did we not have any candy because I did not keep candy in the room, but also I did not keep any small nonedibles like that simply because the kids like Freddie or Max or Susannah would put them into their mouths. No, he couldn't be getting them at school, I reassured her. But I promised I would keep an eye on him to be sure.

The next few days went as usual. Whitney was still gone and I got bogged down with end-of-term report cards, so I spent part of the after-school time working while Sheila played by herself. The weekend came and went, then Monday again.

In the afternoon when I came back from taking the other children to their buses, I found Sheila on her knees in front of the cupboard under the sink. She had a colorful assortment of phrases she saved to use when she was especially perturbed. No matter what I did, she persisted in stringing them out when things did not go her way. Now as I came back into the room, I heard her muttering them half-aloud.

"What's wrong, Sheil?"

She leaped to her feet and whirled around. "Nothing."

"What were you swearing about?"

"Nothing."

I came over to the sink. "Didn't sound like nothing to me. What's going on?"

"Someone takeded something that be mine."

"Like what?"

"Just some stuff." She frowned. "I be gonna make an art project out of. I be looking for it and someone stealed it. It ain't in here where I put it."

"Why did you put it there in the first place? You ought to keep your things in your cubby. You know that. Nobody knows what they find under there is yours. What was it anyway?"

"Just some stuff."

"What kind of stuff?"

She shrugged. "Just stuff. That belong to me."

"Well, you go over to the art box. Maybe there are some scraps in there you can use."

About an hour later, there was Mrs. Crum at my door again. Oh so sorry, she began apologizing, but Freddie vomited again. More little colored balls. She had brought some with her this time, all wrapped up in a paper napkin. Despite her timidity, she insisted I look at them and convince her they did not come from my room.

Gritting my teeth I unwrapped the damp napkin. There were eight or ten little not-quite-round spheres in bright, Day-Glo colors. Taking a pencil, I poked at one. It mashed easily to reveal a dark, greenish-brown center. I could not imagine what they were.

Anton, who had been down in the teachers' workroom, came into the room. I beckoned him over.

"Have you seen anything like this around here?" I asked.

He leaned over my shoulder for a closer look. "What the hell?" Taking the pencil from me, he mashed a second one. It, too, crumbled easily.

"Apparently Freddie has been finding them somewhere, eating them and then throwing them up when he comes home from school. Mrs. Crum thinks they're from around here."

"What are they?" Anton asked, skepticism undisguised.

"I haven't the foggiest idea."

Sheila had gotten curious and came over. She tugged at my jeans. "Lemme see."

I pushed her off. "Just a sec."

She went off to drag a chair over and climbed on it to be closer to our height. "Lemme see."

"You know," Anton said, now holding the napkin with its mysterious contents, "this is going to sound dumb, but they look like rabbit turds to me."

"Anton, they're red and green and blue," I replied.

"I know it. But look at the middles. Don't they look like it to you?"

I started to laugh in spite of myself. The ridiculousness of the situation struck me.

Sheila was balancing precariously on a chair beside me, one hand on my arm, one on the collar of my shirt. "Lemme see, Torey."

Anton leaned over toward her and showed the napkin. When she saw the contents of the napkin, she jerked back suddenly, throwing herself off-balance. Both she and the chair fell over.

"You all right?" I asked as she picked herself up.

She nodded. Something about the way she looked at me made me suspicious. Or more precisely, the way she did not look at me.

"Do you know something about this, Sheil? What these little things are?"

Taking a step backwards, she gave a huge shrug.

Anton's eyebrows came down in his I-mean-business look.

"Sheila, did you give something to Freddie he shouldn't have?"

She looked up at us. Innocence written all over her. Big, wide eyes round as china plates. Hair escaped from her ponytail, wispy around her face. She held her lower lip between her teeth and continued to move backwards. For Sheila such innocent demeanor implied guilt.

"Sheila, I want you to tell me about this," I said. Still no response.

"We know you know," Anton added.

We stared at one another.

"Sheila." My most serious voice. I was having a hard time sounding that way. She looked so damned innocent in the face of such obvious guilt. How she could look that way and betray herself so badly, I did not know.

Finally I approached her, slowly, because fear had creeped into her expression and she still spooked occasionally if someone rushed at her. Putting a hand behind her shoulder, I propelled her back to the table. I kept my fingers on her back and stood behind her so she could not get away again.

"Now suppose you tell us what this stuff is, kiddo. I want to know and I want to know right now."

She stared at the damp napkin full of the colorful little balls which Mrs. Crum had laid on the table. I could feel Sheila pressing back against my hand. I jostled her shoulder.

"I'm losing patience, Sheil. Don't make me

angry. These things could hurt Freddie and we need to know what they are. Now tell me."

"Rabbit poop," she said softly.

"Then how come they're all those colors?"

"I painted them with temperas."

The situation got the better of Anton and he began to giggle. A hand over his mouth, he smothered the sound.

"For crying out loud, Sheila," I said, "why were you painting rabbit poop?"

"For Whitney."

As I wormed the story out of Sheila, we learned that she and Whitney had been planning to play a joke. For Easter, we were making a large mosaic in the back of the room, which was to be hung in the hallway of the main school building for Parent's Night. It was to be titled "Hopping Down the Bunny Trail." Apparently Whitney had thought it would be funny to substitute the mosaic chips with painted rabbit dung. Sheer adolescent humor. Sheila had been given the ignominious task of wrestling the dung away from Onions, who did not like anyone messing around in his cage for any reason. She was painting it and then drying it under the sink where no one looked much. Freddie must have discovered all this covert activity and assumed the painted dung was candy. Or something. He ate it. From the way Sheila related the whole deal, I gathered that the last week must have been a frustrating one for her. Onions had been uncooperative, Whitney had been absent and Sheila's cache of painted poop kept mysteriously disappearing. No wonder I caught her cursing into the cupboard after school.

Anton could barely contain himself through this recital. Lips tight between his teeth, he rolled his eyes heavenward repeatedly, and coughed into one hand. Mrs. Crum did not see the humor inherent in the whole mess. I might have felt differently too, if it were my son. None of us knew about the toxicity of the substance. I knew the temperas were nontoxic but had no idea about rabbit dung. Anton went to call the poison center. However, since Freddie had been eating them over the last week and had apparently suffered no ill effects, aside from his upset stomach, I was not too worried. Besides, he had been throwing them up unchewed and undigested anyway.

I pointed out the quiet corner to Sheila and suggested she go sit there the rest of the time. She went without protest, but deep, melodramatic sighs were issued so frequently that I was afraid she would hyperventilate. Anton returned with the report from the poison control center and assured Mrs. Crum that no harm would come to Freddie. I apologized to her for the kids' foolishness and escorted her to the door.

Anton and I discussed the situation and decided that we ought to have Whitney come in right then. She lived near the school and I felt it was better to get the matter taken care of when the other children were not around. Although it had been meant as a joke, the affair could have had serious consequences. I preferred to talk it over with Whitney and see how things were.

Anton left to call Whitney. I came over to the quiet chair. Sheila looked up.

"Listen, it's just about time for you to go to your bus. You get your jacket and get started. Anton and I are both too busy to walk you tonight, so you're going to have to take responsibility for yourself. I don't want to hear one single word from anybody that you messed around between here and the bus. Is that clear?"

Sheila nodded.

"Good-bye then. I'll see you tomorrow."

"I do be sorry."

"That's okay. We've talked about it and it's over now."

"You be mad at me?"

"I'll live through it. I know you guys did it as a joke and didn't mean to hurt anybody with it. I understand that. And you know now that it was a kind of dumb thing to do. So we'll just forget it, now that it's over."

She stood up but did not move away from the chair.

"Hurry up or you'll miss your bus."

"You be mad at me?"

"No, Sheil, I'm not mad at you. Now get moving."

"How come you don't smile at me, if you ain't mad?" The worry showed too plainly in her eyes.

Grinning, I came down on my knees to be her height and hugged her against me. I kissed her soundly on the cheek. "You're still a little short on

208

faith, aren't you?" I pushed back her bangs. "Now don't you go home and worry about it, because I'm all done being mad. I wasn't very mad to begin with because what you did wasn't on purpose. Mostly I was just worried about Freddie and when I get really worried, it comes out like I'm mad. But it's all over. Okay? Does that settle it for you?"

She nodded.

"All right. Then scoot or you'll miss that bus."

Whitney was another matter entirely. She arrived with her mother about ten minutes after Sheila left. I had not meant it to become that big a deal. I simply wanted to talk to her. I was not angry. As I had told Sheila, I never really had been. Mostly, I had been worried and also a little embarrassed in front of Mrs. Crum. Yet there had been potential danger in the situation and I felt Whitney needed to be aware of that. However, Whitney's mother made a federal case of the deal.

Anton had had to talk to her on the phone and had explained a little bit of the problem. She came storming into the school, hauling Whitney by the arm as if she were a little girl. A tall woman with starched blond hair, Whitney's mother marched into my room and demanded I tell her what happened. I explained best as I could. At that she turned to Whitney with an anger I could not have managed if Freddie had died from the stuff.

"Mrs. Blake? Mrs. Blake?" I kept trying to interrupt. "If I could just talk . . . Mrs. Blake?"

Anton was in the middle of the fray too, trying

to distract her. "Would you like a cup of coffee, Mrs. Blake?"

All the time Whitney sat in one of the little chairs and sobbed.

I don't remember how we shut her mother up. We did finally, and Anton took her down to the lounge for coffee. I figured that was a just reward for her. By that time of day, the coffee would have been in the pot for over eight hours.

Whitney and I were alone. I was embarrassed to be there, to have heard her mother talk to her like that. She must have felt humiliated. I was embarrassed to the point that I did not know what to say. Bringing over a box of tissues, I set them on the table in front of her. I hesitated momentarily, wondering if I should apologize or something. I mumbled something about giving her a few minutes to collect herself while I sorted out the kids' papers and put them in their cubbies for the next morning.

When I came back, I sat down beside her and put an arm around her shoulder. Whitney turned and clutched me. The move had been unexpected and my chair wobbled with her weight against me but I closed my arms around her; she was so hungry for comforting.

"Listen, things aren't this bad, Whitney." I smoothed her hair back from her face. "Anton and I, we're not that mad at you. I'm not that mad at all."

She straightened up in her chair and took an umpteenth Kleenex. "I was just joking."

"I know you were. And I'm not mad. I didn't mean to get you in all this trouble. Believe me, I wouldn't have had you come over if I'd known it would be this bad for you."

"Oh, my mom gets mad at anything."

"Yeah, well, it wasn't that big a deal. I just wanted you to know that you have to be a little careful around here. These aren't normal kids, Whitney. You have to watch things so much more around them."

She nodded and wiped at more tears.

"Kids like Freddie don't know what's edible and what isn't. And Sheila's too little to know she shouldn't be doing that sort of thing."

"I didn't think anybody would get hurt. I didn't mean this to happen."

"Oh, sweetheart, I know that. And this time, nobody did get hurt. We just came awfully close. It was only a silly thing you did without thinking. I love your sense of humor, Whitney, and I love the way you show the kids how to laugh. But these are special kids. We need to take extra good care of them."

She braced her head in her hands and stared at the tabletop. "I never do anything right. I screw up everything I do."

"It just seems that way right now. But you know that isn't true."

"My mom's going to kill me."

"This isn't any of your mom's worry. It's just yours and mine. Anton will take care of your mom and if he doesn't, I'll talk to her."

"I am sorry, Torey."

"Yeah, I know you are."

"What's going to happen to me?"

"Nothing."

Whitney would not look at me; she continued to stare at the table. I had a hand on her shoulder still and could feel the warmth through her shirt. We sat a long, long time in silence.

"Can I tell you something, Torey?"

"Yeah."

Still no way she could look at me. "This is about the only place in the world I like to be. Everybody teases me about it. All the time. They say: Why do you want to hang around with a bunch of crazy people all the time? They think I'm crazy too. You know, not nice crazy, but really mental. Because otherwise why would I want to be here so much?"

"Well," I replied, "then they must think the same thing about Anton and me. We must be crazy too."

"Do people ever say that to you?" For the first time she looked at me.

"Not to me. But I suspect there are more than a few who think it."

"Why are you here?"

I smiled. "I guess because I like very honest relationships. So far the only people whom I've found to be that honest are either children or crazy. So this place seems to be a natural for me."

Whitney nodded. "Yes, I guess that's what I like too—the way everybody shows exactly what they feel. So at least if someone hates you, you know it." She smiled wanly. "The funny thing is, these kids don't seem as crazy to me sometimes as normal people do. I mean . . ." her voice trailed off.

I nodded. "Yes, I know what you mean."

Chad was waiting for me when I arrived home, none too patiently. He had brought over a couple of cartons of moo goo gai pan from Jeno's Chinese Take-Out.

"Where on earth have you been? It's practically seven o'clock." He had been trying to keep the food warm by setting cartons and all in a frying pan. The kitchen smelled of scorched paper.

"At school."

"This late? Jesus, I've been here practically an hour. What were you doing?"

"Well, one of my kids had been vomiting up these little colored balls at home and his mom was suspicious that it was something he got into at school. So she brought this soggy napkin full of what he'd been throwing up."

Chad began to giggle. He had turned away from me to jiggle the frying pan with the cartons in it. I could see his shoulders shake.

"So Anton and I began dissecting these little balls and they turned out to be rabbit turds."

Chad's giggles became full laughter. And contagious. I began to chuckle.

"Anyway, Sheila had been getting the turds out of Onions' cage and painting them with temperas. God only knows when she was doing it, but evidently Freddie found them and was eating them.

I guess he thought they were candy or something."

Both of us were laughing. I could hardly get the last words out. The smell of scorching cartons wafted up between us but by that time the tears were rolling down our cheeks. My side hurt. And still we laughed.

"I'm sorry I asked," Chad finally gasped.

"I'm not," I replied.

Chapter 15

The call that I had been dreading came the third week in March. Ed Somers' low, rumbling voice came over the telephone. When the secretary had called my room that evening after school to tell me I had a phone call, I had a premonition this was the one. When I heard Ed's voice I knew, even before he said it.

"Torey, the director called today. They have an opening at the state hospital."

My pulse began to race when I heard him say that. The beating was so hard in my ears that I could not hear easily. "Ed, she doesn't have to go, does she?"

"Tor, I told you this was only a temporary placement. The court ordered that she be placed in the state hospital when an opening came up. It really is out of our hands. Your placement was only temporary."

"But she's changed so much. She's not the same child. Ed, she won't make it in the hospital."

"Listen, it was all settled before either of us got into it. You know that, we discussed it before. Besides, it'll be in her best interest. Look at that terrible home situation she has. She hasn't got a chance in hell to make it anyway, Tor. You know that. Christ, you work every day with these kids. You, of all people, should know when a kid's got too much stacked against her."

"But she hasn't, Ed," I cried. "This kid has so much. She could make it. She can't go into the hospital now."

Ed could be heard making clucking noises on his side of the phone. There was a long silence as he lit a cigarette. "Tor, you've done a hell of a good job with those kids. I honestly don't know how you do it sometimes. But you've gone too far with this one. You've gotten too involved. I could tell that back with that incident in January. This kid's case was decided long before she ever reached us."

"Then undecide it."

"It's out of my hands. After that burning incident, the state committed her. To placate the boy's parents, that was the only alternative."

"Ed, this is ludicrous. God Almighty, the child is six years old. This can't happen."

"I know how you're feeling, Torey, I really do. I'm awfully sorry this is having to happen this way because I know you've gotten involved with the girl. But she's a court case. We both knew how it would turn out. And I am sorry."

I went down to the teachers' lounge, unable to go back to my room where Sheila was playing. I sat and drank coffee, which I normally never touch, all the while trying to keep the tears back. Ed was right. I had gotten too involved; she mattered too much to me. I could not verbalize my frustration; I was not finding the right words. The chattering over lesson plans and art projects and the school carnival got to me. Finally I ended up going back to my room to get away from the lounge-dwellers who were so filled with after-school merriment.

When Anton saw me, he did not ask what had happened—he knew. He motioned Sheila over to the table where he was setting up a project for the next day and asked her to help him. I stood in the doorway looking around the room. Not a very remarkable place by the looks of it, I thought. Too long and narrow, too dark, too crowded with animal cages that smelled and pillows that lost all their stuffing on the carpet. Not even room for a teacher's desk. I could have used a teacher's desk right then; something to go and hide behind; something that shouted, "LEAVE ME ALONE," without my saying it. But there was none. Wearily, I went over to the pillows behind the animal cages and sank down onto them.

Within seconds Sheila was standing before me, her eyes scrutinizing my face. "You ain't happy," she stated quietly. She had her hands stuffed into the pockets of her overalls. How much she had grown, I thought. There must have been two inches between the overalls and her shoes. Or perhaps there always had been and I hadn't noticed.

"No, I'm not happy."

"How come?"

"Sheila, come over here," Anton called. Sheila remained motionless, her eyes piercing mine, probing my mind. I was wondering if I really had gotten too involved. She was such a beautiful child to me. To be sure, an ordinary passerby would have thought she looked like any of a hundred thousand other children. But she alone was more important to me than all the rest of them together. I loved her, although I certainly hadn't intended to. And loving her had made her so important to me. Now I was " 'sponsible." I could feel the tears in my eyes.

Sheila knelt beside me, the worry rippling across her face. "How come you cry?"

"I'm not very happy."

Anton came over and lifted Sheila to her feet. "Come on, tiger, you come help me put away papers."

"Uh-uh," Sheila twisted out of his grasp, moving out of reach.

I waved a hand at him. "That's okay, Anton. I'm all right." He nodded and left us.

For a long moment Sheila regarded me, her eyes flooded with concern. The tears remained unfallen in my own but I could not make them go away. Nor could I bring myself to look at her. I was embarrassed to show such shaky composure and I was worried about frightening her.

But she stood apart watching me. Then slowly

she came over and sat beside me. Touching my hand tentatively, she spoke. "Maybe if I hold your hand, you'll feel better. Sometimes that helps me."

I smiled at her. "You know, kid, I love you. Don't ever forget that. If the time ever comes and you're alone or scared or anything else bad ever happens, don't forget I love you. Because I do. That's really all one person can do for another."

Her brow wrinkled. She did not understand what I was saying. I suppose I knew she wouldn't because she was so young. But I had to say it. I had to know, for my own peace of mind, that I had told her I had done my best.

I rolled over on the bed to look at Chad. We had been watching TV all evening and not talking. I was too preoccupied to concentrate on conversation. At first I had not even told him the particulars of what had happened; but as the evening wore on, my mind was coming out of the first haze of shock and beginning to tick again.

"Chad?"

He looked in my direction.

"Is there a legal way to contest what they plan to do with Sheila?"

"What do you mean?"

"Well, you know. Is there a legal way to fight the commitment? I mean could someone like me do it? Someone who isn't her guardian?"

"*You* fight it?"

"Someone has to. I think the school district would back me. Maybe."

"I suppose you could try."

I frowned. "My problem is that I can't figure out where to start. To whom do we appeal? The courts committed her and you can't take a court to court, can you? I don't have any idea how to go about this."

"I imagine you'd have to call a hearing with her father and the parents of the little boy she abused and the child protection workers and all that. You could go through due process. You know all that."

I did not know. I had about as much understanding of the judicial system as I did the theory of relativity. But I hated Chad to think so. "Would you take it on, Chad?"

His eyebrows shot up. "Me?"

I nodded.

"I don't know anything about that kind of thing. What you need is someone specializing in that sort of law. Cripes, Tor, my experience is confined to getting the drunks out of jail."

I smiled. "Your experience and my bank account are about equal. I'm supposing that if I advocate, I'll have to pay for it."

Chad rolled his eyes. "Another charity case, huh?" He grinned. "I guess no one ever promised me I'd get rich."

"Oh, someday you will. Just not this year."

When the superintendent of school discovered that I had engaged a lawyer to look into the case, there was a meeting scheduled immediately. For the first time I met Mrs. Barthuly, Sheila's former teacher, face-to-face. She was a petite woman in her early forties with a delicate smile. As all five-foot-nine-inches of me in my Levi's and tennis shoes towered over her, I could well imagine Sheila might have been a trial to her. She wore an Anne Klein scarf and platform shoes and looked like a model for a Chanel No. 5 advertisement on television. Smelly, earthy-minded Sheila must have been hard to contend with.

Ed Somers was also there, as well as Allan, the psychologist, Mr. Collins, Anton, the superintendent and the resource room teacher who had had Sheila in kindergarten the year before. In the beginning it was not a particularly comfortable meeting for me. Not knowing my relationship with Chad, the superintendent felt that I had overstepped my boundaries in consulting a lawyer on this case without going through him. Perhaps he was right. I explained that I had discussed the matter with Ed and he felt there was no way we could touch the case, so I had simply checked into the legal recourse available.

Despite our touchy start, once the meeting got underway, a transition took place. I had brought along examples of Sheila's schoolwork and some videotapes that Anton had made of her in class. Allan reported on the test results. Sheila's former teachers were impressed and said so. Even Mr. Collins, whom I feared would be angry about this next example in a long history of my impulsive acts, commented on the overall improvement in

Sheila's behavior. Unexpectedly, I felt a rash of affection toward him as he spoke.

The superintendent was less enthusiastic, saying that this really wasn't our matter because of the abuse incident. Yet he was encouraged by Sheila's progress and by her unusual IQ. He cautiously agreed to stand behind me in stating that the state hospital was not the most appropriate placement for Sheila and that he thought she could be maintained in the public school system without endangering the other students. He asked that Chad come in and see him. Despite the superintendent's attempt to keep the mood of the meeting low-key, I left in jubilant spirits.

The other major person to involve was Sheila's father. Anton went on scouting duty. The next time he saw the man home, Anton called me, and Chad and I came out immediately.

As the time before, Sheila's father had been drinking. He had had a bit more this second time and was a little jollier.

"Sheila doesn't belong in the state hospital," I explained. "She's doing very nice work in school and I think she might even be able to go back to a regular class next fall."

He tipped his head slightly. "Why do you care what they want to do with her?"

The question echoed in my head, a repeat of what Sheila so often asked me. Why *did* I care? "You've got a special daughter," I replied. "Going to the state hospital would be the wrong move for her. I don't want to see that happen to her because

I think she can lead a normal life."

"She's crazy as a loon, that girl is. They told you what she done, didn't they? She damn near burned that little kid to death."

"She doesn't need to be crazy. She's not. Even now, she's not crazy. But she will be if she goes down there. It'd get worse in the long run. You don't want your daughter down in the state hospital."

He heaved a great sigh. He did not understand me. All his life people had been after him. Things had always gone wrong. He'd been in trouble, Sheila had been in trouble. He had learned to trust nobody. And so had his daughter. In their world it was safer that way. Now I came and he could not understand.

We talked far into the night. Chad and Anton drank beer with him while I made notes. Sheila, who was keeping her usual vigil on us from the far corner, fell asleep on the floor while we talked. I did not know if she understood why I was there and what was going on. I had not told her anything specific because I did not want to frighten her needlessly, nor did I want to give her false hopes. But after that night I suspected she would know. It would be better in the end, I supposed.

Her father agreed with us eventually. At last we convinced him that it was not "charity" or "do-gooding" or a nasty trick. He began to perceive the real reasons, which I had trusted he would if we persisted long enough. I had trusted that he did have some paternal instinct under that crust. In his own way, he loved Sheila and needed as much compassion as she did.

That was a strange evening. All of us were a little tipsy. Chad with his experience of defending the skid-row residents seemed to get along with Sheila's father better than the rest of us. He and her father would slap each other's backs in boozy camaraderie when I tried to get the conversation back onto the track and then they'd ply Anton and me with another can of beer. In a way, I was glad the hospital situation came up. It forced us to recognize each other's places in Sheila's life; that was better for everybody.

The hearing was held on the very last day of March. It was a dark, cold, windy day, promising snow on the eve of April. Not a good day to boost spirits. I had to take the afternoon off from school as did Anton. Mr. Collins came with us too. Surprisingly, in my opinion, he was very supportive of me, coming into my room in the morning and talking in a warm, fatherly way. Of all the people I had encountered, I would have least expected this change in him, because I had nursed a childish one-dimensional picture of him since the incident in Mrs. Holmes' room. At first I was suspicious of him, wondering what prompted this change, if he were simply protecting his own interests. But as I aired out some of the closed portions of my own mind I came to see that he cared in his own way as much for the children as I. Even for Sheila.

It was a closed hearing. Across the room from

us were the parents of the little boy and their lawyer. Milling about were a multitude of state and county people. With us were Anton, Allan, Mrs. Barthuly, Ed, and the superintendent. Sheila's father arrived late, but he did come finally and he was sober. My heart ached seeing him. He had on a suit that must have been a reject from Goodwill. The seams were frayed, the jacket stained and worn, the pants mended. His huge belly pulled the jacket tight and made it gape, straining on the buttons. Obviously, though, he had tried to look nice. His face was freshly shaven and he reeked of dime-store after-shave.

Outside the courtroom on a hard oak bench sat Sheila. Chad felt it would be best if she could be there. He thought perhaps he might need her if things did not go smoothly.

Sheila had come dressed in her overalls and T-shirt. I had so wished we could have dressed her nicely, but time had run out. So over the lunch hour I had given her a very thorough bath in the sink and brushed her hair until it was neat and shiny. If nothing else, she was clean. She had to sit alone outside the courtroom so we had brought a number of books to entertain her. However, when the judge found out that the child in question was being left unattended, he sent a court clerk out to sit with her.

The hearing went much differently from what I had expected. I had never been in a court before and all my information came from television. But this was not like TV. The lawyers spoke quietly and each of us presented our material. I had brought along the videotapes to illustrate Sheila's growth in my classroom in the three months she had been with us. Allan reiterated his findings from the tests. Ed spoke of the possible programs for her in the public schools should she continue to need special services after my class.

Then the parents of the little boy were questioned about the incident in November. Sheila's father was asked about how carefully he watched his daughter and if, in his opinion, she had seemed to improve in the last months. It was a very quiet hearing. No one raised a voice. No one even appeared emotionally involved. It was so different from what I had expected.

Then we were all asked to leave the courtroom while the lawyers and the judge finished up the case. I was so proud of Chad. Despite our long, enduring relationship, I had never seen him work professionally. Now in front of me I saw a different man from the one I knew lounging on the bed in front of the TV. He seemed so sure of himself, so at ease in the court surroundings. I was so proud of him for taking on the hassle of a case he knew would never earn him any money and for taking my bewildered queries and turning them into a real chance to keep Sheila with us.

Down the hallway the boy's parents sat. The strain showed on their faces. Mouths pulled tight and grim. Eyes staring without seeing. I wondered what they were thinking. I could not tell from their faces. Did they have the compassion to forgive

Sheila for what she had done? Or were their hearts still too burdened with grief and with fear? Were they still nursing in deep, unspeakable recesses the hope that her life would be as crippled as they feared she had made their son's? I could not tell from looking at them.

The father turned his head and met my eyes briefly. Both of us looked away. They were not bad people. Not the kind I could work up a hate for. When they had testified, their voices had been soft without detectable anger. If anything, they spoke sadly. Unhappy to have the issue reopened. To be in court a second time. To have their lives once more disrupted by this child. In a way I wished I could have hated them; it would have made the decision either way easier for me to accept. But I could not. They had only done what they thought best. Their fault, if anything, was nothing more than ignorance of mental illness. And fear. Now a judge, a man who did not know either of us, nor either of the children, would be the one to decide— on an issue that had no black or white. I wondered how they felt. I wished I had the courage to get up and go to them and ask. I wished there were a way it could be different.

Sheila was sitting on my lap. She had been drawing a picture when we had come out and was now trying to tell me about it. My self-absorption was annoying her. She put a hand up and physically moved my head to look at her. "Look at my picture, Tor. It be a picture of Susannah Joy. See, she gots on that dress she wears to school so much."

227

I looked down. Sheila had long been envious of Susannah Joy. Susie was the only child in our classroom to come from an affluent family. She was always immaculately dressed and had a splendid wardrobe of frilly little frocks. Sheila was inelegantly envious. She longed for a dress, just one dress like Susannah had. Day after day, she would page through catalogues and pick out dresses she would like to have. Time and again would come entries on the subject into her journal. Only the week before I had found in the correction basket Sheila's creative writing paper.

I do my best writing for you Torey from now on I do be a gooder girl and do my best work I promise. I want to tell you what I do last night. I go down and wait for my father he be at the opptomrix who fistes eye glasses. So I got to walk around for a while and I look in them windows sometimes. Some times I wish I could by the things in them windows. Some times they be so pretty. I seen a dress that be red and blue and be white too and it gots lace on it and be long and beautiful. I ain't never had a dress like that and it was prety torey. I sort of wish I could have it. It be my size to I think. I ask my pa if I could by it but he sad "no". That be too bad cos it be so nice and I aint never had a real dress. And I could a wored it to school like Susannah Joy do. She gots lots of dresses. But I couldnt so we went home and my pa he by me some M&Ms

*instead and toled me "to go to bed Sheila" so
I did.*

That little essay had hurt me in a funny, uniden-
tifiable way. It seemed one of the saddest things she
had ever written. But Sheila went on, knowing she
could not have a dress, accepting it and continuing
to dream.

Sheila pattled on about the picture she was
holding, showing me intricacies in the drawing. Yet
she noticed my mind was wandering. She hadn't
been called in, which I took as a good sign, but she
was aware of the tension among us.

Then at last the doors to the judge's chambers
opened. From the minute I saw Chad's face, I knew
what the ruling had been. He stopped about eight
feet from us, a crisp smile tight on his face. Then
he grinned. "We won."

Noise erupted in the hallway and we danced
about hugging one another. "We won! We won!
We won!" Sheila shrieked, bouncing midst everyone's legs. We all laughed at her jubilance although
I doubted she knew the impact of what she was
saying.

"I think this calls for a celebration, don't you?"
Chad asked. He was pulling on his trench coat.
"What do you say we go down to Shakey's and
order the biggest pizza they have?"

The others were beginning to leave. I glanced
briefly down the hallway toward the boy's parents,
who were putting on their coats. Once again I
wished I had the courage to walk those twenty feet

down the corridor and speak to them. Chad was talking to me about pizza, Sheila was jumping around my legs, scrabbling at my belt to be acknowledged, school people were yelling good-byes.

"Well, what do you say?" Chad asked again. "You want to go or are you going to stand there all evening?" He gave me a playful nudge.

I turned back to him and nodded.

"What about you?" Chad said to Sheila. "You want to come with Torey and me to get pizza?"

Her eyes widened and she nodded. I bent down and picked her up to bring her up to our level of the conversation.

Apart from us stood Sheila's father. Alone. His hands stuffed into the pockets of his ill-fitting suit. He stared at the floor. He seemed lonely to me, lonely and forgotten. This had not been his battle we had just won and it was not to him Sheila had gone. She had waited with us in the hallway and now she celebrated with us. It was our victory. He had not been a part of it. Courts had only been bad places for him in the past; they were frightening places. In his tattered suit and cheap aftershave lotion, he made a strange and striking contrast to the school district and government people. I realized with great sadness that even his daughter was not his own. She was one of us; he was not.

Chad must have perceived the same loneliness I did. "Do you want to join us?"

For a moment I thought I saw a flicker of pleasure on his face. But he shook his head. "No, I have to be going."

"It is all right if Sheila comes with us, isn't it?" Chad asked. "We'll bring her home later."

He nodded, a soft smile on his lips as he regarded his daughter. She was still in my arms, still wiggling with excitement, mindless of her father.

"You're sure you won't come with us?"

"No."

For a long moment we looked at each other, the universe between us never bridging. Then Chad reached into his pocket and took out his wallet. Pulling out a twenty-dollar bill, he handed it to Sheila's father. "Here. Here's your share of the fun."

He hesitated and I did not think he would accept it, knowing his disdain for charity. But uncertainly he extended his hand and took the bill. He mumbled a thank you, then he turned and walked away down the long corridor.

Sheila, Chad and I all piled into Chad's little foreign car and sped off to the pizza parlor. "Hey, Sheila, what kind of pizza do you like?" Chad asked over his shoulder to Sheila in the back seat.

"I don't know. I ain't never had no pizza."

"Never had pizza?" Chad exclaimed. "Well, we might have to do this more often, huh?"

If she never had pizza before, one would never have known it from Sheila's behavior. Her eyes were wide and shiny when the pizza arrived and she grabbed for it like a pro. Chad ordered the biggest, fullest-topped pizza he could find on the menu as well as a pitcher of soda pop. It was a magical moment. Sheila was alive and animated, talking constantly. She was intrigued by Chad and ended up sitting on his lap while we listened to the piano player entertain us. Chad commented that he had never seen a little kid eat so much food in one sitting in his life. Teasingly, Sheila told him she could eat at least a hundred pizzas if he had money to buy them and burped loudly to prove it.

Except for having seen her briefly the night we had gone to visit her father, Chad had never met Sheila. Early in the evening it was clear he thought she was one special person. Obviously the feeling was mutual. They laughed and kidded each other throughout the stay at the pizza place.

Night had fallen and the evening crowd was beginning to drift in. We had eaten the entire gigantic pizza, plus the pop, plus a round of soft ice cream. We had listened to the piano player so long that he coaxed Chad up to play "Heart and Soul" with him. But it was apparent that Chad and Sheila were not ready to part company.

Chad leaned way over the table to look at Sheila. "What's the thing you'd like best in the world, if you could have it?" he asked. My heart flinched because I knew Sheila would answer that she wanted her Mama and Jimmie back and that would dampen our mood.

Sheila pondered the question a long moment. "Real or pretend?"

"Real."

Again she sat pensively. "A dress, I think."

"What kind of dress?"

"Like Susannah Joy gots. One that gots lace on it."

"You mean all you'd want in the whole world is just a dress?" Chad's eyes wandered above Sheila's head to me.

Sheila nodded. "I ain't never had a dress before. Once a lady from a church bringed us out some clothes and there be this dress in it. But my Pa, he don't even let me try it on. He says we don't 'cept no charity from no one." She frowned. "I didn't think it would hurt just to try it on, but my Pa, he said I'd get a pounding if I did, so I didn't."

Chad looked at his watch. "It's almost seven o'clock. I don't think the stores in the Mall close until nine." He looked from me to Sheila. "What if I told you this is your lucky day?"

Sheila regarded him quizzically. She still did not know what was going on. "What do you mean?"

"What if I told you that in a few minutes we were going out to the car and go buy you a dress? Any dress you want."

Sheila's eyes got so big I thought they would break her face. Her mouth dropped and she looked at me. Then suddenly she was crestfallen. "My Pa, he wouldn't let me keep it."

"I think he would. We'll just tell him that's your share of the fun. I'll go in with you when we take you home. I'll tell him."

Sheila was beside herself. She leaped from her chair and danced in the aisle, colliding with unsuspecting patrons. She hugged me. She hugged Chad. Surely she would have exploded then and there if we hadn't left.

The next hour was a giddy one. We walked the aisles of the two big department stores in the Mall, Sheila holding on to our hands and swinging between us. Once we found the little girls' dresses, she turned unexpectedly shy and would not even look at them, instead shoving her face into my leg. Dreams close up can be quite hard to handle.

Finally I selected a few that were pretty and had lace and I dragged Sheila into a fitting room to try them on. Once we were alone she came back to life. Stripping off the overalls and shirt until she stood naked except for her underpants, Sheila lifted the dresses up to inspect them carefully. She was such a scrawny little thing with a sway back and a little kid's fat stomach that only emphasized her skinniness. Now alone with the dresses she became too excited to try them on and danced around the small room in circles. I captured her around the waist and shoved her into one dress. What a magic moment. Sheila preened herself in front of the three-way mirror and then ran out to show Chad. We must have spent a half hour closeted in that little room while Sheila tried to decide among three dresses. She tried each of them on at least four times. At last she chose one, a red-and-white dress with lace at the neck and around the sleeves.

"I'm gonna wear it every day to school," she said enthusiastically.

"You look so pretty."

She was watching me in the mirror. "Can I wear it home?"

"If you want."

"I do!" Her sudden smile faded and she turned to me. She climbed onto my lap, touching my face softly with one hand. "You know what I wish?"

"That you could have all three dresses?"

She shook her head. "I wish you was my Mama and Chad was my Daddy."

I smiled.

"It almost seems that way now don't it? Tonight, I mean. It almost seems like you are really my folks, huh?"

"We're something better than that, Sheil. We're friends. Friends are better than parents, because it means we love each other because we want to, not because we have to. We choose to be friends."

She looked at me for a long time, sitting on my knees and gazing into my eyes. Finally she sighed and slid off. "I wish we could be both. We could be family and friends both."

"Yes, that would be nice."

Her forehead wrinkled. "Could we just pretend?" she asked tentatively. "Just for tonight, could we pretend? Pretend that you and Chad was my folks and you was bringing your little girl out to buy her a dress? Even though she gots lots of dresses at home, you was bringing her out to buy another 'cause she wanted it and you loved her a lot?"

All my psychology class training urged me to say no. But as I saw her eyes, my heart wouldn't let me. "I suppose just for tonight we could pretend. But you have to remember it's just pretend and just for tonight."

She leaped up in a great bounce and tore out of the dressing room, still in her underwear. "I'm gonna tell Chad!"

Chad was amused to find out that while we were in the fitting room he had become a father. He played the part to the hilt. It was a mystical night filled with a lot of unspoken magic for all three of us. Sheila fell asleep in my arms on the way out to the migrant camp and after Chad parked the car, I woke her.

"Well, Cinderella," Chad said opening the door, "it's time to go home."

She smiled at him sleepily.

"Come on, I'll carry you in and tell your Daddy what we've been up to."

She hesitated a moment. "I don't wanna go," she said softly.

"It's been a nice night, hasn't it?" I replied.

She nodded. A silence fell between us. "Can I kiss you?"

"Yes, I think so." I enveloped her in a tight hug and kissed her. I felt her soft lips touch my cheek. And she kissed Chad as he lifted her out of my lap and carried her into her house.

We drove home in silence. Pulling up in front of my place we sat in the car, not speaking. Finally

Chad turned to me, his eyes shining in the wan glow of the streetlight. "She's a hell of a little kid."

I nodded.

"You know," he said, "it probably sounds dumb to say, but I pretended right along with her tonight. I wished we were a family too. It seemed so easy. And so right."

I smiled into the darkness, feeling a comfortable quiet drift down around us.

Chapter 16

April came in with a snowstorm. Although everyone bemoaned this parting shot of winter, it was one of those deep white fluffy snowfalls that are so lovely to look at. However, it stalled everything with its fierce depth, so school was suspended for two days.

When we returned, Sheila announced during the morning discussion that her Uncle Jerry had come to live with them. He had been in jail according to Sheila, although she couldn't remember what for, and now he was out looking for a job. She seemed quite excited about this new member of her family, telling us how Uncle Jerry had played with her all day during the snowstorm when she was bored.

We quickly returned to our routine. There was a trace of euphoria remaining from our victory in court. Although the children were not aware of what had happened, both Anton and I remained in highs spirits. And if we were happy, Sheila in her new dress was positively radiant.

Every day she wore the red-and-white dress, parading in front of the other kids in an obvious attempt to evoke the same kind of jealousy that Susannah had so successfully caused in her. She told them how on her "trial day" she won and got to go to dinner with Chad and me and got her prized dress. Before long, everyone wanted a trial and I had to ask Sheila not to dwell on it. But while her speech with the other children lessened on the topic, with me after school it was the only topic. Like our incident in February over my absence, this had to be gone over repetitively, in minute detail: we had gone to Shakey's, we had had a tremendous pizza, Sheila had eaten lots and lots. Then we went to buy the dress and pretended we were a real family. Over and over and over she would recount the details, her face animated with memory. I let her go on about it because there seemed to be something therapeutic for her in it, just as in the February incident. Interestingly enough, Jimmie had been all but forgotten. I did not hear his name mentioned for days on end. That had been an evening of sheer, unspoiled happiness for Sheila and she didn't seem able to savor it completely enough. But then I suppose when those moments are far and few between, they are even rarer treasures. So I patiently listened, again and again and again.

One morning almost halfway into April Sheila arrived at school subdued. Anton had gone to meet her at the bus, but the bus had been late and she came in after morning discussion had started. She was wearing her old overalls and T-shirt again and was pale. Sitting down on the outer fringe of the group, she listened but did not participate.

Twice during the half-hour session she got up and went into the bathroom. I worried that she might be ill because she looked so pale and seemed so restrained. But the others were clamoring for attention and my mind was distracted.

When I was handing out math assignments I could not find Sheila, only to discover that she was in the bathroom again. "Don't you feel well today, hon?"

"I'm okay," she replied, taking the math papers from me and going over to her place at the table. I watched her as she went. She was speaking more now, using the proper verbs and I was pleased.

Late in the hour, just before freetime, I came over and sat down with Sheila to show her how to do a group of new math problems. I took her on my lap. Her body was surprisingly rigid as I held her. I felt her forehead to see if she were hot. But she wasn't. Yet she was certainly acting oddly. "Is something wrong, Sheil?"

She shook her head.

"You're all tense."

"I'm okay," she reasserted, and returned to the math problems.

As the lesson concluded, I lifted her off from my lap to the floor. On the leg of my jeans was a widening red spot. I stared at it not fully comprehending what it was. Blood? I looked at Sheila. "What on earth is going on?"

She shook her head, her face emotionless.

"Sheila, you're bleeding!" Down the inside of her right pants leg spread a red stain. Picking her up I rushed into the bathroom and shut the door behind us. Unbuckling the overall straps, I let them fall around her ankles. Blood had stained her underpants and ran down both legs. Wadded into her underwear were paper towels. Apparently that had accounted for the numerous trips to the bathroom earlier. She had been trying to staunch the blood flow so that it would not come through and show.

"Good God, Sheila, *what* is going on?" I cried, my voice sounding louder and more alarmed than I had meant it to. Fear rose in me as I pulled away the last of the towels from her clothing. Bright red blood trickled from her vagina.

But Sheila stood immutable. No emotion ran across her face. Her eyes were blank, looking at but not seeing me. She was paler than I had thought out in the dimmer classroom light; God, she was white. I wondered how much blood she had lost. In an attempt to wake her out of her stoicism, I grabbed her shoulders and shook her. "Sheila, what happened? You have to tell me. You can't play games now. What happened to you?"

She blinked like one coming out of a heavy sleep. She was paying a great price to cut off the pain and the emotion. "Unca Jerry," she began softly, "he tried to put his pecker in me this morning. But it wouldn't fit. So he tooked a knife. He said I was keeping him out, so he put the knife inside me to make me stop."

I went numb. "He put a knife in your vagina?"

She nodded. "One of the silverware knives. He said I'd be sorry for not letting him put his pecker in me. He said this'd hurt a whole lot more and I'd be sorry."

"Oh God, Sheila, why didn't you tell me? Why didn't you let me know?" Fearful that she had already lost too much blood, I wrapped a towel around her and picked her up.

"I's scared to. Unca Jerry told me not to tell. He said he'd do it again if I told on him. He said worser thing would happen if I told."

Rushing out of the bathroom carrying Sheila, I told Anton to watch the class. I grabbed my car keys and raced toward the office. Briefly I tried to explain to the secretary that I was taking Sheila to the hospital and to have someone find her father and get him there. Time had wound down to that eerie slow-motion pace it assumes in an emergency. Everyone around me seemed to react as if they were in a movie running at an improper speed. What was happening? The junior high aides peered out of the workroom. What was going on? All the time I could feel the warmth of Sheila's blood against my arm, soaking into my shirt as I held her.

Sheila was whiter now. Clad only in her T-shirt and shoes with the towel I had wrapped around her her only other protection, she was getting sluggish, closing her eyes and leaning heavily against me. I ran for my car. Still holding her in my lap, I turned the ignition and jammed the gears into reverse.

"Sheila? Sheila? Stay awake," I whispered, trying to maneuver the car and keep a hold on her at the same time. I should have taken someone with me, I thought absently, but there hadn't been time. No time to tell them what had happened.

"I do be awake," Sheila muttered. Her small fingers dug into my skin, pulling the tender area of my breast painfully tight as she gripped my shirt. "But it hurts."

"Oh, I'm sure it does, baby," I replied. "But keep talking to me, okay." The distance to the hospital seemed interminable. The traffic impossible. Maybe I should have waited for an ambulance. I had no idea how much blood she had lost, nor how much was too much, nor what I could do about it. I cursed myself for never having followed through on my Red Cross training.

"My Unca Jerry, he said he was going to love me. He said he was going to show me how grown-up people loved each other." Her voice sounded small and childlike. "He said I better know how grown-up people loved. And when I screamed, he said nobody ain't gonna never love me if I can't learn how."

"Your Uncle Jerry doesn't know anything, lovey. He doesn't know what he's talking about."

She caught her lips in a tearless sob. "He said that be how you and Chad loved each other. He said if I want you and Chad to love me, I had to let him show me how, so I'd learn."

We neared the hospital. "Oh lovey, he's wrong. Chad and I love you already. He was just saying that so he could do something wrong to you. He had no right to touch you like he did. What he said and what he did were wrong."

Two young orderlies came running down the emergency ramp with a stretcher. Apparently Mr. Collins had alerted the hospital of our coming. As I placed Sheila on the stretcher for the first time she appeared to register pain and alarm. Moaning, she began to cry loudly but tearlessly. She refused to let go of my shirt and struggled fiercely as the men tried to pry her fingers loose.

"Don't leave me!" she wailed.

"I'm coming right along with you, Sheila. But lie down. Come on now, let go of me."

"Don't leave me! Don't let them take me away! I want you to hold me!" In a contorted mass the four of us and the stretcher moved toward the door. Sheila retained her terror-wrought grasp on my shirt, ripping the pocket. I did not know what brought her to life so fully. Perhaps she was frightened that I would leave her with these strangers; perhaps she could finally feel the extent of the pain. Whatever it was, she fought so valiantly that in the end it was easier for me to pick her up and hold her again than to pry her off and listen to her scream.

The emergency room doctor examined her briefly while I held her on my lap. Her father was still not there, so I signed a form stating that I would be responsible for emergency treatment until her father could be found.

A nurse came in with a needle and gave her a shot. Sheila had once again become docile and silent, not even flinching when the needle came. Within a short time after the shot, I could feel her fingers relaxing and I laid her on the examining table. Another nurse started an IV in one of her arms while a young Mexican-American intern was hanging a pint of blood above the table. The doctor gestured for me to come away. With a last look at Sheila, who lay with her eyes closed, pale and tiny on the table, I followed the doctor outside the swinging doors. He asked me what had happened and I told him to the best of my knowledge. At that point we saw Sheila's father stumbling down the corridor with the social worker. He was stone drunk.

The doctor explained that Sheila had lost a tremendous amount of blood and they had to stabilize that first. Apparently, from what he could see in the examination, the knife had punctured the vagina wall into the rectum. It was a very serious injury because of the likelihood of infection and the vast damage done. Once they had stabilized her blood level, the doctor believed there would have to be surgical intervention. Sheila's father weaved uncertainly beside us as the doctor spoke.

There was no more I could do. Undoubtedly my class back at school was in chaos. If Susannah had seen the blood, Anton would have more on his hands than he could handle alone or even with the other aides. And the children would be alarmed that I had left so suddenly. It was best that I get back to my job. I looked down at my clothes. Blood had stained the entire front of my shirt. The first spot on my Levi's had already dried into a dark blot. I stared at it. I was wearing part of somebody's life on me, little red tablespoons of a liquid more precious than gold. I was made uncomfortable by it, startled by how fragile life really is, reminded too fully of my own mortality.

I was back in school by eleven. When I looked up at the clock and saw how little real time had passed, I was shocked. Less than an hour had passed since I had lifted Sheila off my lap during math and seen the blood. The entire drama had taken place in barely fifty minutes. I had even gone home and changed my clothes before returning to class. I could not fathom that. To me it had felt as if a hundred years had been compressed into that fifty minutes. I had aged much more.

That night I did not go back to the hospital. I had called the doctor after school and he told me that they had just taken her into surgery and she was not yet out. Despite the blood administered, her condition had not stabilized but remained critical. He did not expect her out of the recovery room until quite late. She had been semicomatose most of the day and he doubted that she was aware of who had been present. Sheila would go into intensive care after surgery to make sure the hemorrhaging stopped and she would stabilize before she was moved to the children's ward. I asked if I could come up, explaining I was as close to family as the child probably had aside from her father. He suggested I wait until the next day. She would not be conscious enough to know me tonight and I would be in the way in the intensive care unit. They would make her as comfortable as they could, he assured me.

I asked if her father were still there, but the doctor replied no. They had sent him home shortly after I had gone. He was not sober enough to be coherent. The father's brother, Jerry, had been taken into custody.

In a way I was relieved not to have to go back. It had happened too fast and I could not conceive of the severity of the situation. She had talked to me. She walked all the way from the high school to our room and sat through an hour of class. And she had talked to me during the drive to the hospital. She could not be critically injured. I could not believe it.

The blood-stained shirt and jeans lay in a pile where I had hurriedly changed from them before returning to class in the morning. I put the Levi's to soak in the bathtub, but held the shirt, examining the pocket torn when Sheila had struggled with the emergency room attendants. Gently I folded the shirt and put it in the back of my closet. I could not bring myself to throw it away. Neither could I put it in the sink and wash it. I knew there was too much blood in it and if I did, the water would color. At that moment I was unable to wash the blood out, unable to see the water redden and go down the drain like so much filth. I would not be able to stand that.

After supper Chad came over and I related what had taken place. Chad was explosive. He paced the room at first saying nothing and shaking his head in disbelief. The anguish was not so much in the seriousness of the injury but in how it had happened. Chad raged with hatred, threatening to do physical harm to Jerry. He had no compassion for a man who would do such a thing to a little girl and I was frightened by the change in Chad, having never seen him so angry.

Although I was heartsick about the incident, a strange feeling twinged me. Five months earlier, Sheila had been the abuser and someone else had been the victim. Undoubtedly the boy's parents had felt very much the same way as Chad was now feeling toward Jerry. While it did not by any means excuse the gross inhumanity of the crime, it made me aware that the hurt and damage I had found in Sheila was probably in Jerry too. Neither was innocent, but neither was solely evil either. I was sadly plagued by knowing that Jerry was undoubtedly just as much a victim as Sheila. It made things so much more complicated.

The police called later in the evening and asked if I would come down and give them a statement. Together Chad and I went to the police department. In a gray-painted room at a gray-painted table, I told an officer what had happened in my classroom that morning. I repeated what Sheila had said to me and what I had done. It was a grim recounting of an even more grim occurrence.

During recess the next morning I called the hospital again to see how Sheila was coming along. The doctor's voice was more at ease this time. She had tolerated surgery well and had stabilized in intensive care during the night. By morning she was alert and coherent, so they had transferred her down to the children's ward. I could see her any time I wanted. I asked if her father had been in. The doctor said he had not. Please let her know I would be in right after school let out, I asked. The doctor agreed, his voice warm. She was a tough little kid, he said. Yes, I replied, there weren't any that were tougher.

Perhaps the most difficult task had been explaining what had happened to Sheila to the children in my class. We had already talked about abuse, both physical and sexual, in our room. My kids came from a high-risk population for abuse and I felt it was important for them to know what to do if they found themselves in such a situation or saw it happening to someone else. However, sexual abuse was hard to talk about. In a district where sex education had not made great popular strides in the schools, sexual abuse was taboo. I had worked up an informal unit for my children in which we simply discussed the appropriate and inappropriate ways of being "touched." An adult who held you and hugged you was okay. An adult who held your penis and hugged you was not. We discussed what one should do if that happened, because no one had the right to touch a boy or girl in some places. Neither should they ask to be touched there. We had done the unit in October and had gone over it a few times since. It provided a measure of relief for the kids to be able to talk about those things, expressing fears about not knowing what to do when someone touched them and it felt "funny."

But Sheila's case, I did not know how to handle. Sex and violence together are not good topics for primary-age disturbed children. Yet, I had to say something. They saw us leave so unexpectedly and they did see the blood. Then they saw me return without Sheila. I told them briefly that Sheila had been hurt at home and I had had to take her to the hospital because of it. Beyond that I said nothing.

The children made her get-well cards the next afternoon when I said I had called the hospital and Sheila was in the children's unit and feeling better. Poignant, brightly crayoned messages piled up in the correction basket. The event, however, affected the kids more than I had perceived. At closing time William burst into tears.

"What's wrong?" I asked as I sat down on the floor. The children were gathered around the Kobold's Box with me. William too was there but had suddenly dissolved into tears.

"I'm scared about Sheila. I'm scared she's going

to die in the hospital. My grampa went to the hospital once and he died there."

Unexpectedly, Tyler also began to sob. "I miss her. I want her back."

"Hey, you guys," I said. "Sheila's doing really well. That's what I told you after lunch. She's getting better. She won't die or anything."

Tears coursed over Sarah's face although she made no noise. Max began to wail in harmony, although I doubt he had any concept of why everybody else was crying. Even Peter was teary-eyed, despite the fact that he and Sheila were sworn enemies most of the time.

"But you won't let us talk about it," Sarah said. "You never even said Sheila's name all day. It's scary."

"Yeah," Guillermo agreed. "I kept thinking about her all the time and you kept acting like she never was here. I miss her."

I looked at them. Everyone but Freddie and Susannah were in tears. I doubted they were all that loyal to Sheila, but what had happened had frightened everyone. Moreover, it had affected me. I had worried and in an attempt to keep things calm I had said nothing. In my classroom we had spent the better part of seven-and-a-half months learning openness and putting ourselves in other people's places. They had learned too well perhaps, because I could not disguise things from them.

So normal closing exercises went undone; the Kobold's Box was unopened, while I talked to them, telling them how I felt and why I had not been as honest as I usually was. We sat down on the floor, all of us together, and had a roundtable.

"Some things are kind of hard to talk about," I said. "What happened to Sheila is one of those things."

"How come?" Peter asked. "Don't you think we're old enough? That's what my mom always says when she don't want to tell me stuff."

I smiled. "Sort of. And sort of because some things are just hard to talk about. I don't even know why. I guess because they scare us. Even us big people. And when big people get scared about things, they don't like to talk about them. That's one of the problems with being big."

The kids were watching me. I looked at them. Each of them, individually. Tyler with her long, ghoulish throat scars. Beautiful black-skinned Peter. Guillermo, whose eyes never really looked anywhere, even when he was paying attention. Rocking, finger-twiddling Max. Sarah. William. Freddie. And my fairy child, Susannah.

"Remember I told you that Sheila got hurt at home. And remember back when we were talking about the ways people can touch you? I was telling you how sometimes people want to put their hands places on a little kid's body that they have no right to touch."

"Yeah, like down where it's private on you, huh?" said William.

I nodded. "Well, someone in Sheila's family touched her where he shouldn't have and when Sheila got unhappy about it, he hurt her."

Foreheads wrinkled. Their eyes were intent. Even Max stopped rocking.

"What did he do to her?" William asked.

"Cut her." As I listened to myself tell these kids, I wondered if I was doing the right thing. Instinctively I felt I was. Our relationship was grounded in the truth, however bad it might be. Moreover, I could not believe knowing could be worse than not knowing, nor worse than the many things these children had seen already. The fact that nothing in their lives was so bad that it could not be talked about had been a cornerstone in this room. Yet, deep inside of me nagged the knowledge that once again I was breaking the rules that I had been taught, overstepping the boundaries of proven educational and psychological practice. And as in all other times I had done that, the worry came that this occasion might be my downfall, that this time I might hurt more than I helped. The war between safety and honesty raged once more.

"Who done it to her?" asked Guillermo. "Was it her father?"

"No. Her uncle."

"Her Uncle Jerry?" Tyler asked.

I nodded.

For a minute there was silence. Then Sarah shrugged.

"Well, at least it wasn't her father."

"That don't make it any better, Sarah," Tyler replied.

"Yeah, it does," Sarah answered. "When I was

little, before I came to school, my father sometimes he'd come in my room when my mother was at work and . . ." she paused, looked from Tyler to me, then down at the rug. "Well, he done that kind of stuff. It's worse when it's your father, I think."

"Let's not talk about this anymore, okay?" William said. Fear had creased his brow. He wrung his hands.

"No, I wanna," Sarah said. "I want to know how Sheila is."

"No," William said again. Tears returned to his eyes.

"You're scared, William," Guillermo stated. "What are you scared of?"

I reached a hand out. "Why don't you come over here and sit with me."

He rose and came over. I put an arm around him.

"This is a scary thing to talk about, isn't it?"

He nodded. "There's dust under my bed sometimes if my mom doesn't use the vacuum."

"William, that's off the subject," Peter said.

"That dust scares me. Sometimes I think maybe that used to be people. Maybe it's dead people under my bed."

"That's stupid."

"No, sir. It says right in the Bible, Peter, that you came from dust and you turn to dust after you die. It says so. My mom showed it to me. You ask Torey."

"I don't think that's what the Bible means, William," I said.

"And that might have been people under there, that dust. Might have been my grandpa after he went to the hospital. He might be under my bed now. Maybe it's Sheila."

"No, it's not Sheila. Sheila isn't dead, Will. She's in the hospital and she's going to get better," I replied.

"Torey?" Tyler asked.

"Yes?"

"How come Sheila's uncle did that to her? She just told us the other day that he was nice and played with her. How come he cut her?"

I regarded her. I did not have an answer. No matter how long I waited, an answer did not come to me. "I don't know, Ty."

"Did he have problems?" Sarah asked. "Like my father? They put him in the ward at the state hospital 'cause he had problems. That's what my mother told me. He never came back."

"Yes, I guess you could say he had problems. He didn't understand the right way to touch little girls. Or rather, I suspect he understood, but sometimes people do things without thinking first. They just do what sounds good to them at the moment."

"Is he going to go to the state hospital like my father?"

"I don't know. It's against the law to hurt people."

"When's Sheila coming back?" Peter asked.

"As soon as she's better."

"Will she be the same?"

"What do you mean?" I asked.

Peter frowned. "Well, if she got cut down there will she be the same?"

"I'm still not following you, Peter. Explain what you mean."

He hesitated, glanced nervously around the group, back at me. "Can I say some dirty words? I got to so you'll know what I'm talking about. I need to use dirty words."

I nodded. "This is different than yelling them at people. They aren't dirty when they mean something. Go ahead."

Again a hesitation. "Well, down there, that's a girl's cunt, isn't it?"

"Yeah."

"And down there, that's where a girl goes to the bathroom. Well, what if he cut her there? That's where babies come out. What if he cut her there?"

I still did not have the exact question Peter was asking. I decided to turn the question back on him to see if I could pull further information out of him. "What if he did cut her, Peter? What do you think would happen?"

His eyes widened with anxiety. "What if she grows up and has babies?"

"What if she does?"

There were tears in his eyes. "She might crap on them when they're being born." His mouth pulled down in a sob. "That's what my mom done to me. That's why I'm crazy."

"Oh, Peter, that's not true," I said.

He came crawling over on his hands and knees. I was sitting cross-legged on the floor with William against my right side. Peter laid his head in my lap. "Yes, it is."

"No, it isn't. I don't know where you got that idea, but it's wrong."

"Peter, you're not crazy," William said. "Nobody's really crazy. That's just a word. Isn't it, Torey? Just a word. And nobody's a word."

We talked a long time. The bell to go home rang, the buses came and went and we talked. About sexual abuse. About Sheila. About ourselves.

Afterward, I loaded all eight of them into the hatch of my car and drove them home. We never lost the seriousness of the discussion. Even in the car, the questions kept coming. No one ever kidded or made a joke or goofed off. The things we had to talk about were not funny to anyone. The need to talk about them surpassed all other needs that afternoon. And all our differences.

After I had dropped the other children off I collected the get-well notes and a few books I knew Sheila especially liked, and headed for the hospital. She had been placed in an observation room right off the nurses' station and the doorway I was to use was pointed out to me. I entered.

She was alone in the large room with glass windows on one whole wall, like a cage at the zoo. She was lying in a crib with high metal sides. An IV dangled above one post and next to it a unit of blood. The arm that the needles were in was tied to a rung of the crib with a restraint to immobilize it. She looked so young and small.

Tears filled my eyes before I could stop them and they spilled over my cheeks. The only thing I could think of was why had they put her in a crib? Sheila had a lot of dignity for a little kid. I knew that would humiliate her. I knew she would be embarrassed to have me see her in it. Why hadn't they given her a bed like a nearly seven-year-old child should have? Not a crib. Cribs were for babies.

Sheila turned her head toward me when I entered. In silence she regarded me. "Don't cry, Torey," she said softly. "It don't hurt much. Really it don't."

Humble in the presence of such courage, I stared at her. "Why did they put you in a crib?" I asked, my mind blank. I let down the side nearest me and touched her free hand. "You shouldn't be in a crib."

"I don't mind really," she said. I knew that was not true. We had been friends long enough for me to know the extent of her carefully guarded sense of self. She smiled softly, as if I were the one to be comforted, and reached up to touch my face. "Don't cry, Torey. I don't mind."

"It makes me feel better. You scared me so much and I was so worried about you, Sheil. It makes me feel better to cry a little bit and I can't help it."

"It don't really hurt bad." Her eyes had lost some of their expression. Perhaps the medication was causing the glassy effect. "But I do get sort of scared sometimes. Just a little bit. Like last night,

I didn't know where I was at. That was kind of scary. But I didn't cry none or anything. And pretty soon the nurse comed over and talked to me. She be right nice to me. But I still be a little scared. I wanted my Pa."

"I bet so. We'll see if we can't get someone to be with you when you get scared."

"I want my Pa."

"I know, honey. And he'll be here when he can."

"No sir. He don't like hospitals none."

"Well, we'll see."

"I want you to stay with me."

I nodded. "I will as much as I can. And Anton will come sometimes too. And I know Chad will want to. He's been asking all day about how you are. We'll do the best we can. I don't want you to get scared, love. I'll try my hardest to help."

She turned her head away from me for a moment and looked up at the IV. "My arm hurts some." Her eyes wandered back to me and suddenly the hurt and the fear were alive in them. Her face contorted in a grimace. "I want you to hold me," she whimpered. "My arm hurts fierce bad and I do be so lonely. I want you to stay here and hold me and not go away."

"Kitten, I don't think they would like me to hold you. I think it'd mess up all the stuff they have hooked up to you. I can hold your hand, if you want."

"No," she whined. "I want you to hold me. I hurt."

I smoothed back her hair and leaned close to

her. "Oh I know you do, sweetheart, and I want to. But we can't."

She looked at me a long moment and then that glaze of control filmed over her eyes. She took a deep, shuddery breath and that was all. Once again she was passive, locking up one more thing she could not bear to feel.

"I brought some books. Maybe you'd like me to read to you. It might take your mind off things."

Slowly she nodded. "Read me about the fox and the little prince and his rose."

Chapter 17

Sheila remained in the hospital through the rest of the month of April. During that time her uncle was arraigned and tried for sexual abuse. He returned to prison. Her father didn't go to see her the entire time she was hospitalized, pleading a phobia of hospitals. Instead he drowned his fears at Joe's Bar and Grill. I went every night after school to see her and usually stayed through dinner. Chad came up most evenings and played checkers with Sheila even after I had left. Anton visited regularly and Whitney was allowed on the unit for a couple of brief stops even though she was underage. Oddly, even Mr. Collins came to see Sheila and I surprised him one Saturday afternoon playing a game with her. To the astonishment of the hospital staff Sheila turned out to be one of the most popular children on the unit with a whole entourage of well-wishers coming and going each day. I was thankful for the interest shown in her because much as I wanted to, I could not afford to spend more than a couple of hours up there every night. Yet I knew that I probably would have stayed longer if no one else had shown up.

In a way the hospitalization was good for her. Being so physically attractive and having come through such a harrowing experience, she was the darling of the nursing staff. They showered her with attention. Sheila responded delightedly. She was cheerful and cooperative in most instances and, of course, never cried. Best of all, she was getting three balanced meals a day and was beginning to put on much-needed weight. It was not until the very end of her hospital stay that she began to get restless, not wanting to stay in bed, and getting cranky with those who insisted she did. Her emotional problems seemed totally eclipsed by this event. Certainly for as severely disturbed a child as she had been, there was almost no evidence of her acting up in the hospital. To the contrary the nurses were forever commenting on her outstanding behavior. This concerned me. While it made the stay more pleasant for everyone, I knew neither the hospitalization itself nor the reason she had gone in were anything other than vastly traumatic events. I feared that like her absurd ability to keep from crying, she had sublimated this misery, making it seem as if it had never happened. That was to me a greater indicator of the seriousness of her disturbance than anything else.

In the meantime the rest of the children had

adjusted to life without Sheila. We enjoyed the April sunshine and the resurrecting earth around us. Things calmed down and, except for weekly letters to her, Sheila ceased to be a major topic of conversation.

During this time I learned for certain that my class would be disbanded permanently. A number of things had contributed to that situation and I had been aware of all of them. First, the district was doing some shuffling within itself and now felt that placement of many disturbed children such as Freddie and Susannah could be accomplished without maintaining another separate class as had been done this year. Second, the others had all made enough progress that, realistically, they could go into a less restrictive placement. Perhaps most important, rumblings were coming down of a new bill in Congress on mainstreaming handicapped children back into the normal classrooms. In response to this federal law, a number of special rooms were being eliminated altogether in an attempt to free some specially trained teachers for consultation to the regular classroom. As I had the most severe level, those in charge of placement were most interested in eliminating my level entirely. And last, and certainly most consequential, money was running tight. Maintaining children in classes like mine was very expensive. The low ratio of children to teachers, the greater training of the teachers who could thus command higher salaries, the special equipment all cost a great deal of money. The district could not afford to run as many special classes in the future as they had this year.

While I was saddened by the news, it was not unexpected. My sadness was only the same one I felt every year as it drew to a close and I wished we could start all over. In fact I had my own personal plans. The school district had offered me another position; however, I had applied to graduate school and had been accepted. I already possessed a master's degree in special education and my regular teaching certificate. But I did not have full certification for teaching special children. While the state was not yet requiring this full certificate in addition to the regular certification, I could see it on the horizon. Too many good teachers I had known had lost their jobs simply because they had not been able to keep up with the certification requirements. If the day came and I found myself in a job that I did not want to give up to go back to school, I would not want to be caught short of credits. This job was essentially over; I wouldn't be able to go back to the same kids and the same class in the fall anyway; so now seemed as good a time as any to return to school.

I was also toying with the idea of pursuing a doctorate. I had become increasingly involved in research during the previous years and had been appalled by the huge gaps in research in the areas of childhood withdrawal and depression.

While I loved teaching, the months just past had been filled with soul-searching about my future. In addition, Chad was renewing pressure to marry

and settle down. That night after the trial with
Sheila had affected him and he now openly acknowledged he wanted a family. Yet I was getting
restless. When the acceptance from the university
had come on April sixth, I had agreed to go, which
meant when school let out in June, I would be
moving half a continent away from Chad and
Sheila and a place that had given me several of the
best years of my life.

Sheila returned to school early in May. She came
back with the same extroverted gusto she had displayed in the hospital, giving the distinct impression that she had been on an extended holiday. As
I watched her resume her old place in the class I
was more unsettled than ever by her attitude. Onc
could not swallow that much pain and get away
with it. I feared she might be even more disturbed
than I had thought; that perhaps she was slipping
off into some fantasy to protect herself from the
horrors of the real world. But throughout the day
and then the next couple of days she gave no indication of any problem. For all the world she
seemed like some normal child who had stopped
by to participate in our classroom activities.

By the end of the week the veneer was beginning
to wear thin. The old hassles had begun to raise
their heads again. I started demanding more out of
her and she found herself making mistakes. This
put her in a sulk for a few hours on Thursday. The
other kids were readjusting to her return and were
not giving her the attention to which she had

grown so accustomed. This provoked a bit of angry fussing when things did not go her way. But most important she slowly began to talk to me again. That, I decided, was what had been missing. While she kept up a constant chatter in school and after, she never really did say anything. It was all just prattle over the immediate situation. Unlike before when she was open and voluntarily brought up her feelings, now she spoke only about safe things. Bit by bit, however, a statement would creep in that mirrored what was below the carefree surface.

She had returned to school wearing the old overalls and T-shirt. The blood stains were still visible and after having gained weight in the hospital, Sheila was too large to wear the overalls comfortably. They were too short and too tight. I wondered what had become of the red-and-white dress, so finally on Friday evening after school, I asked. Sheila was helping me cut out figures for the bulletin board; so we sat together at one table, the work spread between us.

She pondered my question a moment. "I ain't gonna wear it no more."

"How come?"

"That day . . ." she paused, concentrating on her cutting. "The day my Unca Jerry . . . Well, he says it be a right pretty dress. He could feel under it. He done it before but this time he wouldn't stop. He kept putting his hands under there. So I ain't wearing it no more. I ain't having nobody feel there."

"Oh."

"Besides, it got all blooded up. My pa, he throwed it away when I was gone."

A long, heavy silence fell between us. I did not know what to say next so I just continued to work on what I was cutting out. Sheila looked up. "Torey?"

"Hmm?"

"Do you and Chad ever do that stuff together? Like Unca Jerry did to me?"

"What your uncle did to you, no one should do. That was wrong. Having intercourse is something grown-up people do with each other. It's not something kids do. And no one ever uses a knife. That was wrong."

"I know what it is. My Pa, he brings home ladies sometimes and does that. He thinks I be asleep but I ain't. It makes a lot of noise, so I wake up. I seen them. I know what it is."

Her eyes were cloudy. "Is it really love?"

I took a long breath. "You're not really old enough, Sheil, to understand altogether. Sometimes it's called love. But it isn't exactly. It's sex. Usually two people do it when they really love one another and then it's good and they like it. But sometimes people just do it but they don't love each other. It's still sex, but it's not love. Sometimes a person forces another to do it. And that's always wrong."

"I ain't never gonna love anybody if I have to do that."

"You're too little. Your body isn't ready to do those sorts of things yet, so it hurts you. But it isn't love, Sheil. Love is different. Love is a feeling. What happened was a really wrong thing. No one should do that to a little girl. It hurt you because it was not something that should have happened. You're too little."

"Then why did he do it to me, Torey?"

Putting down the figure I had been cutting, I pushed back my hair. "You're asking me awfully hard questions, sweetheart."

"But I can't understand that. I liked Unca Jerry. He played with me. Why did he want to hurt me?"

"I don't really know. Sometimes people just lose control. Like remember you and me back in February when I went to the conferences? I mean we sort of did that to each other. It's something that happens."

Sheila stopped her cutting, letting the paper and scissors drop through her fingers to the tabletop. For a long, silent moment she sat motionless, staring at the paper and scissors and at her still spread hands. Her chin quivered. "Things never are the way you really want them to be, are they?" She did not look at me.

I did not respond, not knowing how to.

She lay her face down on the table in a gesture of defeat. "I don't wanna be me anymore. I just don't."

"Sometimes it's hard," I replied, still not knowing what to say but feeling the need to say something.

She turned her head so she could see me but let it remain on the table midst the shambles of her cutting. Her eyes were dull. "I wanna be somebody like Susannah Joy and have lots of nice dresses to wear. I don't wanna be here. I wanna be a regular kid and to go a regular kid's school. I just do not want to be me anymore. I'm sick of it. But I can't figure out how to do it."

I watched her. Somehow I always think I have finally lost my innocence. I always think, my God, I've seen the worst, the next time it isn't going to hurt me as bad. And I always find it does.

Chapter 18

I decided as a last major activity of the school year, our class would put on a Mother's Day program. One of the greatest tragedies to befall special education is that the special children almost never get to participate in the traditional fun activities of regular children. For the special kids, just getting through from day to day seems to be enough of an achievement. But I always hated that. Just "getting through from day to day" makes for a life hardly worth living. We all know it's the icing and not the cake that causes most people to eat cake. So I tried to make up for it by creating some of the more popular activities of the regular school program in our room.

We had had an assembly for the families in October that had gone off . . . not too badly. So I decided that was just what we needed to perk up

May. To devise a program that children like Susannah and Freddie and Max could participate in was no easy task. But with the help of my parents' group we put together a few songs, a poem or two, and a skit full of the traditional spring flowers and mushrooms that always seem to bloom in small children's plays.

The kids were all excited about the event, except that Peter wanted to do a more ambitious skit. Most of them had just seen *The Wizard of Oz* on its umpteenth yearly run on television and were determined we should do that. I explained that with only five reliable actors that might be a bit difficult especially since no one except Sheila could read much. Peter in particular was adamant that he would not be any woodland flower and instead he wanted to be a Tin Man. Sarah agreed. Out on the playground they had been playing *Wizard of Oz* and she thought it went very nicely. I finally gave in, stating that if Peter and Sarah could develop a rough skit that would include parts for Freddie and the others, and Guillermo could play a good part despite his handicap, I would let them do it.

So we began practicing. Actually we had started working on the songs back in April, but Peter's change in script did not occur until Sheila was back with us in May. Obviously, our Mother's Day play was going to be a little late. I was eternally grateful for Sheila and her agile memory. She had a reasonable singing voice and could remember anything she was given. So I padded the pro-

gram with her and with Max, whose disturbance
had equipped him with the ability to repeat vast
quantities of materials, although not necessarily
on demand.

I had asked Sheila if she wanted her father to attend. Many of the other fathers were coming, since
although the play was billed as a Mother' Day
show, it was one of the only opportunities parents
had of seeing their kids in a joyful and frivolous
school activity. Besides, I wanted all the families to
feel free to attend any of our school functions. So I
asked Sheila about her father, knowing that if she
wanted him, special arrangements would have to
be made to get him there.

She screwed up her face a moment in consideration. "He wouldn't come."

"Anton could go out and get him, if he wanted
to come. As long as we know ahead of time, it
wouldn't be hard."

"I don't think he'd come anyways. He don't like
school stuff too good."

"But he could see you in the play and singing
your song. I bet your Dad would be proud to see
you do all those things." I sat down on one of the
little chairs so that I would be more at her level.
"You know, Sheil, you've really come a long way
in here since January. You're like a different girl.
You don't get into trouble nearly as much as then."

She nodded her head emphatically. "I used to
wreck stuff all the time. But I don't anymore. And
I used to not talk when I got mad. I used to be a
bad girl."

"You've done a lot better, alright. And you know what? I bet your Pa would like to see how well you've done. I think he'd be proud of you because I don't think he realizes what an important girl you are in this class."

Sheila ruminated a moment while studying me through squinted eyes. "Maybe he would come."

I nodded. "Maybe he would."

The morning of the program Chad arrived in the classroom carrying a big box. Anton was setting up props and Sheila was brushing her teeth. "What are you doing here?" I asked, surprised to see him.

"I came to see Sheila."

Excitedly, Sheila leaped down from the chair she was standing on and ran over.

"Spit our your toothpaste first," Chad warned her. She scurried back to the sink to return in seconds, toothpaste still outlining her lips. "I understand you're going to have a play today."

"Yeah!" she cried, bouncing around him in excitement. "I'm gonna be Dorothy and Torey's gonna braid my hair up in pigtails. An' I'm gonna sing a song and say a poem, and my Pa's gonna be here and *watch* me!" She was out of breath after the exclamation, having said it so rapidly. "Are you gonna come?"

"Nope. But I brought you a good-luck present for your debut."

Sheila's eyes widened. "Me?"

"Yes, you."

In glee she hugged his knees with such gusto

that Chad wobbled unsteadily.

I knew what was inside the box—a long dress, red, white and blue with lace around the front placket. A beautiful and expensive dress that Chad had brought back with him from a recent trip to New York. I had told Chad about what had happened to the other dress and about Sheila's feeling that dresses made her too vulnerable. For that reason he had bought a long dress instead of a short one. The night he had come in to show me the dress, his eyes were all sparkly like a little boy's. I could just picture him in the New York stores, his tall football player's frame towering over miniature racks of little girls' dresses; his arms spread wide attempting to describe for the salesclerk the special little girl back in Iowa for whom he needed that very special dress. Chad had great confidence that he had found just what Sheila would dream for. That it would erase the horror of the last month and recapture at least a little of the magic we had found the night of the court hearing.

Sheila ripped open the paper and lifted the lid on the box. Momentarily she hesitated, gazing at the tissue paper still partly obscuring the contents. Very, very slowly she lifted the dress out of the box, her eyes huge and round. She looked at Chad who knelt on the floor next to her.

Then she let it drop back into the box and lowered her head. "I ain't wearing dresses no more," she whispered hoarsely.

Chad turned to me in bewilderment, his own

disappointment clear in his face. I came over and knelt down with them. "Don't you think it might be okay this once?"

She shook her head.

I looked at Chad. "I think we need a minute alone, if you'll excuse us." I rose and took Sheila to the far side of the room behind the animal cages. I knew the confusion that must be filling Chad's head. I knew as well that Sheila must have been in torment. She loved pretty things so much and that was a stunning dress Chad had brought, far lovelier than the red-and-white one he had gotten her in March. Yet, what had happened to her was too fresh, the hurt too raw.

Her face contorted into a teary-eyed grimace by the time I had her behind the cages. She pressed her fingers to her temples in an effort to keep the tears back, but for the first time since she had come to my class she was unable to. Over her cheeks coursed rivulets and she dissolved into sobs.

The time had finally come. The time I had been waiting for through all these long months that I knew sooner or later had to occur. Now it was here.

For several minutes I sat with her behind the cages. She had surprised me so much by actually crying that for a moment I did nothing but look at her. Then I gathered her into my arms, hugging her tightly. She clutched onto my shirt so that I could feel the dull pain in her fingers digging into my skin. When it became apparent that she had lost all control and was not going to regain it, I picked her

up and came out of hiding. I needed to go somewhere where the other kids were coming in and all
the preparations for the program would not interrupt us.

"What did I do?" Chad asked worriedly, his gentle face distorted with concern. "I didn't mean . . ."

I shook my head. "Don't worry about it. Put the
dress over there. I'll get back to you after a bit,
okay?" I turned to Anton. "Can you take care of
things for a while?"

The only place I could think of where we would
be entirely alone and undisturbed was the book
closet. Attempting to manipulate a kiddie chair along
with me while carrying Sheila, I unlocked the closet
and went in, securing the door behind me. I put the
chair against a stack of reading books and sat down,
shifting Sheila to make her more comfortable.

She sobbed hard, but not in the hysterical manner in which she had started. But she cried and
cried and cried. I simply held her and rocked the
chair back and forth on its rear legs, feeling my
arms and chest get damp from the tears and her
hot breath and the smallness of the room. At first
my mind was busy, wondering how Anton was
managing alone with all the kids so high about the
play, thinking about the program itself and how it
would go, mulling over Sheila's situation. After a
while my mind ran dry and I just sat and rocked,
thinking of nothing in particular, except that my
arms were getting tired.

Ultimately the tears stopped. Sheila had been
reduced to a quivery, soggy lump. All her muscles

had relaxed from exhaustion. The little room was humid and overly warm and both of us were awash with the saliva and tears and mucus that crying always brings. I smoothed her damp hair back from her face and wondered what had happened in her head to make Chad's gift the final snapping point.

"Do you feel a little better?" I asked gently.

She did not reply but lay against me. Her body convulsed with the hiccupy gasps and shudders that are the aftermath of hard crying. "I'm gonna throw up."

My teacher's reflexes came instantly into action and I let us out of the book closet and into the girls' rest room around the corner. When she came out of the toilet stall she looked battle-weary, her face red and swollen, her steps tottery. Faint lines of toothpaste were still visible on her chin. I picked her up.

"Sometimes that happens," I said as we returned to our haven in the closet. "Sometimes when you cry real hard, it makes you sick."

She nodded. "I know."

We had only the one chair between us but she willingly clung to my lap, leaning heavily against my soggy shirt. We sat for a while saying nothing.

"I can hear your heart beat," she said at last.

I touched her head gently. "Do you think we ought to go back to class? It must be the middle of math period by now."

"No."

Again silence drifted around us. A million things

were running through my head, none of them finding words.

"Tor?"

"Yes?"

"Why did he buy me that dress?"

Across my mind trickled the thought that perhaps Sheila believed Chad had gotten her the dress for the same reason that her Uncle Jerry had told her he liked her red-and-white one. What a horrible thought that must have been for her; safe, kind, lovable Chad wanting her in a dress so he could have the same access to her that Uncle Jerry had had. It was no more than speculation on my part, but it made me certain not to reply that Chad had done it for "love."

"Because I told him your other one was ruined. He thought you might like something pretty to wear in the play." I ran my fingers through her silky hair. "I forgot to tell him you weren't wearing dresses anymore. That was my fault."

She did not respond.

"You know, don't you, that Chad would never do things to you like your Uncle Jerry did. He knows you shouldn't do those things to little girls. He didn't bring the dress to hurt you. He wouldn't ever hurt you."

"I know it. I didn't mean to cry."

"Oh, sweetie, that's okay. Chad knows that things have been hard for you. No one minds that you cry. Sometimes that's the only way to make things better. We all know that. Nobody cares if you cry."

"I wanted the dress," she said softly, pausing. "I wanted it. I just got scared, that's all. And I couldn't stop."

"That's okay. It really is. Chad knows what little girls are like. We all do."

"I don't know why I cried. I don't know what happened."

"Don't worry about it."

The pressure of being gone so long when I knew the children would be excited about the play was getting the better of me. "Sheil, I have to go back to the room. The kids are all there and Anton's by himself. I have two ideas for you. You can come back with me or maybe if you don't feel up to it you could go down to the nurse's office and rest awhile."

"Do I gotta go home 'cause I threw up?"

"No. You're not sick or anything."

She slid off my lap. "Can I rest a little? I'm tired."

I explained to the secretary that Sheila needed to lie down but didn't need to be sent home and I would be back in half an hour at recess to check on her. The secretary gave us a blanket and I settled Sheila down on one of the cots.

"Torey?" she asked as I tucked the blanket around her. "Do you suppose I could still have the dress? I wouldn't really mind wearing it."

I nodded and smiled. "Yeah. Chad left it for you."

I came back to the office at recess time and

Sheila was asleep. She slept the rest of the morning until I came down and woke her for lunch.

With good reason both L. Frank Baum and Judy Garland probably turned in their graves that May afternoon. Except for bearing the same title and characters as the famed story, the children's production had little in common with the book or the movie.

Sheila played Dorothy mostly by virtue of her ability to think fast and make up dialogue quickly. Both Tyler and Sarah had wanted the part, which resulted in some not-too-good-natured arguing for a while and a near-split of the Sarah-Peter production team. But Peter seemed to have authority in casting parts and he selected Sheila. Tyler was given the ignominious task of portraying all the wicked witches. Sarah was transformed into the Scarecrow. William played the Cowardly Lion and Guillermo was the Wizard himself. Oddly, Peter selected Susannah to play the Good Witch Glenda, another fought-over part. The only reason for his choice I could think of was that Susie was so delicately pretty that she made a very realistic fairy even without a costume; but Peter had his own reasons that he would not disclose. Freddie was the sole Munchkin and Max a lone winged monkey. Peter, of course, was the Tin Man.

Only parents, teachers or folks with an uncanny love of unintentionally funny children would have properly appreciated *The Wizard of Oz* as produced by my class. Sheila had fully recovered from her troubles in the morning and had donned the dress Chad brought, refusing to wear the costume Whitney had made for her. Refreshed by a two-hour nap, she bounced all over as she spoke, knocking over scenery and props. Freddie on the other hand would not move. He simply sat in his place, a ridiculous Munchkin hat stuck on his head, and waved at his mother in the audience. His fat legs tripped Sheila on one occasion causing her to fall into his lap. At last Anton had to drag him off when his part was over. The Cowardly Lion was typecasting for William and perhaps because he knew the feeling of fear so well, he gave the truest performance of all, quivering and quaking about on the stage. Most surprising, Susannah Joy did quite well as Glenda. She drifted onto the stage and floated around as out of touch with reality as always, muttering to herself in a high-pitched little squeak. But in the setting of the play, it looked astonishingly natural.

The only major problem suffered during the course of the play was when Sheila got long-winded in her dialogue and often felt the need to narrate parts of the play in case the audience hadn't figured out for themselves what was happening. This left everyone else standing around dumbly while Sheila launched into lengthy monologues. Finally Peter walked out onto the stage during one of her soliloquies and told her to get off.

The remainder of the program was delightful. No one forgot their lines in the poems and the songs were sung with rousing, albeit off-key, gusto. Afterwards we had cookies and punch while the children showed their parents things they had done in school.

Sheila's father did come. Dressed in the tattered suit that buckled over his tremendous stomach and reeking, once again, of cheap after-shave, he had eased his mammoth bulk into one of the tiny chairs. All through the program I kept praying it would not break as it creaked ominously with his weight shifts. For the first time I saw him smile at his daughter when she came bounding over to him after the first performance. He had had the kindness to come sober and appeared to enjoy being with us. He never commented about Sheila's new dress until I finally came over and told him toward the end of the party that Chad had bought it for her. He regarded his daughter carefully and then turned to me, pulling out a worn wallet from his coat pocket.

"I ain't got much here," he said quietly. I was terror-stricken, thinking that he was going to offer to pay for the dress and knowing it was obviously an expensive item. But he had other ideas. "If I give you money, would you take Sheila to buy some everyday clothes? I know she needs something and, well, you need a woman for that kind of thing . . ." His voice trailed off and he averted his eyes. "If I keep hold of the money . . . well, I got a little problem, you know. I was wondering . . ." He had ten dollars in his hand.

I nodded. "Yes, I will. I'll take her out after school next week."

He smiled at me, his lips pressed tight together in a faint, sad smile. Then before I knew it, he was gone. I stared at the bill. Not much clothing could be bought for that anymore. But he had tried. In his own way he had tried to make sure that the money went where it was supposed to before it went for a bottle. I liked the man in spite of myself, and I was flooded with pity. Sheila was not the lone victim; her father undoubtedly needed and deserved as much care as she did. Once there had been a little boy whose pain and suffering were never relieved. Now there was a man. If only there could be enough people to care, enough people to love without reservations, I thought sadly.

Chapter 19

Suddenly, only three weeks remained until school was through. My head was awhirl with all the things that had not been done. And there were plenty of them. I was also beginning to plan my move, which would occur shortly after school terminated. My evenings were filled with packing boxes and cleaning out all the garbage I had accumulated over the years.

I had not told the children yet that the class was to be disbanded. Some of them already knew that they would be returning to less restrictive placements the next year. William was going to a regular fifth grade class with resource help. For the last three months he had been going out of the room for both reading and math with a fourth grade class down the hall in the main building. Tyler was also going to a new program. She would still be in a self-contained room most of the time, but she would be closer to the life of a regular student.

We hadn't decided what to do with Sarah yet. Although she coped nicely in our room, she still withdrew in a larger group. I suspected she would need at least another year in a special class, but she was almost ready. Peter would never leave a special setting, I feared. His behavior continued to deteriorate as a result of increasing neurological destruction. He was too violent and disruptive, his behaviors too impulsive for anything but a tightly structured classroom. Guillermo's family was planning to move. And Max, Freddie and Susannah would all go to special programs. Freddie was being placed in a room for the severely and profoundly retarded, and the teacher hoped he would not be too much of a problem. She had been over to observe him several times to see how his behavior was managed in our class. Max was doing beautifully. He was using much more normal speech and less echolalia. Both he and Susannah were going to a special program for autistic children.

And Sheila? Sheila. I had not spoken with her yet about the impending termination of class. I had put it off because I did not know what would happen when I did tell her. In short, I was scared. She had come a long way from that frightened little lump that was dragged into our room in January; far from the dependent belt-hanger of February. Jimmie had been forgotten and she almost never referred to being put on the highway anymore. But she was fragile. I did not think she would need a special classroom any longer. In fact, I feared she'd be ignored in one because she was so verbal and able to look out for herself. I was afraid that to place her in one now would force her to readopt some negative behavior just to get the share of attention she required. What she needed was simply someone who cared. I was tentatively thinking of suggesting to Ed that she be advanced to third grade, even tough she was small, so she would be closer academically and socially to the other children. Despite her emotional problems, she was mature for her age. Besides, I had a good friend teaching third grade on the other side of town. The district would bus her there if requested because it was closer to the migrant camp than my school was and because maintaining her in a regular classroom was much less expensive than in a special one. And Sandy would take good care of Sheila for me. That assurance I needed for myself.

In an attempt to see Sheila into regular classroom life, I decided to mainstream her into a second grade class in our school for math. One of the second grade teachers, Nancy Ginsberg, was a pleasant, dedicated woman who had been among the first to invite my class and me to share activities with her group. So I approached her one afternoon in the lounge and asked if she would be willing to take Sheila for math. I explained that Sheila was considerably advanced beyond second grade math, but I wanted her out of the room for a period or so during the day in order that she could become readjusted to the strain of a regular classroom. Math was her most secure subject, so that seemed the best place to start. Nancy agreed.

"Guess what?" I said to Sheila as we were putting away toys from freetime.

"What?"

"You're going to do something neat from now on. You're going to go into a regular class for part of the day."

She looked up sharply. "Huh?"

"I talked to Mrs. Ginsberg and she said you could come have math in her room each day."

"Like William does?"

"That's right."

She bent back over the pieces of an Erector set she was putting away. "I don't wanna."

"You're just not used to the idea. You'll want to. Just think, it'll be a regular class. Remember once, you told me that you wished you were in a regular class? Now you will be."

"I ain't going."

"Why not?"

"This here be my class. I ain't going in nobody else's class."

"It's just for math."

Her nose wrinkled. "But that's my favorite in here. It ain't fair you make me leave my favorite time in here."

"You can have math in here too, if you want. But you'll have math in Mrs. Ginsberg's room too, starting on Monday."

"No, I ain't."

Sheila was not keen on the idea at all. For every reason I had, she had a counter reason. The rest of the day she alternately sulked and stormed, not letting me ever change the subject. By afternoon I had had enough and flatly stated that I had heard all the protests out of her I wanted to hear. She was going, she had two days to get ready and I would do all I could to make the change easier, but she was going.

Sheila stomped her feet angrily and stalked off to rattle the bars on Onion's cage. After listening to the persistent clatter of the cage, which Onions fortunately was not in at the time, I went over and dragged her to the table, giving her the alternative of getting her act together better or sitting in the quiet corner. At that Sheila sprung to her feet and marched defiantly off to the quiet corner. Banging the chair around, she sat.

I let her sit. I went back to helping William with his art project and ignored her. She sat the remainder of the afternoon despite both Anton and my telling her she could leave if she calmed down, and even Sarah's offering to let her help with afternoon snacks.

Since she was obviously interested in making me feel bad, I left her with Anton after school and went down to the teachers' lounge to make lesson plans. If Sheila got into one of her moods, she was best left alone. When I returned just before five, she was lounging on a pillow reading a book.

"You done being mad?" I asked.

She nodded casually, not looking up from the

book. "You're going to be sorry you made me go."

"And what is that supposed to mean?"

"I ain't going to be good if I have to go. I'm gonna be bad and she'll send me back here. Then you can't make me leave anymore."

"Sheila," I said in exasperation, "think about that one a while. That's not what you want to do."

"Yes, it is," she replied, still not looking up from her reading.

I glanced at the clock. It was dangerously close to the time when she had to leave. I hated it when she was like this. Coming over to where she was sitting, I dropped on my knees beside her. "What's up, kiddo? Why don't you want to go? I thought you'd like it, being in a regular class again."

She shrugged.

I lifted the book out of her hands so that she had to look at me. "Sheil, I want your thoughts. You know I can't send you in there if you're going to cause trouble. You got me on that one because I don't want Mrs. Ginsberg to have problems. But you can't want to do this."

"I do."

"Sheil . . ."

She finally looked directly at me, her blue eyes fluid. "How come you don't want me in here no more?"

"I never said that. I want you in here. Of course I want you in here. But I want you to learn what's happening in a real class too so you can go back to one."

"I already know what a real class is like. That's

where I was before I came here. I wanna be in this crazy class."

The clock edge toward five. "Sheil, listen, we're out of time. You're going to have to run to catch the bus as it is. I'll talk to you more about it tomorrow."

Sheila would not discuss it further and she was true to her word. I sent her off on Monday morning for thirty-five minutes in Mrs. Ginsberg's class. Within fifteen minutes Anton had to go retrieve her. She had ripped up papers, thrown pencils and tripped some poor unsuspecting second grader twice her size. Anton came dragging her in kicking and screaming. The second the door shut behind them and they were safely in the classroom, Sheila stopped. A pleased smile touched her lips. I sank into a chair beside Max and covered my eyes while Anton escorted her to the quiet corner.

Because her behavior made me extremely angry and I did not trust myself for a while, and also because I knew the time had come to discuss the whole matter of what was going to happen to her the next year, I did not confront her immediately about her behavior in Mrs. Ginsberg's room. After I had calmed down I told her she could leave the corner and rejoin us and then I went about our normal routine.

Directly defying me apparently frightened Sheila considerably. The remainder of the day she was oversolicitous toward me, trying to make sure I saw how good she was being. Also, the fact that

I did not deal with the infraction except for the quiet-corner stay was novel, and this troubled Sheila even more. She asked me once when I was going to get mad at her. I smiled, not wanting her to think that my sudden indifference was another indication of my desire to be rid of her. So I told her we'd discuss the matter later when we had more time. But she was nervous the rest of the day, shadowing me from a distance.

I walked out to the buses with the other children after school. When I returned to the room Sheila stood against the far wall by the animal cages, her eyes wide and fearful. I jerked my head in the direction of one of the tables. "Come over here, kiddo. I think it's time we talked."

Hesitantly she approached, sitting in a chair across the table from me. Her face expressed her wariness, her eyes dilated. "You mad at me?"

"About this morning? I sure was this morning, but I'm not now. No, I just want to find out what is going on with you. I don't really understand why you don't want to go. Last week you refused to talk to me about it. So I just want to find out. You usually have good reasons for what you do; I trust you in that way."

She studied me.

"Well?"

"This here be my class," she replied, falling back on the word "be" which had become almost extinct.

"Yes, it is. I'm not trying to kick you out of it. That's just thirty-five minutes out of a whole day.

Besides, I think it's time that you start thinking about a regular class for next year."

"I ain't going in no regular class. This here be my class."

I regarded her a long moment. "Sheil, it's May. The school year will be over in a few weeks. I think it's time to think about next year."

"I'm going to be in here next year."

My heart was sinking. "No," I replied softly.

Her eyes flashed. "I am too! I'll be the baddest kid in the whole world. I'll do terrible things and then they'll make you keep me. They won't let you make me go away."

"Oh, Sheil," I wailed.

"I ain't going anywhere else. I'll be bad again."

"It isn't like that, kitten. I'm not kicking you out. God, Sheila, listen to me, would you?" She had her hands over her ears.

She raised her stormy eyes at me. They were angry and hurt-looking, the old flare of revenge glinting in them.

"This class isn't going to be here next year," I said so softly that it came out almost inaudibly. Yet she heard it through her hands.

Like a wave the expression on her face clanged and she lowered her hands. The anger drained away leaving her pale. "What d'you mean? Where's it going?"

"This class won't be here. The school district decided they didn't need it. Everybody can go to other classes."

"Didn't need it?" she shouted. "Of course they

need it! I need it! I'm still crazy. I need a crazy kid-ses class. So does Peter. And Max. And Susie. We're all still crazy kids."

"No, Sheil, you're not. I'm not sure you ever were. But you're not now. It's time to stop thinking that."

"Then I will be. I'll do lots of bad stuff again. I ain't going nowhere."

"Sheil, I'm not going to be here either."

Her face froze.

"I'm moving in June. After school is over, I'm going away. It's really hard for me to say that to you, because I know we've gotten to be such good friends. But the time has come. I don't love you any less and I'm not leaving because of anything you did or didn't do. It's a separate decision I made. A grown-up decision."

She continued to look at me. With elbows on the table, her hands were clasped together and she rested her cheek against her fist. Her underwater-colored eyes studied my face without seeing.

"All things end, Sheil. I'm a teacher, so my ending comes in June. We've had terrific times together and I wouldn't have changed it for anything in the world. You've changed so much. And so have I, really. We've grown together and now it's time to see how good the growing was. I think we're ready. You too. I think you're ready to try it on your own. You're strong enough."

Tears suddenly filled her eyes and spilled over, making fast paths over her round cheeks and down to her chin. Yet she remained motionless and unblinking, her face still propped in her hands. I was running out of words to say. I often forgot she was only six. She would not even be seven until July. I forgot because her eyes were so old.

Slowly she lay her hands on the table and lowered her head. She sat a moment, still not wiping away the tears that continued to fall noiselessly. Then she rose and turned away from me, went over to the far side of the room and sat down amidst the pillows on the floor. Once there she covered her face with her hands. Still no sound came from her.

I sat in silence feeling acutely the pain she radiated, which I suppose was my own pain too. Had I gotten too involved, I wondered? Despite her apparent progress, had I let her grow too dependent on me? Would it have been better to have left her as I found her in January and simply taught her, rather than have accustomed her to the everyday trials of loving someone? I had always been a maverick among my colleagues. I belonged to the better-to-have-loved-and-lost school, which was not a popular notion in education. The courses, the professionals, all preached against getting involved. Well, I could not do that. I could not teach effectively without getting involved, and in my heart, because I did belong to the love-and-lost school, when the end came I could leave. It always hurt, and the more I loved a child, the more it hurt. But when the time came that we had to part or I had to honestly give up on the child because I could do no more, I could go. I could do it because I took with me, every time, the priceless memories of what we had had, believing that there is no more one can give another than good memories. Nothing I could do, even if I worked with Sheila the rest of her school career, could ensure happiness for her. Only she could do that. All I could give her would be my love and my time. When the end came, the parting would be just as painful. In the end my efforts would be reduced once more to memories.

Yet in watching her, I worried that there had not been sufficient time to heal her hurts enough, that she might not be strong enough to tolerate my painful way of teaching. While it was right for me, perhaps I was unfair to her in giving her no choice about it. But what should I have done? My heart ripped with worry that at last I had been given the wrong child, the one I hurt instead of helped. Being a maverick is admissible when one is an academician. When one is a practitioner, it is usually safer to be a conformist.

Slowly I rose and came over to where she sat still noiseless, except for snuffling. "Go away," she stated quietly but firmly through her hands.

"Why? Because you're crying?"

The hands came down and she looked at me briefly. "No." She paused. "Because I don't know what to do."

I sat across from her, arranging a pillow and leaning back on it. For the first time I did not feel like putting my arms around her to soothe away the hurt. Dignity sat as tangible as a cloak about

298

her. We were equals then, not one the older, one the younger. I no longer was the wiser one, the smarter one, the stronger one. We were equal in our humanity.

"How come you ain't staying to make me good?" she asked at last.

"Because it isn't me that makes you good. It's you. I'm only here to let you know that someone cares if you are good or not. That someone cares what happens to you. And it won't matter where I am, I still will always care."

"You're just like my Mama," she said. Her voice was soft and unaccusing, as if she had already resolved how things were and why.

"No, I'm not, Sheil." I regarded her. "Or maybe I am. Maybe leaving you was just as hard for your Mama as it will be for me. Maybe it hurt her that much too."

"She never loved me really. She loved my brother better. She left me on the highway like some dog. Like I didn't even belong to her."

"I don't know about that. I don't know anything about your Mother or why she did what she did to you. And really, Sheila, you don't either. All you know is how it felt to you. But your Mama and I are different. I'm not your Mother. No matter how much you want it to be that way, I'm not."

The tears renewed in intensity. She played with the waistband of her pants. "I know that."

"I knew you did. But I know you dreamed. In the same way, I guess I did too at times. But it never was any more than a dream. I'm your teacher and when the school year ends, I'll just be your friend. But I will be your friend. For as long as you want me, I'll always be that."

She looked up. "What I can't figure out is why the good things always end."

"Everything ends."

"Not some things. Not the bad things. They never go away."

"Yes, they do. If you let them, they go away. Not as fast as we'd like sometimes, but they end too. What doesn't end is the way we feel about each other. Even when you're all grown up and somewhere else, you can remember what a good time we had together. Even when you're in the middle of bad things and they never seem to be changing, you can remember me. And I'll remember you."

Unexpectedly she smiled, just a little smile, and rather sadly. "That's 'cause we tamed each other. Remember that book? Remember how the little boy was mad because he'd gone to all that trouble to tame the fox and now the fox was crying 'cause he had to leave?" She smiled in memory, looking within herself, almost unaware of me. The tears had dried upon her cheeks. "And that fox said it had been good anyways because he would always remember the wheat fields. Remember that?"

I nodded.

"We tamed each other, didn't we?"

"We sure did."

"It makes you cry to tame someone, doesn't it? They kept crying in that book and I never 'xactly knew why. I always thought you only cried when someone hit you."

Again I nodded. "You take a chance at crying when you let someone tame you. That seems to be part of being tamed, I guess."

Sheila pressed her lips together and wiped the last traces of tears from her face. "It still hurts a lot though, don't it?"

"Yeah, it sure still does hurt."

Chapter 20

Sheila went back to Mrs. Ginsberg's room the next morning and made it through the thirty-five minutes without too much trouble. Our problems were by no means resolved. Despite Sheila's recognition that the school year was ending and that we would no longer be together, she could not accept it gracefully. I doubted that she would in the two weeks left to us. Her behavior became a little less polished as she vacillated between anger at me for leaving and fear that I was going to. She could not separate out clearly that what was happening to us was different from what had happened between her and her mother. Time and time again we had to discuss the issue in far more detail than her previous conversational obsessions had required. She clung to *The Little Prince* as literary proof that people did part and it did hurt and they did cry, but they all still loved each other. The book was never far from her hands at any time and she could quote parts of it from memory. Because it was in print, it seemed to have more validity to her than my words.

She certainly had learned to cry. Most of the next days found her in tears or on the verge of them. Her eyes were almost like leaky faucets after a while; tears streamed over her cheeks even when she was smiling or playing. When questioned about them she often did not know why she was crying. I let the tears run and did not worry about them. So long had passed since she had cried that I believed she had to accustom herself to it, finding the width and breadth of the emotion, and if it helped her to prepare for what lay ahead, so much the better. Slowly the tears began to disappear.

Underneath it all her marvelous core of joy and courage gleamed. This was her hardest task. All else that had happened in her life had not been voluntary and she had had no choice but to let it happen and try to survive in the aftermath. But she knew this was coming and she struggled valiantly to take control of herself. As I watched her coping with her tears, hugging the mauled copy of *The Little Prince* to her chest and relentlessly plaguing me with questions about what was happening and why, I knew she would make it. She was strong; probably stronger than I. My work with the emotionally disturbed had deeply impressed upon me their resilience. Despite many popular notions, they were far from fragile. To have survived at all was testimony of this. Given the tools that so many of us take for granted, given love and support and trust and self-value that we often do not notice when we have it, they go beyond survival to prevail. In Sheila this was self-evident. She would not give up trying.

In the midst of all the flurry over the ending of the school year, my birthday came. We made a big thing about birthdays in our room, partly because most of the children did not get a celebration anywhere else and partly because I like parties. It seemed only reasonable that the kids should get to celebrate Anton's and Whitney's and my birthdays as well. After all, we had all been born too, and I did not have the modesty to pretend it did not matter. So when my birthday came I brought in a big yellow elephant-shaped cake and chocolate ice cream.

The day did not go well. Nothing especially terrible happened, just the little annoying things that kids seem to be best at doing. Peter had gotten in a fight on the bus and arrived with a bloody nose and a grudge. During recess Sarah got mad at Sheila, who in turn got mad at Tyler, who cried. Then Sheila kicked sand on Sarah and she cried. The quiet corner did a booming business all day long. However, it wasn't until afternoon that I lost my patience. When Whitney went down to the teachers' lounge for the ice cream, she found out one of the fifth grade classes had mistakenly thought it was theirs. I set the cake out anyway. Peter and William were horsing around with each other while we were getting ready. They had a couple of blocks which they were pretending to juggle. I had asked them to stop but they hadn't. One of the other kids was pulling on my arm and I was momentarily distracted. Then *crash*. William had thrown a block to Peter who, while backing up to catch it, bumped into Sheila sitting on the floor. He fell on her and they both came up swinging. Before I knew it Sheila had one of the blocks poised to throw at Peter. He picked up a chair and flung it angrily in her direction. The chair hit the table, then Max, then the cake. My yellow elephant splattered.

"Okay, you guys, that *is* it!" I shouted. "Every single one of you in your chairs with your heads down."

"But it wasn't my fault," Guillermo protested. "I didn't do anything."

"*Everybody.*"

All the kids, even Max and Freddie, found chairs and sat down. Everyone except Sheila.

"It don't be my fault dumb old Peter tripped on me." She was sitting on the floor where Peter had knocked her.

"Get in a chair and put your head down like everybody else. I've had it with the whole lot of you. All you've done all day is bicker. Well, this is where it gets you. Sitting in a chair with your head down."

Sheila remained on the floor.

"Sheila, get up."

With a great sigh she rose and took a chair. Pulling it over next to Tyler, she sat and put her head down.

I looked at them. What a ragtag lot. Whitney and Anton were picking cake out of the carpet. Anton rolled his eyes when I came over. I smiled wearily. What I really felt like doing was crying. For no particular reason except that I had wanted a special day and had gotten an ordinary one. And for my yellow elephant cake that had taken so much time to make and ended up being ground into the rug.

When I turned around to look at the kids, Peter had one eye peering over the side of his arm. I pointed a finger at him and gave him the evil eye. He covered his face again. I looked at the clock and watched the second hand revolve.

"Okay, you guys, if you can act like human beings you can get up. There's about ten minutes left. Help pick up the rest of the cake and then find something quiet to do. I better not hear one single word of fighting."

Sheila remained at the table with her head down.

"Sheil, you can get up."

She remained unmoving, her head in her arms. I came over to her and sat down in a chair beside her. "I'm not so mad anymore. You can get up and play."

"Uh-uh," she said. "This here's my birthday present for you. I ain't gonna be no trouble for the rest of the day."

After school Whitney took Sheila out and Anton and I went down to the teacher's lounge. I was sitting in the one comfortable chair, my head back,

307

my feet up on the table, my arm over my eyes.

"What a hell of a day," I said. When Anton did not respond I sat up and opened my eyes. He was gone. I had not even heard him leave. Oh, well, I leaned back again. I almost fell asleep.

"Tor?"

I looked up. Anton was back, standing over my chair.

"Happy Birthday." He handed me a fat envelope.

"Hey, you shouldn't have done anything. That's the deal around here."

He grinned. "Open it."

Inside was a crazy cartoon card with a green snake on it. Out fell a piece of folded paper.

"What's this?" I asked.

"My present to you."

I opened the paper. It was the photostated copy of a letter.

Dear Mr. Antonio Ramirez:

With great pleasure Cherokee County Community College announces that you have been chosen as one of the recipients of the Dalton E. Fellows Scholarship.

Congratulations. We look forward to seeing you in our program this fall.

I looked up at him. Even though he was trying, he could not keep a smile on his lips in check. It spread from ear to ear. I wanted to congratulate him. To tell him how much this piece of paper pleased me. I said nothing. We just stared at each other. And smiled.

I had called Ed about Sheila's future placement and we held a team meeting. I continued to hold out for placing Sheila with my friend, Sandy McGuire, at Jefferson Elementary School. Sandy was a young, sensitive teacher whom I could trust not to lose Sheila in the crowd. She had talked to me about Sheila a number of times when I had first had the notion that Sheila might be ready to go back to a normal setting.

At first Ed did not favor the plan. He disliked advancing children ahead of their chronological peer group. Moreover, Sheila was a small child for her age. Most of the eight- and nine-year-olds would be half a head above her. We did a lot of soul-searching. She was at least two grades ahead of the second graders academically and she was smaller than they were as well. In her case there were no perfect solutions. I was more in favor of placing her with a teacher I could trust to continue supporting her emotional growth than worrying about her size or IQ. Clearly, she would never be normal academically, so there was no point in providing a source of new trouble. I feared that Sheila's unchained mind would go so unchallenged in second grade that she would get into trouble just keeping herself occupied. In the end the team agreed to try Sheila in Sandy's room. She would also get two hours a day in a resource room to help meet her emotional needs and her advanced academic status.

The second to the last week of school I told Sheila she would be at Jefferson the following year. I said I knew her teacher very well and that we had been friends a long time. I asked Sheila if she would like to go visit Sandy in her classroom some day after school. The first time I suggested it was coupled with telling her where she was going the next year. Sheila could not accept that all at once and vehemently announced that she would not now nor would she ever want to meet Sandy. But later in the day, after the other kids had heard of Sheila's placement and had been all excited because she was skipping a grade, Sheila decided that she might not mind meeting Sandy so much after all.

Wednesday afternoon Sheila and I climbed into my little car right after the bell rang and started off for Jefferson Elementary on the other side of town. Because we had almost a half hour before Sandy's class was finished at three thirty, I stopped at Baskin-Robbins for ice cream cones. Sheila selected a double scoop of licorice. The mistake I made was in not taking any napkins with us when we got back into the car.

By the time we arrived at Jefferson, Sheila looked as if she had changed races. She had black ice cream all over her cheeks and chin, on her hair and down the front of her shirt. I looked at her in surprise because only fifteen minutes earlier she had been clean. I did not even have a Kleenex with me, so I wiped what I could off with my hand. With Sheila clutching at me tightly we went to see the school.

Sandy laughed when she saw Sheila. I couldn't blame her. Sheila looked like a four-year-old with all that ice cream on her and her fear gave her a waif-like solemnity. She pressed close to my leg.

"Boy, you look like you had something good," Sandy said, smiling. "What was it?"

Sheila stared at her wide-eyed. "Ice cream," she whispered. I wondered what Sandy must have been thinking just then. I had enticed her into accepting Sheila mostly by elaborating on Sheila's incredible giftedness and verbal ability. Right then Sheila sounded anything but the epitome of intelligence.

I should have trusted Sandy more. Bringing over chairs, she sat down with us and proceeded to get all the details of Sheila's ice cream passions. Then she took us on a tour of the room. It was a typical-looking classroom. Jefferson was an ancient, bulky, brick building with huge rooms. The room easily accommodated twenty-seven desks and a variety of "learning centers" around the perimeter. As usual for Sandy's room, it was messy. Stacks of work-books defied gravity on the corner of a table, bits of construction paper were strewn through the aisles. I had never been known for my neatness, but Sandy's clutter surpassed even mine. The children must have had half-a-dozen projects going in all states of completion. In the back of the room was a well-stocked bookcase and a gerbil cage.

Slowly Sheila began to thaw out and come to

life. The books interested her and finally got the better of her timidity. Soon she was wandering around on her own, inspecting the premises. Sandy flashed me a toothy, knowing smile as we watched Sheila in silence. She'd make it.

Standing on tiptoe to see the covers of the workbooks, Sheila took one from the top of the stack and paged through it. Still holding it, she came over to me. "This here's different than them you got, Torey," she said.

"That's probably the kind you'd use in here."

She continued to look through it. Then she turned to Sandy. "I don't like doing workbooks so well."

Sandy pursed her lips and nodded slowly. "I've heard other kids say that too. They aren't a lot of fun, are they?"

Sheila eyed her a moment. "I do 'em though. Torey makes me. I didn't use to, but I do now. This here one don't look too bad. I'd probably do this one." She examined a page carefully. "This here kid made a mistake. Look, it gots a red mark by it." She showed it to me.

"Sometimes people make mistakes," Sandy said. I made a mental note to tell her of Sheila's allergy to correction. That would be one of next year's tasks: reducing Sheila's anxiety about her errors.

"What d'you do to them?" Sheila asked.

"When they make a mistake?" Sandy said. "Oh, I just ask them to do it over again. If they don't understand, I help them. Everybody goofs up once in a while. It's no big deal."

"Do you whip kids?"

With a grin Sandy shook her head. "Nope. I sure don't."

Sheila nodded toward me. "Torey, she don't either."

We stayed with Sandy for almost forty-five minutes, Sheila becoming bolder and bolder with her questions. Finally, I suggested we leave so we would get back in time for Sheila's bus. As we went out the door, Sandy mentioned that perhaps Sheila would like to come over for part of a day before school let out and see how it was in the third grade when the children were there. I thanked her for her time and we trotted out to the car.

Sheila was quiet through most of the ride back to our school. Just as I turned the car into the parking lot, Sheila turned to me. "She ain't so bad, I guess."

"Good. I'm glad you liked her."

We climbed out of the car. Sheila took my hand as we walked toward the building. "Tor, do you suppose I could go over to Miss McGuire's class sometime?"

"You want to?"

"I wouldn't really mind."

I nodded. Stretching up to pick a dogwood flower off the tree that leaned over the school doorway, I fastened it into her hair. "Yeah, Sheil, I reckon we could arrange that for you."

Monday of the final week Anton drove Sheila over to Sandy's class. She had elected to remain the entire day, although I had suggested she go just for the morning. But she wanted to eat in the cafeteria, paying for her own lunch and getting to select what she wanted to eat like the other children. At our school my class was the last to eat and their trays were all fixed for them and laid out on the table. Sheila wanted to see how it felt to be a regular kid. My heart lurched a little watching her leave with Anton, her small hand in his. She had come wearing the red, white and blue dress Chad had bought her rather than her everyday jeans and shirt that we had gotten with the money her father had given me. She asked me to put her hair in a pony-tail and had found a piece of yarn from the scrap box to tie around it. She looked so tiny next to Anton as they left, and so vulnerable.

Sheila returned that afternoon a satisfied veteran. The day had gone smoothly and she smiled with pride as she related how she had carried her own lunch tray clear across the cafeteria without spilling anything, and how a girl named Maria, who had the longest, shiniest, prettiest black hair she'd ever seen, had saved a place for Sheila to eat with her. There had been hitches. She had lost her way coming back from the girl's rest room. In the tone of voice she used telling the incident, I gathered she must have been very frightened to find herself in such a spot. But she finally made it back. And, she smiled proudly, she never let on to anybody that she'd been lost. At recess she discovered the long dress, despite it being so pretty, was an impediment to play. She tripped while running and skinned her knees. Sheila pulled the dress up to show me. The scratches weren't very visible, but they hurt, she informed me. She hadn't cried about it. Sandy had seen it happen and had given Sheila comfort. Beaming, Sheila told me Sandy smelled good when she held you real close and she would blow on your knees 'til they felt better. All in all, it had been a successful day. Sheila affirmed that it would be an okay class to be in although she hoped Maria flunked, so she'd still be in it next year and they could be friends. I hastened to mention Maria and she might still be friends without wishing poor Maria such bad luck. For the first time Sheila did not get that stricken look about leaving my class; she didn't even mention it. Instead, her conversation was punctuated with "Next year, Miss McGuire says I can . . ." or "Miss McGuire's going to let me . . . when I'm in her room next year." It was a sweet-sad moment for me because I knew I had been out-grown.

On the last day of school we had a picnic. I contacted everybody's parents and a number met us over in the park a few blocks from school. We brought packed lunches from the cafeteria and the makings for ice cream sundaes, while the parents brought cookies and other goodies. The park was a huge one, old and sprawling with a small zoo and large duck pond. It had gardens of flowers all gleaming in the June sunshine. Children scattered in every direction with a parent in tow.

Sheila's father did not come; we had not really

expected him. But when Sheila showed up in the morning she was dressed in a bright orange-and-white sunsuit. She seemed embarrassed about having so much of herself exposed and walked around clutching her body for the first half hour with us. But Anton raved about the beautiful color and teased her about stealing it if he got the chance. This loosened her up in a fit of giggles at the thought of Anton wearing her sunsuit and she danced for us across the floor of the classroom while we waited for the other children. Her father had bought the sunsuit for her the night before at the discount store and it was the first new thing she could ever remember him getting her. Her mirth bubbled up in her so brightly that she could not stay still. All the way to the park she pirouetted down the sidewalk, her blond hair swirling in the air as she turned.

Once at the park she continued her joyous movements and Anton and Whitney and I sat in the sun by the duck pond after lunch and watched her. She was apart from us, thirty or forty feet down the walk that circled the pond. She was listening to some inner music and gliding in harmony around on the sidewalk. Others on the walk had to step around her, their faces amused. A skip, now a twirl, then a few rhythmic bends. It was almost eerie watching her dance alone in the sunlight, her hair glistening in a wide yellow wheel. Completely oblivious to the strollers on the walk, to the other children, to Anton and Whitney and me, she satisfied some inner dream to dance. The others must have felt the same eldritch fascination that I did. Anton watched without speaking. Whitney cocked her head as if trying to catch the music none of us was hearing.

Anton turned to me. "She looks like a spirit, doesn't she? Like if you blinked too hard, she'd be gone."

I nodded.

"She's free," Whitney said softly. And that indeed was what she was.

The end of the day came all too quickly. We packed up our things and returned to the classroom to pass out the last of the papers and say our final good-byes. The narrow, wood-paneled room was almost empty now. Pictures and stories were down from the walls. The animals had all gone to my apartment. The names were removed from the cubbies.

The finality of what was happening dawned on Sheila and she lost her merry spirit. By the time we had given out all the papers and awaited the ringing of the bell to go home, Sheila had retreated to the corner, empty now of its pillows and animal cages. Lacking those, she squatted on the floor. The other children were all chattering, excited about summer vacation and their changes for next year. So while Anton led them in songs, I broke away to Sheila.

The tears coursed silently over her now-tanned cheeks. Without a Kleenex, she used her hair to wipe away the wetness. Her eyes were filled with hurt and sorrow. "I don't wanna go," she wailed. "I don't want this to be over. I wanna come back, Torey."

"Of course you do, honey." I took her in my arms. "But that's just how it feels now. In just a little while you'll have a whole summer ahead of you and then you'll be in third grade, a regular kid. It's just a little hard right now, that's all."

"I don't wanna go, Torey. And I don't want you to go."

I smoothed away her bangs. "Remember, I told you I'd write you letters. We'll still know what's happening to each other. It won't be like we're really apart. You'll see."

"No, I won't. I want to stay." She was struggling to regain control and her wiry little body shuddered in my arms. "I'm gonna be bad. I'm not gonna be nice at all in Miss McGuire's class and then you'll have to come back."

"Hey, I don't want to hear that. That's the old Sheila talking."

"I won't be good. I won't. And you can't make me."

"No, Sheil, I can't. That's your decision. But you know it won't change things any. It won't make this year come back or this class. Or me. I'll be going to school myself, like I told you. What you do with yourself only you can decide. But it won't bring this year back."

She was staring at the floor, her bottom lip pushed out.

I smiled. "Remember, you tamed me. You're responsible for me. That means we'll never forget we love each other. That means we'll probably cry a little right now. But pretty soon we'll only remember how happy we were with each other."

She shook her head. "I won't ever be happy."

Just then the bell rang and the room was alive with shouts. I rose and went to the other children. Hesitantly Sheila trailed over too. The good-byes came. Tyler and William were teary-eyed. Peter whooped with joy. We all exchanged hugs and kisses and they were gone, running out into the June warmth.

Sheila was catching the high school bus back to the migrant camp. On this last day, it left only a short time after the bus for the grade school children. I figured that, after saying good-bye to Anton and Whitney and collecting her things, Sheila would have just enough time to walk the two blocks to the high school and meet her bus.

Parting from Anton was hard for her. At first she covered her face and refused to even look at him. He kept coaxing her to smile, saying little things in Spanish, which I did not understand but Sheila did. After all, he reminded her, they'd still see each other at the migrant camp. He promised to bring her over to play with his two little boys. Finally I delivered an ultimatum. I'd walk her to her bus, but she had to leave right away. With this she turned to Anton and hugged him, her tiny arms locking him in a wrestler's hold. Then she waved to Whitney and took my hand. At the doorway she paused, broke away and ran to hug Anton again. She kissed his cheek and trotted back to me. Tears sparkled as she picked up her things, a few papers and the worn copy of *The Little Prince,* a tangible memory of what had been. We descended the steps and went down the walk to the high school.

She did not speak the entire way. Neither did I. We had gone beyond needing words. Talking would have spoiled what we had. The bus was waiting in the semi-circle drive of the high school, but the students had not yet loaded. The bus driver waved to us and Sheila ran over to put her things on a seat. Then she came out of the bus again, walking back to where I stood.

She looked up at me, shading her eyes from the light. I looked at her. It seemed a small eternity in the bright sunlight. "Bye," she said very softly.

I sank to my knees and embraced her. My heart was roaring in my ears, my throat too tight to speak. Then I rose and she ran to the bus. All the way to the steps of the bus she ran, but as she started up them she stopped. The older kids were there now and she had to wait to get in. She looked over at me. Then suddenly she came running back.

"I didn't mean it," she said breathlessly. "I didn't mean it when I said I would be bad. I'll be a good girl." She looked up solemnly. "For you."

I shook my head. "No, not for me. You be good for you."

She smiled slightly, oddly. Then in a second she was gone, back to the bus already, scurrying up the stairs and disappearing. In moments I saw her face at the rear window, pressed tight against the glass.

The driver shut the door and the bus began to rumble. "Bye," she was mouthing, her nose squashed flat against the window. I could not tell if she was crying. The bus pulled around and down the drive. A small hand waved, frantically at first then more gently. I raised my hand and smiled as the bus turned onto the street and disappeared from sight.

"Bye-bye," I said, the words squeezing themselves almost inaudibly from my stricken throat. Then I turned to go back.

Epilogue

In the mail a year ago came a crumpled, water-stained piece of notebook paper inscribed in blue felt-tip marker. No letter accompanied it.

To Torey with much
"Love"

All the rest came
They tried to make me laugh
They played their games with me
Some games for fun and some for keeps
And then they went away
Leaving me in the ruins of games
Not knowing which were for keeps and
Which were for fun and
Leaving me alone with the echoes of
Laughter that was not mine.

Then you came
With your funny way of being
Not quite human
And you made me cry
And you didn't seem to care if I did
You just said the games are over
And waited
Until all my tears turned into
Joy.

The Tiger's Child

Prologue

It was a moment of déjà vu.

Home in Montana visiting my mother, I had nipped out alone on a Sunday morning while she and my young daughter went swimming. It was just after eleven and I was walking through the shopping mall. Most of the stores weren't open yet, and as a consequence, the broad concourse was shadowy, illuminated only by security lighting.

Suddenly I saw her. Some distance ahead of me down the mall, she was standing in the shadows of a large planter. Long, unkempt hair tumbled down over her shoulders; bangs hung into her eyes; thick, sensual lips were pushed out in a dramatic pout. She stood with arms crossed tightly over her chest, her shoulders pulled up, her face set in an expression of fierce defiance; and yet there was a poignancy about all that fierceness. I suspect she already knew she wasn't going to win. I was well down the mall when I first saw her, but I recognized her so instantly that adrenaline shot through my veins. *Sheila*.

A second or two later my intellect caught up. It wasn't Sheila, of course. More than twenty years have passed since I watched Sheila depart from my classroom on that warm June afternoon. I am no longer the angry young teacher I was. My teaching days are, at least for the time being, behind me and I have exchanged youth—with some reluctance— for middle age. Yet, for those brief few minutes in the shopping mall, the years disappeared. I was pulled back into the seventies, into my workaholic twenties, to feel once again, however fleetingly, the person I had been and the world as it was then.

Then reality began to impose, layering itself down over the incident rather the way one lays a transparency down over a page. I approached the girl with curiosity, drew up even with her and paused, feigning interest in a nearby shop window so that I could unobtrusively study her. She was older than Sheila had been. She was perhaps seven or even eight. Her hair was darker, more mouse-brown than blond.

My nearness didn't put off her anger any. I was a stranger, so she ignored me and concentrated all her attention on the open doorway of the huge department store behind me. I couldn't discern who had upset her so. They had disappeared into the store, but she stood on, her small fists clenched, her tousled hair falling forward, her hopeless, helpless anger emanating from her. Anonymous and silent, I remained where I was, half a dozen feet away, and marveled at how such a small encounter could wipe away so many years, how Sheila could still set my heart beating fast.

Sheila and I, as student and teacher, were only together for five months. Our relationship over that short time evoked dramatic changes in Sheila's behavior and vastly altered the course of her life. Although less obvious at the time, our relationship also dramatically changed me and vastly altered the course of my life too. This little girl had a profound effect on me. Her courage, her resilience and her inadvertent ability to express that great, gaping need to be loved that we all feel—in short, her humanness—brought me into contact with my own.

The five months Sheila was in my class I chronicled in *One Child*. It was a private book, never initially written with the intention of publication, but only as my own effort to understand more fully this deeply felt relationship. I was teaching a university graduate class in special education at the time and it is to a student in that class that I owe my thanks. The last day of class she gave me a copy of Ron Jones's *The Acorn People*, and inscribed it in the front: To Torey, in hopes that someday you might write about Sheila, Leslie and all the others.

One Child now spans the world in twenty-two languages and has brought me into contact with individuals from Sweden to South Africa, from New York to Singapore. One reader wrote from a base in Antarctica; a handful of letters came from behind the Iron Curtain before it fell; and I have just recently received my first correspondence over *One Child* from mainland China. The universal appeal of watching Sheila grow and change has only been matched by one thing, a question: What happened next?

One Child is a true story, based on real people and real people's experiences. I hesitated to write a sequel simply because six-year-old Sheila was so appealing and the period we spent together was so positive. Indeed, my *One Child* editor went so far as to suggest I not include in the epilogue of the book what had actually been happening to Sheila in the time since we had parted. Real lives are seldom as satisfying as fiction, or even as satisfying as judiciously edited nonfiction, and it was felt the interim period between my class and the time I wrote *One Child* would make too grim an ending for such an upbeat story. Thus, the book concluded with Sheila's beautiful poem, but no details.

I've now changed my mind, not only in response to the countless queries from my readers, but also in response to Sheila, who, against remarkable odds, has grown into an engaging, articulate young woman. Those five months we spent together did have a profound effect on her, but *One Child*, although I hadn't meant it to, tells my story. The experience for Sheila was quite a different one and here, to quote Paul Harvey, is the rest of the story.

Part 1

Chapter 1

The article in the newspaper was tiny, considering the crime. It told of a six-year-old girl who had lured a local toddler from his yard, taken him to a nearby woodland, tied him to a tree and set fire to him. The boy, badly burned, was in hospital. All that was said in what amounted to no more than a space filler below the comic strips on page six. I read it and, repulsed, I turned the page and went on.

Six weeks later, Ed, the special education director, phoned me. It was early January, the day we were returning from our Christmas break. "There's going to be a new girl in your class. Remember that little girl who set fire to the kid in November ...?"

I taught what was affectionately referred to in our district as the "garbage class." It was the last year before congressional law would introduce "mainstreaming," the requirement that all special needs children be educated in the least restrictive environment; and thus, our district still had the myriad of small special education classrooms, each catering to a different disability. There were classes for physically handicapped, for mentally handicapped, for behaviorally disordered, for visually impaired ... you name it, we had it. My eight were the kids left over, the ones who defied classification. All of them suffered emotional disorders, but most also had mental or physical disabilities as well. Out of the three girls and five boys in the group, three could not talk, one could but refused and another spoke only in echoes of other people's words. Three of them were still in diapers and two more had regular accidents. As I had the full number of children allowed by state law for a class of severely handicapped children, I was given an aide at the start of the year; but mine hadn't turned out to be one of the bright, hardworking aides already employed by the school, as I had expected. Mine was a Mexican-American migrant worker named Anton, who had been trawled from the local welfare list. He'd never graduated from high school, never even stayed north all winter before, and certainly had never changed diapers on a seven-year-old. My only other help came from Whitney, a fourteen-year-old junior high student, who gave up her study halls to volunteer in our class.

By all accounts we didn't appear a very promising group, and in the beginning, chaos was the

byword; however, as the months passed, we metamorphosed. Anton proved to be sensitive and
hardworking, his dedication to the children
becoming apparent within the first weeks. The
kids, in return, responded well to having a man in
the classroom and they built on one another's
strengths. Whitney's youth occasionally made her
more like one of the children than one of the staff,
but her enthusiasm was contagious, making it
easier for all of us to view events as adventures
rather than the disasters they often were. The kids
grew and changed, and by Christmas we had
become a cohesive little group. Now Ed was sending me a six-year-old stick of dynamite.

Her name was Sheila. The next Monday she
arrived, being dragged into my classroom by Ed, as
my principal worriedly brought up the rear, his
hands flapping behind her as if to fan her into the
classroom. She was absolutely tiny, with fierce eyes,
long, matted blond hair and a very bad smell. I was
shocked to find she was so small. Given her notori-
ety, I had expected something considerably more
Herculean. As it was, she couldn't have been much
bigger than the three-year-old she had abducted.

Abducted? I regarded her carefully.

Bureaucracy being what it is in school districts,
Sheila's school files didn't arrive before she did; so
when she went off to lunch on that first day, Anton
and I took the opportunity to go down to the office
for a quick look. The file made bleak reading, even
by the standards of my class.

Our town, Marysville, was in proximity to a large mental hospital and a state penitentiary, and this, in addition to the migrants, had created a disproportionate underclass, many of whom lived in appalling poverty. The buildings in the migrant camp had been built as temporary summer housing and many were literally nothing but wood and tar paper that lacked even the most basic amenities, but they became crowded in the winter by those who could afford nothing better. It was here that Sheila lived with her father.

A drug addict with alcohol problems, her father had spent most of Sheila's early years in and out of prison. He had no job. Currently on parole, he was attending an alcohol abuse program, but doing little else.

Sheila's mother had been only fourteen when, as a runaway, she took up with Sheila's father and became pregnant. Sheila was born two days before her mother's fifteenth birthday. A second child, a son, was born nineteen months later. There wasn't much else relating to the mother in the file, although it was not hard to read drugs, alcohol and domestic violence between the lines. Whatever, she must have finally had enough, because when Sheila was four, she left the family. From the brief notes, it appeared that she had intended to take both children with her, but Sheila was later found abandoned on an open stretch of freeway about thirty miles south of town. Sheila's mother and her brother, Jimmie, were never heard from again.

The bulk of the file detailed Sheila's behavior. At home the father appeared to have no control over her at all. She had been repeatedly found wandering around the migrant camp late at night. She had a history of fire setting and had been cited for criminal damage three times by the local police, quite an accomplishment for a six-year-old. At school, Sheila often refused to speak, and as a consequence, virtually nothing was contained in the file to tell me what or how much she might have learned. She had been in kindergarten and then first grade in an elementary school near the migrant camp until the incident with the little boy had occurred, but there were no assessment notes. In place of the usual test results and learning summaries was a catalog of horror stories detailing Sheila's destructive, often violent, behavior.

At the end of the file was a brief summary of the incident with the toddler. The judge concluded that Sheila was out of parental control and would be best placed in a secure unit, where her needs could be better met. In this instance, he meant the children's unit at the state mental hospital. Unfortunately, the unit was at capacity at the time of the hearing, and thus, Sheila would need to await an opening. A recently dated memo was appended detailing the need to provide some form of education, given her age and the law, but no one bothered to mince words. Her placement was custodial. This meant she had to be kept in school for the time being, because of the specifics of the law, but I need not feel under any obligation to teach her. With Sheila's arrival, my room had become a holding pen.

Youth was my greatest asset at that point in my career. Still fired with idealism, I felt strongly that there were no problem kids, only a problem society. Although initially reluctant to take Sheila, it had been because my room was crowded and my resources overstretched already, not because of the child herself. Thus, once I had her, I regarded her as mine and *my* class was no holding pen! My belief in human integrity and the inalienable right of each and every one of my children to possess it was trenchant.

Well, almost. Before she was done, Sheila had given all my beliefs a good shaking and she started that very first day. As Anton and I were sitting in the front office that lunch hour, reading Sheila's file, Sheila was in our classroom scooping the goldfish out of the aquarium and, one by one, poking their eyes out.

Sheila proved to be chaos dressed in outgrown overalls and a faded T-shirt. Everything she said was shrieked. Everything she touched was broken, hit, squashed or mangled. And everyone, myself included, was The Enemy. She operated in what Anton christened her "animal mode." There was not much "child mode" present in the early days. The slightest unexpected movement she always interpreted as attack. Her eyes would go dark, her face would flush, her body would take on alert rigidity, and from that point it was a finely balanced matter as to whether she would fight, or panic and run away. When she was in her animal mode, our methods were a whole lot more akin to taming than teaching.

Yet ...

Sheila was different. There was something electric about her, about her eyes, about the sharpness of her movements that superimposed itself over even her most feral moments. I couldn't articulate what it was, but I could sense it.

I loved my children dearly, but the truth was, they were not a very bright lot. Most children with emotional difficulties use so much mental energy coping that there simply isn't much left for learning. Additionally, other syndromes often occur in conjunction with psychological problems, either contributing to them or resulting from them. For example, two of my children suffered from fetal alcohol syndrome and another had a neurological condition that was causing a slow deterioration of his central nervous system. As a consequence, none of the children was functioning at an average level for his or her age, although undoubtedly several were of normal intelligence. Thus, it came as a surprise to me to discover during Sheila's early days with us that she could add and subtract well, because she had managed only three months of first grade.

A bigger surprise came days later, when I discovered she could give the meanings of unusual words. One such word was "chattel."

"Wherever did you learn a word like this?" I asked when my curiosity finally overwhelmed me.

Sheila, little and dirty and very smelly, sat hunched up on her chair across the table from me. She peered up through matted hair to regard me. "*Chattel of Love*," she replied and added in her peculiar dialect, "it be the name of a book I find."

"Book? Where? What book?"

"I don't steal it," she retorted defensively. "It be in the garbage can. I *find* it."

"Where?"

"I do find it," she repeated, obviously believing this was the issue I was trying to explore.

"Yes, okay," I replied, "but where?"

"In the ladies' toilets at the bus station. But I *don't* steal it."

I smiled. "No, I'm sure you didn't. I'm just interested in hearing about it."

She regarded me suspiciously.

"What did you do with the book?" I asked.

Sheila clearly couldn't puzzle out why I wanted to know these things. "Well, I read it," she said, her voice full of disbelief, as if I'd asked a very silly question. There was a worried edge to it, however. She still sensed it was an accusation.

"You read it? It sounds like a rather grown-up book."

"Well, I don't read all of it. But on the cover it say *Chattel of Love* and so I do be curious about it,'cause of the picture,'cause of what the man be doing to the lady on the cover."

"I see," I replied uncertainly.

12

She shrugged. "But I couldn't find nothing good in it, so I throw it away again."

With an IQ we soon discovered to be in excess of 180, Sheila was electric all right. Indeed, she was more like nuclear.

Discovering Sheila was a highly gifted child intellectually did nothing to change the facts of her grinding poverty, her abusive background or her continuing and continually outrageous behavior. Uncertain where to start when there was so much that needed improving, I began with the very smallest things, those I knew were within my power to change.

Sheila's hygiene was appalling. She literally had only one set of clothes: a faded brown-striped T-shirt and a pair of worn denim overalls, a size too small. With these went a pair of red-and-white canvas sneakers with holes in the toes. She had underwear, but no socks. If any of these were ever washed, there was little evidence of it.

Certainly Sheila wasn't washed. The dirt was worn in on her hands and her elbows and around her ankles, so that dark lines had formed over the skin in these areas. Worse, she was a bed wetter. The smell of stale urine permeated whatever part of the classroom Sheila occupied. When I quizzed Sheila about washing facilities, I discovered they had no running water.

This seemed the best place to start. She was so unpleasant to be near that it distracted all of us from the child herself; so I came armed with towels, soap and shampoo and began to bathe Sheila in the large sink at the back of the classroom.

I was washing her when I first noticed the scars. They were small, round and numerous, especially along her upper arms and the insides of her lower arms. The scars were old and had long since healed, but I recognized them for what they were—the marks left when a lit cigarette is pressed against the skin.

"Does your dad do things that cause these?" I asked, trying to keep my voice as casual and conversational as possible.

"My pa, he wouldn't do that! He wouldn't hurt me bad," she replied, her tone prickly. "He loves me." I realized she knew what I was asking.

I nodded and lifted her out of the water to dry her. For several moments Sheila said nothing, but then she twisted around to look me in the eye. "You know what my mama done, though?"

"No, what?"

She lifted up one leg and turned it for me to see. There, on the outer side just above the ankle, was a wide white scar about two inches long. "My mama, she push me out of the car and I fall down so's a rock cutted up my leg right here. See?"

I bent forward and examined it.

"My pa, he loves me. He don't go leaving me on no roads. You ain't supposed to do that with little kids."

"No, you're not."

There was a moment's silence while I finished drying her and began to comb out her newly

14

washed hair. Sheila grew pensive. "My mama, she don't love me so good," she said. Her voice was thoughtful, but calm and matter-of-fact. She could have been discussing one of the other children in the class or a piece of schoolwork or, for that matter, the weather. "My mama, she take Jimmie and go to California. Jimmie, he be my brother and he be four, 'cept he only be two when my mama, she leave." A moment or two elapsed and Sheila examined her scar again. "In the beginning, my mama taked Jimmie *and* me, 'cept she got sick of me. So, she open up the door and push me out and a rock cutted up my leg right here."

Those early weeks with Sheila were a roller-coaster ride. Some days were up. Delighted awe at this new world she found herself in made Sheila a sunny little character. She was eager to be accepted into the group and in her own odd way tried desperately to please Anton and me. Other days, however, we went down, sometimes precipitously. Despite her brilliant progress right from the beginning, Sheila remained capable of truly hair-raising behavior.

The world was a vicious place in Sheila's mind. She lived by the creed of doing unto others before they do unto you. Revenge, in particular, was trenchant. If someone wronged Sheila or even simply treated her a bit arbitrarily, Sheila exacted precise, painful retribution. On one occasion, she caused hundreds of dollars' worth of damage in another teacher's room in retaliation for that teacher's having reprimanded her in the lunch-room.

What saved us was a complicated bus schedule. In the months prior to coming into my room, Sheila's behavior had gotten her removed from two previous school buses and the only one available to her now was the high school bus. Unfortunately, this did not leave for the migrant camp until two hours after our class got out. Thus Sheila had to remain after school with Anton and me until that time.

I was horrified when I first found out, because those two hours after school were my planning and preparation time and I couldn't imagine how I would get on with things while simultaneously having to baby-sit as unpredictable a child as Sheila. There was, however, no choice in the matter.

Initially, I let her play with the classroom toys while I sat at the table and tried to get on with my work, but after fifteen minutes or so on her own, she'd inevitably pull away and come to stand over me while I worked. She was always full of questions. What's that? What's this for? Why are you doing that? How come this is like this? What do you do with that thing? *Constantly*. Until I realized we were talking much of the time. Until I realized how much I enjoyed it.

She liked to read and she could, I think, read virtually anything I placed in her hands. What stopped her was not her ability to turn the letters on the page into words, but rather to turn them into something meaningful. Sheila's life was so deprived that much of what she read simply made no sense to her. As a consequence, I began reading with her.

There was something compelling about sharing a book with Sheila. We would snuggle up together in the reading corner as I prepared to read aloud to her and Sheila would be so ravenous for the experiences the book held that her entire body'd grow taut with excitement. Winnie the Pooh, Long John Silver and Peter Pan proved sturdier magic than *Chattel of Love*. However, of all the books, it was Saint-Exupéry's *The Little Prince* that won Sheila's heart. She adored this bemused, perplexing little character. His otherness she understood perfectly. Mature one moment, immature the next, profound, then petty, and always, always the outsider, the little prince spoke deeply to Sheila. We read the book so many times that she could quote long passages by heart.

When not reading, we simply talked. Sheila would lean on the table and watch me work, or we would pause at some point in a book for me to explain a concept and the conversation would go from there, never quite returning to the story at hand.

Progressively, I learned more about Sheila's life in the migrant camp, about her father and his lady friends who often came back to the house with him late at night. Sheila told me how she hid his bottles of beer behind the sofa to keep him from drinking too much, and how she got up to put out his cigarettes after he had fallen asleep. I came to hear more about her mother, her brother and the abandonment. And I heard about Sheila's other school and her other teachers, about what she did to fill her days and her nights, when she wasn't with us. In return, I gave her my world and the hope that it could be hers as well.

Those two hours were a godsend. All her short life Sheila had been ignored, neglected and often openly rejected. She had little experience with mature, loving adults and stable environments, and now, discovering their existence, she was greedy for them. The busy atmosphere of the classroom during the day, supportive as it was, did not allow for the amount of undivided attention Sheila required to make up for all she had lacked. It was in the gentle silence of the afternoon when we were alone, that she dared to leave behind her old behaviors and try some of mine.

Chapter 2

The real issue for Sheila was what had happened between her and her mother on that dark highway two years earlier. Given her extraordinary giftedness, the matter did not remain inarticulate. With exquisite clarity, she gave a voice to her agony.

The relationship between the abandonment and Sheila's difficult behavior became most obvious over schoolwork. Despite her brilliance, Sheila simply refused to do any written papers. I hadn't made the connection initially. I saw the aggressive misbehavior as waywardness and only afterward realized it was a ploy to keep her from having to sit down at the table and take a pencil in hand. Coercing her to the table proved a major battle and even then she held out, refusing to work. When she did eventually start accepting paperwork, she would still crumple two or three imperfect efforts before finally finishing one.

On one occasion, she wasn't even in class but alone after school with me. She had found a ditto master of a fifth-grade math test in the office trash can, when she had come down with me while I ran off some papers. Sheila loved math. It was her best subject and she fell upon this with great glee. It was on the multiplication and division of fractions, subjects I had never taught Sheila, but as she scanned the paper, she felt certain she could do them. Back in the classroom, she settled across the table from me and began to write the answers on the paper—a very unusual response for Sheila. When she finished, she proudly showed it to me and asked if she had done them right. The multiplication problems were done correctly, but unfortunately she had not inverted the fractions for the division, so those were all wrong. Turning the paper over, I drew a circle and divided it into parts to illustrate why it was necessary to invert. Before I had even spoken, Sheila perceived that her answers weren't right. She whipped up the paper from under my pencil, smashed it into a tiny ball and pounded on the table before flopping down, head in her arms.

"You didn't know, sweetheart. No one's taught you this."

"I wanted to show you I could do them without help."

"Sheil, it's nothing to get upset about. You did nicely. You *tried*. That's the important part. Next time you'll get them right."

Nothing I said comforted her and she sat for a few moments with her hands over her face. Then slowly her hands slid away and she uncrumpled the paper, pressing it smooth on the tabletop. "I bet if I could have done math problems good, my mama, she wouldn't leave me on no highway, like she done. If I could have done fifth-grade math problems, she'd be proud of me."

"I don't think math problems have anything to do with it, Sheila."

"She left because she don't love me no more. You don't go leaving kids you love on the highway, like she done me. And I cut my leg, see?" For the hundredth time the small white scar was displayed. "If I'd been a gooder girl, she wouldn't have done that."

"Sheil, we just don't know what happened, but I suspect your mama had her own problems to straighten out."

"But she copeded with Jimmie. How come she copeded with Jimmie and left me?"

"I don't know, love."

Sheila looked across the table to me, that haunted, hurt expression in her eyes. "Why did it happen, Torey? Why did she tooked him and leaved me behind? What made me such a bad girl?" Her eyes filled with tears, but as always, they never fell.

"Oh, lovey, it wasn't you. Believe me. It wasn't your fault. She didn't leave you because you were bad. She just had too many of her own problems. It wasn't *your* fault."

21

"My pa, he says so. He says if I be a gooder girl she'd a never done that."

My heart sank. There was so much to fight, so little to fight with.

The issue colored everything: her work, her behavior, her attitude toward other children and toward adults. As the weeks passed and particularly as we spent so much of the after-school hours in close contact, I knew very well what was being encouraged to happen. I was the first stable, nurturing adult female Sheila had occasion to spend much time with and she grasped at the relationship with greedy desperation.

Was it right to let her? This question was never far from my mind. My training, both in education and in psychology, cautioned rigorously against getting too personally involved with children, and I strove to keep the proper balance. On the other hand, I had always rebelled against the idea of not becoming involved at all. The cornerstone of my personal philosophy was commitment. I felt it was the unequivocal commitment of one individual to another, of me to the child I was working with, that evoked positive change. How could there be genuine commitment without involvement? That was a contradiction in terms.

On a gut level I felt Sheila *had* to have this relationship and without it she could never go forward. She needed the esteem that comes only from knowing others care for you, others value you sufficiently to commit themselves to you. She needed to know that while her mother might not have been able to provide this kind of commitment, this did not mean that Sheila was unworthy of it. Yet on an intellectual level I knew I was treading a dangerous path.

Just how dangerous came home to me in February, after Sheila had been with us about seven weeks. I had to attend an out-of-state conference, which meant I would be gone from class for two days. Having ample warning, I endeavored to prepare my class for my absence and the anticipated substitute teacher. Sheila reacted with rage.

"I ain't never, *never* gonna like you again! I ain't *never* gonna do anything you ask. It ain't fair you go leave me! You ain't supposed to do that, don't you know? That be what my mama done and that ain't a good thing to do to little kids. They put you in jail for leaving little kids. My pa, he says."

Tirade after tirade and nothing I said, no effort I made to explain I would be gone only for two days abated Sheila's anger. In my absence she reverted to all the worst of her old behaviors. She fought with the other children, bloodying noses and cracking shins. The record player was destroyed and the small window in the door was cracked. Despite Anton's efforts to keep her in check, Sheila devastated the classroom and the substitute ended her days in tears.

I had expected better from Sheila and my anger, when she proved so uncooperative, was not a whole lot less than hers. She was a bright girl. She knew how long two days were. And I had gone to strenuous efforts to explain where I'd be, what I'd be doing and when *precisely* I would be back. She *knew*. Why could I not trust her to keep herself together for two lousy days?

To be more exact about the matter, I felt betrayed. Having known I was following such a dangerous course in allowing her growing dependence on me, I had wanted straightforward evidence that I was doing the right thing, that her dependence was natural and healthy and not *too* serious. I was, after all, going to have to walk out of her life in, at most, three and a half months' time, when the school year ended, and in even less time, if the opening in the children's unit at the state hospital occurred. For my own peace of mind, I needed reassurance I was helping more than hurting and—I suppose if I'm honest—I expected it from her. I had given her so much that, in my heart of hearts, I had trusted her to give this bit back to me. When she hadn't, I reacted with an anger I didn't control at all well.

We had, to put it mildly, a bad day, and even after school, when we were alone, the strained silence remained between us. I offered to do the things we'd come to enjoy so much: to read aloud to her, to let her help me correct my papers, to come down with me to the teachers' lounge and share a soft drink, but she simply shook her head and busied herself in the far corner of the room with some toy cars. The first after-school hour passed. She rose and went to look out the window. When I next glanced up, she was still there but had turned to watch me.

"How come you come back?" she asked softly.

"I just went away to give a speech. I never intended to stay away. This is my job, here with you kids."

"But how come you come back?"

"Because I said I would. I like it here. I belong here."

Slowly, she approached the table where I was working. Her guard had dropped. The hurt was so clear in her eyes.

"You didn't believe I was coming back, did you?"

She shook her head. "No."

Chapter 3

Our falling-out over my absence did not appear to have any lasting effects. Indeed, just the opposite. Sheila developed an intense desire to discuss the incident: I had left her; I had come back. She had gotten angry and destructive; I had gotten angry and, in my own way, destructive. Each small segment she wanted to discuss again and again until it slowly slotted into place for her. The fact that I *had* come back was, of course, very important to her, but so too was the degree of my anger. Perhaps she felt that now that she had seen me at my worst, she could more fully trust me. I don't know. Intriguingly, Sheila's destructiveness virtually disappeared after this incident. She still became angry with great regularity, but never again did she fly into one of her rampaging rages.

Sheila bloomed, like the daffodils, in spite of the harsh winter. Within the limits of her situation, she was now quite clean and, better, she recognized what clean was and endeavored to correct unacceptable levels of dirtiness herself. Increasingly, she interacted with the other children in the class in a friendly and appropriate manner. She had gone home to play with one of the other little girls in the class on a few occasions and they indulged in the usual rituals of little girls' friendships at school. Academically, Sheila sailed ahead, excited by almost anything I put in front of her. We were still coping with her fear of committing her work to paper, but that too improved through March. It seldom took more than two or three tries before she felt secure enough with what she had written down to let me look at it. She was still extremely sensitive to correction, going off into great sulks, no matter how gently I pointed out a mistake; and on moody days, she could spend much of the time with her head buried in her arms in dismal despair, but we were coping.

It was after school and Sheila and I had returned to *The Little Prince* yet again. Snuggled down in the pillows of the reading corner together, we had just begun the book. I had come to the part where the little prince demands that the author draw him a sheep.

"A sheep—if it eats bushes, does it eat flowers too?"

"A sheep," I answered, "eats anything in its reach."

"Even flowers that have thorns?"

"Yes, even flowers that have thorns."

"The thorns—what use are they ...?"

The prince never let go of a question, once he had asked it. As for me, I was upset over the bolt. And I answered with the first thing that came into my head:

"The thorns are of no use at all. Flowers have thorns just for spite!"

"Oh!"

There was a moment of complete silence. Then the little prince flashed back at me with a kind of resentfulness:

"I don't believe you! Flowers are weak creatures. They are naive—"

Sheila laid her hand across the page. "I want to ask you something. What's 'naive' mean?"

"It means someone whose ways are simple. They haven't much experience with the world," I replied.

"Do I be naive?" she asked, looking up.

"No, I wouldn't say so. Not for your age."

She looked back down at the book. "The flower thinks she has experience."

I nodded.

"But the prince knows she doesn't." She smiled. "I do love this part. I love the flower."

We read on:

28

So, too, she began very quickly to torment him with her vanity—which was, if truth be known, a little difficult to deal with. One day, for instance, when she was speaking of her four thorns, she said to the little prince:

"Let the tigers come with their claws!"

"There are no tigers on my planet," the little prince objected. "And anyway, tigers do not eat weeds."

"I am not a weed," the flower replied sweetly.

"Please excuse me ..."

"I am not at all afraid of tigers—"

The door to the classroom opened and the secretary stuck her head around the door. "Sorry to interrupt, Torey, but there's a telephone call for you in the office."

Handing Sheila the book, I rose and went down to take it.

It was the call I was dreading. The director of special education was on the other end of the line: a vacancy had come up in the children's unit at the state hospital. Sheila's time in my classroom was over.

To say I was devastated diminishes the enormity of the emotions I felt at that news. Whatever her difficulties, Sheila in no way belonged in a mental hospital. Intelligent, creative, sensitive, perceptive, she belonged here with us and, eventually, back in a normal class in a regular school.

I moaned, I pleaded, eventually I raged. The director listened. We got on well, he and I. I had always counted him among my allies in the district, the sort of man I relied on as a mentor, and this, if anything, made his call harder to take.

"It was settled long before any of us got into it, Torey," he said. "You know that. There's nothing we can do."

Pathetic little flower, I thought, so proud of her fierce thorns, and when the tigers really came, the thorns gave no protection at all.

I simply couldn't let it happen without a fight. When she had arrived in January, she had presented as bleak a case as I had ever encountered, and if they'd come for her then, I might have accepted it. But now ...? The very thought of a child of Sheila's caliber ending up institutionalized at six froze me to my soul.

That evening when I was home, ostensibly watching television with my boyfriend, Chad, a plan formed in my mind. I had so much evidence of both Sheila's intelligence and her progress that I wondered if there might be a chance of changing things. It would have to be approached in a formal, unequivocal manner to be taken seriously and it would have to be undertaken rapidly. I glanced over at Chad. He was a very new junior partner in a law firm downtown and was spending much of his time as a court-appointed lawyer to those who couldn't afford their own legal advice. So he knew the ropes.

"Is there a legal way to contest what they want to do with Sheila?" I asked cautiously.

"*You* fight it?" he replied, sensing the meaning under my words.

"Someone has to. I'm quite sure the school district would support me. The school psychologist has been in to administer IQ tests. He had evidence of her giftedness. And Ed knows."

A pause. A few mutterings. I was the sort of person inclined, as Chad described it, "to get the bit between my teeth and run," so I think he could guess the obsessive nature of what was going to happen.

"Would you take it on for me?" I asked.

"*Me?*"

Yeah, him.

And so it was. With admirable solidarity, the school district did back me fully. They even paid for Chad's services. I marshaled together the videotapes I'd made of Sheila in class, her schoolwork, the psychologist's evaluations and whatever other examples I could find to support Sheila's steady improvement. The weakest link in the chain was Sheila's father, who had been in and out of so many institutions himself that he didn't seem to believe there was any point to pursuing a different life for his daughter. He was deeply suspicious of us because we did. Beneath his boorish behavior, I felt he did genuinely love Sheila, but it took several rather beery evenings between us to convince him we were right.

The hearing was held on the very last day of March, a dark, windy day that promised to bend the daffodils down yet again with snow. Sheila had

had to come along, still dressed in her T-shirt and now badly outgrown overalls. They were clean and I had managed to get her father to accept socks and mittens for her from our church donation box, but that was the best I could do. She sat outside the courtroom with an attendant, in case we needed to call her in.

Inside, I saw the parents of the little boy whom Sheila had abducted and set alight. It was the first time I'd encountered them. Up to that moment, the incident that had placed her in my class had seemed distant to me. In truth, I suppose I had kept it distant in my mind in an effort to make such an act of calculated cruelty unreal. Sheila certainly *had* done some outrageous things and she had done plenty of them in my presence, so I'd always felt I had a realistic picture of her, but for the first time I had to confront the veracity of another point of view. This upset me, if for no other reason than that I had so desperately wanted to feel a hundred percent right in what I was doing just then. In a way I still did. Revenge would not undo the harm done to their son and it would cripple Sheila for life. This was the only right route for this girl. Yet the hearing brought home to me the enormity of what she had done.

The judge ruled in Sheila's favor. She was to remain under Social Services supervision, but the order for detainment in the children's unit was rescinded. Joy broke out in the halls of the courthouse, and afterward, Chad and I took Sheila out to celebrate.

It was a magical evening, one of those times when the experience is greater than the sum of its parts. Still high from our success, we went for pizza in a place Chad and I haunted frequently, full of smoke and jazz music and people speaking Italian. Sheila had never had pizza and took to the new experience with animated delight. Indeed, she took to Chad, and he, likewise, to her. He was soon as much under her spell as I was.

They got into a silly contest, the two of them. What would you like best? To eat a worm sundae or brush your teeth with a spider toothbrush? That sort of thing. Until Chad went serious and asked what was the thing she would like best in all the world—for real. A dress, as it turned out. Something pretty to wear. Unable to resist this opportunity to play Santa Claus, Chad soon had us out to the shopping center. Despite all Sheila's fears that her father wouldn't let her accept a dress, Chad reassured her and helped her find the one she liked best.

Sheila fell asleep on the way back to her house in the migrant camp.

"Well, Cinderella," Chad said, coming around to my side of the car and opening the door. He reached down and lifted her up. "The ball's over."

She smiled sleepily at him.

"Come on. I'll carry you in and tell your daddy what we've been up to."

She buried her face in my hair. "I don't wanna go," she whispered.

"It's been a nice night, hasn't it?" I said.

She nodded and she pressed tighter against me. "Can I kiss you?"

"Yes, I think so," I said and enveloped her in a tight hug and kissed her first.

Chapter 4

My class would cease to exist at the end of that school year. The mainstreaming law with its edict that every handicapped child should be placed in the least restrictive alternative was the primary cause. Most of the special education classes were being closed and teachers like myself were being redeployed as "resource people" to provide support to the regular classroom teachers, who would now have special education children among their students.

I wasn't terribly comfortable with this change. While I would have liked to accept the law on the ideological grounds it was being put forth on—that it would promote greater equality and opportunity for handicapped children—I was too much of a natural cynic. The far more obvious factor to me was that it was a cheaper way to educate handicapped children.

On a personal level, my style of teaching was best suited to the closed environment of a self-contained classroom. It was in this setting I was at my best. I could create the tight-knit, supportive milieu that became my trademark and it was under these circumstances I could encourage the most positive growth among my students. Consequently, I was loath to become a floating resource person with my children reduced to a catalog of educational problems I was given twenty minutes a week to sort out. Most difficult, however, was being boxed in theoretically. I was an eclectic, picking and choosing my methods of operation from a wide variety of sources, some of them entirely outside education. This seemed the only sensible approach when dealing with such varied difficulties as one comes across in human behavior. However, with the new law we were going to be restricted, generally to some form of behavior modification. I was competent enough with this approach but felt it vastly overrated as a method and rather dangerous as a theory. Thus, not feeling that I was ready to commit myself to all of this, I applied and was accepted at an out-of-state university to do further graduate work.

It was May and school would end the first week in June. In the four and a half months Sheila had been with us, she had metamorphosed into a lively, sunny-natured girl. We had had no serious breaches of behavior since that week in February when I had gone to the conference, and while she was still capable of a hearty tantrum when provoked, normal methods of discipline brought her back into line. She could now express anger without destructiveness; she could be reasoned with; and she could even accept a small amount of gentle criticism without falling to pieces. In short, I didn't feel Sheila would need a special class any longer. She was still fragile and the placement would need to be well thought out, but I was convinced she had the capacity to get on in a normal classroom.

I had a good friend, Sandy McGuire, a third-grade teacher in another school who I felt would be an ideal next teacher for Sheila. She was young, innovative and had a reputation for sensitivity toward her students, many of whom came from minority backgrounds or extreme poverty. And while we had quite different styles of teaching, we shared similar philosophies. I felt confident that if Sheila went with her, she would receive the support and encouragement she would need to make the transition back into the mainstream.

In the beginning, Ed, the director of special education, was not in favor of this, as it would mean not only releasing Sheila back into regular education, but also advancing her a grade, a practice he frowned upon; however, after much discussion we mutually concluded this was the best choice. Academically, Sheila was at least two grades above her chronological peers and she had no current peer friendships to disrupt anyway. Moreover, I feared that if Sheila did not receive a certain amount of academic challenge, she would get herself into trouble just to stay occupied. The most important factor, however, remained the teacher. Sheila *had* to have a flexible, supportive teacher to cope with the transition from me and my room to a new setting and I held tight to my belief that Sandy best fulfilled this capacity. In the end, Ed and the placement team agreed.

Sheila didn't.

I approached the whole issue cautiously, although not tentatively, as Sheila would home in on anything done with uncertainty. Moreover, there was nothing to be tentative about. June was coming and that was the end.

Tears, anger and great silences met my early efforts to broach the subject. We spent the better half of a week dancing nervously around the matter, once it had been raised.

"This here be my class," Sheila muttered to me after school. Her peculiar usage of the word "be" had almost disappeared over the months since she had been in our room, but now it came back. "I ain't going in no other class. This here be mine."

"Yes, it is, but the school year will be over in a few weeks' time. We need to think about next year."

"I'm gonna be in here next year."

My heart sank. "No, sweetie."

"I am too!" she shouted. "I'll be the baddest kid in the whole world. Then they won't *let* you make me go away!"

"Oh, Sheil. Oh, sweetheart, that's not what's happening. I'm not kicking you out. I'd *love* to have you with me."

She remained angry, her face flushed, her eyes hurt. She pressed her hands over her ears.

"This class isn't going to be here next year," I said softly.

She heard me, even through her hands. The color drained from her face. "What d'you mean? Where's it going?"

"It's a grown-up decision. The school district decided they don't need it and everyone can go into other classes."

Tears filled her eyes. Taking out the chair across the table from me, she slumped into it, folded her arms on the table and lay her head on it. The tears just fell. Her pain was palpable. I'm sure I could have touched it, had I reached out, and when I didn't, it pressed in against me.

All I could think of at just that moment was how much we expected from her in terms of tolerance, acceptance and understanding, and here she was, only six. *Six*, for God's sake, not even seven until July.

What had I gotten her into? There I was with all my ideologies on commitment and how it was better to have loved and lost than never to have loved at all. But did *she* think that? Had I ever given her a choice?

On the other hand, what choice was there? To have done what I did, or to have left her as she was and simply counted off the days until they would come for her? There hadn't been many alternatives. Watching her as she wept, I did not know if even with so few alternatives I had chosen the right one.

Sheila rose from the table and went to bury herself among the pillows in the reading corner. I remained at the table, listening to her as she cried. At last, I rose and went over.

"How come you ain't staying to make me good?" she asked me, her voice confused.

"Because it isn't me who makes you good. It's you. I'm here to let you know that someone cares if you're good or not. And in that way, I'll never leave you, because I'll always care."

"You're just like my mama," she said.

"No, I'm not, Sheil."

"You're gonna leave me, just like her."

"No, Sheila, this is different."

"She never loved me really," she said softly, matter-of-factly. "She loved my brother better than me. She left me on the highway like some dog, like I didn't even belong to her."

"I'm not her. I don't know what her reasons were for what she did, but this is different, Sheila. I'm a teacher. My ending comes in June. But I'll still love you. I won't be your teacher any longer, but I'll still be your friend."

"I don't wanna be friends. I wanna be in this class."

I reached over to her. "I know you do, sweetheart. I do too. I wish it could go on forever."

She pulled away. "You're bad as my mama."

"This is *different*."

"It don't feel any different to me."

They were an emotional few weeks, those last ones. Sheila was in tears as often as not. Not angry tears, though, just tears, popping up at the most unexpected moments: while we were baking cookies on Wednesday afternoon, while giving water to our cantankerous rabbit, while reading on her own in the book corner. I felt they were a natural part of the separation process, so I accepted them, giving her what comfort she sought and otherwise letting her come to terms at her own pace. And tears were by no means her only expression. There were plenty of boisterous, happy moments too.

I took her over to visit Sandy and her classroom and then we arranged for Sheila to go spend a trial day there. As I suspected would happen, Sheila was seduced by Sandy's warm, cheerful personality and by the more stimulating environment of the third-grade classroom. These children were actively learning, busy with intriguing projects and undertakings, many of them self-generated. All in all, quite a different atmosphere from our classroom, where going to the toilet was considered an achievement. Sheila came back vibrant from her visit, her conversation full of "Next year, when I'm in Miss McGuire's class ..." I knew then I had been outgrown.

Then the last day.

We had a picnic in the park to celebrate our year together. All the parents were invited and we brought packed lunches and ice cream and all the trappings for a good day out. Ours was an extraordinarily beautiful municipal park with a long, winding lane lined with locust trees, a babbling brook that tumbled down through natural rock cascades to empty into a large duck pond ringed with weeping willows. In all directions there were large expanses of grass stretching out beneath ancient sycamores and oaks.

Sheila loved the park. She had never been there before coming to our room, as it was a long way from the migrant camp; but it was only a few blocks from the school, so I had taken my class over on several occasions. Her father did not come that day, but it was obvious he was making more of an effort with Sheila. She came dressed in a bright-orange cotton sunsuit and excitedly told us how her father had taken her down to the discount store the night before and bought it, especially for her to wear to the picnic. She was so ebullient that day, skipping, dancing, pirouetting in the sunshine, that I still call to mind that bobbing form of sunlit orange every time I smell locust blossoms or see duck ponds.

And then, finally, the end—the last good-bye at the door of the classroom to Anton, the last walk together over to the high school to meet her bus. I had given her the now dog-eared copy of *The Little Prince* to take with her, a tangible reminder of these last five months, and she clutched it to her as we walked.

Running up the bus steps, she went straight to the back and clambered up on the bench seat to wave to me from the back window. The bus rumbled to life and diesel fumes overpowered the scent of locust blossoms. "Bye," she was saying, although I couldn't hear her because of the glass and the noise of the engine. The bus began to pull away and she waved frantically.

"Bye-bye," I said and lifted my hand to wave too, as the bus turned the corner and disappeared from sight. Then I turned to walk back to my classroom.

Chapter 5

When autumn came, I was a thousand miles away from the school, the migrant camp and the locust trees. Settled into graduate school, I was devoting most of my spare time to research. Some years earlier I had become intrigued by psychologically based language problems, elective mutism in particular, where an individual can speak but does not do so for emotional reasons; however, I had had to put this on the back burner while teaching full-time, because there just hadn't been time to pursue it. Now I was able to devote the kind of attention to the work I wanted. As a consequence, I was still in daily contact with children, but it was of a different kind and quality to what the classroom had given me. This was okay. I had been ready for the change, and thus was finding this new work rewarding.

Chad and I had parted ways over the summer. We'd been together for much of the previous three years and the last year, in particular, we'd grown close. Sheila, in her own way, had brought us closer still. Previously, Chad had only been part of my personal life, a world I tended to keep strictly separate from my life in the classroom, but with Sheila's hearing in March, he had been drawn into that too. The magic of that night when Chad had taken Sheila and me out for pizza had been powerful and all three of us, I think, got caught up in a dreamy moment of believing we were a family. It'd seemed so right just then—Chad, Sheila and I; however, in the cold, hard light of day, I knew it wasn't right. Chad was older than I was and had sown his wild oats, but I was still very young. I knew I was not yet ready for the commitments that a closer relationship with Chad would entail. Because commitments were so important to me, I wouldn't make them lightly. So, seductive as the vision of family life was at that point, I knew I would fail at it if I tried it now. So this, too, lay behind my decision to change tracks and move away from the area. I loved Chad and I didn't want to break up our relationship, but I didn't want to intensify it either. Putting distance between us seemed a reasonable solution.

Chad, of course, figured out what I was doing and he wasn't particularly happy about it. For him the time was right to settle down and get married. If anything, those last eight weeks with Sheila had verified for him that this was what he wanted and he chafed at my uncertainty, angry with me one moment for my immaturity, poignantly vulnerable the next, when he bemoaned the unfairness of the fact that no matter how much a man might be ready to be a father, he couldn't be one without a woman. I felt awful, as one always does when relationships crumble, but I went ahead with my plans regardless, knowing in my heart even more certainly that this was the right thing to do.

Sheila went into Sandy McGuire's third-grade class, and for all intents and purposes, she did extremely well. Sandy kept me well informed with letters each month or so. I was gratified to hear that Sheila was settling in, making friends and achieving good academic results, and even more so to hear that she was coming to school cleaner and better fed, which made me hope the home situation was improving.

My only other source of information was Anton, who still lived in the migrant camp himself and occasionally saw Sheila there. Despite my misgivings when Anton had first come to my classroom the previous autumn, he had turned out to be a natural teacher. He had tremendous rapport, particularly with the slower children and with the Spanish-speakers, of whom there were many in our migrant population. As a consequence, he had decided to work on his teacher qualifications at the nearby community college while still continuing as an aide in the school district. He was well informed on how all my former students were doing, and thus, a letter from Anton was a real treat.

I wrote to Sheila, as I had promised her I would do, and Sheila occasionally wrote back. She was, however, only seven, and as with all seven-year-olds, no matter how gifted, letters were clearly a chore. They came erratically and if I had not had Sandy's letters in the interim, I really wouldn't have had any idea of what was going on. Indeed, the contents of Sheila's letters were even more erratic than their number. She was given to sending me her homework for some reason and that was all I sometimes received for months on end.

All went smoothly. Sheila finished her year with Sandy an enthusiastic, if somewhat quirky, student, and was promoted to the fourth grade. I received a school picture of her from Sandy, showing her in a bright-yellow dress, her smile sweet and toothless. She looked well, if not too clean.

Autumn came but Sheila didn't. I received a puzzled note from Sandy saying that Sheila had been withdrawn from the register. It was Anton who investigated the matter and wrote back to tell me that Sheila and her father had moved to a small city on the far side of the state, some two hundred miles away. They had left in June, just after school had let out, apparently because her father thought he had found a job.

I wrote to the only address I had, her old one, and received no answer. Distressed at the thought that I had actually lost contact with Sheila, I made a few phone calls in an effort to trace her. During the course of these, I discovered that she had apparently gone into foster care at the end of the summer, but it was only a rumor and I couldn't confirm it. I knew no one in this new city to which she and her father had moved and I was twelve hundred miles away. It proved impossible to find out where she was and how she was doing.

This upset me profoundly. Confiding in an older colleague one afternoon after an abortive effort to trace Sheila, I was reassured that this was better, that I shouldn't try to hold on to old students. She smiled gently and patted my shoulder. "Never look back. You've got to love them and leave them."

It was three years before I managed to go back to Marysville to visit my old friends. By then Anton was gone. He had completed his two-year course at the community college and won a scholarship to the state university to finish his bachelor's degree. I visited with Sandy, however, and Whitney, who was now a senior in high school; and I went back to walk through my old classroom, now converted into a resource center.

Chad and I had separated amicably and we'd stayed in touch. He was married now to a fellow lawyer named Lisa and she was expecting their first child in a month's time.

We decided to lunch together and I came up to his law office to meet him. He had been held up in a meeting, so I paced languidly about the reception desk waiting for him. It was then I noticed a paper lying in the outgoing basket. I just caught it with the corner of my eye, but the name pulled me back. It was Sheila's father's name. Glancing at the receptionist, I realized I couldn't really look, but I was desperate to hear what Chad had to say.

"Didn't you know he's back in prison?" Chad replied to my query.

"*No.* When did this happen? You never told me."

"Well, I couldn't really, could I?" he said apologetically. "I mean, confidentiality and all. Besides, I assumed you did know." What he didn't mention was that we had never exchanged much more than Christmas cards anyway since we'd parted. But still, I felt somehow cheated.

Chad smiled gently. "I'm not handling many legal aid cases these days, so I didn't know myself until I saw the folder."

"What's happened?"

"I can't really discuss it, Torey."

"I'm not just anybody, Chad. I was the one who brought him to you in the first place." I was feeling hurt and heartsick. I knew it was hardly Chad's fault and I fully understood his need to keep confidence with clients, but the shock made me irritable.

"Well, suffice it to say he's been wholly predictable. He's up for the same tricks as always."

"Where's Sheila then?"

"Don't know. He's been living over in Broadview for a couple of years now and he was arrested and booked over there. They sent over here just looking for files. I've never seen him or anything."

"But where's Sheila?" I murmured, lowering my head.

Heartbroken at this discovery, I endeavored to find out about Sheila's fate, but I had few resources at my fingertips. Broadview was still two hundred miles off and was a much bigger city. Finding one small girl was no easy matter. The most I could confirm was that she had been taken into foster care as a direct result of her father's arrest and imprisonment and was, apparently, still placed. Where, with whom and for how long I could not determine. Rumor had it that she had been repeatedly in and out of foster care from the time they had moved.

Foster care. Practically the whole time Sheila was in my class, all of us had viewed foster care as a panacea to her problems. If only Sheila were away from the poverty, if only she were in a stable home with loving parents, if only ... We hadn't been able to get her into foster care then simply because the Social Services were so overstretched in Marysville and she did have her natural father. Now she was in foster care and I should have felt glad. The fact was, I didn't.

Back home, I sat down and wrote a very long letter to Sheila. I told her about my visit to our old school and our old friends. I mentioned that I knew her life had been disrupted in the last eighteen months and that I knew she was now with foster parents. I said that I hoped all was well and that if there was any way I could help, I would be happy to try. Including my phone number, I said she could call me collect any time, if she wanted. Then I added a photograph from the visit of Sandy and me and an old one I had taken of Sheila on our last-day picnic. Folding everything together, I put them in a large envelope. But where would I send it? In the end, I sent it to her father, in care of the prison, and asked him to forward it to her.

I never heard whether Sheila received my letter or not, whether she ever knew that I was trying to find her again. There was no answer, and as the months went by, I began to accept there wasn't going to be one.

This was difficult for me to come to terms with. It seemed inconceivable to me that she had disappeared from my life. Yet the words of my colleague kept returning to me: you've got to love 'em and leave 'em.

Two years later, a small envelope arrived on my desk. It was addressed not to my home, but rather to the university where I now taught. I recognized Sheila's loose, scrawly handwriting immediately and tore the envelope open. There was only one sheet of paper inside, a crumpled piece of lined notebook paper. The writing was done in blue felt-tip marker with many of the words watermarked, as if the paper had gotten splattered by rain. Or was it tears?

To Torey with much Love

All the rest came
They tried to make me laugh
They played their games with me

Some games for fun and some for keeps
And then they went away
Leaving me in the ruins of games
Not knowing which were for keeps and
Which were for fun and
Leaving me alone with the echoes of
Laughter that was not mine.

Then you came
With your funny way of being
Not quite human
And you made me cry
And you didn't seem to care if I did
You just said the games are over
And waited
Until all my tears turned into
Joy.

There was nothing else, no letter, not even a note. As with the days when she had sent me only her homework, Sheila seemed to feel no need for explanations. It was my turn to cry then and so I wept.

Part 2

Chapter 6

I can remember the moment precisely when the magic began. I was eight, a not-very-outstanding third grader in Mrs. Webb's class. I didn't care much for school. I never had. My world in those days was the broad, swampy creek that ran below our house; that and my beloved pets. School was something that got in the way of my enjoyment of these things.

On one particular morning, my reading group had been sent back to our desks to do our seat-work, while Mrs. Webb listened to the next group read. On my desk, under my workbook, I had hidden a piece of paper, and instead of doing what I should have been doing, I sneaked the opportunity to write. At home I had a dachshund, which had been a present to me from my mother on my seventh birthday, and I made him the hero of a rather lurid tale involving our old mother cat and a band of marauding, eye-plucking crows. So absorbed did I become in spinning this tale that I failed to notice Mrs. Webb on the move, and what inevitably happens to eight-year-old girls who do not do their reading workbooks happened. Mrs. Webb snatched the story away from me and I had to stay in from recess to do my work.

The incident itself was minor, the sort of thing to which I was unfortunately rather prone, and as a consequence, I forgot all about it. Then, a couple of weeks later, I was ill and kept out of school for a few days. When I returned, I had to stay after school that afternoon to make up some of the work I had missed. Mrs. Webb apparently took this opportunity to clean out the drawers of her desk. Anyway, when I had finished, she handed over a piece of paper to me. "Here, I think this is yours," she said. It was the story about my dog and the crows.

Collecting my coat and belongings to go home, I began to read it as I walked down the school corridor, dark and silent because all the other children had left so long before me. Once at the end of the hall, I pushed open the heavy double doors of the school and then sat down on the concrete steps at the entrance to finish reading.

That precise moment I remember with such exquisite clarity—the feel of the cold concrete through my skirt, the late-autumn sunshine transposed against the darkness of the school entranceway, the uncanny silence of the empty playground, even the faint anxiety of knowing that I should be on my way home because my grandmother would worry if I was too late. The paper, however, held me spellbound.

It was all there: my dog, his adventure, the excitement such melodramatic experiences always created in me. I felt just as excited by the story reading it as I had been writing it. Astonished when I realized this, I lowered the paper. I *remember* lowering the paper, looking over the top of it, seeing someone's hopscotch game chalked onto the playground asphalt, and being overwhelmed by a sense of insight. *Wow*! I had always written because I found writing like pretending: an opportunity to turn myself into someone else for the moment I was doing it and be that individual, feeling his or her feelings and experiencing his or her adventures; but once the act of creation was over, I had never really gone back to what I had written. Now here it was, two weeks later, and I was feeling exactly what I had experienced earlier when I was writing it. Exactly. Again. As if the two weeks hadn't happened. I had *stopped time*. There, on the school steps, I knew I had stumbled onto magic of the first order. *Real magic*!

For the rest of my childhood, through my adolescence and into adulthood, writing compelled me. It was an internal, almost autonomic, activity, like circulation or digestion, that happened simply as a natural part of me. I wrote in all forms: diaries, anecdotes, stories. I wrote to understand other people, to give myself the opportunity to be inside them a while and see what it felt like to see the world from another point of view. I wrote to understand emotions and experiences I had not yet encountered. And I wrote to understand myself.

It proved a powerful, if somewhat unusual, education. In particular, it fostered my abilities to be objective and to empathize, which in turn allowed me a greater general acceptance of differences; and, of course, it made me a keen observer.

I was in the final year of a doctorate I hadn't meant to find myself doing. I had weathered the mainstreaming law that had so disconcerted me the year I'd had Sheila. Although still not happy with all aspects of its implementation, I'd returned to the classroom a couple of years later and taken up teaching again as a "centered" resource teacher, which meant I stayed in the same room but the children came and went. It wasn't quite as fulfilling as having my own class, but at least I saw the same boys and girls on a regular basis.

Then the administration in Washington changed and with it, the general attitude of the country. Issues I'd fought heart and soul to see achieved a decade earlier were swept away with a single signature. Lower taxes and cuts in public spending became the bywords of the day. Because treating handicapped children in the public schools is labor intensive, and thus expensive, ours were among the first programs to be targeted. Further emphasis was put on placing special education children in the regular classroom as the cheaper alternative.

We were being forced to respond to children in ways that were not necessarily the most beneficial to the child—or the teacher, either, for that matter, as many regular education teachers had little grounding in dealing with handicapped children. These philosophies, however, were the only ones that allowed us to process children through the system at the cost demanded of us by the government. The market economy was now being applied to education.

Angry at this change and all too aware that if I continued in the classroom, I too would soon find myself unemployed, I'd decided to work on a doctorate in special education. This was a stupid decision. The degree would overqualify me for the only part of the special education hierarchy I genuinely loved: teaching. Worse, it threw me into the hotbed of those creating the theories that I was trying to escape. Consequently, my heart was never in it.

I coped by finding other outlets. In this case, it was the continuation of my long-standing research into psychological language problems. This work was of little interest to my colleagues in special education; however, I soon found a niche across campus in the university hospital complex. There, in the department of child and adolescent psychiatry, among others, I discovered willing partners among the psychiatrists and other professionals. Despite my hybrid credentials, my ideas were accepted and encouraged and my research flourished.

As always, I continued to fill my spare time with writing. Indeed, I was writing more then than at any previous time; in part, I suspect, because I wasn't fully engaged in my work.

The desire to write about my experiences with Sheila had been with me for some time. I had saved a lot of material from that class, not with the intention of using it to back up writing at a later date, but just because I was a bit of a hoarder and a sentimental one at that. Although I hadn't kept a daily diary while working in the class, I had kept copious anecdotal records; moreover, I had had liberal use of a video camera, and as a consequence, had quite a lot of Sheila on tape. I went through these things periodically, and all the while I could hear Sheila in my head: the inflections in her voice, the strange lilting grammatical constructions. I had to write it down. I had to liberate those five months from the onward rush of time.

Then, driving home on the freeway from work one dark January evening, the beginning came to me: *I should have known*. I went home and started writing. Eight days and 225 pages later, I was finished.

It was only in the aftermath that I realized what had happened. At 225 pages, this wasn't a little something done for my own amusement, it was a book. I knew then that I had to find Sheila and let her read it before the matter went any further.

Chapter 7

The job advertisement that caught my eye was for a small private psychiatric clinic in a major city about four hours' drive west of Marysville. In all my years back east, I had missed the Midwest. Admittedly, Sheila also crossed my mind. Broadview, where she had last been living, was a satellite community of the city. Six months had elapsed since I had written the book and I was no closer to finding Sheila. The idea of living near her, of perhaps reestablishing contact and renewing our relationship was appealing.

I was accepted at the Sandry Clinic as a research psychologist to coordinate and oversee the various research projects among the staff, as well as to continue my own research work with elective mutism. There were seven staff. Five, including the director, Dr. Rosenthal, were established child psychiatrists.

They had founded the clinic together several years before and overseen the conversion of the elegant old building into a series of quality offices and therapy rooms.

I liked the Sandry Clinic very much. My colleagues were creative people, all lively and articulate, who worked well together as a team. The pinnacle among us in more ways than one was our director. Dr. Rosenthal was a giant of a man physically, standing over six and a half feet tall, with a giant-sized intellect to match. He had about him that charisma powerful men seem to have, which make them handsome whatever their actual physical characteristics. I was in awe of him much of my first year there. Although born and bred in America, he had a European formality about him. For instance, he never called any of us by our first names. "Doctor" was his usual method of catching someone's attention, but as I didn't merit that, I remained steadfastly Miss Hayden. This gave him a certain aura of unapproachability, which, combined with his formidable intellectual reputation, kept me shy around him. Nonetheless, I came to know him as a gentle man, firm but kind with his staff in much the same way he was with the children he worked with, and always, always fair.

Life at the clinic was luxurious compared to what I had become accustomed to while teaching in the state school system. We had wonderful facilities, including a large, sunny therapy room full of things I would have killed for when in special education, such as a five-foot-tall doll's house, complete with extended doll family, a pony-sized wooden rocking horse, an indoor sandbox and a water tray.

Similar luxury applied to my workload. Children were parceled out to me for therapy mostly by virtue of their language or lack of it, but I was also allowed a generous amount of time to work on the research projects or to consult with colleagues. Not completely comfortable with the fifty-minute "psychiatric hour," I was given the freedom of seeing my own clients two or three times a week, if I preferred that to the more traditional one session or of seeing them in their own settings, rather than at the clinic.

The only fly in the ointment from my point of view was that the majority of my colleagues were committed Freudians, which boxed in their views as tightly as behaviorism had with my education colleagues. And there I was, the atheist admitted to the monastery. To me, there is no single framework upon which we can hang all interpretations of human behavior. We create theories as a way of ordering the chaos sufficiently to have a chance of effecting change, but it is *we*, the practitioners, who have created this order, because it is we who need it. Any given theory, to my way of thinking, simply provides one route to interpretation and, like climbing the proverbial mountain, there are many other paths one could take.

I could cope with this disparity most of the time, as the general ethos of the clinic did not demand I practice as my colleagues did, and given that I was not qualified in psychiatry, they didn't expect me to. Indeed, it was my varied point of view, I suspect, that had attracted Dr. Rosenthal. Nonetheless, I found myself having to do a lot of tongue-biting.

Not being a full-fledged psychiatrist, I didn't merit one of the offices up front. Instead, I shared an oversized closet in the back of the building with Jeff Tomlinson.

Jeff, already a doctor, was in his last year of training as a child psychologist. He was one of those individuals so intellectually gifted that it is taken for granted. No modesty with him. He was brilliant and he knew he was brilliant, and he knew everyone else knew. "Does Superman fly?" he would say casually whenever I evidenced amazement at some mental feat, but he was so ingenuous when he said it that one never minded. Too much.

Unfortunately, Jeff might as well have been Freud's grandson. Indeed, he might as well have been Freud himself, for all his ability to quote what the old master said. With a near photographic memory, Jeff could bludgeon me into silence with word-for-word regurgitation of endless cases the old boy had worked on. It became a game with us after a while, to see who could outdebate the other.

Truth was, I loved Jeff. We were the youngest members of staff by quite some years, if not decades, and ours was like a sibling relationship there among the grown-ups. The other psychiatrists all had magnificent offices up front with cornices and fireplaces, carpets and leather couches. In the back of the building Jeff and I shared a windowless closet of an office, which had once housed another psychologist's research animals and still smelled. Here we had festooned the walls with posters, cartoons and matching Pink Panther nameplates. And here we worked, fought and shared our problems.

What saved Jeff from certain annihilation for his Freudian idiocy was an extraordinary sense of humor. He had a particular gift for funny voices and mimicry, which he displayed with the aplomb of a stand-up comic. As a consequence, the inanimate objects in our office—the filing cabinet, the desks, the radiator—were all inclined to join unexpectedly into conversations, each with its own weird little Robin Williams-type voice. The kids, of course, adored this when they heard it, but it even worked on me. It was difficult to get angry with a guy who had the furniture on his side.

All in all, I was pleased with this career move away from special education. It still felt funny to dress for work in wool skirts and dangly jewelry, to know that I could leave my long hair unbound because no one was likely to try and pull it out of my head; and, indeed, I found I missed my jeans and track shoes too much and was back in them after the first few months. But I fully enjoyed the ample resources and stimulating colleagues and felt that for the moment, at least, this had been the right move.

Chapter 8

Sheila was three months short of her fourteenth birthday when I finally located her. I hadn't seen her in seven years—half her lifetime past—and other than the poem I'd received through the mail two years earlier, I hadn't heard from her in five. I found her back with her father, living in an outlying suburb of Broadview. After a telephone conversation with her father, I asked if I could visit.

They were living in a duplex, a brown-colored building with peeling paint, in a run-down area where the yards were littered with car bodies and rusting appliances; however, compared to Sheila's home in the migrant camp, this was luxurious.

I knocked at the door. A long moment passed with no sound beyond the door and I found to my surprise that my knees were shaky. All the ghosts of long ago came crowding in around me as I waited on the doorstep and I could hear them so clearly. A child's laughter echoed, shouting, squealing, the sounds of a classroom, and then the dark, blowy silence I remembered experiencing as I had stood on the doorstep of Sheila's tar-paper shack in the migrant camp. Then, back to the present. Footsteps came toward the door and it opened.

I don't think I would have recognized Sheila's father if I hadn't assumed it would be he opening the door. He had changed dramatically in seven years. The dumpy, overweight boozer I recollected was not there. Instead, the man opening the door was slim and athletic-looking and, most startling to me, *young*. I had been in my early twenties when I had last seen him and I had always regarded him as being in my parents' generation. Now, with shock, I realized he was, in fact, not much older than I was.

"Mr. Renstad?" I asked tentatively.

He nodded.

"I'm Torey Hayden."

He smiled in a genuinely welcoming fashion and held the door open. "Come in. Sheila's not here at the moment. She's just run over to the store for some milk, but she'll be back in a few minutes." He opened the door to let me into the living room. It was small, with a television, a well-worn brown sofa and two old-fashioned armchairs. Indeed, the whole room had a sort of brownish quality to it, but it was comfortable.

Sudden shyness struck us both. All these years I had pondered this moment and now that it was here, I didn't know quite what to say. He obviously felt just as uncertain.

After a moment, he snatched a photograph from the top of the television. "Here, you want to see this? These are my boys."

It was the photo of a baseball team, the boys appearing to be about ten or eleven. They were posed in two rows, the first kneeling, the others behind. Mr. Renstad was on the left of the back row.

"I been coaching a year now," he said, moving beside me to look at the picture. "See that kid? His name is Juma Washington and you listen out for that name, because he's going to be great someday. Like Hank Aaron, that kid. And it was me that taught him to hit. Wouldn't do nothing for us when he first came. Was a wild, jazzy kid. And now he's gonna make the major leagues. You watch and see. I know he's gonna make it big."

"That's super."

He looked at me. "I'm clean now, you know. Sheila tell you that? No more booze or stuff. I been clean eighteen months now and now it's me helping them."

"I'm pleased," I said.

"I mean it. I'm not having no trouble at all anymore, and now I got these boys. We won four games already this season. Didn't win no games at all before I took 'em over. Were wild kids, crazy as monkeys. But we're making it big now. Got Juma. Got a couple of other good ones too. Here, let me show you." He took the photograph. "Him, that's

Salim. And him, Luis. You ought to see 'em play. Can you come down some Saturday?"

Just then the door banged and there stood Sheila.

Sheila?

Who stood there was a gangly adolescent with—honest to God—orange hair. Not strawberry blond, not red. Orange, like a road cone. It was longish, and permed into frizzy ringlets, a Cubs baseball cap pulled down over the top of it.

Would I have known this was Sheila if I had encountered her on the street? She'd grown taller than I'd expected. She'd been such a tiny, malnourished thing when I'd had her, that I had always kept her small in my mind, but here she was, a good five feet four or so and only thirteen. Adolescence hadn't worked its full magic with her yet, however. She was gangly and still had the undeveloped figure of a child.

No question about whether or not she recognized me. On seeing me, she stopped abruptly, as if seeing a most unexpected sight. Her cheeks colored. "Hi," she said and smiled shyly. That smile did it. Her features grew familiar instantaneously.

"Hi."

All three of us were uncomfortably self-conscious. After anticipating this reunion for so long, I hadn't expected to find myself at a loss for words, but that's what happened. Sheila, equally thunderstruck, clung on to her half gallon of milk and stared at me. Only Mr. Renstad seemed able to find his voice. He went back to talking about his baseball team; however, he never asked me to sit down, so we all continued standing there in the middle of the living room.

Sheila's father just kept chattering. Several times he reassured me that he had given up drugs and alcohol and put his past behind him. This embarrassed me, making me feel as if he were interpreting my visit as checking up on him. He appeared to think Sheila and I had had much more contact with each other over the years than we'd had and so alluded to events that I knew nothing of. I felt it would be indelicate of me to inquire further at this point and thus said nothing, but from what I could make out, Sheila had been in foster care between the ages of eight and ten and then again for a while when she was eleven. They had been living together since his last parole, about eighteen months earlier.

Sheila said absolutely nothing. Like her father and me, she still stood in the middle of the living room, but she made no effort to join in the conversation. I stole glances at her, particularly at her dyed hair, because it was such an unusual color. Then at her clothes. When in my classroom, she had had one single outfit—a brown-striped boy's T-shirt and a pair of denim overalls—which she had worn day in, day out until her father had finally accepted the dress Chad had bought for Sheila after the March hearing. Sheila didn't look as if she was faring much better these days. She wore an enormously oversized white T-shirt with a ragged jeans jacket minus the arms layered over the top.

Underneath the T-shirt I assumed there was something besides underwear, as I could see what might be the fringed edge of cut-off jeans, but I wasn't sure. Contemplating the outfit, I assumed this was fashion and not poverty showing.

Finally, when her father paused, I turned to her. "I passed a Dairy Queen coming over. Would you like to go get a sundae with me?"

Alone in the car with me, Sheila remained silent. It was by no means a hostile silence, but it was uncomfortable enough. I found myself wandering back to the very first day I had met Sheila. She had been silent then too, fiercely silent, breaking it only to announce with tigerish vehemence that I couldn't make her talk. I kept calling back to mind that charismatic little girl I had known and trying to find her in this nervous adolescent. I was only too aware that I didn't know this strangely clad, deer-like thing at all.

Pulling into the parking lot of the Dairy Queen, I looked over. "Remember when I used to take everybody over to the Dairy Queen and buy those boxes of Dilly bars? And how Peter always wanted something different? Never mattered what it was, he never wanted what everyone else was having."

"Who's Peter?"

"You remember. In our class. He used to always tell those awful jokes. The real groaners. Remember him?"

A pause. "Yeah ... I think. He was Mexican, wasn't he?"

"Well, actually, he was black."

We chose our sundaes and then went out to sit at a picnic table in front. Sheila hunched over her ice cream in a manner that evoked memories of her early days in the class, when she would clutch her lunch tray up close to her, wary, like an animal, in case someone tried to take it away from her before she finished. She began to stir her sundae. The ice cream, chocolate sauce and whipping cream all went together in a gooey mess.

"So how's school?" I asked.

"All right, I guess."

"What courses are you taking?"

"Just the usual stuff."

"Anything good?" I asked.

"No, not really."

"Anything hard?"

"Not really," she said and stirred more energetically. "Boring, most of it."

Looking for some angle to get a conversation started, I resorted to an old trick I'd used in the classroom to stimulate a child to talk. "So what do you hate most about it?"

"Being youngest," she said without hesitation. "I *hate* that."

An accusation? She knew I had been responsible for moving her forward a grade. Was there a second meaning here? "What do you hate so much about it?"

She shrugged. "Just being youngest, that's all. Littlest. I was always so much shorter than everyone else, right up until just this last year. And always the baby of the class. Everyone picked on me."

"Yes, I can see where that might cause problems," I said, "but it was hard for us to know what was best for you."

Another shrug. "I'm not complaining or anything. It's just you asked."

Then silence. I wondered whether to draw her out on this issue and chance getting into something heavy, which I didn't feel would be appropriate just at the moment, or whether to soldier on searching for new topics of conversation. I felt amazingly uncomfortable. This wasn't the Sheila I had expected at all.

More silence. Taking small bites of my sundae, I concentrated on the flavors.

Suddenly, Sheila expelled a noisy breath and shook her head. "This is so weird," she said. "Like, I always think of you as someone I know well." She looked over. "But really, we're no more than strangers."

That broke the ice, that admission. Truth was, we *were* strangers and neither of us had anticipated that. Once it was acknowledged, talking became far easier than it had been when we were pretending that the previous seven years hadn't intervened.

Spontaneously, Sheila began to talk about her school. She didn't like it. She was just finishing ninth grade and apparently doing well academically, but in listening to her I could tell virtually none of it had touched her. The authorities were getting after her about her hair and her clothes and her general attitude, and the way she related it, I suspected she was dealing with it by playing truant.

Perversely, the only subject that appeared to be engaging her was Latin, a language I didn't realize was still being taught in schools. The teacher, an elderly man, was unfashionably strict and held unenlightened views about girls' academic abilities, but this combination had somehow goaded Sheila into working hard enough to "show him." As a consequence, she talked animatedly about the class and the curriculum, even though she professed to hate it.

In turn, I told her what I had been up to over the interceding years, about my other classes of children since leaving the one we had shared, about my stints at graduate school, and about the change to the clinic in the city. And about writing the book.

"I have it in my car," I said. "I want you to read it."

"A *book*?" she said incredulously. "You wrote a book? I didn't know you could write."

I shrugged.

"It's got *me* in it? Our class? God. Weird." Then a slight smile. "That's, like, mega-weird, you know?"

"You need to be prepared for the fact that it's going to sound a little different to what really happened. Everybody's gone on from there, so it wouldn't really be right to invade people's privacy. Consequently, I've had to change the names and things and put some events out of order, but still, I think you'll recognize everything."

"This is so weird. A *book*? About me?"

"Anyway, I want your thoughts on it," I said. "It is your story, well, yours and mine, but you're the big part in it. I wouldn't want to include anything you didn't think was right."

She smiled. "It doesn't matter much. I hardly remember a thing about it."

"Oh, you will," I said and grinned back.

She shrugged, her expression still benevolent. "You got to keep in mind, Torey, that I was nothing but a little kid then. That all happened more than half my life ago. Like, I'm going to love to read this, but if you want to know the truth, you could write anything you want. Honest, I remember nothing."

Chapter 9

"God, did it really happen like this?" Sheila asked, a curiously amazed tone to her voice. It was the following Saturday. We were in her bedroom and she was curled up, the pages of the manuscript fanned out around her.

Smiling, I nodded.

"Wow, you were pretty brave to take me on, if I was like this."

"A lot of people thought that at the time. I did a bit myself, sort of."

"It wasn't your choice, was it? They just said you got to take … me." She looked back down at the sheaf of papers. "I think I might remember Anton now. I didn't when you first mentioned him the other day, when we were at the Dairy Queen, but reading this kind of brings him back to mind."

"You know what he's doing now?" I asked.

"He's working on his master's degree in special education. He works with mentally handicapped children and has had his own classroom for three years now."

Sheila looked up. "God, you're really proud of him, aren't you? I can tell by your voice."

"I think it's amazing, what he's achieved. That's taken hard work. He's had a young family to support through all of this and his whole history had been with the migrant workers."

Regarding the typewritten pages, Sheila didn't speak for a few moments. "All I can recall is this really tall Mexican guy. He seemed like about seven feet tall to me then, but I don't remember a thing about what he did."

"Do you remember Whitney?" I asked.

"No. But I do recall that time with the rabbit poop. I remember painting all those little balls. God, it'd disgust me now. Imagine. I was actually picking up shit with my bare hands." She laughed. "What a disgusting kid."

I laughed too.

"The weird thing is, you never think you are when it's happening to you," Sheila added. "I remember being really serious about painting those things."

"What about Chad?" I asked. "My boyfriend, the one who defended you at the hearing? Remember him?" I asked, but before she could answer I grinned. "Guess what? He's married now and he has three kids. And guess what he's named his oldest girl?"

A blank look. "No idea."

"Sheila."

"After me?" she asked in amazement.

"Yes, after you. I mean, he thought the world of you. We had such a marvelous time that night after the hearing."

A pause followed. Sheila glanced down again at the pages in her hand and appeared to be reading the top one for a moment. "Shit. Shit. This is just so weird. I can't get over it."

"Weird in what way?"

"I dunno. Seeing my name here. It's somebody else here, really, but it's me, too."

"You don't think I've done it right?" I asked.

"Well, no, not that ... Maybe it's just seeing myself as a character in a book ... I mean, mega-weird." Another pause. "*You* seem real enough. This is just like I remember you. Reading this makes me feel like I've been sitting down and having a nice chat with you, but ... Was that class really this way?"

"How do you remember it?" I asked.

"Mostly, I don't. Like I said last week ..."

Silence again.

What entered my mind as I listened into the silence was the horrible nature of some of the things that had happened to Sheila over the course of the time she was in my room. In bringing the book here for her approval, I hadn't given serious consideration to the possibility that she might have dealt with her past by forcing it from memory. Such a reaction seemed un-Sheila-like to me and I hadn't anticipated it from her. Now, suddenly, I feared for what I had done. It was an upbeat story, but that was from my point of view.

Turning her head, Sheila gazed out the window beside her bed. It was an insignificant view—the side of the neighboring house, its gray-green paint peeling, the neighbor's window, a venetian blind hanging crookedly across it. She seemed to study it.

I, in turn, studied her with her long, straggly orange hair, her thin, undeveloped body clad in torn jeans and a rather strange, clingy gray top that looked like a piece of my grandpa's underwear. This gangly punk fashion plate wasn't quite what I had expected to find and I was having to fight the disappointment.

"What *I* remember are the colors," she said very softly, her tone introspective. "As if my whole life had been in black and white, and then I went in that classroom ... Bright colors." She made a little sound. "I always think of them as Fisher-Price colors, you know? The toys? Fisher-Price red and blue and white. All those primary colors. Remember that riding horse you could sit on and move around by pushing with your feet? *That's* what I remember. Every single color of him. Of sitting at the table when I was supposed to be working and looking at his colors. And where it said 'Fisher-Price' on him. God, I wanted that horse so bad. I used to dream about that horse, about how it was mine, that you let me take it home and keep it."

I probably would have, had she ever said it meant that much to her, but she never did.

"And that parking garage," she said. "Remember that? With all those little cars that'd go down the ramps and those little people who didn't even look like people. They were just plastic pegs with faces, really. Remember how I used to steal them? I was so desperate to have them. I used to line them up on the floor beside where I slept, this whole line of them—the guy in the black top hat, the guy in the cowboy hat, the Indian chief—do you remember me taking them?"

Over the years there had been so many toys in so many classrooms. I remembered garage sets and riding horses, but they could have been any of a dozen such I had had.

"You never got mad at me for it," she said, turning to look at me. She smiled. "I kept stealing them and stealing them and you never got angry with me."

In the hurly-burly of that class, truth was, I probably hadn't even noticed she was doing it.

"That's what seems so weird to me about this book, Torey. You make out like we're always fighting. Like, in it you seem to be getting mad at me about every other page. I don't remember you *ever* doing that."

I looked at her in surprise.

Then she wrinkled her nose and grinned conspiratorially. "Are you just spicing it up, like? So they'll want to publish it?"

My jaw dropped.

"I mean, I don't mind at all. It's a terribly good story. And, like, it's brilliant, thinking of myself as a character in a book."

"But, Sheila, we *did* fight. We fought all the time. When you came into my class, you—"

Again she turned to look out of the window. Silence ensued and it lasted several moments.

"What exactly *do* you recall?" I asked at last.

"Like I said ..." And then she didn't say. She was still gazing out of the window and the words just seemed to fade away. A minute or more passed.

"We *did* fight," I said softly. "Everybody fights, whatever the relationship, however good it might be. It wouldn't *be* a relationship otherwise, because two separate people are coming together. Friction is a natural part of that."

No response.

"Besides," I said and grinned, "I was a teacher. What would you expect?"

"Yeah, well," she said, "I don't really remember."

I couldn't come to terms with the fact Sheila had forgotten so much. Driving home on the freeway that evening, I turned it over and over in my mind. How *could* she forget Anton and Whitney? How could the whole experience be reduced to nothing more than a fond recollection of colorful plastic toys? This hurt me. It had been such a significant experience for me that I had assumed it had been at least as significant for her. In fact, I had assumed it was probably more significant. Without me, that class, those five months, Sheila most likely would now be on the back ward of some state hospital. I had *made a difference*. At least that's what I'd been telling myself. My cheeks began to burn hot, even in the privacy of my car, as I realized the gross arrogance of my assumption. I was further humbled by the insight that those five months might well now mean more to me than to her.

She had been only a very young child. Was I being unrealistic in expecting her to remember much? At the time she had been so exquisitely articulate that it had given her the gloss of a maturity even then I knew she didn't really have, but I had been accustomed to associating verbal ability with good memory.

As I sped through the darkness, I tried to recollect being six myself. I could bring to mind the names of some of the children in my first-grade class, but mostly it was incidents I could recall. There were a lot of small snippets: a moment lining up for recess, a classmate vomiting into the trash can, a fight over the swings, a feeling of pride because I drew good trees. They weren't very complete recollections, but if I tried, I could identify the locations and the names and appearance of the individuals involved. Still, they were nothing akin to the clarity of my memories as an adult. I was probably being unrealistic in expecting her to remember more.

Yet, it nagged at me. Sheila wasn't just any child, but a highly gifted girl who had blown the top right off almost every IQ test the school psychologist had given her that year. Sheila's prodigious memory had been among the most notable of many outstanding characteristics. She had used it like a crystal ball for gazing in, as she spoke to us all so poignantly, so eloquently of love and hate and rejection.

Love and hate and rejection. It couldn't be all arrogance on my part to expect that she should be remembering more. Her amnesia seemed so uncharacteristic, but still, it was not hard to imagine what might be causing it. Although I didn't know any specifics about what had happened since Sheila had left my room, I knew these hadn't been easy years in between. She had been in and out of foster homes, had moved to different schools and coped with her father's instability. If these years only half mirrored the nightmare she had been living when she'd come into my class, they would have given her ample reason for forgetting. She'd been such a brave little fighter that I didn't like to think she had finally buckled under the strain, but in the back of my mind, that's what I was beginning to accept. Yet ... why had she so thoroughly forgotten *our* class? The one bright spot, the one haven where she had been loved and regarded so well? Why had she forgotten us?

Chapter 10

At home, I rummaged through the things I had accumulated from the class, which I had used to write the book, looking for things to take with me on my next visit to see Sheila. The vast majority of the materials were just school papers and anecdotal records, neither very useful for the purpose. What I really wanted to share were the videotapes, but this was in the era of the old reel-to-reel videotapes and the only machine I had for playing them on was at the clinic; so those would have to wait for the time when Sheila came in to visit me. In the end, I resorted to going through my picture album.

I had surprisingly few photographs of that year. There was the class picture, all of us lined up against the blue curtain on the school stage, looking like felons in a group mug shot. The camera had caught Sheila full on, washing out her pale features. She wouldn't smile on demand in those days, so she had just a blank stare. Unfortunately, several others in the class had been equally uncooperative and many of them were consequently rendered unrecognizable.

In total, I had only three other photographs of Sheila and these included the individual school picture, taken at the same time as the group photo. I had kept this one, as her father had declined to buy it. It was the only one I'd ever had of her smiling. Normally, she'd simply refused to smile for cameras, but on this occasion, the photographer had tricked her into it while trying to get her to grab his pen. Taken only a short time after she had arrived in our classroom, it caught her full grubby glory and I adored it.

The other two photographs I had taken myself. One was to commemorate the first time I'd really gotten her cleaned up and she sat in deep solemnity on the school steps, hands clasped upon her knees. Her hair was combed smooth and put into pigtails; her clothes were washed; her face was cleaned; and the truth was, it didn't look like Sheila at all. She was not nearly so engaging as the filthy character in the school photograph. The other picture I had taken on the last day of school when the class had gone down to the park for our end-of-school picnic. I had taken several photographs that day, but unfortunately, Sheila was in only one of them. She was standing beside the duck pond with two of the other little girls in the class. Both of them were neat and clean and beaming cheerfully, but Sheila, in the middle, stared back at the camera with a guarded, almost suspicious gaze. Despite the new orange sunsuit her father had bought for the occasion, she had come to school very scruffy that day, her long hair uncombed, her face unwashed, and she stood in stark contrast to her two classmates. There was a compelling aspect to the photograph, however. It was the wariness of her expression, which made her seem fierce and yet surprisingly vulnerable.

I decided in the end to take that photograph, as well as the others taken on that day, which showed the other children, Anton and Whitney.

The following Saturday, Sheila and I went to watch her father's baseball team play. They were an inauspicious-looking group, those boys. Grubby ten- and eleven-year-olds dressed in mismatched uniforms, they were almost all minority kids from a mixture of backgrounds, united, I suspect, only by their poverty. But they were noisy and cheerful in the way of all children, and they greeted Sheila's father like a returning champion when he ran out onto the baseball diamond.

From all I could gather, Mr. Renstad appeared to be doing well. He was enormously proud of the small duplex where they lived. It wasn't large; it wasn't in a particularly good part of town, and he didn't own it, of course; but he had *chosen* it himself, rather than have it foisted upon him by Social Services. Moreover, he was paying the rent himself out of the steady salary he now earned as a laborer for the parks department. He had taken me right through the duplex, showing me each and every thing he had managed to buy—the beds, the sofa, the television, the kitchen table. *He* certainly remembered the circumstances in which we had last met, and he was enthusiastic to show me how far he had come in the interim. These things were his and I could tell acquiring them meant a lot to him.

His real love, however, was the baseball team— "his boys." Again and again, he told me how it was they who had made him go straight for good. They depended on him, he said. The team had nearly been disbanded for lack of a coach until he took over. More to the point, he admitted, he would lose them if he messed with drugs again. He was still under the watchful eye of the parole officer.

I enjoyed that baseball game. They didn't win, but they played well and it was apparent that winning wasn't so important to them. They *were* a team, in the true sense of the word, and I identified immediately with that. Whatever his past, Mr. Renstad's present was going well.

I'd made plans to take Sheila out after the game. On the other two occasions I'd come to her house, so I thought it would be pleasant to go somewhere with her. Sheila, however, was unable to decide where she wanted to go.

I suggested we go for a pizza. I thought I might take her up to the city, partly to give her a change of scenery, and partly because there were nicer places to eat up there. So after the game, we got into the car and headed north.

Somewhere within the first five miles, I took a wrong turn. As I was still learning my way around this new area, this wasn't unusual; however, I didn't realize I'd done it until the thinning houses made me suspicious that I was not going toward the city. Normally I have an excellent sense of direction, and while I do take wrong turns, even then I can usually discern if I'm going in the right general direction. On this occasion, I managed to get myself completely turned around, because while I still felt that I was going toward the city, evidence outside my window said otherwise. I voiced my concern to Sheila.

"No, you're all right. I know exactly where you're at. Just keep driving this way," she said confidently. So I did.

Another fifteen minutes and I hit open country. I knew I was irredeemably lost and knew I wasn't going to right myself without taking drastic action, probably in the form of stopping and digging out the road map. I pulled the car over into a gateway to a field.

"What are you doing?" Sheila asked in surprise.

Reaching my arm over the backseat, I groped for my road atlas.

"Looking for the map. I'm lost."

"No, you're not."

"We're lost."

"No, we're not. I've been out here millions of times."

I raised an eyebrow.

"Yeah, I have," she said. "I used to be in a children's home near here. Just down that road over there. I know exactly where we are."

"So, where are we then?" I asked.

"Well, here, of course."

"But *where's* here?"

Sheila looked out the window.

"Tell me. Where are we?"

"Don't get so bitchy."

"You don't know either, do you?" I said. "We are lost."

Unexpectedly, Sheila smiled. It was a beguiling smile. "I'm always lost," she said cheerfully. "I've gotten used to it."

I tugged the atlas over into the front seat and opened it. Locating us on the map, I discovered where I had turned wrong and figured out what I would need to do when eventually we headed back to Broadview. "Okay. I'm happy now," I said, closing the book. I started the engine.

"You're really a control freak, aren't you?" Sheila said. "I never realized that about you before."

"Not really. It's just I feel uncomfortable when I'm disoriented."

"Ah, not only a control freak, a defensive control freak."

If she wanted to go in this direction, I thought, well and good, we'd go. So we took off down a minor highway in a direction I'd never been before.

The better part of an hour raced past, along with the scenery.

It was a pleasant drive. Sheila talked, launching into a most amazing conversation about Julius Caesar. She had read his account of the Gallic wars in Latin class and this caught her fancy, particularly his descriptions of the native Celts in Gaul. I had done Caesar myself when I had taken Latin in high school, but in those days I had been more interested to see if I could get good grades without having to read the assignments, rather than find out what the books actually said. Consequently, I had emerged from school clever but culturally illiterate and had spent most of my adult life catching up. I hadn't managed to work myself around to Caesar yet in Latin or English, so for most of the conversation I just listened, which was probably no bad thing.

Passing through a small town, Sheila spotted a bowling alley. "Oh, look, there! Could we stop and play a game? I love bowling."

So we went in and had three games. Afterward, I bought us Cokes in the bar. "What about pizza?" Sheila asked. "You said we could get pizza."

"I'm thinking we might be better going back toward Broadview. We're quite a ways out and it's going to take a good hour and a half to get back. I'd probably find my way back better if it weren't pitch dark."

"God, Torey, do you get lost a lot or something? You are really hung up on it."

"I'm driving, that's why."

"So, relax. We're okay. And let's eat around here. It's late and I'm starving."

"I haven't seen a pizza place," I replied.

"Well, let's just keep driving."

I was hungry too and finding myself in a not particularly good mood. The day wasn't working out quite as I had planned. We had wandered from one thing to another, with none of it being very special. I became aware of wanting to impress Sheila. I wanted to win her over.

"There! There!" Sheila called out, interrupting my thoughts. "There's a pizza place."

Sure enough, there was. And like the rest of the day, it was nothing special. I thought of the old days and how my boyfriend Chad and I had taken Sheila out for her very first pizza after the hearing that had kept Sheila out of the state hospital. The place we went into now had none of the jazz-piano atmosphere of that pizzeria; this was just a branch of one of the faceless pizza chains found everywhere.

Too hungry to care, I stopped there and we went in. Placing our order at the counter, we then located a quiet table in the corner. Sheila pulled off her baseball cap, letting her long, crinkled orange hair spill down over her shoulders, and she sat down.

"I thought you might like to see some pictures from our class," I said, opening my handbag, "so I dug some out."

"Like, cool. Let's see."

"They're from that picnic we had on the last day. We went over to the park. Do you remember

89

that park? It had that duck pond and the little stream."

Taking the photographs from me, Sheila bent over them, studying the faces. "Who's this kid?"

"Emilio."

"What's wrong with him? Is he handicapped?"

"He's blind," I said.

"Oh, yeah, the blind one. What did you call him in the book?"

"Guillermo."

"Oh, yeah, I know who you're talking about now."

Tongue protruding slightly between her lips, Sheila remained intent on the photos. "I think I remember that park," she said slowly. "Did it have trees that bloomed or something? They had a really sweet scent? Because I seem to remember that."

"Yes. The locust trees."

"Who are these girls?" she asked, handing over one of the pictures.

"Don't you recognize her? In the middle? That's you. That's Sarah and that's Tyler, but that there is you."

"*Really*? God, is that me? Shit." She craned forward to study it more closely in the dim light. "*Shit*. Did I really look like that?" She looked up in amazement. "My dad doesn't have any pictures of me when I was little ..."

My heart sank. She didn't even remember herself. Watching her as she bent back over the photos, I felt so lonely. What was I doing here with this punky-looking adolescent? This wasn't Sheila.

This was just some kid.

The pizza came just in time. We had ordered a huge one, loaded with everything save the proverbial kitchen sink, and we both tucked in enthusiastically. For several moments our attention was focused on the food.

"I've had so much fun today," Sheila said as she maneuvered most of a full slice of pizza into her mouth. "You know, I think it's brilliant that you live so close by now."

"Good, I'm glad."

"It's just like the old times, isn't it?"

"Yeah," I said, probably not too convincingly.

Sheila's expression grew rather sheepish. "I'm sorry I don't remember more about when I was in your class."

"Well, you were little."

"Yeah, but I can tell I'm, like, a real disappointment to you."

"Of course not!" I said a little too heartily. "You were *very* young when we were last together and nobody remembers much from that age."

"But you want me to, don't you?"

"Yes, if I'm honest, I suppose I do, but just because it was a meaningful year for me and it was you who made it meaningful."

This disarmed her. She smiled. "Really?"

"Yes, really."

"You liked working with little kids, didn't you?" she said.

I nodded. "I still do."

"It showed."

Silence came then and we went back to our food. Then Sheila looked up.

"Can I ask you something, Tor? It's from the book."

"All right."

"How come you didn't marry that guy Chad?" she asked.

"I was too young. I wasn't ready," I said. "If I had, it wouldn't have worked out."

Pensive over her pizza, Sheila picked at it, ferreting out the olives and eating them with her fingers. "Too bad," she said. "It would have made for a brilliant ending to your book."

"Probably, but this was real life."

"Real life never follows the script, that's the problem," she replied. "You and him getting married and adopting the little girl. That's how every single person who reads it is going to want it to come out."

"Yes, I know, but it isn't how it did come out."

"Yeah, I know." She smiled faintly. "But you know, his eldest daughter? The one called Sheila? Well, that's right. She should be called Sheila, but by rights, she should have been me."

Chapter 11

The summer program at the clinic had been my idea. I had always felt there was a better chance of effecting change when I was with a child several hours a day, day in, day out, rather than in just one or two hourly sessions, which was one of my original reasons for choosing teaching over psychology as a career. This was borne out to me at the clinic, which was the first place I'd worked that stuck so strictly to the fifty-minute "psychiatric hour." I felt there must be some other way.

My office partner, Jeff, was intrigued with the idea of working with children in a different setting from the therapy room; so together we developed the idea of a morning summer-school program to run for eight weeks in June and July. We made plans to use a nearby school that was normally vacant over the summer, and from the clinic client list, we began to handpick the children we felt would benefit most. Because of the experimental nature, we decided to keep the number modest. It was just Jeff and I supervising, and I thought it was best to start out with something I knew we could keep in control. Thus, we settled on having eight.

In the group, three of the children were severely handicapped. Joshua, five, and Jessie, six, were both autistic and couldn't speak, and Violet, eight, was labeled a childhood schizophrenic. Of the five remaining, there were two girls, Kayleigh, a five-year-old who persistently refused to speak in group settings, and Tamara, eight, a startlingly beautiful girl with dark, exotic features, who suffered from depression and bouts of self-mutilation. Of the three boys, there was David, a bright, beguiling six-year-old arsonist, Alejo, a seven-year-old Colombian boy who had been adopted at four by American parents, and a six-year-old tornado named Mikey.

Experience had long since taught me that the higher the adult-to-child ratio, the more effective a program generally is. I didn't want a one-to-one situation, as I felt this would destroy the benefits of the group, but I felt we needed enough adults in charge to minimize the chance of any given situation degenerating into total chaos.

Jeff took umbrage at the idea that we couldn't handle eight children between us. He pointed out that he was, after all, a fully qualified doctor, ready to sit for his final board exams in child psychiatry, and well on his way to certification as a

psychoanalyst. I pointed out in turn that this setting required rather different skills. Over the
course of the three hours each day that the children were with us, they would need not only therapy, but entertainment, exercise, refereeing and
nurturing, to say nothing of Band-Aids, drinks,
snacks and taking to the toilet. This was more
than two adults could sanely do, if we wanted to
accomplish something more than baby-sitting.

Thus, together we approached Dr. Rosenthal to
fund us more staff for the project. He agreed to do
the best he could. As a result, we gained Miriam, a
former teacher. She was an older woman, lively
and decisive, with silvery hair and an enviable
figure. I liked her instantly. She had a sensible,
down-to-earth approach, but with that touch of
class I admired but didn't possess myself. Yet, even
with Miriam added to our staff, I was still eager for
more help. With such young, handicapped children, we didn't need many expensive, highly
trained professionals. We just needed *hands*, real
hands, plain and simple.

I was editing *One Child* during the period when
Jeff and I were setting up the summer-school program, and the contrast of reading about my situation with Sheila's class in comparison to the luxury
I was currently working in struck me dramatically.
There were eight children then, every bit as severely
handicapped, and what did we have but a young,
fairly inexperienced teacher, an ex-migrant worker
without a high school diploma and a junior high
student. Junior high student. *Junior high student*!

Sheila! Of course.

This seemed an ideal solution. Old enough to be responsible, yet young enough to be flexible and cooperative, Sheila was at an age to be very useful in a setting like this. In return, it would give her the chance to spend the summer in a structured, stimulating environment with supportive adults. Best of all, it would allow the two of us to spend time together in a natural way. I wanted to get to know Sheila again. The child I had loved so much had to be somewhere in that gangly adolescent. I wanted the chance to seek her out.

Sheila was delighted with this proposition. She had had no work lined up for the summer and even when I explained that the pay would be very small indeed, covering not much more than her bus fare and lunch, she remained enthusiastic.

Jeff didn't have a chance to meet Sheila before the first day of the summer program. We had discussed the need for an extra pair of hands and he had been pleased that I could come up with a volunteer so easily. I gave him a brief summary of Sheila's background and my previous relationship with her, but I didn't go into great detail, as it seemed inappropriate. If anything had become obvious to me over the previous weeks, it was that Sheila had moved on from her former self; and just as I would not have expected an employer to take into account what I had done when I was six, I didn't feel it was necessary to discuss her background.

Privately, I was looking forward to introducing Sheila to Jeff. In the summer-school program,

Sheila'd find herself surrounded by adults who were all intellectually formidable, but among us only Jeff was probably Sheila's equal. I doubted she had previously encountered another person of her ability, and as a consequence, I was keen to acquaint them. Both showed similar personalities, given to quirky, somewhat unpredictable behavior, and both emanated that aura of isolation so common to highly gifted individuals. I was tickled to think of the possibilities in bringing them together.

On the first day, Sheila arrived forty-five minutes early. What she was wearing looked—honest to God—like thin white long johns. Over this she had layered a pale-colored, flower-sprigged shift. To complete the outfit, she'd laced on heavy, black work boots more befitting of a lumberjack. And, of course, on her head was the ever-present Cubs baseball hat.

I gaped. I'm embarrassed to admit it, I, who has cultivated the ability to disregard the most bizarre of behaviors, but my mouth dropped right open.

"Like it?" she asked ingenuously.

God, was I getting old? Was this what teenagers were wearing now and I hadn't noticed? I was dressed in a pair of Levi's and a work shirt and thought *I* was being avant-garde at the clinic. "Well," I sputtered, "it's unique."

"My dad doesn't let me wear things I like."

"Where did you get it?" I asked.

"Different places. I got this dress at a rummage sale and I got these down at the Goodwill place," she said, indicating the longjohn things. "They didn't cost me much. My boots cost me the most."

I found myself startled. The ghost of that six-year-old in her ratty brown T-shirt and outgrown overalls still haunted me. I had been unprepared for this adolescent fashion plate.

"You don't mind, do you?" she asked and I realized that for her to ask, she must have read my surprise.

I shook my head. "No, I don't mind." And I suppose I didn't, really. The fact was, she looked surprisingly good in her long johns and little flowered dress. Weird, yes, but still attractive, if one suspended personal taste and just looked at her. And confident. That's what really struck me. For the moment, anyway, Sheila was clearly very pleased with who she was.

Jeff arrived shortly afterward. He was carrying a huge box of Pampers. "Yo, catch, Hayden!" he shouted and lofted the box at me. Sheila leaped back in surprise as I lunged to catch it. I set it on the ground.

"What are those for?" she asked.

"Help, help! Let me out!" came a little voice from the direction of the box.

Sheila looked alarmed and I thumped Jeff's arm. "This is Dr. Tomlinson's sense of humor."

"Jeff to you, sweetheart," he said and chucked Sheila under the chin. "Like your outfit."

Sheila recoiled from his touch.

I grabbed the box of Pampers and took them into the book closet alongside the room. Sheila followed.

"Is that your office partner you're always talking about? That's Jeff?"

I nodded and pushed the box up onto a shelf.

"Yuck."

"Oh, he's all right. Got a weird sense of humor, but he's good fun. You'll like him."

"Don't count on it." She leaned back against the wall. "How come you've got those diapers?"

"Because one little boy isn't toilet trained yet," I replied.

"You're kidding. You mean he shits in his pants?" she asked.

I smiled.

"Oh, gross. You didn't tell me this. I'm not going to have to change him, am I?"

"We'll see."

"We *won't* see," she replied. "We shall close our eyes!"

I laughed.

The first child to arrive was Violet. She was a large girl for her age, although not really fat, with pallid skin and pale, crumpled hair. Her clinical diagnosis was childhood schizophrenia, manifested by an obsessional interest in ghosts and vampires. She believed all the people around her were either vampires or the victims of vampires, hence, ghosts, and she had much trouble with invisible ghosts talking to her, teasing her and telling her awful things.

"Shhh," she said to me, as her mother brought her in. "I saw him in the hallway, the one with the rainbow-colored hair. He had his ghost cat with him."

"Sheila, could you show Violet where to sit down?" I asked.

"Not going with her!" Violet shrieked. "She's got fangs!"

Eyes wide, Sheila looked over at me.

"Here, I'll take her," said Jeff. She was his client and when she saw a face she recognized, Violet relaxed visibly.

Just then, in whooshed Mikey. Mikey was six, short and stout, and capable of moving at light-speed. This gave him the appearance more of a ball than a boy, rather like the sort used in pinball. Zip! Bang! Whoosh! He careered around the classroom, leaving all of us stunned in his wake. His mother looked only too relieved to be rid of him for the morning.

Next came Kayleigh, my elective mute. In contrast to Violet, Kayleigh was tiny for her age, her small features overpowered by long, thick bangs and a heavy mass of hair. It was in the back of my mind that Kayleigh might be a good child for Sheila to work with individually, as Sheila herself had been electively mute when she had come into my class at six. Moreover, Kayleigh had a sweet, loving nature, which made her easy to like and pleasant to work with. I was keen for Sheila to enjoy the challenge of being with us and longed for her to understand my own attachment to such children; so Kayleigh seemed an ideal choice.

"Sheila, do you suppose you could take Kayleigh over to the table and show her some of our toys?"

Sheila just stared at the girl.

"Kayleigh loves putting puzzles together. Perhaps you could help her do one while we're waiting for the rest of the children to arrive."

Uncertainly, Sheila held out her hand. Kayleigh responded with a delighted smile.

Joshua and David arrived together in a car pool driven by Joshua's father. Of all of our children, Joshua was the most severely handicapped. It was he we had the diapers for. Diagnosed at eighteen months as autistic, Joshua neither spoke nor engaged people in any other way.

David was Joshua's opposite number. Smily and gregarious, he could worm his way into the coldest heart. And he was such a lady-killer with his big blue eyes and curly blond hair. In truth, I think he was one of the most appealing-looking children I had come across. He was also one of the most disturbed.

Alejo came next. He was a new child at the clinic, having started only at the beginning of April, and he was seeing Dr. Freeman, so I didn't know him personally. His parents, a wealthy professional couple who had been childless through sixteen years of marriage, had decided to adopt a Third World orphan when it finally became apparent to them that they would not bear a child of their own. On a trip to Colombia, they found Alejo, then age four, in an orphanage run by a group of nuns. Adopted and brought to the United States, he had now been with his current family for almost three years, but he had never really settled into his new suburban surroundings. He was restless and aggressive and, although he had learned English, he spoke only rarely, preferring his fists to do his talking. His school performance had been uniformly poor and there was now a question of whether his deprived early life had caused permanent brain damage. Alejo himself was a small, rather unattractive boy with thick black-rimmed glasses. He had the flat features of the native South American Indians and a thatch of unruly dark hair that fell forward into his face. He appeared shy in the midst of so many strangers and clung tightly to his father's hand until Jeff came and knelt down beside him.

Behind Alejo came Jessie. A small black girl with her hair meticulously corn-rowed, she, like Joshua, was autistic. She was not as severely afflicted as Joshua and could talk after a fashion. Recognizing this as a school, she ran past us all to the table, sat down in one of the chairs and began drumming loudly with her hands while shouting out the alphabet song.

Last to arrive was Tamara. Of Mediterranean lineage, with long black hair and huge, soulful dark eyes, she reminded me rather uncannily of the opera singer Maria Callas, which gave me trouble the entire eight weeks in keeping her name straight. Now eight, Tamara had been coming to the clinic for over two years, ever since her parents had first noticed the myriad of small cuts along her arms. Despite intensive therapy, Tamara continued her obsession with self-mutilation. Consequently, she arrived that warm summer's morning wearing a long-sleeved T-shirt and jogging-suit bottoms to cover the myriad of sores and scabs on her arms and legs and to discourage her attempts to create more.

So we started. Like all first days, it was a bit chaotic; however, we had planned well to provide an engaging but low-key morning. Thus, there were no disasters.

Sheila befriended Kayleigh, or perhaps it was Kayleigh who befriended her. Whichever, Sheila spent most of the morning with the little girl, helping her with her activities, taking her to the toilet, finding good cookies for her at snack time. As part of my ongoing therapy with Kayleigh, I had insisted she speak to Sheila from the onset, which she did with only a little urging.

This is right, I thought, watching the two of them together at one of the tables, their heads bent over what they were doing. Sheila was talking to her, pausing occasionally to glance over at the child. Seven years earlier, she had been that small girl. There was something deeply rewarding in seeing her come full circle.

Indeed, as I stood there surveying the group, I became aware of how very happy I felt at that particular moment. The morning was going well; the program was off to a good start. The children were challenging but engaging. Jeff was my absolute favorite colleague to work with in the whole world. When we were getting fired up, the two of us could operate as one mind in two bodies, challenging, growing, building upon one another's ideas so easily that everything felt possible to me. Miriam, whom I had not known previously, was full of energetic initiative and had a far better sense of organization than either Jeff or I. Consequently, all the small things, like finding the paper cups at break time, happened as they should. Best of all, there was Sheila, back in the classroom with me and it was the first day, with all the future stretching ahead of us. I regarded her. It *was* Sheila there. For the first time since we had been reunited, I felt certain of that.

Chapter 12

After the morning ended and all the children had gone home, the four of us went out to lunch. Miriam, who lived locally, suggested a whole-food restaurant down by the lake and so we found ourselves on benches gathered around a wooden plank table in the cool interior of the restaurant.

We discussed the morning's events, evaluating how the various activities had gone and making plans to adjust them as necessary. Sheila didn't say much, even when we went over our observations of Kayleigh in the group. She appeared absorbed in a tradescantia hanging in the window beside our table, its long branches stretching down to a point where she could fiddle with them.

After lunch, I offered to drive her the five miles down to Fenton Boulevard, where she could catch a direct bus back to Broadview.

"So, what did you think?" I asked, once we were alone in the car together.

Sheila was silent for several moments. "I don't like your partner very much. What's all this crap about regression motivating neuroses and stuff?"

"Jeff's a Freudian. You've got to excuse him that."

"It's crap. Why doesn't he just talk English?" Sheila asked.

"Freud's ideas have had very wide-ranging applications. While a lot of people don't agree with all of them anymore, they've still done a great deal to help us understand how minds might work. And people like Jeff, who have really studied the theories, seem to make good progress using them."

Sheila raised her lip in an expression of disgust.

We went a few moments in silence before I looked over again. "So, Jeff excepted, what did you think? Did you like it? Did you enjoy working with Kayleigh?"

"Yeah, pretty much. Why doesn't she talk?" she asked, her head turned away from me to watch out the window. "And not Jeff's kind of explanation. Not 'cause she's got an anal fixation or something."

"I don't know why."

"I told her that when I was her age, I didn't talk either," Sheila said.

"Did Kayleigh respond to that?" I asked.

"Dunno. She just kept coloring." There was a pause. "I wanted to ask you about that other kid. The kid with the Spanish name."

"Alejo?"

"Yeah. What's wrong with him?"

"He's very difficult at school. He fights with the other kids all the time, quite a vicious little boy, and he does very poorly at his work. We're trying to determine at the clinic whether this is as a result of psychological problems or a mental handicap."

"Jeff said he's adopted."

"Yes. He's from Colombia."

"Where are his real parents?" Sheila asked.

"I don't know. I don't think anybody knows. He was abandoned. The report I read said that someone had found him living in a garbage can and had then taken him to these nuns who ran the orphanage."

Forehead puckered, Sheila looked over. "Really?"

"Apparently there are a lot of street kids in some of these South American cities. It's a serious problem in some places."

"His folks abandoned him in a garbage can?"

"Maybe he was just sheltering in one. I don't know. The report's pretty scant and probably about fifth-hand."

Sheila was pensive a long moment, before turning back. "Did I hear you guys saying that the parents he's got now were going to send him back to where he came from?"

"I don't know. There's some talk of it. They're an older couple, both professionals, not very used to accommodating children, and he's been quite a handful."

"Can they really do that?" Sheila asked. "Just send him back to Colombia, like he was damaged goods or something?"

"I guess."

Then came silence. Plagued by red lights and roadwork, I wasn't making very speedy progress toward Fenton Boulevard. Sheila leaned her head against the window and gazed out. She looked tired. Had it been the rigors of the morning? Or had she come tired? The thought suddenly struck me that I was taking the stability of Sheila's home life for granted. Sneaking a look, I studied her. God, that orange hair!

"I think ... well, I guess I can see now what got you attracted to this kind of work," she said, her voice quiet and rather distant-sounding. "'Cause you hear about these things happening to people, and they are so unfair that they make you feel you just got to do something. That's my reaction, anyway." She paused. "Well, that's one reaction."

"What's the other?" I asked.

"I just want to put my hands over my eyes and my fingers in my ears and stop it from getting in. I mean, I already know the world's bad. I'm not sure I can stand knowing it's really worse."

Our first "incident" happened the next morning. The school was across the street from a small park. It wasn't an elaborate place, but there were swings and a large wooden structure built for climbing and plenty of room for running around. What made it particularly hospitable on a hot summer's morning were the trees. There were a dozen or more, with enormous trunks and long, overhanging branches. Some particularly forward-thinking person in the parks department had had attractive wooden seating built around three of the trees nearest the play equipment.

We decided to take our juice and cookies outside and let the children play on the swings and climbing frame during their break time. David and Mikey thought this was wonderful and went tearing off at such a rate that Jeff had to run after them and catch them before they went into the street.

Although I had agreed happily when Jeff had suggested that we take the children over to the park at break time, I realized the moment David and Mikey ran off that it was a mistake. We were all too new to each other. But by that time, we were already underway.

Right from the beginning, it was small-scale chaos of the sort that kids adore and grown-ups abhor. Joshua went into a self-stimulated frenzy on the swings. Jessie just stood on the grass, arms out, and spun dizzyingly around and around. David, Mikey and Alejo immediately fell into playing some dreadfully noisy war game that required an enormous amount of tearing around and much shouted large-artillery fire. Violet appeared to get rather turned on by this. I couldn't tell if she simply wanted to join in and did not have the appropriate social skills to get the boys to include her, or whether she found it all genuinely sexually stimulating.

Whichever, she began to indulge in open masturbation, while shouting out cheers and gunfire noises to the boys as they tore by.

Needless to say, our break time was quickly turned into a rowdy, deafening affair. Only Kayleigh and Tamara did not join in. Clinging to Miriam's hand, Kayleigh watched the other children apprehensively. Tamara, on the other hand, didn't seem particularly frightened by the mayhem, but she withdrew away from all of us. Taking her paper cup of juice and her cookies, she went off into a cubby-hole formed by tires on the underside of the climbing structure.

After fifteen minutes, Jeff and I went to herd everyone back together, while Miriam sat down on one of the benches and tried to keep hold of those we had captured. Sheila proved fairly hopeless. Whether it was the noise or the sudden hyperactivity around her, I don't know, but she simply froze in the midst of it all and the more I shouted at her to go get one child or another, the more solidly she seemed to be rooted to her spot.

One by one, we rounded them up, until we only had David, Mikey and Tamara left. I was chasing David down when I heard Jeff cry out. "Oh, my God!"

We all stopped then and looked over. He was extracting Tamara from her tires and as she stood up, I saw she was covered in blood. While the rest of us had been absorbed elsewhere, Tamara had taken the opportunity her privacy afforded her to gouge long lines into the skin along her jaw with a small, sharp stick she had picked up from the mulch put down to cushion falls from the climbing frame. They were not particularly deep cuts, but they bled dramatically.

Then, abruptly, from the group of children with Miriam, frantic screaming started up. Instinct told me it was Violet and I spun around, but it wasn't. It was Alejo. Seeing Tamara's blood, he put a hand to either side of his face and screamed and screamed. I ran toward him, but this seemed to make matters worse. Shrieking incoherently, he fled across the grass until he came to one of the other trees and then, like a little monkey, he swarmed right up it and into the branches.

We all stood there, stunned. Even Tamara, Jeff's handkerchief pressed to her face, gazed up in amazement. Alejo kept climbing until he must have been the better part of fifty feet in the air.

"Oh, Jesus," Jeff muttered. "What now?"

I glanced around us and then back up in the tree. "Alejo? Are you all right?"

He wasn't screaming any longer, wasn't doing anything other than standing on a branch and looking down at us.

"It's okay. Everything's fine here. Nothing wrong with Tamara. She just scratched herself. But it's nothing serious. Why don't you come on down now?" I called.

"Alejo?" Jeff said. "It's time to come down."

He didn't budge.

"You reckon I can climb up?" I asked Jeff.

"Don't be stupid, Hayden."

Miriam was beside us now. She was holding Kayleigh in her arms. "How about the fire department? Do they do these kinds of things?"

I looked around at the others just in time to see Joshua strolling out into the road. "Oh, cripes. Josh? Come here, Josh." I ran after him. Snagging him by the T-shirt, I hauled him back into the group. It was then I noticed Sheila sitting on the ground. She was unlacing her work boots.

"I can get him," she said, and before any of us had a chance to protest, Sheila had leaped into the branches and was pulling herself up.

"Oh, God," Jeff cried, "*two* of them up there. Why did you let her do that, Hayden?"

"Well, at least we've got a doctor on the premises."

Then silence, as we all watched.

"We're gonna get sued out of our lives ..." I heard Jeff mutter under his breath.

Sheila climbed the tree with no difficulty, shimmying up through the branches as easily as Alejo had done until she reached the one just beneath him. I heard her talking to him, but I couldn't discern what she was saying.

Minutes went by. All the while I was racking my brains for the best solution, as no doubt Jeff was doing as well. Should we call the fire department? The police? Dr. Rosenthal? Alejo's parents? Or could we risk just waiting him out? What about the other children? It was only ten forty-five and the program ran for another hour and forty-five minutes. Should Miriam and I take the rest back in and try to pretend everything was normal?

Then, just as I was about to suggest phoning for help, I saw Sheila begin to descend, and within a few moments, Alejo started down behind her. Jeff, Miriam and I all sighed a collective sigh of relief.

"Hey, you're a hero," Jeff said to Sheila as we all finally started back to the school. He reached an arm out and slipped it over her shoulder. "You really did great there. I bet you're proud of yourself."

Nodding, Sheila ducked to free herself of his touch.

"I hope you *are* proud of yourself," I said to Sheila as I drove her down to Fenton Boulevard after lunch. "What you did was very brave."

She shrugged. "Yeah, I guess." She put her hands behind her neck and lifted her hair up off her shoulders. "I didn't think about it."

"What did you talk about when you were up there? How did you convince him to come down?" I asked.

"I spoke Spanish to him. I didn't say anything special, just, like, I knew he was scared and I would help him come down, but I spoke in Spanish."

I raised an eyebrow. "I didn't realize you spoke Spanish."

"You don't know everything about me."

"No."

"I mean, like, you have been gone a few years, Torey."

"Yes, you're right."

There was a few moments' silence, while Sheila, her face turned away from me, watched out the window. Then she added, "All those years in the migrant camp and not learn to speak Spanish? Shit, I would never have had anybody to talk to."

I didn't answer. There was a sparky undercurrent to Sheila that showed itself more often than I was comfortable with. Much as she seemed to want to be with me, she also seemed easily irritated with me. Probably just adolescence. I wasn't particularly gifted with adolescents, so that didn't help any either. Whatever, I found it mildly upsetting.

Sheila seemed to sense this and came back with a conciliatory tone. "I thought talking in Spanish might make him feel better. Like, more secure. It was just an idea."

"It was a good one. And did he understand you?"

"I *am* fluent," she retorted.

"No, I mean, it will have been a long time since Alejo heard anyone speak Spanish to him, and even then it may have been a dialect."

"Yeah, he understood me. He came down, didn't he?"

Silence. I was approaching a major interstate junction on the freeway. There was the omnipresent roadwork and quite a lot of congestion, so for several minutes I concentrated on my driving. Once the traffic eased and I could relax, I listened into the silence.

"You know, Sheila, I get this sort of ongoing feeling that you're angry with me," I said.

"*Me?*" she replied with disbelief.

"If there are things or people I like, you seem to go out of your way to show you dislike them. If I say something, you seem to make a point of proving me wrong. And there's just this general tone of voice."

"Shit, you're just listening to, like, every little thing I say, aren't you?" she retorted. "And *judging* it."

"I'm not trying to."

"Well, you know, I don't think you're so great either," she said. "In that book you wrote, you come off sounding so patient with everything and you're not, you know."

I looked over. "What do you mean?"

"You get angry with everything. Like, you swear at all these drivers."

"I'm not *swearing.*"

"You might as well be," Sheila said. "It's like 'Come *on*, lady!' 'Hurry up and get out there, mister,' every second sentence, Torey. And, like, you got mad at me when I tried to get in the car and had hold of the door handle so you couldn't unlock it."

"I didn't get mad at you."

"You did! You said, 'Let it *go*' in a really bitchy tone of voice. Not like you talk in your book at all. In there, you're so patient and kind. You wait forever in your book and never say a cross word, but now I can see how you really are and you get mad every other second."

"Not every other second, I'm sure."

"Seems like it to me," she replied.

"I'm human, Sheila. I get irritated sometimes. And irritable."

"That's not like you are in *One Child*."

"No, maybe not. That's a character in a book. People are too complex to be portrayed in their entirety on paper. And, in some parts, too boring."

Sheila snorted. "So you're saying it's *not* you."

"That character is the essence of me, but it isn't me, no. I'm me. Here. Now."

Sheila snorted again. "Hot shit."

Chapter 13

From dropping Sheila off at the bus station on Fenton Boulevard, I returned to the clinic. The conversation in the car had upset me, confirming as it did what intuition had already told me. She was angry with me. Why? Because I was annoyingly human, when she had expected the character from a book? I couldn't imagine that would provoke the strength of feeling I was sensing from her.

On the wall above my desk in the office, I'd hung the poem she had written me when she was twelve. Sitting down in my chair, I looked up at it.

... Then you came
With your funny way of being
Not quite human ...

Whatever she wanted from me, it was different from what she was getting.

Jeff opened the door and entered our small shared office. He was returning from a therapy session and had obviously had a close encounter with his client, because his hair was mussed and there was blue tempera paint on one cheek.

"You look like I feel," I said.

He set his notepad down on his desk. "I am never going into infant psychiatry, I can tell you that," he muttered none too good-naturedly. "Rosenthal can have that field entirely to himself. I am restricting myself to those who do not need finger paints."

"I don't think I'm going to go in for adolescents," I replied.

Jeff raised an eyebrow. "Who's getting to you? Your little orangutan?"

I nodded and told him about the conversation in the car.

Although I had filled Jeff in about Sheila's past in general terms, such as the fact that she had been a student of mine, I had never gone into any great detail, including never having told him she was the subject of my book. Book publication being the lengthy process it is, *One Child* was not due for release for several more months; and being a little leery of how my venture into popular nonfiction would be received in professional circles, I had never talked much about it to any of my colleagues. Now I found myself not only explaining Sheila's darker past but also our complex relationship.

"Hoo," Jeff said when I paused. "You do land yourself in some tortured situations, Hayden."

"So, what are your thoughts?" I asked. "What have I done wrong with this girl? I've stirred something up unintentionally."

He smiled gently. "You know what I think the real problem is here? You and Sheila both have a dose of the same disease. All she remembers is this wonderful teacher who never got mad at her and now she's upset to discover just how ordinary and human you are; but, you know, Hayden, you're doing the very same thing. What's coloring your behavior toward her now is the fact that what you remember, too, is not Sheila as a real child, but rather the six-year-old character in a book."

"I do *not*."

"We all do," Jeff replied. "That's all memory is, our interpretation of what we've experienced. The only difference here is that most of us never get the book written."

"How much do you remember about your mother?" I asked Sheila the next afternoon, as I was driving her to the bus station.

"What do you mean?"

"Just what I asked. How much do you remember about her?"

Sheila didn't answer. Turning her head away, she looked out the window.

I listened into the silence, trying to discern what her emotions were. It had been a fairly good morning. After the drama of the previous day, everyone seemed content to keep things quiet. Jeff, Miriam and I were beginning to get a feel for each other's working style and weren't tripping over one another quite so often. Sheila still remained an outsider among us. She did not initiate much, either with the kids or with the three of us adults, and she didn't participate easily, preferring, instead, to hover on the perimeters. This was all right, to my mind, as this wasn't a field she was particularly familiar with and these were still early days. All in all, the day had gone quite well for everyone and we had gone off to lunch in high spirits, Sheila included.

"Have you ever seen your mother again? I mean, since leaving my class?" I asked.

Sheila shook her head.

"Do you know where she is?"

"No," she replied, her voice quiet.

Silence.

"Do you remember her?"

Again, Sheila did not answer me. Seconds rolled by and became minutes.

I glanced over.

"No," she said quietly. "I don't."

"Do you remember Jimmie?"

"Jimmie ...? You mean my brother?" A pensive silence. "I think I do. Maybe. I got this image in my mind ... of someone with brown hair. It's a memory, you know, from long ago and when I try to place it ... I think perhaps it's Jimmie." She looked over. "Why? Why do you ask?"

"Just wondering. Do you miss your mother?"

Sheila's eyebrows rose in surprise. "What's there to miss? I don't know her. I don't even remember her. How could I miss her?"

"Just wondering," I replied.

"You wonder a lot."

We had hit the roadwork section again and traffic had come to a standstill. Self-conscious of what Sheila had said the previous day regarding my attitude toward other drivers, I sat in silence.

"There's no reason I should miss my mother," Sheila said quietly. "She was a lousy parent. It's my dad who's done everything for me."

"Well, I was just wondering. It was a big issue for you when we were together last time."

"I was still a little child then. I suppose it mattered more to me when I was six."

The next morning, we broke the children down into three small groups. The idea had been initially to let one person be in charge of Jessie and Joshua, who needed the most individual attention, and then to split the other six by age, so that one of us would have Kayleigh, David and Mikey, who were younger, and the other would have Alejo, Tamara and Violet, the older three. However, after Alejo's extreme reaction to Tamara's behavior, it seemed unwise to put the two of them together just yet; so we substituted David for her.

I had this group of David, Alejo and Violet and I had decided on doing what I liked to call "guided drawing," the making of pictures after a short period of visualization. I found this a useful technique for bringing out children's emotions and it worked well with a small group. So we all sat down at one of the tables. I gave out large sheets of white paper and set in the middle of the table a variety of materials to choose from—thin felt tips, fat felt tips, crayons, colored pencils and plain pencils and pastel chalks.

Sheila came and sat down with us. I had hoped she would help Miriam, who had Joshua and Jessie, as they needed virtually one-to-one attention, but she seemed uncomfortable with these children. Feeling it was better to let her warm up at her own speed, I said nothing and let her take out the chair at the end of the table.

"All right," I said and looked with enthusiastic anticipation at each of the three children sitting across from me, "know what we're going to do today? We're going for a ride in space."

"Hey, cool!" David said.

"No, put your pen down, David. We don't need pens yet. Instead, I want everybody to close their eyes. Closed? Alejo? Close your eyes. That's right." I closed my own eyes to encourage the others. "Now, here we go: Keep your eyes closed so that you can see the rocket ship. Can you see it? Make a picture of it in your mind. This is *your* rocket ship, the one that is going to carry *you* into space. Can everybody see it?" I looked around to see nodding heads.

"Okay, here you go. You're strapped into your seat in the rocket ship. There go the engines. Feel them rumbling? They shake your seat a little."

David was very much into the fantasy. I saw his small body shake with the movement of his imaginary spaceship. I noticed, too, Sheila at the end of the table, her elbows braced on the table edge, hands interlaced to shield her eyes from my view. She was participating, I suspected, but didn't want me to realize she was joining in as another of the children.

"It's liftoff. Up, up, up you are going. The blue sky is rushing past you. It's getting paler. See it? Look out your window and see how the earth is falling away and you are zooming into outer space. Ooooh, there you are, out in space.

"Now, you can unfasten your seat belt and walk around, but ooh! What happens?"

"You're weightless," Sheila said without a moment's hesitation.

"That's right. You're weightless. You float. What's it feel like? Do you like it? Where are you going? Look around. What kind of rocket ship are you in? Is it big? Is it small? What colors are there? Is there lots of room to move around in? And where are you going? Where is the rocket ship headed? Look out the window. What do you see? Stars? Planets? Do you see Earth, or are you far away already? Is it crowded with things out there or is it very empty? Are there other spaceships out there? Look around your rocket ship again. Are you alone? Or is there someone traveling with you? Is it someone you like? What are you doing in the rocket ship just now?"

I paused, watching the children, all deep in their fantasy. "Okay, now, when you're ready, you may open your eyes and then I want you to draw me your spaceship."

As virtually always happened with this kind of activity, the children aroused from their imaginings excited and reached enthusiastically for the drawing materials.

"I seen Dracula, Torey," Violet said cheerfully. "And he had this big blob of blood hanging off his teeth."

"You're weird," David replied and reached across her for the felt tips.

As I would soon discover happened every time we asked Violet to create something, she made a cross, as this symbol kept her safe from vampires. On this occasion, she made one large black cross before going on to make several more smaller crosses and around this she dotted small round faces, all with pleasant, fang-toothed smiles.

David was drawing busily. He made a great red-and-white-striped rocket ship with a bright-yellow light shining out of its nose and was now surrounding it with an array of multicolored stars.

Alejo had reached quickly for a felt-tip marker, but once he had it, he paused a long time over the blank paper, then slowly he began to draw. His spaceship was a tiny speck in a huge, black universe.

It was this blackness that eventually got him into trouble. There was such a huge area of paper to cover that it soon became obvious he couldn't do it with the small black felt tip he was using. Setting it down, he surveyed the available drawing materials before spying a large black marking pen on the far end of the table. Rising, he reached across David to get it. In the process, he accidentally bumped David's hand.

"You spaz!" David shouted and flung his arm out angrily.

Within a split second, Alejo had him by the shirt. Indeed, it happened so very fast, I didn't anticipate it and was alarmed to discover Alejo had pulled David off his chair and down to the floor before I had even managed to rise. Grabbing David by the hair, he slammed his head down against the linoleum.

I dashed around the table, but before I could reach him, Alejo was off. In blind panic he ran. The room we had chosen in the school was normally a double classroom and we had picked it for its size. With so few children, however, we had not needed the many tables or chairs used by the ordinary pupils in the school; so we had shoved the large metal teacher's desk into a far corner and then nested all the other tables and stacked them around it, before piling the chairs on top. It was here Alejo went, sliding in through the tangled legs of the tables and under the teacher's desk to become virtually unreachable without moving them all.

David was my immediate concern. He had gotten a nasty bash against the floor and was crying lustily, so I knelt to comfort him. Both Jeff and Miriam had come to my aid, and we all stood regarding Alejo in his hiding place. He, in turn, watched us with huge, dark eyes.

"What should we do?" I asked Jeff. I was unsure whether fishing him out and making him sit in our "time-out chair" would be the appropriate action or whether he was too frightened to benefit from that.

"Can I talk to him?" It was Sheila. "I could speak to him like I did the other day. Maybe I could get him to come out."

"Yes, I think that's a good idea," Jeff said. "You be in charge of Alejo, Sheila. You talk to him, and if you get him out, you keep him aside individually."

This seemed to surprise Sheila. "What should I do with him?"

Jeff gave her a reassuring smile. "What seems right. You'll know when the time comes."

The time didn't come. Alejo stayed under the tables for the remainder of the morning.

During the drive down to the bus station on Fenton Boulevard, Sheila was lost in pensive silence. "What was the point of that exercise with the rocket ship?" she asked after a long while in thought.

"To help the children experience themselves, I suppose. That's what creativity is all about, basically."

"So it was just an exercise in creativity?"

"In expression. Most of the children in this group find it difficult to express their inner feelings, and I've found these kinds of activities often provide a good way to start."

Again Sheila fell silent. We went for five or six minutes without speaking.

"Torey?"

"Yes?"

"I remember you doing that."

"Doing what?"

"In our class. I remember you taking us on one of those imaginary trips. We went under the sea." Her face suddenly lit up. "We were all sitting in a circle on the floor. On my knees. I was on my knees. You showed us these pictures of tropical fish in this magazine, and then you told us to close our eyes and we were going under the water. Under the sea to see the fish. And I remember all these fish swimming around, yellow-striped and turquoise, all colors." Sheila was smiling.

I smiled back and nodded.

"Suddenly, I can remember that. Really clearly. Like it just happened. I can see us sitting there in that circle on the floor. I can see the blackboard behind you."

"Yes, we did it quite a lot. It was a favorite activity with almost everyone."

She smiled broadly. "And now I remember it. I can really remember."

Chapter 14

Apparently Alejo felt we were too dangerous a group to deal with, because when he arrived the next morning, he wouldn't get out of the taxi. Jeff went out and tried to talk him into coming into the school, but Alejo was having none of it. He cowered in the small floor space of the backseat. Jeff, who was not accustomed to his clients so vehemently not wanting to see him, was inclined to let Alejo go home again. He felt Alejo needed more time to work through this matter and would only make positive therapeutic progress if allowed to move at his own speed. I disagreed, feeling that if Alejo left now, he would never come back. Sensing that any possible future of staying with his adoptive family hinged on his learning more appropriate behaviors over the course of the summer, I doubted we could afford that kind of therapeutic luxury. So, despite Jeff's misgivings and Alejo's loud protests, I extracted him from the back of the taxi and carried him in.

He was a really vicious little boy. Most children, when I had to deal with them physically, fought back in a reasonably predictable, "fair" way and I was able to hold them and move them without hurting either one of us. I got the odd knock on the shins, but that was about all. Not so with Alejo. When he fought, it was with fierce, no-holds-barred desperation, biting, scratching and squirming so violently that I found it almost impossible to hang on to him.

Both Jeff and Miriam tried to help me move the boy up the steps and into the school, but, if anything, Alejo struggled more as each additional pair of hands took hold of him. In the end, I asked them to let go and just make sure the exits were guarded, in case I accidentally let go of him before we got into the classroom.

Once we reached the classroom doorway, I did release Alejo and he bolted off to the same far corner that had succored him the day before. Dropping down, he slid back behind the stacked chairs and tables and under the teacher's desk.

"Oh, good," muttered Jeff and turned to me. "You're the expert in these kinds of things. Now what?"

What came back to me was my own first encounter with a seriously disturbed child. I was eighteen at the time and a volunteer in a preschool program. There had been a small girl there who, day after day, spent the whole time hiding behind the piano. The director of the program, a marvelous, innovative individual who was to serve as my mentor for several years afterward, had set me the same kind of task. I was to go spend time with this little girl and get her to come out. He didn't tell me how to do it or what to do, just that this was my task and that he had faith in me. He said, whatever I chose to do, it would make the child's life better than it was at the moment. Whether or not he realized that the months that followed would change my life forever, I never knew, but my entire career in special education could be traced straight back to that one small girl.

What had affected me indelibly in this encounter had been the director's faith that I, a rather awkward and self-conscious teenager, had the ability to think for myself, to discern what needed to be done and to do it. Looking at Sheila, I thought how much I wanted to give her that same gift.

"You go with him," I said to her.

She looked disconcerted. "And do what?"

"He must be terribly frightened. Talk to him. If he wants to come out, great, but otherwise, just use your judgment."

For a long moment, Sheila regarded me, her expression flickering between puzzlement and uncertainty, then she glanced over at Alejo behind his barricade.

"Remember how you felt when you first came to my class?" I asked. "Talk to him as if he were you, then."

"I don't remember," she said. "So I don't think I can do that."

"I'm sure you can."

Going down on her stomach so that she could see under the tangle of chair and table legs, she spoke softly to him in Spanish throughout the morning. Not fluent myself in the language, I could not understand most of what she was saying, but her voice grew gentle and encouraging.

Alejo didn't come out. Safe behind his barricade of metal legs, he kept himself curled up and resisted Sheila's charms. Indeed, I don't believe he even talked to her that first day. Sheila, however, proved just as persistent. She got up a couple of times and came and joined me, working with the children I had that morning, but she always went back to sit on the floor beside Alejo's den. I was impressed with her concentration. It was the first time, I think, we had managed to fully engage her.

For the following two weeks, Alejo continued to take refuge among the table legs. Each morning he would arrive, be carried in from the taxi, shoot across the room and under the tables to lurk until extracted again at lunchtime to go home. Jeff and I discussed the merits of hanging on to him when we got him inside the door of the classroom and not allowing him to get into his hideaway, but in the end felt it was perhaps better that he be allowed this form of security. So each day went the same.

Sheila accepted the ongoing challenge of trying to charm Alejo out. For several days she lay on her stomach on the floor and talked to him, sometimes in Spanish, sometimes in English. She was surprisingly good at keeping up these one-sided conversations. I had never perceived Sheila as particularly garrulous and would not have expected her to tackle the situation in such a manner, but she did, maintaining a pleasant chatter full of questions to him about what he might like in the way of food or sports or other activities, what he did with his day when he wasn't here, what his preferences were in regards to animals, school subjects and a host of other areas.

Occasionally, Alejo could be drawn into answering, although he never said much. He seemed to appreciate her efforts at Spanish, as we often heard him murmuring back to her then. And so they went, three and a half hours a day, five days a week.

As she continued to share floor space with him, Sheila grew intensely interested in Alejo's circumstances. Nothing was known about his real family, not even their names or whether or not any of them were still alive. Repeatedly, Sheila queried the possibility of finding out. I tried to explain the impracticality of it, and most likely the total impossibility of it as well, but Sheila's curiosity remained.

The tale of how Alejo had been found, living in the garbage can, provoked a particularly large amount of conversation from Sheila. She mused on everything from how cold and hungry he must have been to the logistics of a young child's actually surviving in such circumstances. My suspicion, of course, was that in some unconscious way, Sheila was relating this to her own abandonment. I could recall how, at six, she used to recount over and over and over again the incident where her mother had left home, taking her and her younger brother Jimmie, and how her mother had stopped the car and pushed Sheila out onto the verge of the freeway, before speeding off into the night, never to be seen again. Sheila's need now to recount Alejo's abandonment caused all those long-ago conversations to echo in my mind.

Whatever was happening psychologically, Sheila became increasingly committed to Alejo. She was desperate to reach him, to convince him that he could trust her, and it was this desire that engaged her so completely in her work with him.

Despite this newfound intensity in her work, however, there were still plenty of hot moments with Sheila. One of the most dangerous areas was her appearance.

Having known her as a child, I must admit Sheila did not now look at all as I had expected she would. She had been a very pretty girl, even through the dirt and grime of her early days in my class. Her long hair, a dark honey-blond in color, had been very, very straight, of the sort to slide off the fingers in a fluidlike motion when lifted. Her features were bold, with a cheeky little cleft in her chin and a particularly attractive mouth.

The chin, the mouth, the bold features were, of course, all still there, but the permed, brightly colored hair diminished them, and everything was overshadowed by Sheila's wardrobe. *Where* she got her fashion sense I could only guess at. It was so far out as to be almost in.

We had been treated to various combos involving the white long johns and an assortment of dresses and T-shirts. Indeed, one of her favorites included wearing nothing over the long johns except a very baggy peasant-style shirt, which made her look like an extra from *Fiddler on the Roof* who'd been interrupted in the changing room. She also had an assortment of what appeared to be lacy, white Victorian nightshirts, which she wore as dresses, usually layered over long-sleeved striped T-shirts in loud, occasionally neon, colors. And all of these were complemented by the thick black lace-up workman's boots.

She had had her ears pierced, the left one five times, the right one twice, although, thank God, no other parts of her anatomy seemed to have received this treatment. She wore nothing more than thin gold rings in her ears, but the sheer quantity made up for their simplicity.

Admittedly, it did all take a bit of getting used to, but the fact was I didn't mind it. In fact, as I did grow used to it, I found some of the sartorial combinations attractive, if a little bizarre. She did have an obvious flair for clothes, and, moreover, she had the slim, waiflike build needed to carry such outfits off. Had Sheila been among people a little more in the fashion vanguard than Jeff and I could lay claims to, I suspect her imagination would have been admired.

Sheila's father, however, did not appear to admire Sheila's dress sense whatsoever, and from what I could make out, there were many arguments over the matter. Moreover, her school hadn't taken a very enlightened view either and she had, on more than one occasion, been sent home to change. This, I assumed, was what accounted for Sheila's touchiness over the matter, because it became obvious from the first day that she wanted to wear these things and look the way she did and not have a single person even allude to the fact that she might appear a smidgen peculiar.

Jeff was always landing himself in it. He had nicknamed her the Orangutan as a result of her orange hair and her climbing feat on that second day and this was guaranteed to make her shout, just by his saying it. Worse, he could never resist commenting, "Shall we turn the air-conditioning down for you so you won't have to come in with your nightgown on over your clothes?" or "Isn't Grandpa missing his underwear yet?"

Sheila reacted to these comments, like most of his tongue-in-cheek humor, with the spitting rage of a wildcat kitten, and I was quite certain the rage was genuine. Whatever hopes I had had about bringing two such powerful minds together had long since evaporated. Sheila appeared to feel nothing short of hate for Jeff and Jeff was never much help. I tried to get him to turn off his undisciplined mouth, but it made no difference whatsoever. He enjoyed winding her up.

Once I'd adjusted, I didn't find it too difficult to keep my own mouth shut regarding her appearance. I'm fairly unshockable and can screen out unwanted sensory information quite easily, so except for mediating over the matter between her and Jeff, I could generally steer clear. This was just as well, because on the few occasions when I accidentally got drawn in, Sheila came out with all guns firing. In fact, I suspect there was a provocative aspect to Sheila's appearance, which, when I didn't react to it, made her have to come after me occasionally.

On one such time, we were at the back of the room after the session ended. Some of the children had done painting and Sheila was helping me wash out the paint pots. The sink was full of soapy water and Sheila had her arms plunged into it almost up to her elbows.

"Could you get my hair back?" she asked, as I came around the side with more paint pots. "I got a ponytail holder in my left pocket. Could you just pull it back and fasten it for me?"

I reached in her pocket, extracted the holder and began smoothing the hair back to fasten it. What came immediately to my mind were memories of doing Sheila's hair when she was little. It had been wonderful hair, so silky straight that it was lovely to feel, and I had always enjoyed our mornings before school when I had brushed it. What I felt now was quite a different matter. Treated and colored, it was a crinkly mass.

"I'm thinking of doing my hair yellow this weekend," Sheila said. "I saw this stuff at the drugstore and it was only two dollars and ninety-nine cents."

"Do you ever think of letting it grow back like it was?"

In a split second, Sheila had whirled around and whacked my hand down, soapy water flying everywhere. "Stop it! Just stop it!" she shouted in fury.

I jumped back in surprise.

"That's what you want, isn't it? To control me! To make me back into your little darling. Well, I'm *not* her. I'm me! And you can't tell me what to do anymore."

She had gotten so angry so quickly that I was stunned into silence. Both Jeff and Miriam were in the room too and they stopped short and stared.

"I'm not your property anymore. You don't own me. You didn't create me!"

Chapter 15

The following Monday morning, I was playing "empty chair" with David, Tamara and Violet. A variation of the therapeutic technique developed by the renowned psychiatrist Fritz Perls, it involved setting an empty chair in the middle of the group and talking to it, as if a person were sitting in it. We were discussing angry feelings and sad feelings and how the two sometimes got mixed up. I had asked the children in turn to think of an occasion when someone had made them each feel that way, then to imagine that that person was sitting in the empty chair and to talk to him or her, telling that person about their feelings. It took us a while to get going. I gave an example, placing in the chair a neighbor of mine who disliked my cat, and then telling the empty chair how angry it made me feel when I saw him abusing my pet. Then the children had turns. It wasn't until we were on our second round that everyone began to pick up the right mood.

Tamara's second turn came. "I'm going to put my mom in that chair," she said.

"Okay," I replied. "And what do you want to tell your mom?"

"I'm fed up with the baby."

"Okay."

Tamara looked over at me. "I want to tell her I don't want to take care of the baby anymore. Why did she have so many kids that she can't take care of them all herself?"

"Can you tell her that?" I asked. "Imagine she's sitting just there and you tell her how you feel."

"I don't want to take care of the baby anymore," Tamara said. "I'm sick of the baby. He's not mine. It's not fair, just because I'm oldest. Why do I have to take care of him?"

Tears came to her eyes and she stopped. Looking over at me, she said, "I'm too little to take care of him."

I pointed to the chair. "Why don't you tell her you feel like that? That you feel too small for such a big responsibility?"

Tamara nodded tearfully. "I'm just little, Mama. I need you to take care of *me*."

She sat down, and for a long moment everyone was absorbed in a pensive silence.

"Okay, Violet?" I said gently. "How about you?"

Violet lumbered to her feet. She approached the chair, walked around it, all the while regarding the seat. During the first round, she had seated a girl from school in the chair. Violet told me that she wanted to ask the girl why she always treated her in such a mean way, but when redirected to imagine the girl sitting in the chair and to address her comments there, Violet had degenerated into silly chatter about ghosts. I wasn't holding out much hope for this new attempt. Violet's problems were so all-pervasive that she didn't appear able to cope with such a direct approach.

"I'm going to put Alejo in the chair," Violet said, much to my surprise.

Alejo wasn't far away. We were in a circle only feet away from where Sheila had been lying prone on the floor and talking to him; however, over the course of the empty-chair exercise, Sheila had gotten caught up listening to us and was now sitting cross-legged on the edge of the circle. She ducked her head slightly to see Alejo under his tangle of furniture when his name was mentioned.

"All right," I said. "What do you want to say to Alejo?"

"Why don't you come with us, Alejo?" Violet said, approaching the chair. She cocked her head and regarded it closely, as if really seeing the boy. "Why do you keep hiding from us? It isn't scary here and I miss you. I wish you would come out."

She circled the chair and then came to stand on the left side of it. "I feel angry with you when you go hide, because I think you don't like me. I feel sad, because I want to be your friend. Why don't you come out? I want you to be with us."

"All right."

Stunned, we all jerked our heads over to see Alejo standing beside the stacked table.

"He's come out!" David shrieked with such loudness that I fully expected Alejo to bolt back under, but he didn't.

"Do you want to join us?" I asked. I snagged a chair from an adjacent table and pulled it into our circle.

Alejo remained right where he was.

"Would you like to play too? Do you want to talk to someone in the empty chair?" I asked.

He shook his head.

Sheila, still sitting cross-legged on the floor, reached her hand out. "Come here, Alejo. Sit down beside me."

Without hesitation, he went over to her and sat down.

"Let's change things. You've had a chance to talk to the empty chair. Now, let's pretend the empty chair can talk back," I said. "Tamara, you just talked to your mom, sitting in the empty chair. Now you go sit in the empty chair."

Hesitantly, she rose from her place, walked across the circle and sat down in the empty chair in the center.

"Now you're your mom. You just heard what Tamara said. You answer her back."

Tamara sat silent a long moment. "I don't mean to make you work so hard," she started quietly. "I just got too many children." She paused. "Don't get married, Tamara. Don't have babies." Then she stood up and walked back to her place.

"My turn now. I get to be Alejo," Violet said and beamed at him. She went over to the empty chair and sat down. "I'm glad you asked me to come out, Violet. I was tired of being under there. You acted good to me. Now I'm going to be your friend."

I smiled at Violet and then looked over at Alejo. "Can you share with us how it made you feel, when Violet said how much she wanted you to come join us again?"

"Good," he said.

Sheila and I didn't join Jeff and Miriam for lunch as we usually did. I had a client meeting very near the school in the early afternoon, so I'd brought my lunch with the idea of eating it over in the park across the street. Deprived of her usual ride down to Fenton Boulevard, Sheila needed to make the rather complicated set of connections from the main road two blocks over. She left immediately after the program ended that morning and I assumed she was headed for the bus stop; however, she returned, a McDonald's bag in hand, and joined me on my picnic bench in the park.

"I don't have to go home right away," she said, "It's just an empty house anyway."

"I'm always glad for company," I said, as I unwrapped my sandwiches.

We spent a moment with our food.

"What do you usually do in the afternoons when you get home?" I asked.

Sheila shrugged. "Depends."

"Do you get together with friends?"

She hesitated over her food, then shrugged again. "Not usually."

"I don't hear you mention friends very often," I said.

"Doesn't mean I don't have any, if that's what you're asking," she said a bit testily. "Just I don't do much with them, that's all." She took a bite of her hamburger. "It's a dorky school I go to. There's not really anyone there I'd want to be friends with, if you want the truth."

"What do you do?"

"Like I said, depends. I always got the housework, you know. My dad sure wouldn't do it. If it's left to my dad, we'd live in a pigsty. And the shopping. And the cooking. Who do you think does our cooking?"

I nodded.

"He's very lucky he's got a daughter, you know. Somebody to do all this for him. He'd have been stuck, if I was a boy."

"How's it work out? Does he give you the shopping money and you make the decisions about what the meals will be?"

"I got to get it off him." She finished her hamburger in two big bites. "I learned that, like, ages ago. I got to get the money off him within minutes or it's not there to get."

I regarded her.

"Mostly he gives it to me when I ask. He's getting used to me doing it now, but if he doesn't, I'm still pretty good at getting it. I tell him I'm going over to the Laundromat and I got to have the pants he's wearing right away, so would he change? Then he takes his wallet out. Or sometimes I just wait till he's asleep."

"I thought he was done with the alcohol and stuff. I thought all that was in the past."

She snorted derisively. "Don't kid yourself."

"He's still drinking?" I said in dismay. "I thought the baseball team ..."

"People don't change. Didn't you know that? Circumstances change, but people never do."

Now that Alejo had come out from his hideaway of his own volition, Jeff and I decided to take definitive measures to prevent him from returning there; so we arrived early the next morning and humped the extra tables and chairs down the hall to a room we were not using. This had the added advantage of leaving us with a much larger working space.

When the taxi arrived, Alejo again showed reluctance to get out, but Sheila climbed in and sat with him a moment before finally coaxing him out with her. For the first time in three weeks he did not have to be dragged into the room, but instead walked in, holding Sheila's hand.

"Can I just take him and work with him on my own?" Sheila asked.

"If you'd like. Do you have something planned?" I replied.

She shrugged. "All that time I was with him on the floor I was thinking of different things. And I thought maybe he would find it easier than being in a big group."

They went to the far end of the room near a small, low bookcase and sat down on the floor. I saw Sheila tip out the canister of Lego bricks in the middle between them and then both bent forward to begin building.

It was my day to take Joshua and Jessie, our two autistic children, and between them, they were a full load, so I did not get much of a chance to over-see what Sheila and Alejo were doing together. They remained absorbed in the Lego bricks all the way to snack time and the break.

While they were outside, I took the opportunity to walk over and see what they had been building. It didn't appear to be much. There were several rectangular forms, looking like half-started houses or the like, and a few long strings of bricks clicked together.

"Should we let them continue?"

Startled, I jumped at the unexpected voice and turned to see Jeff. He crossed over to where I was standing. Bending down, he picked up one of the rectangular structures. "I think they'll go back to this after the break. Do you think we should leave them to it?"

"What do you think?" I asked.

"I was eavesdropping. It was quite an interesting conversation. They seemed to be building jails with the Lego and putting the little Lego people in it. From the sounds of it, Alejo was putting his mother in jail. He said, 'She says No! No! No! You do that again and I will lock you in your room. I won't talk to you for two days. You are a wicked boy to do that and you can't watch TV.' And Sheila says, 'Lock her in the jail. This is the bad moms' jail. Put her in there and we'll give her punishment. What shall we do to her?' And Alejo says, 'Cut her throat. Make her bleed. Drop bombs on her till she's dead.' So that's what they were doing, dropping hunks of Lego." Jeff looked over. "It was a little difficult to tell who was leading whom."

"So it sounds," I replied.

"I think we should let them go on, if they want," Jeff said. "He's talking more than I've heard yet, but ... I want to keep an ear tuned."

I felt unnerved by the content of the conversation. As much as I wanted to give Sheila a positive experience here with us, she was an untrained teenager and not a therapist; moreover, she still carried plenty of her own emotional baggage. Was she encouraging Alejo's play in an effort to imitate Jeff's and my therapeutic activities? Or was she fulfilling her own needs? Or both?

We didn't get a chance to find out. When Miriam and Sheila came back in with the children after break, Alejo quite happily joined the others at the painting table and Sheila retreated to the back to clean up the things from snack time and to polish off the remaining cookies.

When the morning was over, Sheila came over to me as I was putting things away. "Let's not go to lunch with them," she said, as she handed me the materials to put up on the shelf.

"You don't feel like it?"

"Let's do what we did yesterday and eat in the park. I liked that. It's so nice and sunny out and then we spend it sitting around in that dingy restaurant," she replied.

"The problem is," I said, "I haven't brought my lunch today, so I don't have anything to eat. Moreover, I have an appointment back at the clinic at two, so if I don't eat promptly, I won't be able to take you down to Fenton Boulevard before I have to be back."

"I don't care. I can take the bus from here." She bent down and unlaced one boot. Lifting the boot up, she tipped it and out spilled a five-dollar bill. "If you don't eat too much, I could buy you something from McDonald's."

"All right. McDonald's it is, but I'll buy," I said. "You can provide the delivery service and go get it when we're done here."

We'd had a messy morning, using finger paints at the table, soft colored chalk on the blackboard and water in the sand tray. In addition, there was the usual debris. Jeff was at the back sink washing out paint pots, while Miriam was sorting through books and putting them back into the bookshelf.

"Have you told them?" Sheila asked, coming over to where I was wiping down a table.

"Told them what?" I asked.

"Well, that we're not going out to lunch with them," she replied, a little exasperated.

"No, but I will. Let's just finish the cleaning up. We were really mucky in here today."

"We can clean up," she said. "Why don't you tell Jeff and Miriam they can go now. Then you and me can clean up." When I didn't respond immediately, Sheila continued. "This is the only problem with this work. You and I never get to spend any time alone. I thought we would more, but there's always them around. Sometimes I just want to be with you."

I smiled. "Well, go tell them we'll do the room on our own then."

I was hoping that Sheila's request to be alone with me was an indication that she wanted to talk. The conversation Jeff had reported earlier between her and Alejo still disconcerted me a little and I was anticipating that she might want to discuss it or at least discuss Alejo with me; but this didn't seem to be the case. Once there were just the two of us, we continued to clean up the room.

Taking a set of fresh erasers from the cupboard, Sheila erased all the colored drawings from the chalkboard, while I tacked up the finger paintings on the bulletin board. When I next looked over, she had a box of the colored chalk in her hand and was drawing on the board. I didn't say anything, but Sheila quickly became aware that I was watching her.

"The only other problem with this place is that I don't get to play too," she said and grinned sheepishly. "I keep wishing, like, I was one of them instead of one of you guys. God, it looks like so much fun, what these kids get to do. Like a dream school."

I grinned back.

"Can I make a picture with these?" she asked hesitantly, holding up the box of chalks. "Like, maybe it could be decorative? For when they come in tomorrow? It'd look better than just a blank blackboard, don't you think?"

"Yeah, sure. Go ahead."

Sheila threw herself wholeheartedly into making an enormous picture that took up a whole section of the chalkboard in the classroom. This intensity of concentration surprised me; she worked as if it had been bursting to get out of her all along. As I finished my work and the time drew near to go for lunch, I was reluctant to pull her away, as she was so deeply involved in what she was doing.

"Shall I go for the hamburgers?" I asked.

"Would you?" she replied in surprise. "God, like, great."

When I returned about twenty minutes later, Sheila was putting the finishing touches on the blackboard drawing. It was an intriguing picture: a desert of gold sand stretching the full length of the board with hardly anything above it. There was one lone saguaro-type cactus and a couple of branched, leafless bushes. Below the level of the sand, however, were an incredible number of little burrows filled with snakes, mice, scorpions, rabbits and beetles. And at the very far end was a female backpacker in hiking boots and shorts with a red scarf on her head.

"Hey, that's good. I didn't know you were such an artist," I said.

"There's lots you don't know about me, Torey."

"It's really good. You have the woman's expression very realistic. But I especially like all these things down under the sand. Look at the rabbit burrows. A regular warren, with all those individual rooms for the rabbits to go in. And I could never draw a scorpion just out of my imagination."

Sheila grinned. "I like doing things that surprise you."

I regarded the picture. "She looks lonely, though. This lone hiker with everything hiding from her."

"Now, don't go into your psychologist mode. It's just a picture."

"So," I said, "*you* tell me about it then."

"It's just a picture. She's walking in the desert. It's the California desert. I've seen pictures of it, of bushes like those."

California, where Sheila's mother had fled, I was thinking, but I didn't say that. "It still looks lonely from the hiker's perspective."

"Well, yeah, there's a lot of loneliness in deserts. You kind of feel like there's this big stretch of emptiness ahead of you," she replied.

"And everything that's alive is hiding from you?" I ventured.

"Well, yeah, that, or ..." She turned and looked at me, a knowing smile crossing her lips. "Or everything is hiding just below the surface, waiting to be discovered. Touché? I caught you at it? I can interpret pictures too?"

I shrugged good-naturedly.

"You're dying to get your hands on me, aren't you? What you really want is for me to say that this person is me and this desert is my life, isn't it?"

"Only if it's true."

"Oh, it's true," she said. "And you should know it."

Chapter 16

Sheila's fourteenth birthday came in early July, just before the program broke up for three days over the Fourth of July. I told Jeff, saying that as it was the only birthday to occur over the course of the eight-week program, it would be nice to have a little party. All the time I was teaching I had always made a special effort to have class celebrations, in part because they provided a pleasant change from routine, but mostly because the handicaps, the emotional dysfunction in the families and/or the financial circumstances often prevented these children from experiencing parties elsewhere. Many were the boys and girls in my classes who had never been invited to a single birthday party or been the center of one for themselves. So I baked us a huge chocolate cake and decorated it with Sheila's name, while Miriam made up an assortment of small party foods. Jeff provided the paper hats and honkers.

Sheila made no pretense at sophistication when she saw the streamers and balloons, the colorful Pink Panther paper plates and hats, and the cake. Absolutely delighted, she picked up each and every item and inspected it.

"God, you did this for *me? Shit*," she said, trying a hat on. "God, I've never had one of these. How does it look? Where's a mirror? I've got to see." She went over to the corner where the dressing-up clothes were and took up the small hand mirror. "I've always wondered what I'd look like with one of these hats on."

The children were equally delighted, squealing with enthusiasm when they spied the bright decorations and the array of party foods. Having lived through dozens of classroom parties before, I knew what a recipe for disaster they generally were. Everyone got a little too excited, the noise level was unbearable and nothing of measurable worth got done. However, there was magic in this sort of chaos, to my mind, and I always enjoyed the ferment.

We started with party games and ended with a feast of goodies, the finale being the cake. All the children were amazed by the number of candles Sheila got and even more amazed that she had the ability to blow them all out. After cutting the cake and passing out a slice to everyone, Jeff said, "Well, now must be the time for presents."

I had gotten her a gift certificate from a local department store, so that she could have the leisure of picking what caught her fancy. Miriam, who was an accomplished craftsperson, had made an attractive woven belt. Then Jeff handed her a small package, prettily wrapped. It was obvious from its shape that it was a book. Taking the gift from him, Sheila paused to look at it. The wrapping, a shimmery gold, was quite unlike anything I'd seen before and I found it amazing to think that Jeff would take time with things like wrapping birthday presents.

Carefully, Sheila prized the sticking tape off. Inside was a paperback copy of Shakespeare's *Antony and Cleopatra*. Sheila lifted it up and regarded the cover. At a loss for words, she just stared at it.

"Torey said you liked Caesar," Jeff said. "This is set in the same time period." He regarded Sheila's face. "Have you read it?"

Curling her lip in undisguised disbelief, she shook her head. "This is Shakespeare."

"Yes, well, don't hold it against him. Forget who wrote it and just take it home and read it. There's one of the best stories in the world between those two covers and you're going to meet a soul mate."

Sheila looked up, astonished. "Me? Who?"

"You read it and find out."

En route down to Fenton Boulevard after lunch, Sheila was full of ebullience.

"Thanks for that, Torey. That was really nice of you and Miriam and Jeff to do all that for me today," she said.

"We thought it'd be a bit of good fun. I'm glad you liked it," I replied.

She smiled. "That's what I always hated about having a summer birthday. All the other kids at school got some kind of fuss made, you know, like they sang 'Happy Birthday' or something, and I never got anything. And I always wanted it. Just once. You know, just once, so you could stand up and everybody'd think *you* were special." She paused. "It's funny how such a silly thing can matter so much when you're little."

I nodded.

"If you want the actual, honest-to-God truth, this is the first birthday party I've ever had."

I nodded again. I had suspected as much.

"Once, when I was in this one foster home ... I was eight, I think, and turning nine ... they said they were going to let me have a party and she took me out to look at paper plates and junk, but ..." Turning her head, she gazed out the window. "I didn't get it. I did something or another, I don't remember what now, and she told me I wasn't going to have anything for my birthday because of it. But, you know, I don't think she was going to do anything anyway, 'cause she never bought the paper plates. I think she was just winding me up."

"That must have been disappointing," I said.

"Yeah, but then what's new?"

Silence.

Sheila looked down at the presents in her lap. Pulling out the gift certificate I'd given her, she examined it, then put it back in its envelope. Then she felt the weave of Miriam's belt. Finally, she began to page through the play Jeff had given her.

"Why on earth do you suppose he gave me this?" she murmured. "It's a weird gift."

I didn't answer.

"Have you ever read it?"

"Yes, long ago. I did a report on it at school once." I paused, then giggled. "To be truthful, I *didn't* read it. I was about your age and my sole goal in life in those days was to figure out how to short-circuit the work and still get the grades. I was a world-class skimmer. I don't think I actually read a whole book cover to cover until I was about twenty-two."

"*Torey!*" she said, absolutely appalled.

I turned and grinned.

"God, and I thought you were so perfect," Sheila said.

A pause.

"So, you don't know what's in it either?" she asked.

"Well, not other than it's about *Antony and Cleopatra*. You know who Cleopatra is, don't you?"

"Vaguely. A queen in Egypt a long time ago, but that's about all," Sheila replied. "I can't imagine why Jeff thinks I'll want to read this. Holy shit, *Shakespeare*."

"I guess you'll have to read it and find out."

I was coming to the roadwork again, so I slowed the car down.

"I remember that other book," Sheila said. "From your class. *The Little Prince*. Do you remember reading that to me? It was my best book in the whole world for the longest time. I just couldn't get enough of it."

"Yes, I remember it very well," I said.

"I can still quote all my favorite parts." She smiled over at me. "You know who I liked best in the book?"

"The prince?" I ventured.

She shook her head.

"The fox?"

"No, the rose. I loved that rose. It was so conceited, so full of itself and yet ... Remember how it had those thorns, four thorns, and thought itself so brave? Remember that one bit? The rose said to the little prince, 'Let the tigers come with their claws!'" Sheila boomed out in a deep, fierce voice. "And the prince said, 'There are no tigers on my planet, and besides, tigers don't eat weeds.' 'I am not a weed!'" Again, the dramatic rendering. Sheila's voice squeaked over the word "weed." "She was so put out. And then she just kept going on, 'Let the tigers come! I am not at all afraid of tigers!'" Sheila smiled. "I can just imagine that brave little rose."

"I can see why you liked her," I said. "You were a bit of a little rose yourself in those days."

She wrinkled her nose. "Oh God, I wasn't, Torey. God. That's no compliment. A *flower*? No, it's the tigers I identified with. Rrrowrr!" she said and struck playfully out at me with fingers arched as claws. "I was the tigers' kid."

Chapter 17

Over the Fourth of July weekend, I asked Sheila if she would like to come with me for a brief visit to Marysville, where she had been in my class all those years previously. It was a two-hundred-mile journey and I thought it would fit well into the four days we had until the clinic summer school-program resumed.

Sheila accepted enthusiastically. She had been back on only one previous occasion five years before, when her foster family had taken her to visit her father at the penitentiary. It had been almost as long since I'd been there. I'd passed through on one or two occasions since but I hadn't stopped. With the exception of Chad, all the people I had been closest to were now gone.

The plan was that I would pick her up early on Thursday morning and we would work our way

across the state to Marysville at a leisurely pace.
Friday and Saturday we would spend looking
around. Chad and his family had invited us to celebrate the Fourth of July with them on Saturday
evening, and then on Sunday we'd return.

Sheila was waiting outside on the front steps of
the duplex when I pulled up. It was very early, only
just after six, and the sun was not high enough to
dispel all the shadows. Even so, I squinted hard at
the figure by the door. Sheila?

"I've done this *just* for you," she said emphatically, as she flung her duffel bag into the backseat
and got in beside me. She buckled the seat belt. "I
hope you appreciate it."

What could I say? The orange hair was gone,
replaced by bright-yellow hair that stood up all
over her head, as if it had a life of its own. Sort of
Marilyn Monroe meets Bride of Frankenstein.

"You said I looked better blond," she replied to
my stunned silence. "I thought, well, *just* for you,
since you're taking me someplace nice."

I set off in a high mood. I love to drive, and it
was a super time for driving, on an early summer
morning. Although we had been in the midst of a
string of quite hot days, the air was still cool and
the humidity was low, making the far horizon
sharp.

"I wonder what we're going to find," Sheila
said. "Can we go to the school?"

"It'll be closed, but we could look at the playground."

While I negotiated the last of the freeway inter-changes necessary to get us out of the city, Sheila amused herself trying to tune in a rock station, but my radio wasn't very good and she finally gave up.

"After you left my class, where all did you go?" I asked.

She shrugged. "Lots of places. I was in, like, three foster homes. Four? I can't remember now. See, we were in Marysville and then we moved to Broadview and my dad got in trouble, like really soon after we moved. So, I went in this one foster home and then I got in another one and another. Then I got sent to a children's home for a while."

"How come?" I asked.

Another shrug. "Just the way the system works."

"What made you move from Marysville in the first place?" I asked.

"Don't know. Don't remember."

"Do you remember being in Sandra McGuire's class the year after my class?" I asked. "When you were seven?"

"Sort of." She paused pensively. "Actually, I have exactly one memory. I was sitting at a table and we were getting assigned lockers. We had to share and so I got assigned to share with the girl sitting across the table from me. I remember her, this girl. She was the smartest kid in the whole class, you know, the one that always got the best grades, and I was excited to think I was going to have a reason to talk to her now and she was going to have to talk to me; but then, I was also sort of scared because I knew she didn't like me very well."

"*You* were the smartest kid in the whole class, Sheil."

"No, I wasn't. She got the best grades. I tried, but she got them."

"You were the smartest kid, regardless of who got the grades."

"Yeah, I read about what you said my IQ was in your book. I read it and thought, God, you faked that one. That's not me," she replied.

"It is."

"It isn't."

"Has no one ever told you in all this time that you were gifted?"

Sheila shook her head.

Shocked, I looked over. "You're kidding."

"I'm not gifted, Torey. I know I'm not."

"What makes you say that?"

"Well, just 'cause. I mean, I'm me. I know. And I'm not smart. I'm stupid."

"You're not!"

She didn't respond, but I could tell I had not convinced her.

"So, give me one example of why you think you're stupid."

"Well, like, in class, for instance, everybody else gets the information the first time the teacher gives it out, but I never do. I hear it and I think I understand it, but then I start getting questions. I think, what about this? Or, like, oftentimes, I'll think, well, that's true in this instance, but is it true in another instance? And every time I'll see there's a time when it *isn't* true, but then it *is* true some of the time. Then I realize there's this big huge area of junk I don't understand at all, but everybody else is sitting around me, writing like mad. *They* understand it and I don't. And if I ask the questions, then pretty soon the teacher says, 'We've got to move on now. You're holding us up.' And then I know for sure I'm some kind of mega-dumbhead, because I only understand a weensy bit of it."

Her cheeks grew blotched, making me realize the intensity of her emotions over the subject. Pushing the shaggy mass of hair back from her face, she rested her hands against her reddened skin. "And the kids ... Whenever I try to ask something, everybody groans. They say, 'Oh, God, not her again.' Or, 'Shut her up, would you?' This one kid who sat in front of me in math, he turned around to me and said, 'Shit, can't you just *do* it, for once?' I wanted to die, I was so embarrassed. I never asked anything again in there."

Pointed silence hung between us. Sharp, it was, like a small dagger. Sheila turned to me. "It's because I'm the youngest in the class. I haven't had as much school as they have and it isn't fair." Her voice was heavy with accusation. "How can they expect me to know as much?"

"You're youngest in the class, Sheila, because you know *more* than they do, not less. The other kids aren't asking questions, because their minds don't throw up so many possibilities so quickly as yours. They don't even realize questions are there."

She chewed her lower lip a moment. Staring ahead at the far-stretching road, she sighed wearily. "If I'm so smart, how come I feel so stupid then? What kind of gift is it that turns the world upside down, so that less is more and more is less?"

We arrived in Marysville in the midafternoon after a leisurely journey across the state. The day had grown very hot, the sky going white with the heat, and coming into the shady streets of the town was a relief. I booked us into a motel on Main Street that, much to Sheila's delight, had a swimming pool. Unfortunately, she didn't have a swimming suit, so we made a jaunt out to find one at the shopping mall. The mall hadn't been there when I had last been in town, and as with all such places, Sheila was keen to explore. Consequently, we wandered around for an hour or two, by which time we were ready for an evening meal; so we stopped for supper in the mall food court before returning to the motel. Feeling overcome with nostalgia as I drove through the familiar streets, I would have preferred going out then and there to visit some old haunts, but Sheila was desperate to go in the pool. Thus, we spent the evening swimming.

The next morning, it was raining steadily.

"Oh, geez, would you believe it?" Sheila said in dismay, as she pulled the curtain back from the motel window. "In July? It never rains in July."

It certainly did that particular July day and by the looks of the clouds, it was not close to stopping. "Come on," I said, "it won't matter. Let's go."

Sheila wanted to go out to see the migrant camp.
I thought I remembered the road, but it turned out
I didn't and we were soon lost. This left me feeling
a bit irritable, which wasn't a good start.

When we did finally locate it, we found the
camp full to bursting with seasonal workers.
Several types of crops were at a harvestable stage,
which had caused the usual swell in camp numbers, but as it was raining and some crops could
not be worked, many of the workers were milling
around the various buildings.

The camp itself had changed considerably from
what I remembered of it. Two large new housing
units had been erected. They were great green-
painted aluminum structures reminiscent of the
calving sheds I was used to in Montana, and they
dominated the camp. Many of the old tar-paper
buildings that made up my clearest memories of
the migrant camp were gone and the layout of the
old roads in the camp had been disrupted by the
new buildings.

What Sheila was thinking, as we drove through
the rutted tracks around the housing units, I do not
know. She had become increasingly silent as we
approached the camp. Face turned away from me,
she looked out the window.

There was a different atmosphere here to when I
used to come out to see Anton. It didn't strike me
as a particularly safe place for two young white
women to wander around alone and a lot of people
were noticing us, even in the car. As a consequence,
I didn't suggest we get out of the car. It was with a

sense of relief that I drove through the gates and back up onto the main road. Sheila still didn't speak.

Back in town, I took the car slowly down a few of the streets I knew best. I pointed out where my old apartment had been. The pizzeria where Chad and I had taken Sheila after the hearing had been replaced by a bar and lounge, but I showed her where it had been. We had an invitation to Chad's house for a picnic supper and fireworks for the next day, and I mentioned that I hoped the weather would improve.

Down a quiet, tree-lined suburban street I located our old school. A low, one-story brick building with white trim, it fitted in attractively with the neighborhood of ranch-style homes. This wasn't a wealthy suburb by any means, but it was solidly middle class, the type of area that so embodied the American Dream of the fifties and sixties. Most of my teaching career since had been spent in drafty, old, turn-of-the-century buildings in the less-affluent parts of large cities, and I had forgotten just what a small, attractive school this had been. The contrast with the migrant camp struck me forcefully.

Pulling the car over to the curb, I turned off the engine. "Recognize this place?"

Sheila nodded faintly.

"See that window there, three along on the left? That was our room," I said.

Absorbed silence.

"Do you remember any of this?"

"I don't know," she murmured quietly.

I certainly remembered. All the little moments came crowding back, grappling one with the other to reach my consciousness first. There was the door where I lined the children up, observing the military precision my principal had loved so well. There were the seesaws the kids always fought over. There was the wide expanse of asphalt where Anton and I had struggled to teach them dodgeball and kickball and ...

"Are there still special-ed kids in that classroom?" Sheila asked.

"The room isn't a classroom anymore. They've made a counseling center out of it," I said. "I suppose we could get out and walk around, if you want ..."

"No."

I started the engine, then paused, hoping for what I'm not sure. Finally I pulled away from the curb and drove off.

After another half hour of cruising up and down the back streets, I began toying with the idea of visiting the shopping mall again. It was still raining heavily and my mood was going from wistful to something less comfortable, making me realize I'd had enough nostalgia for one day.

"You want to do something?" I asked. "I think I saw where there are movie theaters out at the shopping center. Shall we go see what's on?"

Sheila shook her head. "Let's go to that park," she said, "the one where you took those pictures of the last day of school."

"Why don't we wait until it stops raining? Maybe tomorrow, before we go see Chad."

"No, let's go now."

The park was just as beautiful as I remembered it, with its broad winding entrance road lined with locust trees and flower borders. I parked the car on the street and we walked slowly down amidst the flowers. The floral display being quite stupendous, I was entranced. I am very fond of gardening and was curious about the plants used, so I stopped along the way to examine them. Sheila, however, was totally lost to the here and now. She walked as if bewitched.

The lane ended at the duck pond. When we reached the point where it met the path circling the water, Sheila stopped stock-still. Her brow furrowing, she watched the ducks and geese noisily announce our arrival. One by one, they clambered out of the water and waddled over until we were surrounded, and all the time, Sheila never moved. She just stared down the path to the water, her expression inward, and I suspect she never saw the ducks at all.

The ghosts rose up before my eyes also. With an intensity I hadn't experienced elsewhere, the past came back to me. The rain disappeared and the air was full of children's voices. "Look at me, Torey! Look what I can do! How big the trees are here. Do you see the bunnies they got? Down here, come this way, so I can show you. Can I feed the ducks? Can I wade in the pond? Let's roll down the hill. Torey? Torey, look at me!"

And there on the path around the duck pond was Sheila, little Sheila in her bright-orange sunsuit, running, skipping, laughing. She threw out her arms and spun around, letting her head fall back, her long hair sail out in a sunlit halo. Around and around and around she turned, completely oblivious to the other walkers on the path, the other children, us. Eyes closed against the sun, lips parted in a half-smile, she satisfied some inner dream to dance.

Did she remember? I glanced sidelong at the gangly adolescent beside me. Intuition told me she was remembering something, and I longed to know her thoughts just then, but I dared not ask.

"I was happy here," she whispered after a long silence. It was said so softly that I couldn't detect the emotion it held. Finally she turned away from the duck pond. Crossing the grass to reach the lane again, we started back to the car.

We were soaking wet by then. It was warm summer rain. I wasn't particularly uncomfortable, but everything was dripping. Sheila bent to pick up a long, brown locust pod that had fallen on the walk.

"When I think of Marysville, I always think of locust trees," I said. "I remember how they used to scent the air when they were blooming. I remember driving into Marysville the first time. I'd come along the highway and as it dips down the hill into the valley, I can recall having my car window down, and I could smell Marysville before I got here. And when the blossoms start to fall, it's like snow. I remember coming out in the mornings and my car would be covered."

Sheila stopped, turned and looked back down the lane toward the duck pond, no longer visible. Pausing, she slit open the locust bean with her fingernail and took out the seeds, letting them drop to the wet pavement. "These are poisonous, did you know?" she asked and threw the empty pod out into the road. "They can actually kill you."

Sheila grew increasingly moody. Keen to rescue the situation, I suggested we go for a couple of games of bowling, a sport I knew she enjoyed very much. No, she didn't want to do that. An ice-cream cone at Baskin & Robbins? No. Was she sure? I'd pop for a banana split with extra nuts and whipped cream? No. A browse around the bookstore? No. All she wanted to do was just drive around more.

Having more or less exhausted the town, I tried the countryside, heading north along a network of small rural roads. We were soon into open countryside, comprised mainly of corn- and wheat fields. The area was hilly and Marysville had quickly disappeared from view to leave the fields stretching away from us in an undulating fashion for as far as the eye could see.

I made a few efforts at conversation, but they were useless. Sheila sat absolutely silent. Arms folded across her chest, she gazed out the passenger window so motionlessly that I could have been driving around with one of those inflatable dolls in the front seat beside me and no one would have discerned the difference.

The rain lessened, then finally stopped altogether, and very slowly the clouds began to break up. It was already early evening, so when the first patches of blue sky began to appear in the west, the sun came slanting across the hills.

"Stop!" Sheila cried. Not only was it the first word she had spoken in the better part of an hour and a half, which made it startling enough, but she said it with such suddenness that I fully expected to hit something with the car. I slammed on the brakes sufficiently hard to throw us both sharply forward. This made her smile briefly in my direction, before pointing to the east. "Look at that."

For a short, shining moment, color was sovereign. The wet asphalt of the road gleamed black against the sudden gold of the sunlit wheat. Beyond the ruffling grain rose the dark remains of the storm clouds, pierced through by a rainbow. Only a very short part of the rainbow was visible; there was not even enough to form a clear arc, but that small section shimmered brilliantly above the restless wheat.

"Oh, God," Sheila murmured softly, as she regarded the sight, "why do beautiful things make me feel so sad?"

Chapter 18

Back at the motel, we had our evening meal and then went out to enjoy the pool. The rain had cleared away entirely to give a cloudless night, the stars dimmed by the town's lights but still faintly discernible.

Sheila remained subdued. There was a heavy, almost depressed feel to her quietness. For the first time, she put aside that smoldering anger I always sensed just below the surface. In its place was nothing, just a great emptiness.

The exercise did me good. The pool was cool enough to let me swim hard and I did, blocking out everything except the feel of the water rushing over me, until at last I surfaced, tired and relaxed. Sheila wasn't a very good swimmer. I suspect she had never been taught and just got by on what she'd figured out over the years, but she kept at it almost as long as I did. Then we both retreated to the warmth of the Jacuzzi.

Back in the motel room, she stood before the mirror toweling her hair dry. She studied her reflection as she worked.

"Do you like me?" she asked.

Having finished with my shower and changed into my nightgown, I was lying on my bed and inspecting the TV schedule. Her question caught me unawares. "Well, yes, of course I do."

"I know I look stupid," she said to her reflection. "I know you think I do."

"No."

"Yes," she said. "You do. Everybody does. I do too." She ran her fingers through her hair, smoothing it down. "You see, I just don't want to look like me. That's why I do it. I can put up with looking stupid, if there's a chance that it might make me into someone else."

Once she was in her bed, I turned the light out. It wasn't all that late, only a little after eleven, but the swimming, combined with the emotional rigors of the day, had left me exhausted. I was ready for sleep and drowsy almost immediately.

Sheila turned restlessly in her bed. The room was very dark, so I could only hear her, not see her, but the sound of her movements kept intruding.

"Torey? You asleep?"

"No, not quite."

Silence.

"You wanted to say something?" I inquired.

A second long pause. She turned again. "A lot's changed," she said quietly.

"In what way?"

"In the migrant camp. It's a lot different to what I remember it."

I didn't answer.

"I do remember it. I haven't forgotten everything." A pause. "My memory's like Swiss cheese. It's got big holes in it. But other things ... I saw the camp today and it was, like ... well, like I'd never been away. I can remember it so good."

Silence then, long enough that I felt myself growing drowsy again.

"You know what I used to do at night, when we lived in the camp?" Sheila asked into the darkness.

"What's that?"

"Well, my pa used to always be out drinking," she said, using her old name for her father for the first time since we'd been reunited. "He used to leave me. Nearly every night. He'd give me, like, a bag of corn chips or something and tell me to go to bed, and then he'd go out. And once he was gone, I used to get up and go out into the camp and walk around. It was dark. It was, like, really late at night, and I would look for places with lights on. We didn't have any electricity then, just a kerosene lantern and a flashlight. So, I'd look for these places with lights and then I'd go peek in their windows. All the time. Every night."

"Why? Because of being alone? Or the light?" I asked.

"Yeah. I wanted light, I remember that. But mostly just to see what they lived like. A lot of the people weren't a lot different than us, but I just wanted to see."

A pause.

"I got in trouble for it. My pa catch me and I'd be whipped red for it."

Catch. I heard the word in its present-tense form, echoing Sheila's old childhood speech patterns. We never had found out why she spoke like that and since we had been reunited, she had used remarkably impeccable grammar for an adolescent. It was eerie to lie in the dark and listen to these long-ago words and speech patterns begin to reemerge.

"The police got me once. More than once, I think. People thought I was stealing things, but I wasn't. I'd just been looking."

"I can understand," I said softly. "It must have been lonely, being left on your own so often, when you were such a young child."

"Yeah," came the quiet, disembodied voice through the darkness. "It was."

A long silence followed. I had woken fully up by then and lay staring up. The curtains were heavy to shut out the motel security lights, but the occasional car turning into the parking lot shot a brief spear of light over the top. This threw the stucco ceiling into sudden relief.

"Can I tell you what happened sometimes?" she asked.

"Here? When you were little?"

174

"Yeah. When we lived in the migrant camp. When I was in your class."

"Yes, of course," I said.

"I had a mattress on the floor. That's where I slept. My pa slept on the couch. But he'd go out boozing and when he came home ... there were always people with him. Women, usually. And they'd fuck on the couch."

"Yes, I can remember you telling me once," I said.

"But sometimes ..." She stopped.

I listened into the darkness. She was breathing shallowly, her breaths audible to me in the next bed.

"Well, he was doing drugs. You knew that too, didn't you?" she asked.

"Yes."

"Smack mostly. And these guys got it for him. There were two. Sometimes he'd come home with them. Sometimes it was one or the other, sometimes both of them, but he never used to have enough money to pay them. I can remember lying there listening to him pleading with them. Begging them to give him the stuff, telling them how he was going to get them money. He'd even cry some of the time; I can remember hearing him."

I watched the patterns flash black and headlight-yellow across the ceiling.

"Well, this one guy, he used to give it to my dad cheap if ... He liked me to lay down with him ... He didn't fuck me or anything; it's just he liked little girls. Like to feel them over. And if I sucked his cock, my pa got his stuff cheap."

My blood ran like ice. "Why didn't you tell me?"

"How do you say that when you're six? Besides, it was my life. I was used to it."

I lay awake long after Sheila fell asleep. Memories came back to me, one after another, of the days in our classroom. Things had been *so* bad for her. She had been such a deprived, neglected child that there would have been no way of doing everything that had wanted doing, of undoing all the harm. I had known that then and had approached her one small issue at a time, changing what I could. Yet somewhere between then and now I had come to believe I had saved her from the worst. To realize now that even while in my room she had continued to suffer hurt me; that I had never even perceived it hurt me worse. Over and over and over I pondered on what more I should have done.

The next morning, Sheila was back to her usual, rather off-the-wall self. She spent ages in the bathroom doing her hair to emerge looking not a whole lot tidier than when she had arisen from bed, and her outfit, a cute little number involving exceptionally ragged cut-off jeans and a shimmery green top that would have been more at home in a Las Vegas floor show, needed to be seen to be believed.

It was the Fourth of July and our agenda for the day included the picnic with Chad and his family. I was very much looking forward to this. Chad and I had remained on good terms throughout the metamorphosis of our relationship from the physical to the platonic, and in the last few years it had matured into a genuine friendship. We were now in contact frequently, exchanging stimulating letters and lengthy phone calls, but the fact remained that I had never met his wife nor seen his three young daughters. Bringing Sheila with me created the prospect of an even more enjoyable reunion.

We drove over to Chad's house at three. He lived down a quiet, unpaved lane on the very edge of town. His was a beautiful house, new and huge, with a three-car garage and a tennis court to the side. I must confess to a twinge of remorse, or perhaps it was jealousy, when I saw it, knowing that this could have been mine. Not that I was particularly keen on houses of that sort or wanted that kind of lifestyle, and I didn't even play tennis, but it was impossible to ignore his level of success.

"Wow," Sheila murmured as we pulled into the drive and summed the whole matter up in that one word.

Before we were out of the car, Chad was at the door, opening it wide. "Welcome!" he said and children came spilling out around him.

His wife, Lisa, appeared beside him. Of Latino descent, she had the most exquisite eyes, dark and sparkly. She was a lawyer too and I had heard so much about her reputation as a killer in the courtroom that I had been expecting something quite different from what I saw. She was sweetly pretty and quite petite, rather the way one imagines fairy-tale heroines.

"And here," Chad was saying, as he pulled a small girl in front of him, "here's my Sheila."

His Sheila and my Sheila eyed one another. Like her mother, Chad's daughter was pretty in a girlish sort of way. Her hair was dark and curled naturally in long, loose ringlets down over her shoulders. She was dressed impeccably in a two-tone green designer-brand outfit that beautifully showed off the rich color of her hair.

"Sheila's five," Chad said, lovingly clasping her to his side. She smiled up at him. "And these ... girls, come here. Stand still a moment. This is Bridget, who's four. And this is Maggie. How old are you, Maggie?"

Laboriously, Maggie worked at holding up two fingers.

"That's right. Clever girl! Maggie's just had her birthday last Saturday."

Like their elder sister, both Bridget and Maggie were blessed with dark curly hair and laughing eyes, and both were attractively dressed in practical, but expensive clothes. All three girls were friendly, open children, chatting easily with Sheila and me, inviting us to come around to the backyard and see the picnic table and the box of fireworks.

At the back of the house, we found a large redwood deck ingeniously laid out to include a sandbox near the patio doors and to progress away on one side to a large wooden swing set and climbing frame and on the other to a large, landscaped garden that ended with a fence that overlooked open fields.

"Come see our horses," Chad's Sheila called cheerily and ran down the grass ahead of us. "Do you like to ride, Sheila? Do you want a ride on my horse? I'll take you."

"Thanks," Sheila replied, her voice hesitant. "Thanks, but not just now, okay? Maybe later."

"Well, come down and see them. Mom? Mommy, give us apples." She came running back up to the deck. She took Sheila's hand. "Come on. We'll get some apples and go down. I want to show you."

Chad and I, sitting in chairs on the deck, watched the two girls go off down the lawn toward the fence at the bottom.

"There's something I never thought I'd see," he said, his voice thoughtful.

"No."

There was a long moment's pause. "She's changed, hasn't she?" he said.

I didn't know quite how to respond. That had been my first impression too, but increasingly I was realizing that, no, Sheila hadn't actually changed much at all.

"I mean, that *hair*," he continued, when I didn't speak. "And those clothes! She's going to scare the horses." He laughed. "I suppose it's just adolescence, but I must admit, I didn't expect it of her. She always seemed such a practical little thing."

"She didn't have much choice in those days."

"How's it going for her?" Chad asked.

Sitting in my deck chair, I watched her with little Sheila, feeding apples to the two horses. "I don't know," I replied. "I haven't quite figured that out yet."

I sensed there was trouble fairly early on. Sheila mooched around on the outside of the crowd almost from the beginning. The little girls tried to engage her in various activities, ranging from riding the horses to grilling hot dogs on the barbecue, but for the most part, Sheila resisted their efforts. Initially, she wasn't unpleasant about it, just distant. However, as the afternoon progressed into evening, she became increasingly detached from the group. Long periods were spent wandering around the perimeter of the yard or swinging listlessly on one of the swings.

Feeling responsible for her, I tried to gloss over her behavior, especially to Lisa, who was going out of her way to try and include Sheila. I think perhaps things might have worked out better if Lisa simply could have ignored her and let her join in at her own rate, but this seemed to go against Lisa's innate way of dealing with children. It had become apparent very early on that Lisa was a doer and a joiner. Wanting to see Maggie, Bridget and Sheila sufficiently stimulated and socialized, she had provided schedules so full of lessons and extramural activities for her daughters that they probably maintained their own Filofaxes. Likewise, the picnic had been planned with exquisite attention to detail aimed at giving everyone a Very Good Time. That Sheila was refusing to join in implied she was not having a Very Good Time and this troubled Lisa to no end.

Sheila contributed to this. Discerning that she could bug Lisa so easily, she began to go at it wholeheartedly as the evening went on. Her ennui grew more obvious. The little girls irritated her, making her frown evilly at them when they came around her, and worst of all, she turned her back on the fireworks. Chad would light one, up it would go. Flash! Bang! Then all the oohs and aahs, while Sheila, bored, leaned against the deck railing and stared through the patio doors at Chad's dining-room table.

In turn, I got drawn into this too. Mortified by Sheila's rude behavior, I first tried making excuses, then tried tugging her off to the privacy of the bathroom for a quick word. She was having no quick words. She was having no words at all.

"Why are you so angry?" I hissed.

"You're the one who's angry," she replied in a sensible sort of voice.

"You've been angry with me the whole frigging time we've been back together. You act like everything is my fault."

"Well, isn't it?" she replied.

How we managed through the last hour at Chad's I don't know. I *was* angry. As far as I was concerned, the evening had been totally ruined. Here was my first time of meeting Chad's wife and his daughters, my first time face-to-face with Chad in many years, and what a jolly affair this had turned out to be. I felt like dumping Sheila off at the nearest bus station and buying her a one-way ticket back to Broadview.

The silence during the ten-minute ride back to the motel was lethal. Sheila was gloating, or at least that's what it felt like from my perspective. Having stirred all of us up into a lather, she appeared calm and detached, if not even a bit superior. I got the distinct sense that she thought she was above all this. With each passing minute, my feelings grew fiercer.

"Well, this evening was a write-off," I said crossly, as we got out of the car at the motel. Fumbling with the keys, I unlocked our room.

"You are really a control freak, you know that?" Sheila said. "God, you have got to be in charge of everything."

"I do not."

"You think you own my life. You think you created me. You think I'm just a character in your book."

"I do not!" I retorted.

"You do. I didn't say I wanted to go there tonight. You're the one who arranged it and you didn't ask my opinion of it. Why should I want to go over there? I don't even know those people."

"You *do*. That's Chad, for God's sake."

Sheila shrugged insolently. "I don't know him. Could have been anybody and his stupid kids there, as far as I knew."

"That was *Chad*. Who kept you out of the state hospital. Who stood up for you when nobody else would. All he did—"

She cut me off with one fierce downward movement of her arm, like a sword stroke. "And I'm supposed to be so grateful, aren't I?" Her voice rose. "That's what you want. I'm supposed to be so goddamned, fucking grateful to all of you guys for what you did for me. That's it, isn't it? That's what you want."

"*No.*"

"It *is*. Don't go fucking me around, Torey. That's what you want. To make yourself into such a good guy. That's the only reason you came back."

"It's not!" I cried.

Seeing her face, I realized a monster had been unleashed. Her face went from pink to red to a deeper scarlet, the veins becoming prominent at her temples. Her eyes dilated and her lips drew back against her teeth. Warning bells went off somewhere far back in my mind, alerting me to my own physical safety.

"You think you made my life better, do you?" she yelled, her voice growing louder with each word. "You think you *fixed* things? You didn't. You made them worse. A million, million, million times worse than they ever were before!"

"Whoa, whoa, whoa," I said.

"*No!*" she cried passionately, "you whoa. You're the one who can't stop meddling. You leave my life alone!"

I regarded her.

"You set me up, Torey. You took me in that room and you let me play with all those toys and read all those books and you just made me feel like a million dollars, and then what did you do? Did you stay? Did you take care of me once you got me?" Her mouth drew down to where I thought she was going to cry and there was one very long, shuddery intake of breath. "You set me up, knowing all along you were going to leave."

"I didn't mean—" I started.

"You *did*! You meant every goddamned thing you did with me, Torey. I never knew how fucking awful my life was until then, and then you came along and suddenly there's this whole other world. And you *meant* that. You controlled the whole thing. You created me out of shit and made me think I smelled like flowers."

"Sheila, listen to—"

"You made me believe you loved me."

"I *did* love you, Sheila. I still do."

"Oh, shit, don't give me that. How could you? You left me."

"Sheila—"

"You had so much power, Torey. I loved you such a terribly lot, *so much*. And what did you do? You pushed me out that door and left me."

"Sheila, *please*."

"But you're never the fuck going to do it again!" she cried, and before I realized what was happening, she had opened the door to the motel room and was gone.

Chapter 19

I stood, shell-shocked, for only a moment or two before running to the door to see where she was. In that short time, she had disappeared into the night.

"Sheila? Sheila, where are you?" I called.

A door down the way opened. "Could you keep it down out there?" someone shouted.

Gripped with real fear, I closed the motel door and went back inside. What now? I looked around the room. Her meager possessions lay strewn around her bed. What should I do? Would she come back of her own accord? Should I go looking for her? Or leave well enough alone? I felt paralyzed with helplessness.

Sitting down on my bed, I tried to pull my thoughts together. Where would she be likely to go? The migrant camp came first to mind, but surely not. Surely she would have more sense than to go there, alone, in the middle of the night. And why? Would there still be anyone there she'd know? I doubted it. She had given no indication of still having connections with anyone in Marysville.

Where else? The only places I could think of were those where we had spent time together and I couldn't imagine, given the circumstances, that she would go to any of them. Most likely, she would head for the town center, simply because shopping areas were the places many teenagers escaped to when distressed. Obviously, little was likely to be open so late at night, especially in a community the size of Marysville, but it was Fourth of July night ... Worried, I gathered up my car keys and set out to search for Sheila.

Around and around and around I drove, the streets becoming increasingly familiar again, until old, long-forgotten journeys through Marysville started coming back to me. It was a very still place that late at night. There were a few cars "turning the point" down on Main Street, but otherwise, mine was the only vehicle for blocks, sometimes miles, at a time.

I went downtown three or four times and found no sign of her. From there, I followed the main road leading out to the shopping district that had grown up around the mall. I circled the whole town, using the highway to connect outgoing roads, and finally went out to the migrant camp.

There, unlike the rest of Marysville, people were up and moving around. Indeed, it was lively in certain parts, making me suspect that, as in the old days, not all the residents spent their days in hard labor. There were numerous drugged or drunken men lying about in one area on the lower end and I found myself feeling very ill at ease. Unwilling to roll my window down, I didn't stop and ask anyone if they had seen a girl of Sheila's description.

All my fond recollections of Marysville came crashing down to dust in those early hours spent driving around the town. I hated it by the end and only wanted to reach the highway and head home; however, worry kept me at the ceaseless midnight circling.

At long last, about two in the morning, I saw Sheila. She was in quite an unexpected area of town, walking along one of the larger arterial roads out in the residential part not far from our old school. It was only by chance I happened to be coming that way, as I had had an idea of a different part of downtown to search and was taking a shortcut to get there. I pulled the car up along the curb and rolled the window down.

"Look, I'm sorry. Can we go back to the motel and sort things out?"

Her eyes were wide and dark in the dim illumination of the streetlight, which gave her a wild, almost animalistic appearance. I sensed she was very frightened and not likely to be predictable.

"I am sorry," I said in my most contrite voice. "Come on, please? Come back with me."

She shook her head. "No. Go away. I don't need you."

"Please?"

She regarded me.

"Well, look, let's go get a hamburger or something, if you don't want to go back to the motel. Okay?"

Sheila hesitated, which encouraged me to keep on.

"We could go over to Lenny's. They're open all night. Come on. Please?"

Much to my relief, she opened the passenger door and got in. Indeed, she almost fell in, giving away just how very tired she was. I glanced over at her with her yellow hair and her silly clothes, crumpled in exhaustion. God, how hard it is to be fourteen.

Once in the restaurant, Sheila tucked hungrily into a whole plate of food, while I nursed a cup of coffee and a stale doughnut, but she didn't talk. I didn't press her. We were both too tired for that.

Afterward, she came back to the motel with me without any protest. Once in the room, she sat down on her bed and began to pull off her heavy work boots. "I'm not staying," she said quietly. "Tomorrow comes and I'm getting out of here."

"Yes, I think I'm ready to as well."

"No, Torey. That's not what I mean," she said, looking up. "I'm not going with you. I'm not going to sit in a car for four hours with you. I'm going home on my own."

I regarded her.

"And you can't stop me," she added to my unspoken words.

"No, I won't stop you. If that's what you want, I'll take you down to the bus station tomorrow and we'll get you a ticket. And you can take the first one out."

"*I'll* get me a ticket," she said.

"No, Sheila, I'm quite happy to get it. Save your money."

"No, I said, *I'll* get it, Torey. You don't own me, so don't try."

Wearily, I nodded. "Fine. Do it that way."

Once in bed with the lights out, I lay staring into the darkness. What had gone wrong? What had happened between last night, when we had seemed so close, and tonight, when we felt worlds apart? As if she were reading my thoughts, Sheila spoke.

"You left me. Don't you know how much that hurt me?" Her voice was soft, almost inaudible even in the nighttime silence.

"I didn't want to, Sheila."

"Then why did you?"

"Because it was simply the way things were. I was a teacher. My end came in June when school finished and there was nothing I could do about that ..."

"It wasn't right, what you did," she said so softly. A long pause followed. "You left me behind."

"I'm sorry. I truly am."

"And it wasn't just that. You took it all with you when you went—the sun, the moon, the stars. Everything. What right did you have to give it to me, when you just took it all away again?"

Sheila did not return to the summer-school program on Monday, when we resumed after the Fourth of July break. I had neither seen nor heard from her since putting her on the bus in Marysville. Although I longed to phone, if for no other reason than to reassure myself she had made it home all right, I knew instinctively that I had to stay away.

Jeff, ever keen to perceive my moods, cornered me back in our office after lunch. "Okay, so what's going on?" he asked. "Where'd the Orangutan hie off to?"

I gave him a brief synopsis of what had happened on our visit to Marysville.

"Ooh," he replied, as if touching a bruise. There was a pause while he put away a medical journal that had lain open on his desk for the better part of the last week, then he looked over. "I can see where she's coming from, though. She's already been abandoned by one mother. Then you come along, provide all the attention and nurturing she was so desperate for. Then *you* disappear. At six it's going to be difficult for her to discern that what you've done is any different from what her mother did."

"Yes, I know that, but it *was* different. I was her teacher."

"Okay, so you were her teacher," he said. "But what was on your curriculum, Hayden? Math? Reading? Or was it love? Confidence? Self-esteem?"

"What should I have done with her?" I asked. "Left her alone? Seen this incredible kid in this even more incredible situation and done nothing?"

190

Leaning back in his desk chair, Jeff pursed his lips.

"Are you saying I shouldn't have done it?" I asked.

"Are you?"

Turning away, I sighed. "That's a pointless question, actually. I can't turn back time and change anything. The real question is: what do I do now?"

Balancing a paper clip on his thumbnail, Jeff aimed and then flicked it into the pencil holder on his desk. "You do what all of us do in this business: pray that in the end you've helped more than you've hurt."

Sheila remained absent from the program for the rest of the week and also the following Monday. Late Monday afternoon, when I was in my office at the clinic, there was a soft knock on my closed door.

"Yes? Come in."

Sheila gently pushed the door open. "Can I talk to you?"

I nodded.

"Is Jeff here? I want to talk privately. I don't want him walking in," she said.

"No, he won't. He's over at the hospital and won't be back tonight," I replied.

Sheila closed the door behind her and came across to Jeff's desk. Pulling the chair out, she sat down. She looked around. "So this is your office, huh?"

"Yup." I had been marking a file and returned to finish it off.

She studied Jeff's bulletin board. "You guys sure are alike. Look, you got your junk arranged just like his junk. You even got the identical same Pink Panther things. 'This is where Jeff lives it up' this one says. 'This is where Torey lives it up.' Where'd you get them?"

"Jeff got them," I replied.

"Do you love him?" Sheila asked, rocking herself idly back and forth in the desk chair.

"I *like* him. A great deal. But if you mean romantic love, no. I've got somebody else."

"Oh? Who? I haven't seen you with anybody."

I looked over. "Surely you haven't come all the way up here from Broadview to talk to me about my love life."

"Yeah, well, I was just trying to get your attention," she said. "You've hardly looked up since I walked in. The whole time you've had your stupid nose stuck in that thing you're writing."

Closing the file, I laid it up in the basket and turned in my chair toward her. "I'm all yours."

"Gosh, look. You got my poem up there. You never told me you put my poem on the wall."

"I wasn't hearing from you very much then," I said. "I didn't have your address."

"Yeah, I was in the children's home then, when I wrote that."

Her tone was light and breezy, her attitude, as she lazily rotated the chair, relaxed. One would never have known anything had happened between us. It would have taken her forty-five minutes on the bus to get up here from Broadview, plus a good ten-minute walk from the nearest bus stop, so this was hardly a casual visit. Yet Sheila was giving nothing away.

"Is there anything I can do for you?" I asked.

"Well, it's almost five o'clock. I thought maybe you would like to go out for Italian with me or something. It doesn't have to be pizza. We could go for spaghetti. Or something else, if you want."

I grinned.

"Or you could take me over to your house. I've never been to your place. I got to thinking that if we stopped at the supermarket first, I could get things and make you supper. I make this really good thing with tuna fish and a can of mushroom soup."

"I'd loved to," I said, "but unfortunately, I've already got plans for this evening."

Her face fell. "Is it with this guy?"

I nodded.

There was an enormous silence.

"Look, I'm sorry," I said. "I really would have loved to, it's just I didn't know in time. Maybe we can some other night."

Head down so that the yellow hair fell forward, obscuring her features, she sighed heavily. "I'm *trying* to say sorry to you," she muttered. A pause. "And I wanted to come over to your house."

Chapter 20

Tuesday morning found Sheila back with us. As with me the afternoon before, she behaved as if nothing in particular had happened and there had been no absence. I had threatened Jeff to keep him from making an issue of it. Miriam inquired politely and Sheila blithely lied through her teeth, saying she had been ill.

Alejo was charmingly pleased to see Sheila. When she came through the door, his small face lit up and he ran across the room to throw his arms around her in an enthusiastic hug. This caught all of us by surprise, as Alejo had remained an aloof, unpredictable boy throughout the weeks, but none of us more so than Sheila. An expression of alarm crossed her face first, when the boy so eagerly grasped hold of her, but then she smiled and bent to hug him back.

Throughout the summer program, Sheila, like Alejo, had been a guarded soul. It was apparent by now that this was not a particularly natural setting for her. She did not innately respond to young children in the way that some teenaged girls do, and she found some of the more difficult situations unsettling, because, I suspect, they still came just a little too close to home. Jeff and I had discussed this and felt it was best to let her continue to the end, as we were not that far off now, but we agreed that to expect more in the way of help from Sheila was probably unrealistic.

She appeared genuinely happy to be back with us. Her mood was positive, if not downright sunny. Thus far, among the children she had only responded in a relaxed and natural way to Alejo and occasionally to David. The girls, in particular, she had shunned, which was a pity, as we could have done with a good role model for Kayleigh, Tamara and Violet. However, on this morning, she showed genuine warmth and generosity toward several of the children. Even Violet.

Over the course of the summer, Violet had developed what could only be described as a crush on Sheila. She had struggled vainly to catch Sheila's attention, to sit near her, to hold her hand. A big, ungainly girl with plain features and annoying persistence, Violet wasn't very easy to accept, even in the best of circumstances. Sheila had found her obsessional fervor irritating and Violet's repeated efforts to touch her horrid. I tried to explain to Sheila that such crushes were fairly normal in girls of Violet's age and implied nothing serious, but Sheila, not fully comfortable with her own sexuality, continued to find these advances revolting. On this morning, however, Sheila listened patiently to Violet's various ramblings, and while not allowing Violet to go so far as touch her, she did let the girl sit next to her at snack time.

After snack time, we took the children over to the park across the street and Sheila continued to play actively with them, pushing Kayleigh on the swing, boosting David and Mikey up to the uppermost reaches of the climbing frame.

I realized what was happening. Like the swan, so graceful above water and paddling like hell below the surface, Sheila was working actively on serenity in hopes that all the turmoil brought up between us would disappear, or at least no longer be apparent. Watching her through the morning, I pondered on how much of a behavior pattern this was for her.

Feeling the need to confront this issue, rather than allow her to bury it, I cornered her during the ride down to Fenton Boulevard.

"This might be a good time for us to talk," I said, as I pulled away from the school.

"Oh? About what?"

"About us. About the Fourth of July weekend. There were obviously some very strong feelings and I think it would be better if we cleared them up."

Sheila shrugged, as if I were talking about something completely unknown to her.

"I get the feeling you think I walked out on you when you were little."

"I never said that."

"What I heard was how angry you felt. How you felt that I set you up, how it seemed to you that I didn't care and I just left you."

"It doesn't matter. I'm not angry now," she replied.

"These things need facing, Sheila. If you have such strong feelings, they won't go away just because you pretend they have."

She shrugged. "I don't know. Sooner or later everything else in my life goes away, why not them as well?"

"Sheila."

"Okay, okay, so I was upset," she said wearily. "So what? People get upset. I'm over it now, so let's just leave it at that."

I didn't answer.

Looking over, she smiled beguilingly. "You want me to say I'm sorry, okay? I was stupid. I didn't mean it."

"It's all right to be angry with me," I said. "I don't mind, but let's just be up front about it."

"No, I wasn't angry. Just stupid, that's all. I get like that. So let's forget it. Let's go on like it didn't happen."

"But it *did* happen."

"Not if I say it didn't." She looked over at me. "Things only exist if you believe they exist. That's true. I've read it. And it's true, because I know it."

"So, you're saying that if you don't believe we had the argument, we didn't have it?" I asked.

"Things can only bother you if they exist. And they can only exist if you let them."

Silence came then. I was drawn back abruptly across the years to a dark school closet where I had retreated with Sheila after she had gotten into serious mischief in another teacher's room. That teacher had sent her to the principal, who gave her "swats," the form of corporal punishment acceptable in my school at the time.

Distressed to have lost control of the situation myself and have a child who I already knew was physically abused at home, then experienced swats at school, I had withdrawn with her into the only private place I could find to try and sort the matter out. Sheila, however, had seemed to take the whole experience in her stride. Indeed, she pointed out with some pride how she had not cried at all when the principal struck her.

"Don't you feel like it?" I had asked in amazement. She was six and I was twenty-four and I felt like it.

"Ain't nobody can hurt me that ways," she'd replied matter-of-factly. "They don't know I hurt if I don't cry. So, they can't hurt me."

Seven years later and I realized Sheila was still operating under a variant of that theory.

We had only two full weeks of the summer program to run. Both Jeff and I were immensely pleased with how it had turned out. There had been hiccups, to be sure, and plenty of things we would do differently the next time around, but in general, it had worked well.

One obvious advantage to providing a program of this nature for our clients was the opportunity to work with them in such a natural milieu. Some of the children, among them Kayleigh and Mikey, had responded well to the group situation and the supportive setting and were well on their way to putting their problems behind them.

Equally useful were the diagnostic advantages of such a setting. A few of the children had been with the clinic for some time without any marked sign of progress. Being with them for three hours a day, five days a week, in such varied circumstances allowed Jeff and me to assess their problems much more accurately than had been possible in the confines of the clinic and its psychiatric hour.

Tamara was a good example of such a child. She had first come to the clinic when she was six on referral from her family doctor. He had treated sores on her forearms, which refused to heal, despite all his efforts. His suspicions that Tamara was inflicting the injuries herself and then preventing the wounds from healing were soon confirmed.

Initially, Tamara had seen one of the other psychiatrists at the clinic, but after eighteen months of therapy, she was referred to Jeff in hopes that she might progress faster with a male therapist. Jeff had been seeing her weekly in play therapy for a further ten months and felt he was still no nearer to helping Tamara control her destructive urges.

The summer program showed us a complex, deeply unhappy little girl, who had difficulty relating to just about everyone, young and old alike.

There probably was an element of depression in Tamara's behavior, just as her copious files said, but then depression is a fairly natural reaction to sensing no one likes you. Unable to get the attention she needed through more traditional means, Tamara had discovered that injuries received a lot of notice. Over the course of the program, we saw her draw blood on several different occasions when things didn't go her way. Jeff, armed with these insights, was now working with Tamara to help her improve her interpersonal skills and felt at last that they were moving forward in therapy.

Alejo was another child who had been included for diagnostic purposes. Unfortunately, he wasn't enjoying such a happy ending. Increasingly, Jeff and I were having to acknowledge that the majority of his problems stemmed less from emotional trauma than from low intelligence and, most likely, brain damage. There was no doubt that his traumatic early years had had an effect on him, and this showed itself in his abrupt, sometimes violent, responses to actions around him; however, many of his more trenchant behaviors were simply the result of a boy mentally incapable of coping with the usual demands of school and home. This had become particularly apparent in the ebb and flow of daily activities in the program and Jeff and I were making preparations to discuss the matter with his parents.

I was dreading telling Sheila this, even more than Alejo's parents. Of all the children, Alejo alone was special to her. There had been a natural affinity between them, right from the beginning, and we had encouraged it. Now I regretted having involved her so closely, because I knew Sheila would find the final verdict on Alejo unacceptable.

Unfortunately, I didn't get a chance to tell Sheila. Instead, she overheard Jeff talking to me at the end of one session when we were cleaning up.

"What do you mean, he's got a low IQ? You mean he's retarded?" Sheila asked, coming back to where we were standing.

"Jeff did the official workup last week," I replied.

"Last week? When I was gone? You just waited till I was gone, didn't you?" she retorted.

Jeff turned away, unwilling to get drawn into an argument with her.

"He's not got a low IQ. He's perfectly normal," she said.

Miriam, who was coming back to us with the boxes of crayons and marking pens, said, "He's still a lovely boy."

"He's *not* retarded. That's not why he's not talking. You think he's not talking for that reason, don't you? But it isn't that. He talks to me."

"He talks to us too, Sheila," I said. "But he doesn't say much and why he doesn't say much is because some of the areas of his brain aren't working quite like they should. It's called aphasia."

"I don't care what it's called," she snapped back. "He hasn't got it. He's perfectly normal. He just doesn't talk to *you*. He talks to me just fine. He talks in *Spanish*. So how do you expect him to tell you things when you don't even speak the same language as him?"

Jeff tapped my shoulder. "This isn't worth getting into, Hayden," he murmured quietly.

"Yeah, sure, you'd say that," Sheila said to him. "It's not you they're calling stupid." Throwing down the rag she'd been wiping the tables with, she stomped off.

"You can't let that happen to Alejo," Sheila said to me in the car afterward. The anger had gone from her voice, to be replaced by urgent concern.

"No, it's a very difficult situation."

"But you realize what they're going to do, don't you?" she said. "Send him back to Colombia."

"We don't know that for sure. His parents have discussed a lot of different alternatives and that's just one of them."

"You mustn't let it happen."

There was silence between us then. I focused my attention on getting us out onto the freeway.

"You don't *want* it to happen, do you?" she inquired.

"No, of course I don't."

"So, Torey—"

"It isn't my choice, kiddo. He's a lovely boy, but he is brain-damaged, of limited intelligence and emotionally disturbed. That's a lot to cope with. I can encourage his parents to keep him and I certainly will do so. Both Jeff and I will, but we can't force them."

"But what if they want to send him back to Colombia?" she cried. "What if they put him in the orphanage again?"

"Sheila, I haven't got much control over this situation. In fact, he isn't even my client, or Jeff's. So, technically, we have *no* control. I do desperately hope they don't send him back. It would hurt him and I think it's wrong, morally; but I can't make them do anything they don't want to do. Nor stop them from doing anything they do want to do. They are legally Alejo's parents."

Sheila sputtered in angry frustration. "Look what's happened to him! He's been found living in some garbage can and brought here and people have been giving him nice toys and food and TV and everything. And now what are they going to do? Put him back in the garbage can. And you're going to just sit there and let it happen?"

"We're not going to 'just sit,'" I said. "We're going to *try* to keep that from happening. We're going to try to help Alejo change his behavior. We'll try to find an acceptable alternative for his parents."

"And what if you fail?" Sheila asked.

"I'll feel terribly sad."

"That's it? You'll feel sad?"

"That's all I can do," I said.

Folding her arms across her chest, she turned her head away from me. "You're shitholes," she muttered. "You and your kind. You really are fucking shitholes."

Chapter 21

My personal life was in a state of flux that summer. I tended toward a pattern of exclusive, long-term relationships that often lasted several years, and was, at the time, "between men," as one close girlfriend so succinctly put it. I had actually been "between" for several months by that point and getting fairly fed up with it.

Synchronizing my life at work with my personal life had always been difficult for me. Although I'd mellowed from earlier years, when the intensity with which I'd thrown myself into classroom life left little room for other activities, I still loved my work profoundly. I still felt a thrill of anticipation on Sunday for the approaching Monday and I still found it nearly impossible to exclude the kids I was working with entirely from my thoughts. I didn't dwell on them, but they were simply there, turning over in the back of my mind. This made me a challenging companion, I knew, and it took a secure, tolerant man to cope. At the time, such men seemed rather thin on the ground.

To complicate matters, I preferred men from outside my profession. It kept me from talking shop twenty-four hours a day, as I was inclined to do with colleagues. And it kept rivalry at bay. I had a fiercely competitive streak, which served me well with the children, because it kept me determined to win even when the odds were not at all in my favor; however, it was lethal to personal relationships. I also enjoyed the slightly schizophrenic experience of maintaining separate lives because it allowed me to develop interests and talents that might otherwise seem mutually exclusive.

The newest contender was Allan. The downtown area of the city had been subjected to redevelopment a few years earlier and many of the old buildings had been rescued from decay and now formed part of a rather elite shopping district. Allan owned a small bookstore tucked into a tiny side street in the midst of this redeveloped area.

I had first met him when I was pursuing an obscure book of Greek plays. Intrigued, he had invited me into the back room to show me his classical collection, which was one of the better come-on lines I had heard. From there we went on to a series of rather nice dinners in restaurants quite unlike the greasy spoons I usually patronized.

Allan was, in a word, civilized. He enjoyed the opera, discussed literary novels in the enthusiastically casual way of one who had not only read them, but actually enjoyed them, and he could pick amazingly good red wines. His apartment was in an old, restored town house not far from the city center, and it was immaculately furnished with Indian rugs and antique furniture. He even had a tablecloth on his table, which indicated real class to someone like me, who seldom had enough of the clutter off the table to find the surface.

I knew right from the beginning that Allan and I were not soul mates, the way Chad and I had been. Allan was finicky, which got on my nerves. I was unpredictable or, as he termed it, "uneven," and that got on his. But there was still much to be said for the relationship, not the least the fact that I had met no one else.

Certainly Allan met the qualifications as far as being outside my profession went. Deep quests into the nether regions of human behavior might as well have been space probes into other galaxies from his point of view. Trying to talk with him about my kids was impossible. But this was all right. I had Jeff to talk to if I wanted to mull something over about work, and when I was outside it, I was perfectly happy discussing Greek poets or Australian Shiraz.

That Friday night, Allan and I had a picnic planned. This was no rude affair with Allan. He had European-style picnics, complete with wicker picnic basket, red-checked cloth to lay on the ground and real plates and glassware. This called for something rather grander than Kentucky Fried Chicken and barbecue beans, so I had spent Thursday roasting eggplants and fiddling with pâtés, while Allan sought out French baguettes and the right wine.

Friday night after work, I came home to put the final touches on the food. We were going to a local beauty spot on the lake that bordered the eastern side of the city. This required serious mosquito protection, so Allan was in the back room trying to get my insect lamp to work.

A knock at the door. Thinking it was the paper boy coming to collect his money, I slipped the check between my teeth and wiped my greasy hands before pulling open the door.

Sheila.

"Hi," she said cheerfully.

"Hi. What are you doing here?" I asked.

"I tried to look your address up in the phone book, but you aren't listed yet, so I called for Directory Inquiries," she replied. "Can I come in?"

"They're not supposed to give out addresses," I replied.

"No, I know it, but if you act like you already got the address, say, like, 'Is that the Hayden on Maple Avenue?' they always say, no, and give you the right address. Or at least part of it. Then you hang up, try again to get someone else and then use that part to get the rest. It always works." She looked past me. "Can I come in?"

She didn't wait for an answer, but came on in anyway. Smiling, she looked around at the walls of my apartment. "Wow, this is neat. I like the way you've done this." She flopped down in a chair. "I came over 'cause I thought maybe we could talk."

I didn't want to make her feel unwelcome, but her visit was totally unexpected. It left me momentarily floundering.

"You're always trying to talk to me in the car when you take me down to Fenton Boulevard and I hate that," Sheila said. "It's too short. I know the ride's going to end and I never can get my thoughts organized fast enough. I didn't have anything to do tonight, so I thought I'd come over here and we can talk."

Was this manipulative? I wondered. Did she know that I would normally give over what I was doing to allow her to talk?

Just then, Allan appeared from the back. "Torey? Oh ..." he said, seeing Sheila.

"Oh," said Sheila in return.

"I had plans tonight," I said gently.

"Oh. I see." A long pause followed as she regarded Allan. "Is he the one you're fucking now?" She said it casually, as if she expected it to be normal conversation.

"Sheila, I think you'll need to go," I said. "I'm sorry you came all this way. I wish you'd let me know first."

Her expression hardened. *I know that look*, I thought. Flashing back across the years came the face of six-year-old Sheila, thwarted, angry, bent on revenge. So much about her had changed, but with that expression she became instantly recognizable.

"You know, he isn't as good-looking as Chad," she said to me, her voice still pleasantly conversational. She glanced at Allan. "That was her last fuck. Well, probably not her last. I don't know how many others have been in between."

"*Sheila.*" I put a hand on her shoulder and turned her toward the door. "I'll see you on Monday." I got her through the door and shut it.

"Maybe you will, maybe you won't," she muttered.

As I turned from the door, I saw Allan's face, pasty-white with shock. "Sorry about that," I said.

"*Who* was she?"

"It's too difficult to explain."

Sheila was back on Monday with no indication that anything had happened. She joined in with the children in a helpful manner and chatted pleasantly with Miriam at break time. I was aware of being on my guard with her, expecting I'm not quite sure what from her, but it never materialized. Sheila behaved as any other teenaged helper might be expected to.

In the car down to Fenton Boulevard, I said nothing. If she wasn't comfortable with this as a time for talking, then I'd abide with that. There could be other times.

Her arms folded across her chest, Sheila sat in silence for a mile or two. Out of the corner of my eye, I caught her glancing at me occasionally. I leaned forward and turned on the radio.

Sheila gave a huge sigh. "Oh, God, now she's sulking," she muttered under her breath.

"I'm not sulking," I said. "The other night you said you didn't want to talk during this ride, because it was so short."

"I didn't mean not talk at all. You practically haven't said a word since we got in the car."

I studied the cars on the freeway before me.

Sheila was watching me. When I didn't respond, she let her shoulders drop. She sighed. "Tor?"

"Yes?"

"What's going to happen to me?"

"What do you mean?" I asked.

"Well, I mean when this summer-school thing is over. What will I be? I mean, what am I now? I'm not your student, really, am I? I'm not a client. At least I don't think I am. But you wouldn't treat a friend like you treat me."

That caught my attention. I looked over at her. "How do you mean?"

"You know what I mean, Torey. We're not friends. I don't know what you want to call it, but it isn't friendship." A pause. "And now this program is just about over. Are you going to leave me again?"

"No. I'm not going anywhere. I'll still be at the clinic."

She made a frustrated little clicking noise. "You are, like, *so* dense sometimes," she muttered. "I don't care where you're working, Torey. The thing is, *I'm* not going to be there, am I? What's going to happen to me?"

"What do you want to happen to you?" I asked.

Arms still folded across her chest, Sheila turned

her head away from me and gazed out the window. Several moments passed in pensive silence. "We're going to run out of time," she whispered. "We're one point eight miles from the bus station. Shit."

Turning my car into the parking lot of a large discount store, I pulled over to the far side and turned off the engine. "There are other buses. If you miss the usual one, you can get a later one."

Her eyes had grown huge with the unexpectedness of my action.

"If you're asking what's going to happen in regards to our relationship, that's up to you. I like having you around. I've enjoyed this summer. I hope once the summer school is over, we continue to see each other."

The car quickly grew warm in the summer sun, so I rolled down the window and leaned on it.

"That's it?" Sheila asked. "We might just get to see each other sometimes?"

"There's a hidden agenda here," I answered. "You're asking me more than I'm hearing."

She didn't reply. In the heat, sweat beaded up along her temples and trickled down along the side of her face. Minutes passed. My mind began to wander, and as it so often did when I was with Sheila, it wandered back to the time we were together in the classroom.

Suddenly, I was awash with longing. It had been so much simpler then, when I was the adult and she was the child, when I was convinced my world was right and her world was wrong and it was only a matter of getting her to change sides. Never once had I questioned then the basic value of what I was doing.

"Do you fuck him?" she asked, her voice soft.

Pulled from my thoughts so abruptly, I looked over in surprise. "Who?"

"That guy who was at your apartment. Do you fuck him?" The question was not saucily put at all, as her references to such activities had been on Saturday night, but with genuine inquiry in her voice.

"That's a fairly personal question," I replied.

As if suddenly embarrassed, her head dropped and her cheeks colored. There was a deep intake of air. Then, unexpectedly, it crossed my mind that she was going to cry.

"I'm sorry," I said. "I'm not angry with you for asking it. It's just that it's one of those questions that I'm not prepared to answer."

She was going to cry. I could see her sucking her lower lip between her teeth to keep it from quivering. "You told me before," she said. Her voice was shaky, but the tears didn't fall. "When I was little. I asked you if you and Chad fucked and you said you did."

I wasn't sure I quite remembered that particular phraseology, so I paused, recalling what she might have said.

"You *did*," she insisted, reading my silence. "It was that time after my dad's brother Jerry had … had done what he'd done. You know. And I couldn't figure out what was going on. I couldn't understand why he'd done that to me, because I liked him so much. And you explained all that to me. 'Cause he'd told me it was how you and Chad loved and he was just teaching me, so you'd love me too. And I asked you. And you answered me without even pausing. I know, 'cause I remember you doing it."

"That was different, kiddo. I was explaining," I said. "It wasn't just conversation."

"Why do you call me that?" Sheila asked abruptly, looking over at me.

"Call you what?"

"Kiddo. When I was little, you called me lovey. And tiger. And sweetheart. What was I then that I'm not now?"

What occurred to me when I was back at the clinic and mulling our conversation over was that Sheila had clearly remembered our talking about the matter when she was six. She made precise reference to that early conversation, using real names and details that indicated a very clear recollection of the event. This stood in stark contrast to her hazy memories earlier or, indeed, to her insistence that she had no recollection of Chad. Were the memories coming back? And if that was so, what had happened to make them fade in the first place? Or was it possible that she had remembered all along and had told me otherwise? If so, why?

I was also becoming very conscious of a hidden agenda. Conversation after conversation with Sheila I sensed we were talking on two levels at once, that she was addressing another matter as well as the one at hand. I had the distinct feeling that she was aware of what this hidden agenda was and that it fueled a good deal of the sparky anger Sheila had demonstrated over the course of the summer.

Then again, maybe it wasn't so hidden. Sheila had spoken in no uncertain terms during our visit to Marysville about the pain and anger she'd felt when the school year had finished and I'd departed. Perhaps the fault had been mine in not bringing the subject up again. I had been so startled by the intensity of her feelings that night in the motel room and then distracted by the need to deal with the here-and-now of her running out, that I hadn't handled the issue as deftly as I might have in a more controlled location, like the clinic or the classroom. And she was right: the car after summer school was not the appropriate place for such a discussion.

I looked at my calendar. We were meeting with Alejo's parents on the following afternoon, so I wouldn't be able to see Sheila then. In fact, it was a very busy week, due to the ending of the summer program. Jeff and I had several evaluation meetings, in addition to our usual clinic commitments. Pulling the diary over, I penciled in Sheila's name on Friday. She seemed so desperate to come over to my house, I thought, so maybe Friday evening we could do something special together.

The next morning was one of chaos. It started with the minibus driver, who brought several of the children to the school, announcing to us that Violet had been sick on the ride over, and indeed, she had, everywhere and over everyone. This involved all four of us in cleaning up. Then, when I phoned Violet's mother, she explained that she couldn't come to get Violet, because her husband had the car. Miriam volunteered to take Violet home, but it was quite a distance, so that left us without Miriam for the first half of the morning.

Tamara, who had become quite reliable about not hurting herself, seemed to find all the attention the minibus children were getting was simply too much. While we were all distracted, she managed to locate a large pair of scissors and cut a long gash on her inner arm, almost from wrist to elbow. It wasn't deep, but it was bloody and by that point it was just Jeff, Sheila and I. The other children were becoming very unsettled with all this disruption, and frankly, we did not have control of things.

Jeff, being the doctor, got the job of bandaging Tamara back together, while Sheila and I tried to quell fears and get everyone re-oriented. The summer school had not been running enough weeks to develop the very useful group camaraderie that I'd always cultivated in my classrooms. There was still no real center with this bunch, such that when disaster struck, things flew apart easily. I tried a few songs to keep up the cheer, but Joshua and Jessie, our two autistic children, both screamed and a couple of the others just kept wandering off.

The only humorous moment came when, in the chaos, I noticed David, Alejo and Mikey were gone. Panicked, because I realized that in all the commotion, we had not searched David that morning for matches, as we usually did, I dashed out to hunt for them. It took me five or ten minutes to locate them. The three boys were outside. I was still inside, when I heard their voices through an open window, and I approached cautiously because I wanted to see what they were up to before giving my presence away. Sure enough, David had started a very small fire of grass and twigs in the lee of the school building.

"See, there it is," he said to Mikey. "I told you I could do it."

I was just about to make myself known when, much to my pleased surprise, I heard David say, "But now we got to put it out."

"How?" Alejo asked.

David cast around a moment for something to use, then his small face brightened. "I know. Like this." And he unbuttoned his jeans. "Okay, all together. On the count of three, everybody *pee*."

Afterward, Jeff and I had the meeting with Alejo's parents, so I wasn't able to take Sheila down to Fenton Boulevard. Instead, she left on foot for the bus stop near the school, while Jeff and I headed back to the clinic.

Alejo was the only child in the group who was not a client of either Jeff or myself, so as a consequence, neither of us knew his parents, Mr. and Dr. Banks-Smith. Indeed, my only contact had been with his father, the first day of the program, when he had brought Alejo in. I had never met Alejo's mother at all. Jeff had had a little more contact, as he had done the full workup on Alejo a couple weeks earlier, but for the most part we had relied on Alejo's psychiatrist, Dr. Freeman, for our information on his family.

Alejo's mother was a doctor practicing family medicine, while his father was an insurance man. They were both tall, attractive and Nordic-looking, the kind of couple usually dreamed up by advertising executives. They greeted us warmly, shaking both Jeff's and my hand, and then turned to exchange pleasantries with Dr. Freeman before sitting down. What struck me forcefully as I watched them was the knowledge that a dreadful mistake had been made. This was the wrong set of parents for Alejo.

The second thought to strike me was that Mr. and Dr. Banks-Smith had not bonded with Alejo. As we passed out our various test results, papers and compilations of data, they each examined them in turn and asked articulate, intelligent questions, but they did so in the same thoughtful yet detached way that Jeff, Dr. Freeman and I did. They spoke to us not as parents, but as fellow professionals.

"So, you say Alejo is functioning at a lower level than his age group," Mr. Banks-Smith said to Jeff. "This translates into what, IQ-wise?"

"If you look at it as a bell curve, with the average IQ—i.e., most of the population being here in the middle where it's fattest—"

"No, just his score, please. What is his IQ?" Mr. Banks-Smith asked.

"I'm often reluctant to tie us down to specifics," Jeff replied. "IQ is a relative measure, and tests don't always reflect a true picture."

"Come on, just the numbers," Mr. Banks-Smith replied.

"Well, I gave him the WISC. He had a verbal score of sixty-five and a perceptual score of seventy-nine, which gives him a total IQ of seventy-four."

"That's in the retarded range, isn't it?" Mr. Banks-Smith said.

"We generally regard seventy as the cutoff, but really, sir, we don't like to put a lot of emphasis on single scores, particularly in a case like Alejo's, where cultural issues may have influenced the results."

"And you," Dr. Banks-Smith said, indicating me, "you said there are definite indications that he is brain-damaged?"

"Possible, not definite. It's very difficult to be definite about such matters," I replied.

"What caused it?" Alejo's father asked. "Was it inflicted? A result of his deprivations?"

"No way of saying. He shows indicators of aphasia, which involves an inability to use and understand words in the usual way. The majority of children I've seen with this disability have been born with it."

"So, he could have been damaged all along, is that what you're saying?" he asked.

218

I didn't want to be saying that, but unfortunately, it was probably the truth.

"Alejo's problems can't really be helped, can they?" Dr. Banks-Smith said.

"They can be helped," Jeff said quickly. "Alejo's made very good progress in the summer program in terms of his interpersonal relationships. He is getting on quite well socially and has made friends with some of the other boys. We've seen a nice change in him, haven't we, Torey?"

I nodded.

"I think if he continued at the clinic—" Dr. Freeman started, but Dr. Banks-Smith cut him off with a wave of her arm.

"No, what I'm asking is: he basically can't be helped. You can't make him more intelligent. You can't repair the brain damage."

"Well, no ..." Dr. Freeman said.

I felt myself pulling back, as if slipping down a long tunnel. We'd lost. Perhaps we had lost even before we'd started. I suspect Mr. and Dr. Banks-Smith had already decided to send Alejo back to South America and, indeed, had already begun the process before ever coming in for the conference. Whatever, at that precise moment, I knew there was no hope. Alejo was condemned.

Chapter 22

"I thought perhaps you would like to come over to my place tomorrow night," I said to Sheila as we drove down to Fenton Boulevard the next day. "It's Friday, so we don't have to worry about work in the morning. Maybe I could do us something on the barbecue."

"Barbecue? Where do you have a barbecue in an attic apartment?"

"I have a door out onto the garage roof. Wait until tomorrow. I'll show you."

Sheila smiled sweetly. "Yeah, I'd really like that."

There was a small period of silence before Sheila looked over again. "How did that meeting go last night with Alejo's parents?"

I shrugged.

"What are they like, his folks?"

"All right. Nice, in a way. If I had met them at a party or something, I think I would have liked them," I replied.

She pulled a strand of hair down and examined it. "So, what's going to happen to him? Are they going to try and send him back?"

"I don't know for sure. Dr. Freeman will cover it with them, because he's Alejo's therapist, but we didn't go into it."

"Yeah, but you're going to do something, aren't you? You and Jeff? You're going to try and stop them," Sheila said, an urgency coming into her voice. "I mean, like, you won't *let* them."

Pulling my lips back over my teeth, I sucked my breath in. "I don't want to let them, but I'm afraid if they want to, there won't be much I can do to stop them."

"But you won't let them?"

"Like I said …"

Bending forward in her seat, Sheila put a hand on either side of her head, as if in pain. "Oh, it can't happen. Oh, geez, he's been brought here. He's been given all these things. Everything's so nice."

I could hear the tears in her voice. Unexpectedly, I felt my own tears. They welled up without warning, blurring the road ahead of me. The enormity of what was happening to Alejo, and, through him, all unfortunate victims, suddenly overwhelmed me. "It makes me want to cry too," I said.

Startled, Sheila looked over at me.

I reached up and wiped the tears away. "I feel so

helpless when something like this happens. I want to change things so badly and I just can't."

Her forehead wrinkling, she gazed in amazement. Unlike me, she had remained dry-eyed.

"Sometimes it helps," I said of my tears and wiped the last of them away. "In these circumstances, it's about all there's left for me to do." I smiled at her.

"I want to cry sometimes, but I almost never do," Sheila replied. "I feel it building up and then just when I think I'm going to, the feeling disappears."

I nodded.

"Actually, I make it disappear," she said. "Not that I necessarily mean to. It's just I suddenly think, what is this? It isn't real. What is any of it? A bunch of chemicals rushing around in our brain. A bunch of molecules. What kind? Carbon? Hydrogen? And what does that amount to? Nothing. It's all really nothing."

"Do you believe that?" I asked.

"Yes."

"*Really?*"

She shrugged. "It just comes to me, whether I want it to or not."

We celebrated our last Friday together with a special activity: finger painting using chocolate pudding instead of paints. Both Miriam and I had done this activity on previous occasions, so we were well prepared for the extraordinary mess it generated. Miriam arrived with an assortment of old shirts to protect clothing and we cleared back the tables and set out newspapers on the floor before putting down the large sheets of paper for painting. Then we mixed up huge bowls of instant pudding.

Both Sheila and Jeff were highly amused with our proceedings. Jeff with his Freudian training saw all too much meaning in the gloppy brown mixture, but he was the first one to plunge his hand deep into the bowl and scoop pudding out onto Violet's paper. Exuberantly, he provided all the children with generous splats.

The kids, of course, loved it. More went in their mouths than on the paper, and within a short time, there was chocolate pudding from ear to ear on most of them, but that was the glory of it. Of the various activities I had done through the years with my classes, this had become one of my favorites. All such terribly messy things are releasing, but there is a special freedom in those surrounding food. The squishy, cold feel of the pudding, the copious quantity, the permission to smear with the fingers, to slurp up from the paper with tongues produced an unhindered gaiety. Every child in the room was lively and open.

Sheila was seduced too. Indeed, she had been unusually outgoing all morning, chatting spontaneously with several of the children, lifting Mikey way up in the air above her head. Alejo had initially been reluctant to touch the chocolate pudding, so Sheila sat down beside him on the floor and started off his painting for him, encouraging him to join her. Scooping a fingerful of the pudding up from the paper, she held it out for him to taste. He wouldn't, so she ate it herself, smearing it playfully across her lips. Alejo laughed at this. He had a gorgeous laugh, very bright and boyish, and we all turned in surprise to hear it. Lifting up a finger loaded with pudding, he let it drip into his mouth, then burst into giggles.

I was delighted with the success of the project. Everyone was laughing and talking and I felt a deep sense of fulfillment watching them.

Sheila appeared at my right and said, "I'm going to take Alejo down to the rest room. He needs to go and he's absolutely covered with pudding, so I'll sluice him off." Through a coating of chocolate, Alejo grinned up at me.

"Yes, I think it's time we all clean up," I replied.

Giving the children a five-minute warning before terminating the activity, I went over to Jeff and Miriam and suggested that once we had the worst of the mess off the children, they could take them outside for break time and I would volunteer to clean up the classroom. This met with approval and I was soon left alone with what appeared to be the aftermath of an explosion in a pudding factory.

There was such a mess that I never made it outside at all. I could hear Jeff's voice filtering through the open window, as he supervised a game of Sharks and Mermaids, and it evoked far-off memories of my own childhood. The warm, dry summer heat, the light falling in across the floor, patterned by the cottonwood trees outside the window, the sound of children's voices all combined to lend a moment's transcendence to the mundane tasks I was doing.

A good half hour passed before the kids came back inside and we resumed normal activities. As everyone was getting settled, I surveyed the class-room. "Where're Sheila and Alejo?"

"I was just going to ask you the same thing," Jeff replied.

I looked at him blankly. "What do you mean?"

"Well, I'd assumed they were in here helping you during the break. I thought maybe you'd sent them down to the janitor's room to get some-thing."

"What? They weren't outside with you?"

Jeff shook his head.

"Miriam?" I called. "Have you seen Sheila and Alejo? Weren't they with you outside?"

Surprise crossed Miriam's face. "I thought they were with you."

The meaning of that expression of one's blood running like ice came home to me just then, as a physical sensation of cold flowing down through my body suffused me.

"When did you last see her?" Jeff asked me.

"Ages ago. She took Alejo down to the toilets. I was in here all along and I just *assumed* ..."

I tried to quell the sense of rising panic I felt, as I went out into the hallway and down to the rest rooms. Bursting into the girls', I slammed open the doors to the stalls and looked around the corner where the trash bins were kept. Then I went next door to the boys' and did the same. Nothing and no one.

Back in the classroom, Jeff and I huddled in the back by the sink, discussing what to do next, while Miriam attempted to keep the children occupied.

"What's happened? Where could they have gone?" Jeff asked.

"I don't know. I have no idea what's going on. Sheila was fine when she came in this morning."

"Is she a runner?" Jeff asked.

"No. I don't think so," I replied. "Well, I don't know. She wasn't when she was six."

"That's a long time ago," he said acridly.

"But why would she go? She wasn't unhappy, not that I could see. She was delightful this morning, in very good humor."

"Yeah," said Jeff blackly. "The way suicides are, once they've made their minds up."

Silence then, as we regarded one another.

"But why's she taken Alejo?" he asked. "There's the dangerous question."

The moment Jeff voiced it, I knew the answer. "She was worried about Alejo, about the possibility that his parents might send him back to South America."

"Oh, God. So she's done a bunk with him, you think?" Jeff asked.

A pause.

"Why didn't you tell me this *was* a possibility, Hayden? We should have been alerted that she was capable of this."

"I didn't think it *was* a possibility, no more than I would think it was a possibility that you would take one of the kids and go," I hissed back in an angry whisper.

"Well, you seem convinced enough of the reason now. You had no trouble coming up with that; so you must have known there was the possibility she might act on it."

"I *didn't*. Would I act on it? Would you act on it? We were both upset by the Banks-Smiths' reaction the other night; why not us? Why should I have suspected Sheila?" I cried.

Jeff looked at me darkly.

For all the times I had found Jeff able to keep his humor in adversity, on this occasion he couldn't. He was genuinely angry with me, acting as if I had kept great secrets from him about Sheila's mental stability. Because I hadn't, because this was coming as a big surprise to me too, I felt hurt and angry, as well. This did nothing to help our situation, because for the first fifteen minutes of the crisis, neither of us was thinking straight.

Jeff was right in saying that I was convinced that Sheila had run away with Alejo. While it had never occurred to me beforehand that Sheila might try such a thing, once it had happened, everything fell clearly into place for me. She was desperate, and desperate measures were called for. The first logical step was to search the school thoroughly; so once Jeff and I had gotten over the initial stages of accusing one another, we helped settle Miriam on her own with the kids and then divided up the school building between us.

I went methodically through every room, cupboard and storage area that we had a key for and some that we didn't. My hope was that even if Sheila was serious about taking Alejo away, she would try hiding in the school until we were all gone, so I tried to leave no area unchecked. When nothing turned up, I rejoined Jeff and we went outside to scour the playground and the park area across the road. Nervously, I kept checking my watch. I dreaded the moment when the minibuses and taxi arrived to take the children home, because we would then have to acknowledge to the driver who transported Alejo that we had no Alejo to transport. Jeff had settled down, but he was still prickly. Consequently, I kept my feelings to myself.

Unfortunately, search as we did, there was no trace of them. Twelve-thirty came and Miriam brought the children out front. When we saw the taxi pull in to take Alejo home, we had to acknowledge defeat. I explained nothing to the driver, just said that Alejo wouldn't be coming with him, which he accepted grumpily as an annoying last-minute change to his routine. Meanwhile, Jeff went inside to do the unwelcome task of phoning Dr. Rosenthal and Alejo's parents.

Miriam, who had other commitments after lunch, went home, leaving Jeff and me alone, regarding one another.

"Oh, God," Jeff muttered. "Why did it have to

end like this? We were doing so well. This has been such a super experience. Why did it have to end like this?"

Dr. Rosenthal was next on the scene. When his gigantic frame appeared in the classroom door, the seriousness of the situation really came home to me. He had never visited our site. He'd followed the program closely, because Jeff and I had to submit weekly reports, and he had sat in on several parent conferences, but otherwise, this had been our project. Seeing him here now gave me a sudden sense of a stern parent come to sort out his children's mischief. Jeff and I were so much younger than anyone else at the clinic, so much less experienced that, in contrast to the other psychiatrists' suit-and-tie formality, we'd always seemed like kids. I'd gotten a bit of a kick out of it on other occasions, but now, seeing this tall man in his elegant dark suit and graying hair, all I could think of was what a stupid little twit I was.

He crossed the classroom to where Jeff and I were at the table and lowered himself into one of the small schoolroom chairs. "Did you know this girl was a risk?" he asked me.

Normally I'm quite cool under pressure, but just then I wasn't. It was past lunchtime and I was hungry. I was worried and I was worn down by the guilty suspicion that this might all be my fault. Dr. Rosenthal's question, although straightforwardly put, sounded all too much like those last ninety minutes of Jeff's questioning. Consequently, I started to cry.

This unsettled Jeff, who squirmed and turned away, but with surprising gentleness, Dr. Rosenthal rose and came around to my side of the table. He put a hand on my shoulder. "Don't worry," he said. "It'll come right."

I'm glad he thought so.

Alejo's father arrived at one-thirty. "What's this? What's going on? Who is this girl?" he asked. Like Jeff, his worry took the form of anger. He waved a fist threateningly at us. "Why weren't you watching?"

Dr. Rosenthal relieved Jeff and me of the necessity of explaining. "I understand you're contemplating returning Alejo to Colombia," he said to Mr. Banks-Smith.

This comment caught him completely off guard. He looked blankly at Dr. Rosenthal.

"Yes?" Dr. Rosenthal persisted.

"Well ..." Mr. Banks-Smith foundered a moment, glancing back and forth among the three of us. "What does this have to do with anything?"

"The girl who has gone off with Alejo, she's formed a very close attachment to him. She was worried he might be returned to the orphanage."

Mr. Banks-Smith dropped his eyes to the floor.

"I don't think Alejo is in any danger," Dr. Rosenthal said. "From my staff's experience of her, she's a sensible, streetwise girl. So what I think we need to do is respond to this in a calm, rational manner. It's a very unfortunate thing to have happened, but I'm sure it will turn out all right."

I could have kissed Dr. Rosenthal just then, so grateful was I for his supportive approach. For the first time since it had started, I began to feel perhaps things weren't so bad.

There was one last thorough search of the school and its environs. Dr. Rosenthal contacted the school caretaker, who supplied keys to the areas of the school that we had not been able to get into; consequently, we were able to search every nook and cranny. Unfortunately, there was not a single clue as to their disappearance.

At four, we transferred back to the clinic. Dr. Banks-Smith met us there. Dr. Rosenthal had managed to dispel Mr. Banks-Smith's anger so successfully that he had become a supportive member of the search team at the school. Now his wife joined in the conversation in the conference room, giving us helpful suggestions on Alejo's anticipated behavior in this situation. Sheila's father had been contacted at his work and we all awaited his arrival.

Dr. Rosenthal came over to me as we milled about in the clinic corridor with our coffee cups while waiting for Mr. Renstad. "Come in my office a moment, please," he said.

In contrast to the bright lights and nervous bustle in the area around the conference room, Dr. Rosenthal's unlit office was dim and silent. As director, he commanded the biggest office, a room of late-Victorian elegance with a mahogany fireplace and corniced ceilings. There was a thick carpet on the floor and wonderfully squishy leather chairs—womb chairs, Jeff called them, for their propensity to envelop the sitter in comforting softness—as well as the obligatory psychiatrist's couch.

"Tell me more about this girl," Dr. Rosenthal asked me. "What's her background?"

"She's a former student of mine," I said. I'd already given a brief summary of Sheila's relationship to me in the conference room, but now I went into detail. I told him of her deprived background and her history of abandonment and abuse.

Nodding, Dr. Rosenthal reached across his desk and turned on a cassette recorder that was sitting on the window ledge. Mozart's Piano Concerto no. 20 began. He cocked his head and listened to it. The somber first notes of the allegro sounded foreboding to me.

"It's quite understandable, isn't it?" Dr. Rosenthal said at last. "Here's a child who was, herself, abandoned by her mother. She identifies with the boy, who was abandoned in Colombia. He's been rescued, but now he's about to be abandoned again."

I nodded.

He looked over at me. "It says a great deal for her, really. She's a good girl at heart."

"I think ... if I'm reading my experiences lately with Sheila right ... that there may be even deeper identification. You see, Sheila and I ... well, I've gotten mixed up in the abandonment issue. I think she sees me in the same role as Alejo's parents, that I helped lift her out of her former life by bringing her into my classroom, accustoming her to a more stable environment, more reliable adult relationships, and then, when the school year ended ..."

There was a deep silence. The music, which should have filled it, emphasized it.

"I didn't mean to," I said. "It's hard for me to come to terms with the fact that what I thought of as such a good experience she's interpreted as abandonment ... She doesn't even remember being abandoned by her mother, but she remembers my doing it. And now this."

"Ah," said Dr. Rosenthal and he said no more. Leaning back in his chair, he looked up at the patterned design on the ceiling. The music washed over us.

Sheila's father was in the conference room when I came out of Dr. Rosenthal's office. He had been called over from work and was wearing filthy jeans and a sweat-stained shirt. His metal-toed boots clicked against the legs of his chair and the conference table. The moment I saw him, I knew having him present was a mistake. His scruffy appearance was off-putting, but worse was his mouth. I'd tried to downplay the more lurid aspects of Sheila's childhood, feeling that the things she had done when she was five or six were hardly to be held against her at fourteen. Without anchoring it to this early time, Mr. Renstad readily acknowledged that Sheila had been in trouble with the police. I challenged him and he admitted that, no, she hadn't been in trouble since being in my class, almost a decade earlier, but then he added that she had caused serious problems in her last foster home, because she'd kept running away, and had eventually been sent to a secure children's home. By the time he finished talking, the Banks-Smiths were wild-eyed and they insisted the police be called in.

At six forty-five, two police officers arrived. One was a big, burly fellow named Durante, the other a woman with short blond hair and a steel glint in her eye named Metherson. Still sitting around the conference table in the clinic were Dr. Rosenthal, Sheila's father, the Banks-Smiths and Jeff and I, and once again, Jeff and I recounted our tale. I was numb by then, my emotions having run on high for too long, so I just related it as it had happened and did not try to give meaning to any particular aspect. Afterward, Officer Durante stayed in the conference room with the others, while Officer Metherson, Jeff and I went into our office to review Alejo's file and discuss the summer program in more depth. We returned to the conference room to discover someone had ordered sandwiches from the deli on Nineteenth Street. Neither Jeff nor I had had lunch, so we fell upon them like dogs.

Time ground down, nearly to a halt. The police officers had come and then left, but we all remained, not knowing quite what else to do. In contrast to the hectic urgency of the afternoon and early evening, there was nothing left but to wait. And eat. Another order was sent out to the deli and someone popped across the street to the doughnut shop and brought in a dozen doughnuts. Dr. Rosenthal made fresh coffee and Jeff raided the pop machine. After not eating for the whole course of the working day, I easily overate while sitting there with nothing else to do. This only contributed to the murky, depressed sense of lethargy I felt.

On my way back from the rest room about 9 p.m., I met Mr. Renstad loitering around the front door of the clinic. He wanted to go home; I suspect he had wanted to go home from practically the moment he had arrived, but by now there was an urgency to his restlessness.

"I don't know what we're going to do," he said wearily. "Don't help none staying in this place. She's not going to come here."

I nodded.

"We just got to wait her out, that's all. That's all you can do with Sheila."

"How often has this happened before?" I asked.

He shrugged. "Often enough."

"Where does she go?"

He shrugged again. "She don't tell me and I don't ask. She's got her mother in her. Does what she wants, when she wants, how she wants, and I just sit home hoping it don't cause trouble."

"She *hasn't* been in trouble with the police recently, has she?" I asked, almost dreading his answer.

He shook his head. "No."

There was a small silence between us. I glanced out through the double doors at the summer twilight. "Could you tell me a little about these

235

occasions when Sheila was in foster care? It's something she hasn't talked much to me about. How many has she been in?"

Mr. Renstad puffed out his cheeks and expelled the breath. "Quite a few. I don't know. Ten, maybe?"

"*Ten*?" I said in surprise. I had thought it'd been three or four. "On what occasions? When you were … away?"

"Yeah." He nodded. "Them times I was in Marysville. And I was down at the state hospital. Down twice, getting dried out. You know." He gave an embarrassed smile.

"But it was *ten* times in, what? Six, seven years?"

"She just didn't settle. She was okay the first time. She was, like, eight, maybe, when she went in the first foster home. And they seemed real good. They used to bring her down to see me. That's when I was in Marysville and they used to bring her down every month for a while, then all of a sudden, it stopped. Turns out he was fucking her, the old man. Showing this real good face to me and then fucking my kid at night."

I searched his face.

"She didn't say nothing about it, but she ran away from there. Actually, she never has said, but the guy got done for fucking the next kid they put in with him, so I reckon that's what he was doing to my kid too."

Oh, God, I was thinking, did this never stop?

"He made a runner out of her, that guy. She never run before that, but now anytime you get mad at her, she goes. And just like a hare she is. They keep putting her in different places, but nothing stops her. Got her mother's blood, I tell them. If she wants to go, she's gone, and no one the likes of who's in there," he said, gesturing toward the conference room, "is going to find her."

Chapter 23

Nothing came of all our waiting, and at last we had to give up and go home, leaving the affair to the police. Once home, I couldn't sleep. Around and around in my head went all the aspects of my relationship with Sheila. It had been too easy to think that what I had done with her at six had been enough, that I had made a difference. Now sleepless in the gloom of night, it became too easy to think I had made no difference at all.

The next day was Saturday. I didn't go back into the clinic, as there was little we could do from there anyway, but I remained close at hand for the phone. Allan came over for a little while, but he had come with the intention of our going upstate for the afternoon to nose around in the small antique and secondhand places that dotted the sleepy rural communities of the corn belt. When I explained what had happened, he was astonished and remarked several times about never having known anyone before who got herself involved in such things as I seemed to get into. Although sympathetic, he was a bit disconcerted. I also suspect that he didn't want to spend such a bright summer Saturday afternoon in the city. As a consequence, Allan soon left and I spent the rest of the day on my own.

The phone rang a lot. Dr. Rosenthal rang three times to catch me up on things. Officer Metherson phoned once, as did Dr. Freeman, Alejo's psychiatrist from the clinic. Jeff rang twice. And I telephoned Mr. Renstad late in the afternoon to see if he had heard anything. The police were at his house when I called, so I had another opportunity to talk to Officer Metherson. There was still no news.

Making myself supper, I took it in front of the TV. That not holding my interest, I reread the newspaper and did the crossword. Restless, I toyed with the idea of going swimming at the health club. I could have used some exercise at that point and the thought of a hard workout and a soak in the Jacuzzi really appealed to me, but in the end I decided against it. Gathering my dishes up, I took them to the kitchen to wash them.

A knock at the door.

Sheila? The thought shot through my mind like a brightly sent arrow, lifting my spirits as it went. "Just a minute," I called, lifting my hands from the soapy water and drying them. The knock came again, louder, more insistent. I hurried to open it.

Jeff.

"What are you doing here?" I asked.

"Now there's a friendly greeting, if ever I heard one," he replied and came on in. He glanced around. "So, this is *chez* Hayden, is it? I like your paneling there."

"*What* are you doing here?"

"I just thought I'd come over. You're by the phone, I'm by the phone. We might as well be by the phone together. You play chess? I've got my chessboard along. Could do Trivial Pursuit, but it isn't much good with two people. But I'm wicked at Trivial Pursuit," he said and grinned.

"I just bet you are."

He scanned my bookshelves. "So where's this book you've written?"

"It's not published yet. Won't be out till next April, but that's the manuscript over there." I pointed.

Jeff went over and picked it up, while I returned to the kitchen to drain the sink and finish cleaning up. A few minutes passed before Jeff wandered into the kitchen, the pages of the manuscript in his hands.

"What's this, Hayden?"

"What?"

"Right here, Chapter One, page one. 'The article was a small one, just a few paragraphs stuck on page six under the comics. It told of a six-year-old girl who had abducted a neighborhood child.'" He looked up. "Is this Sheila?"

A sense of horror came over me.

He continued reading. "'... she had taken the three-year-old boy, tied him to a tree in a nearby woodlot and burned him. The boy was currently in a local hospital in critical condition.'" Jeff paused to regard me. "You never told us about this."

"I didn't think of it."

"Didn't *think* of it, Hayden? She's done this before and you didn't think of it?"

That wasn't quite the truth. I had thought of it, at great length, in fact, particularly during the night when I'd been lying awake, but I wasn't quite sure how it fit in. It sounded so horrible, that incident. It *was* horrible. Yet, did it have any bearing on what she was doing now? I doubted it. As with inadmissible evidence in a trial, to have mentioned it at this stage would only have prejudiced people without contributing anything useful. I said this to Jeff.

He raised an eyebrow. "Be careful. You're setting yourself up as judge and jury in this thing."

"So you think it needs to be brought out?" I asked.

"Well, to Dr. Rosenthal, at least. I mean, this was hardly a small incident, was it? All the things you've told me about her, you never gave me the impression she was up to this kind of thing as a child. Sounds like she almost killed the kid."

"It was a one-off. A cry for help. She never did anything else like it," I replied. That I felt was the truth, although this had been the one unspoken area between Sheila and me. When she was in my classroom we'd talked about every other aspect of her life, including her abandonment, her abuse and

241

her difficulties adjusting to our expectations, but we had never once touched on that abduction. I'd thought of it often enough during those five months she was in my class, but I had never pressed the matter. I wasn't a trained psychologist at that point in my career and I didn't feel it was my place to press the issue, if Sheila showed no willingness to discuss it. And the fact was, she never did.

Jeff was uncomfortable with this new knowledge. "She *could* do something," he kept saying, as if it weren't true that we all "could do something" if the circumstances were right. Then came the lawsuit side of the matter. "They could sue us, if something happened and we hadn't told about this."

"They could sue us anyway, if they got the urge, just because we let Sheila in the summer program. She's been a risk all along," I replied. "But for pity's sake, she was a little child when she did these things. I mean, when I was six, I used to steal Hershey's bars from the grocery store. Does that make me a security risk now? Of course not. Because when I was old enough to know better, people expected me not to do it and treated me as someone who wouldn't."

"This is rather different from Hershey's bars, Hayden."

"No, the point is she shouldn't be treated like a criminal now for something she did when she was a very little girl."

Jeff shook his head. "No, Hayden, the point is that this girl already has a history of abducting little boys and harming them, and if we don't tell somebody we know that, we're talking big trouble here."

In the end, Jeff won the argument and we phoned Dr. Rosenthal. He listened solemnly. No, please, not the police, okay? I'd asked, but Dr. Rosenthal gently made all the same points Jeff had. Consequently, half an hour later, Officer Durante was sitting at my kitchen table with Jeff and me.

By the time everyone had gone home, I was well and truly depressed. What was it with this girl? She had so much to offer, so much promise, yet at every turn things went wrong. Running myself a hot bath, I tried to soak the problems away.

The door again. Glancing at my bedside clock, I saw it was almost eleven-thirty. Officer Durante had said he was going to check up the details of the abduction in Marysville and if he had any questions, he'd come back to me. Wearily climbing out of bed and pulling on my robe, I went to the door. Didn't this guy ever call it quits?

It was Sheila. Sheila and Alejo standing in the dim light of the apartment-building hallway. "Can we come in?" she asked.

"Oh, yes," I said in surprise. "Yes, come in." I stood aside to let them pass.

Sheila flopped down on my sofa, with Alejo dropping down beside her. He looked as if he had recently been crying. His eyes were puffy and red-rimmed. Sheila just looked tired.

"Where have you been? Do you know everybody's looking for you?" I asked. "Do you realize the police are involved?"

Sheila grimaced. "Could you make us something to eat? We're so hungry."

I made them tuna-fish sandwiches, and when they'd devoured those, they moved on to peanut butter and toast. All the time, I was trying to puzzle out how to handle this situation. It didn't seem inconceivable to me that Sheila might flee if I was too quick about telling everyone else she was here, but knowing how desperate Alejo's parents were, I was anxious to let them know he was safe.

Alejo answered the matter for me. I turned from putting the peanut butter away to find him sound asleep, face down on the table.

"Come on, lovey," I said and reached down to pick him up. Carrying him into my bedroom, I removed his shoes and slipped him under the comforter. He never really woke up.

Back out in the kitchen, Sheila, sitting slouched down in a chair at the table, looked in about the same shape as Alejo. She braced her head with one hand, her fingers shielding her eyes from my view.

"I'm going to have to call and tell them you're here," I said.

"I know," she murmured wearily.

"Why did you do it? We were so worried, Sheila."

Looking up at me, her face crumpled. "Don't be mad at me. Just do with me like you did with him, okay? Just say, 'Come on, lovey,' and let me know you're glad to have me back."

By the time Alejo's parents arrived, both Alejo and Sheila were asleep. I'd moved Alejo out to the sofa, because he was so far gone that lights and noise scarcely made him stir, and I put Sheila to bed in my bedroom. Alejo's parents roused him briefly with hugs and kisses, but he was asleep again before they had him in the car.

Officer Durante, just going off his evening shift, stopped by on his way home. I showed him the bedroom and he stood in the doorway, watching Sheila asleep in the darkened room. "Silly girl," he murmured and turned back into the living room.

"What's going to happen now?" I asked.

"Depends if the parents press charges or not. Depends what everyone does."

"Could it just end here?"

He shrugged affably. "Possibly." He met my eyes. "Is she really such an okay kid?"

"Yeah."

"Well, tell her to smarten up."

Chapter 24

Sheila roused late the next morning and stumbled out into the living room like an old she-bear just coming out of hibernation. It was past eleven o'clock and I was sitting on the floor reading the Sunday newspapers. She flopped into the armchair and regarded me amidst my sea of newspapers.

"God, how many papers do you get?" she asked and sleepily rubbed her face.

"You want some orange juice?"

She yawned and rubbed her face again. "I'm all stiff. I don't think I moved all night." Then suddenly, realization crossed her features. She glanced around my apartment, then back at me. "I almost don't remember how I got here," she murmured. "But then again, how could I forget?"

"Yes," I said, "we have some serious sorting out to do."

"Yeah," Sheila muttered, "heap big trouble, eh?"

The one person I hadn't called the night before was Sheila's father. I know I should have, but it was very late by then and I reckoned he probably wasn't losing any sleep over his daughter's absence. However, once Sheila was up and moving, I insisted she phone him.

"Do I have to go home right away?" she asked, when I made it plain that she was doing nothing else until she let her father know where she was.

"Don't you want to?"

"Couldn't I just stay here for a little bit? Please?"

"Look," I said, "we'll get you sorted out first, all right? You have a shower and clean up. I'll make you some breakfast and then we'll see what's going to happen with this mess. Then maybe I can run you home later on. Okay? But *phone* your dad *now*."

Begrudgingly, Sheila agreed.

There was something unusually defenseless about Sheila that morning. Perhaps it was just the rigors of her experiences with Alejo leaving her so tired and hungry. For whatever reason, she left her neediness undisguised.

One of the most poignant moments came when she went in to get cleaned up. She had no clean clothes, so I suggested she put on an old jogging suit of mine, while I washed her things. Hearing she was out of the shower, I came into the bathroom to collect the dirty laundry. Sheila stood in front of the mirror, her hair dripping wet.

"Do you like my hair like this?" she asked, as she pulled the comb through.

I hesitated, wondering whether to lie for politeness's sake or gently tell the truth.

"You don't, do you?" she replied, reading my hesitation. "You think it looks stupid."

"No, not really. It's just that I always thought you had very beautiful hair. I've always wanted straight hair myself and had to put up with curly, and yours was so shiny and nice."

Pulling her hair back from her face and into a ponytail, Sheila regarded her reflection. She looked much more like her childhood self that way. For the first time, I saw the little girl I'd known looking back at me. "I don't know why I do this, why I make myself look like I do. Nobody likes it."

"I think you've got quite a good fashion sense," I said. "*I* rather like it. It's different, but there's nothing wrong with being different, and it is quite good."

"I wanted you to like me so much," she said quietly. "I want everybody to like me, but then just as I get to where I think I can do that, I stop myself. I don't know why. I think, I can put this on—like it's some dress or something—and everyone will think it's very pretty. But then some other part of me stops me. I put it away and try something different, something I know is going to drive everyone nuts. I *know* what to do. I *want* to do it. But I never can."

I smiled gently. "That's just being a teenager. It goes with the territory."

"No," she replied. "Maybe in most cases, but not in mine. Because I've done it all my life. Even when I was little, even when I was dying inside for people to like me, I never could do those things that would make it easy for them."

Afternoon came and with it the need to confront and resolve Alejo's abduction. The phone had been ringing all morning and it was finally decided that everyone, including Sheila, would meet at the clinic. Feelings were still running high and I sensed that police action remained a distinct possibility, but I took it as a good sign that everyone wanted to meet and talk the matter through before turning it over to the authorities.

At home with me, Sheila was visibly worried. If the term "clingy" could be applied to a fourteen-year-old, that's what she was, trailing after me from room to room in the apartment. She worried about her hair and her clothes, bit her fingernails and wrung her hands, although she never directly addressed the matter on any more than a superficial level.

"We'll take it one moment at a time," I said, as we got into the car.

"I was just trying to do what I thought was right," she murmured. "That's what's so awful. I wanted to do the right thing."

"I know, lovey." Putting the key into the ignition, I reached across the seat to her. "Come here." I drew her in close in a hug. The years melted away when I did that. Suddenly she was tiny again and the need to protect her made me feel tigerish.

The hug had the same effect on Sheila. She looked at me as I started the car and pulled out of the drive. "Know what that reminds me of? Remember that time I got into that teacher's classroom and wrecked it?"

"Yes."

"Remember afterward? You took me into that little teensy room and I can remember sitting on your lap. I was so scared. What happened? Did the principal whack me or something? I don't really remember that, but I remember it being afterward and you took me in there and held me on your lap."

I nodded.

"I felt so horrible. Just empty inside, like someone had pulled all my guts out. And then you held me. It was dark in there, I can remember that, and I can remember laying against you and feeling your arms, and how you just slowly sort of filled me up again."

Looking across at her, I smiled. "Yes, I remember that well."

A silence came then. It was bright and sunny, the kind of summer day meant for going out on the lake or having a church picnic, and it contrasted sharply with the tense mood in the car. I was watching the traffic and thinking loosely about picnics and how hot it might get, while at the same time never losing completely the reverberations of Sheila's earlier conversation.

"You remember that well," I said suddenly, as the realization dawned on me. "I mean, given how little you were remembering."

"Yeah," she agreed. "It comes back to me. Not in continuous memories, but jigs and jags of it. I don't know why. Things just turn up in my mind."

The meeting included the Banks-Smiths, of course, along with Dr. Rosenthal, Jeff and Dr. Freeman, as well as Sheila's father. Much to their credit, Mr. and Dr. Banks-Smith greeted Sheila with calm understanding. Dr. Rosenthal presided over the small group around the conference table, his soft-spoken civility contributing significantly to the overall composure of the group, but Mr. and Dr. Banks-Smith impressed me.

From them we heard that Alejo was home, tired but safe and happy. He had spent a good night, eaten well that morning and was enjoying cartoons now at his grandmother's house. Dr. Freeman had stopped over just after lunch to chat with Alejo and he felt that Alejo was none the worse for his ordeal. Indeed, he said he found Alejo friendly and chatty, wanting to show him a new toy.

"What we need to understand, Sheila, is why this happened," Dr. Rosenthal said.

Sheila, beside me, lowered her head. She didn't speak.

"It was wrong. I can see you know that already. Taking Alejo caused his parents a great deal of worry and we were very worried for your safety, as well as Alejo's."

"I know I caused a lot of trouble," she mumbled, her head still down. "I'm sorry. I didn't mean to."

"Why did it happen?" Dr. Rosenthal asked.

"Because I thought ..." She lifted her head and looked pointedly across the conference table at the Banks-Smiths. "Because I thought they were going to send Alejo away."

"So you thought taking him would be better?" Sheila nodded.

"Do you still think that?" Dr. Rosenthal asked.

For a long moment, Sheila didn't answer. Hands in her lap, she twisted them and watched as her knuckles went white. Then finally she looked back over at him. "Yeah, I still think so."

"What were you going to do with him?" Dr. Rosenthal asked Sheila.

She shrugged. "I'm not sure. But I wasn't going to hurt him, if that's what you're asking."

"No, I didn't think you would," Dr. Rosenthal replied.

Taking a deep breath, Sheila looked up. "I'm already in trouble, so I might as well say what I think." She turned to the Banks-Smiths. "Don't send Alejo back. He can't help the way he is. He's just a little boy. He doesn't know that not being smart isn't acceptable, that because things happened to him to make him damaged, he isn't as good as other boys."

It was the Banks-Smiths' turn to lower their heads. I saw Dr. Banks-Smith's eyes fill with tears.

"I didn't mean to cause a lot of upset. I didn't think I would, because I thought you didn't want him anymore anyway," she said.

252

"That isn't true," Dr. Banks-Smith said tearfully. "We do love him. We're not sending him anywhere."

Mr. Banks-Smith nodded. "I'm sorry we made you think we didn't love him, Sheila. I suppose if there's any good to come out of this, it's been to show us how much we do."

In the end, the Banks-Smiths decided not to press any charges against Sheila. Indeed, they responded generously to her throughout the meeting, making me suspect that perhaps Dr. Rosenthal had had a private discussion with them about Sheila's own circumstances. Whatever, it was one of those rare occasions when pain and fear give way to growth. I think we all came out of the experience better people.

In talking to Sheila's dad after the meeting ended, I offered to let Sheila come back with me for the rest of the day and said I would drive her home to Broadview that evening. He had been totally silent throughout the whole proceedings, and his reticence remained. I suspect he had been braced for trouble with the authorities and hadn't quite taken in the fact that things had come out all right. Whatever, he appeared vaguely confused by the whole works and seemed not to care too much one way or another where or when Sheila turned up. It did cross my mind then to wonder whether or not he was high or coming off a high.

Sheila, too, seemed stunned by the decision to let things drop. I had expected jubilation from her and the desire to celebrate, but found instead a deep quietness. That, and a desire to touch me. Standing in the conference room as we talked to her father, she slipped her arm through mine and leaned against me. Smiling, I put my arm around her shoulder and she then grabbed me in a warm hug.

I hugged her back, but then started to pull apart. Sheila kept ahold of me. "This feels good," she murmured. "Don't let go. I don't want to lose you again."

I fell back on old favorites and took Sheila out for a pizza, then bowling. I think she was probably still exhausted from her ordeal, because she didn't play at all well, but she seemed to have a good time. Coming out of the bowling alley, I noticed Walt Disney's *Jungle Book* advertised at the multiplex theater across the street at the shopping mall. Impulsively, I asked her if she wanted to go see it. So we did.

By the time we came out from the movie it was dark, and I knew I ought to get Sheila home, particularly as it was a good hour's drive down to Broadview.

The first ten minutes of the drive passed in pleasant chatter, as we discussed the movie, but then silence descended on us. I could sense Sheila's tiredness by that point and, lulled by the ride, I felt no need to talk. The miles ticked by. I came to the outskirts of the city. The freeway lighting ceased and we plunged into country darkness.

I was thinking as we sped through the darkness, and it occurred to me that despite the traumas of the last few days, or perhaps because of them, my relationship with Sheila was the best it had been since we were reunited. While it had been a harrowing day in many ways, it had been emotionally rewarding as well.

"You won't do it again, will you?" Sheila asked softly. "That's all behind us now, huh?"

I looked over at her.

She sat with her head resting against the shoulder strap. She gazed ahead into the darkness. "I remember that night."

Racking my brain to recall what she might be referring to, I finally gave up. "I'm not sure I know what you're talking about," I said.

"Well, you know. That night you left me. When you went."

"When I went? Where?"

Sheila straightened up in her seat and looked over at me. "You remember, of course you do. Remember, I was fooling around in the car and you stopped it and made me get out."

"When?"

"When I was little. When I was in your class, when the class was over. That night." An agitated note had come into her voice. "You had me in the car, you had everybody in the car. What were you doing?" She asked this last question more of herself than me. "Taking us out? For a good time? Like tonight. Like you're doing tonight."

I puzzled a moment, trying to recollect what she might be talking about, but the only time I had ever had Sheila out in a car at night was when

Chad and I had taken her for pizza after the hearing. "I don't think that was me," I ventured.

"Yes, it was. I remember it. And we were on the road. I can remember the lights going by, the streetlights, and then dark, like this. You pulled over to the side of the road and told me to open the car door and get out."

"That wasn't me, Sheila."

"It was, 'cause I can remember your car. That little red one. You called it Bingo. You used to take us all in it and we'd sing that song, B-I-N-G-O, for the little red car."

I smiled. "Yeah, I remember the car, because it was my first one. But I only took you kids out in it two or three times, and never at night."

"It was at night," she insisted. "We were all sitting in back. I had the door against me on one side, and on the other, I was next to … Jamie? No, there wasn't a Jamie, was there? Billy? No. Well, I can't remember his name, but he was next to me and we were fooling around, making noises. Fart noises, I think. And you said to shut up. Shut up or you were going to stop the car and make us get out. We were just fooling around, but you got really angry and I got scared. *I* shut up. That's what made me so upset all these years, Torey, because *I* shut up. But Jamie didn't, he made this other big fart noise and you veered the car over to the side of the road. I remember that really clearly, because there was such a big jerk we all screamed. And you said, 'Get out.' I was crying by then. I knew it wasn't me, but you were so angry. I was scared to say it wasn't and

I could tell I had to get out. And then you just drove off." She took a deep breath. "I mean, like, *that's* why it's been so hard for me to settle down since you got back. You kept saying 'Remember this? Remember that?' and if I tried to remember any of what happened then, all that came into my head was that you left me. You got me used to thinking I was special and then you just pushed me out."

Horrified, I looked over at her. "Sheila, that *wasn't* me!"

"It was you, because I remember your car."

"It was *not* me. That was your mother. And it wasn't Jamie sitting next to you, it was Jimmie, your brother. You've confused me with her."

Sheila's expression was one of utter bewilderment. "It was you. You were the one who left me. I don't even remember my mother."

Seeing a rest stop on the side of the road, I pulled my car in. There were bright overhead lights, which in contrast to the darkness in the car threw everything in sharp relief and I saw a look of genuine terror run across Sheila's features. Caught as she was between confused worlds of memory, I think she half expected me to tell her to get out now, so I hurriedly turned the engine off. The fact was, the conversation we were having was too powerful to carry on and still drive safely. I realized this needed my whole attention.

"Sheila, I never had you in my car at night. You were in Chad's car with me after the hearing and in my red car maybe two or three times when we had class outings, but otherwise, you were never in my car."

She sat as if paralyzed. Gazing straight ahead, her eyes unfocused, she remained stock-still for several moments, then slowly shook her head in a faint, confused fashion. "I *remember* it," she said softly, her voice perplexed. "Telling me to get out. Reaching back and opening the door. I was so scared. I was crying and so scared and I wouldn't do it. I could hear the cars going by and I was just crying and crying and no one came to get me."

"That wasn't me," I said gently.

"I was so sure it was," she replied, her voice going way up into a whimper. Tears came over her cheeks. Putting her hands up to cover her face, she bent forward. "No, oh no," she cried in dismay.

Leaning across the space between the seats, I took her in my arms and held her close against me. "That's because I left you too, didn't I? I'm sorry, lovey. I never realized how much it must have hurt."

Chapter 25

In the end, the only consequence to come out of Alejo's abduction was the general feeling of Dr. Rosenthal and Alejo's parents that it would be better if Sheila did not return to work at the summer program. This was understandable and we all agreed. We were in our last week anyhow, so it didn't make much difference.

Because she didn't come back to the program, I didn't get a chance to see Sheila until the following Wednesday evening. She phoned me that afternoon at the clinic and asked if she could come over to my apartment. She was sounding cheerful but rather lonely, so I agreed to let her make me her famous tuna-fish-and-mushroom soup combo for supper. I arrived home to find her sitting outside on the doorstep of the apartment building, a brown paper bag full of groceries on her lap.

"You shouldn't have spent your money," I said. "I probably have all the ingredients."

"That's okay. I wanted to pay you back for Saturday night. And Sunday." Rising from the step, she followed me into the building and up the stairs to my apartment.

Sheila was ebullient that evening. The contrast between the silent, sullen teenager I'd first encountered in May and this eager, chatty girl was marked, and it was easy to be with her; indeed, to want to be with her. However, there was an undercurrent to her cheerfulness, something poignant that made Sheila seem terribly vulnerable to me.

We had much that needed talking about. The realization on Sunday night that Sheila had confused me with her mother and my departure with her initial abandonment had shocked me deeply, as, I suspect, it did her, and both of us were so overwhelmed with emotion that we were not capable of discussing it in any depth then. However, I definitely did want to discuss the matter with her. The insights from that revelation were causing me to see the whole situation with new eyes.

The problem was, the topic did not raise itself naturally that evening. Perhaps we were still too dazed by the discovery to be ready to discuss it. I don't know. Whatever, our conversation skirted around the edges of it.

Sheila repeatedly got off on complete tangents. She was *very* chatty and for the first time seemed keen to unleash the full extent of her brain power, describing to me the most extraordinary projects

she had in mind. She was quite good with computers, for example, and told me at some length about
working on programs on the school computer. Still
keen on Roman history and Caesar, she had come
up with the idea of trying to develop an extension
to a program on one of the computers that would
allow the machine to construct 3D models of
Roman buildings that you could walk through.
Knowing what school computers were like, I
couldn't imagine what kind of program she might
be thinking of modifying, but it was fascinating listening to her talk.

And so the evening passed pleasantly, as friend
to friend, rather than teacher to student or therapist to client, and perhaps that's how it should have
been. It was only toward the very end, when it was
getting late and I knew I was going to have to send
her home or I wouldn't be worth anything at work
the next day, that Sheila touched briefly on matters
at hand. She had grown rather melancholy toward
the end of the visit. Deep down, I think she had
been angling for an invitation to spend the night
and was sad that this wasn't forthcoming and she'd
have to go home.

"You know what?" she said, as I was rising to collect the odds and ends we had scattered around the
living room and putting them away. "I don't even
remember my mother. My mind is, like, absolutely
blank. I've never even seen a picture of her. Dad
hasn't got any. So she could look like anyone."

A silence came, gently fringed with the clinking
of the mugs as I picked them up.

"I look when I go in crowds. I look at the different faces and think, Are you my mother? I wouldn't know. And she wouldn't know me. And that, like, strikes me as *so* weird. I mean, think of it, Torey. This woman carried me inside her. She made me. She *created* me and half of what I am is from her, yet I wouldn't even recognize her on the street."

Sheila remained in the armchair, the table lamp bathing her in a golden tungsten glow. I carried the dishes out to the sink and came back. All the time, Sheila kept her eyes on me. "Why do you suppose she left me?" she asked.

In the glow of the lamplight, I could see tears in her eyes. They didn't fall, but they shimmered, sparkling faintly as she moved her head.

I paused a moment to think of the best answer. Before I could say anything, she spoke again. "Tor? Do you think it's ever going to come right for me?"

"Do you mean, are you ever going to find your mother?"

She shrugged. "No, not necessarily. Just is it ever going to be all right? Do you think? Am I ever going to have a chance just to be normal?"

Slowly, I nodded. "Yes, I think so. It's going to mean coming to terms with things. Accepting that an appalling thing happened to you when your mother left you ... two appalling things, because I left you too. I didn't mean to, or at least I didn't mean for it to feel like that's what I was doing, but I can see now that it did. And it means accepting that perhaps they both had to happen, that circumstances wouldn't allow otherwise, but that they weren't your fault. They happened to you, but you didn't cause them. And finally, you have to forgive and let go."

"Do you think I can do that?"

I nodded. "Yes. It'll take sinew, but then you always have been a tiger."

I didn't see Sheila for the rest of that week. We were busy with the final aspects of the summer program, with parent conferences and clinic evaluations. Then came the weekend and Allan and I had a flying trip out of town to the ballet planned. It wasn't until the following Wednesday that I realized how long it had been since I'd heard from Sheila and tried to phone. There was no answer.

I'm not particularly good at contacting people. I don't enjoy using the telephone and procrastinate phoning people for an embarrassing amount of time for just that reason. Most of my friends, aware of this bad habit, were accustomed to maintaining the lion's share of keeping in touch. So it had usually been with Sheila. She had almost always telephoned me. When it became my responsibility, another three or four days slid by before it occurred to me to try her again. Again, there was no answer. I did begin to wonder at this point, simply because since we had been reunited in May, two full weeks had never gone by without my hearing from her.

No answer. No answer. No answer. Then, on the Thursday three weeks after the night Sheila had made dinner for me, I tried her house again. This time a recorded message came back: the line had been disconnected.

My first thought was that Mr. Renstad had failed to pay his phone bill. This was certainly within the realms of possibility, knowing him. Nonetheless, I felt disconcerted. So, after work, I drove down to Broadview to investigate for myself.

Given the distance and the traffic, I didn't get to Sheila's house until after eight. The street was already in evening shadows, as I pulled the car up in front of the beige duplex. In the left-hand unit where another family lived, there were lights and the sounds of a television playing. In the Renstads's unit, there was only darkness.

I knocked. No answer. I knocked again. Still nothing. Going around to the side of the house to see if there was a second door, I tried that. Obviously, they weren't home. Coming around to the other side, I rose up on tiptoe and attempted to peer in through the window.

"Hey, what are you doing there?" a voice called.

Startled, I pulled back and looked over to see a man sticking his head out from the door of the other unit in the duplex. "Oh, hi," I said. "Do you know where these people are? No one seems to be home."

"You're not going to find them here," he replied. "They moved out about three weeks ago."

"Moved out?" I said in surprise.

"Yup."

"Where'd they go? Do you know?"

"Nope. No idea. Sorry." Then he shut the door and disappeared inside.

Utterly overcome, I just stood there on the sidewalk beside the house and stared at it. Moved? Sheila had said absolutely nothing about moving to me. And Mr. Renstad had given us no indication when we had seen him that weekend. He had a steady job, he had his baseball team. Why would they move? And where?

Sheila and her father had disappeared. I couldn't believe it. I ran through the whole gamut of emotions over the weeks that followed: shock, anger, dismay, regret, sadness. Very definitely sadness. It had taken me the better part of three months to re-form a relationship with Sheila, then it all evaporated.

I simply couldn't believe it. Over and over again I discussed the whole affair with Jeff and tried to puzzle out where they might have gone and what signs I had missed that were pointing to their leaving. Together, we endeavored to find out where they had disappeared to. This was much harder than I had hoped. We didn't have any legal reasons for finding Sheila or her father, so straight-forward inquiry did not open many doors. I was reluctant to lie or otherwise falsify my intentions, so this left me with nothing more to fall back on than deductive reasoning, persistence and good luck. The first two I probably had enough of, but the third I simply had to wait for.

As much as I hated to consider it, the first thought to come to mind was that Mr. Renstad had committed a new offense and was back in prison. I couldn't find anyone who would willingly confirm this, given privacy laws. Chad seemed my only chance when I ran up against a blank wall, so I called him and asked if he could find out. A stickler for maintaining client confidentiality, he was reluctant to do much, but he did confirm that Mr. Renstad was not on his firm's client list. This seemed to decrease the chances that he was in the penitentiary again.

Jeff suggested that perhaps they had simply fled, from bills or maybe some dodgy loan shark or the like. If we were lucky, he said, perhaps they were still in the city and it would just be a matter of waiting for Sheila to contact me. That, I suspected, was what it was going to boil down to anyway— waiting for Sheila. She knew where I was, and unlike the previous occasions when we'd lost contact, she was now old enough to initiate the process of finding me.

Anyhow, that was the end of it. Sheila, once more, was gone.

Part 3

Chapter 26

Sheila didn't contact me. Summer turned to autumn. New children came. New relationships formed. My work went on.

Then, in October, luck caught up with me. Through a series of flukes, I found out that Mr. Renstad was back in Marysville at the state hospital detox center. I attempted to talk to him by telephone, but was unsuccessful. So, when we had the long Columbus Day weekend, I drove over.

It was a warm, bright fall afternoon when I arrived at the unit. The poplars and the birches had all turned to brilliant shades of yellow and gold, highlighted by long shafts of autumn sunshine.

Mr. Renstad didn't seem all that surprised to see me, nor all that happy, although he went willingly enough with me to the visitors' area.

"Why don't you just leave us alone?" he said,

when I asked about Sheila. "You don't do her any good."

"How do you mean?" I asked.

"You stir things up. She was doing okay before you came in. She was settled down nice and we weren't having no problems."

I regarded him.

"It's you that's caused everything. You upset Sheila and I don't want you around no more. She was settled down nice till you stirred things up."

"I didn't mean to upset Sheila," I said. "I didn't realize I had."

"You put ideas in her head that don't belong there. She was happy before you came along."

"But the things we talked about were things Sheila wanted to discuss. I think she needs to talk to someone about what's happened to her."

"What's happened to her? What *has* happened to her? Nothing she ain't done for herself. And you put her up to it. Her stealing that little boy. It never would have come to that, if you hadn't gotten her going. She was *fine* till you came in."

"I'm sorry, but—"

"So just leave us alone, okay? Keep yourself to yourself. Sheila don't need your help and I don't want you seeing her anymore. I got the right. I can stop you." And with that he rose and walked back into the unit.

Chastened, I returned to my car. It was only after I was seated behind the steering wheel that anger began to overtake the effect of being reprimanded. Me? My fault? What a stupid man.

Still, what was undeniable about the outcome of that meeting was that he had no intention of telling me where Sheila was. If anything, he would make certain I didn't find her, or block my efforts, if I did. Disheartened, I returned home.

Winter came and the year turned. There were reminders along the way. Alejo's parents stopped by one afternoon in January to tell me that they had formally adopted Alejo. He was now in a special class for mildly mentally handicapped children and making good progress. On another occasion, my mother sent me a recipe that included tuna fish and mushroom soup. And Chad stopped by my office one frosty February afternoon with his Sheila. He was on a business trip in the city, and his daughter, now six, was enjoying her first solo trip with Dad. Immaculately dressed, bright, friendly and terribly polite, Sheila showed me a small hand-held computer game her father had bought for her. The contrast between her childhood and the girl she was named after couldn't have been more profound.

I remained hopeful, scanning the mail each evening when I came home for something in Sheila's handwriting, but it didn't come. Winter turned into spring and eventually spring into summer.

We ran the summer program again. It was much less the amateur affair it had been the previous year. We had twenty-four children in three classrooms with three specialist teachers, four aides and rotating on-site psychiatrists. Jeff only came once a week, and while I was there daily, it was in a supervisory capacity, roaming between rooms. The program was excellent, I felt, but it lacked the gung-ho magic of its predecessor.

In early July, I noted when Sheila's birthday came. She would be fifteen now. And then the anniversary of her disappearance. I couldn't help wondering where she was at the moment and what she was doing.

When the summer school finished, I took a month off and went to Wales. The barren, mist-laden mountains in the north of that small corner of Britain had become a second home to me. I was never quite sure what it was that attracted me there in the first place, but there had never been any doubt about what brought me back. I found an innate rightness in being there amidst the heather and the slate-built stone walls. It was an organic thing, something from within me, and I returned for the peace it always brought when I did so.

I had a group of good friends among the locals by that summer and we all shared a love for the mountains. Days were spent spanning the rainy moorlands and communing with Wales's teeming sheep population. Evenings were passed around the coal fires of local pubs, where I could indulge a fondness for draft Guinness and Welsh accents. The city, the clinic and all my former life disappeared like the mountains did when the mist rose up from the sea.

Like all good vacations, this one ended with my returning so exhausted I could hardly see straight. I staggered down off the plane, caught a taxi into the city and then staggered up the stairs of my apartment building. Setting down my rucksack, I fished out my house keys and opened my door. Or rather, I tried to. The mail, pushed through the mail slot, had fallen to the floor and wedged itself under the door as I pushed it open. Several minutes passed before I successfully extracted enough mail from under it to get into my apartment.

Once in, I bent to clear up the rest of the mail when my eyes fell upon one letter. Immediately, I recognized Sheila's handwriting. I ripped it open.

Dear Torey,
I don't quite know how to start, but I think I'm going to kill myself. I got the pills. They're right here and all that I've got left to do is write this letter. I feel so alone, Torey. Nothing seems to work out for me and I'm just so damned tired of trying. This is the only thing to do that makes sense.

But I wanted to write you this first. I wanted to say thank you for everything you've done for me. I know you went the extra mile a couple of times and I'm really honored to think you would. I want you to know I always felt grateful. I'm sorry things just couldn't work out.

With love, Sheila

And across the bottom was a row of Os and Xs, indicating hugs and kisses, as in a very little child's letter.

Quickly, I looked for a date, but there was none. I flipped the envelope over to see the postmark, and to my absolute horror, I saw that the letter had been posted two days after I had left for Wales—a full four weeks earlier. Paralyzed with grief, I just stared at it.

There was an address on the letter, indicating that Sheila was in a group home near a community about an hour's drive east of the city. But what could I do now? Four weeks had elapsed. How did one handle this? Phone up the group home and ask if Sheila was still alive? Knowing Sheila's personality, I didn't think she was the type for gestures. If she said she was going to commit suicide, I had little doubt that was exactly what she would do, and I didn't know how I would cope with a phone call of this sort.

Unfortunately, this wasn't the only chaos to accost me on my return. Another youngster I'd been working with had assaulted a care worker, then run away, and he'd chosen this particular evening of my return to ransack Jeff's and my office in search of a homemade knife I had taken off him. The immediacy of this problem, combined with the pressure from the authorities to deal with this boy, and my general exhaustion after a twenty-hour return trip from abroad caused me to behave toward Sheila's letter in a way that I now feel deep embarrassment about. There I was, with the worst letter I had ever received, and, ashamed as I am to admit it, I did nothing.

I didn't forget the letter by any means. It preyed on me, night and day. Small, quiet moments, particularly those deep in the night when I would awaken, were nibbled by that letter. My problem was, I just didn't quite know how to handle it. I genuinely believed Sheila would do what she threatened, so I didn't know how or whom to ask to confirm this. Moreover, I was saddened and ashamed to think that she had written me in a moment of desperation and would never know that I had been unable to respond. She would think instead that I, like everyone else, had abandoned her.

All this provided an unexpected and rather unwelcome opportunity for intense self-examination. I had failed Sheila. That was the bottom line. Moreover, I couldn't help but feel I was the one who had set her up. I had opened up unimaginable worlds to her when she was six, and, as she had so rightly pointed out to me, I had made her think they could be hers. Young and idealistic at the time, I'd genuinely believed they could be. She was bright, articulate, attractive, charming when she wanted to be and full of grit. I thought I'd given her the passport to a better life. Older and sadly wiser, I now realized nothing was ever as simple as it seemed.

The months that followed were a difficult, disruptive time in several areas of my life simultaneously. My client list was very full, the children on it a more demanding assortment than usual. I was physically attacked on two different occasions and nearly raped on a third. Worse, more than a fair share of my clients were quite unrewarding to work with, requiring long hours of effort for very little response.

I was beginning to chafe under the capitalist ethos of the clinic, feeling uncomfortable knowing that I could only treat those children who could afford to pay for my services, not those who needed treatment worse. This caused me to waste precious time trying to secure special funding for some children, who I believed genuinely needed continued therapy, and to feel resentment toward those with mild problems that could have been dealt with easily in the school or home but whose well-off parents insisted on treatment.

The biggest blow, however, came in midwinter, when Jeff left the clinic in unfortunate circumstances. My colleagues' sexual behaviors were of little interest to me, as long as they did not impinge on work-related matters or my relationship with the individuals. Deep down, I think I was probably aware that Jeff was gay, although it had never been of any consequence to what we were doing together, and thus never something I'd paid attention to. Sadly, society did. When the board of trustees for the clinic found out about his sexual preferences, they felt it unwise for Jeff to be working one-to-one with young children. Jeff was given the opportunity to go quietly with good references, and feeling he had no alternative, he did.

He transferred to a post in California working with alcoholics.

I was devastated. We had been sharing several cases and had built our treatment methods around the partnership. Jeff left very abruptly, having negotiated with the trustees right up to the end to stay. When they'd refused to budge, he'd stormed out in anger. Consequently, I had not been prepared for his departure and was left to clear up the damage. There was plenty, and I was kept unpleasantly busy.

The only bright spot in the winter had been the advent of a new boyfriend named Hugh. Allan had long since passed from the scene and I had been doomed to a number of months of the dreaded dating ritual. Then up popped this incredibly handsome man with a wicked sense of humor and a ten-year-old VW with dead bugs painted all over it. We were definitely an example of the old adage of opposites attracting each other, because Hugh and I couldn't have made a less likely couple. A complete antithesis to Allan and Chad, Hugh was a pull-yourself-up-by-the-bootstraps college dropout, who had set himself up in pest extermination at age twenty-one with the money that should have gone for education. He had a shrewd business mind and a genuine passion for crawling through people's cellars and attics killing small creatures, and after ten years, he owned one of the most successful pest-extermination businesses in the city.

What had attracted me most was his sense of humor, which was of legendary proportions. For me, in my deadly serious profession, humor was the lifesaver I often grabbed hold of just to stay afloat, so it was easy to love someone who was always capable of appreciating the funny side in life's unfunnier situations.

Spring came very slowly that year. It had been a dry, cold winter that lingered uninvited into March, and then the snowstorms finally arrived in April, burying us, paralyzing the city and destroying what few signs of spring there were.

At the clinic I argued with my colleagues over the fate of the summer program. Dr. Freeman had taken over much of Jeff's summer-program involvement and, without consulting me, he had applied for and gotten grants to expand us into two locations. We would now be serving forty-eight children, including a group of severely autistic children who were not clients of the clinic. I sensed a money-making scheme behind all of this, which annoyed me mightily, as I'd wanted to keep it confined to children whose progress we could continue to follow, but it didn't matter much. My position with the program had become almost tangential. In the end, I gave up the fight. It was probably a good enough program, but it was light-years away from what Jeff and I had conceived two summers earlier, so I decided to leave it all to Dr. Freeman.

May came and with it a new office partner named Jules. He was a dramatic change from Jeff in all respects, from appearance to demeanor. Having switched to child psychiatry after many years as a urologist, he was almost fifty, a short, round dumpling of a man with a few whiffs of white where his hair ought to have been. Unlike Jeff, with his rapier wit and showy confidence, Jules was soft-spoken and gentle as a bunny. I liked him. Indeed, the more I came to know him, the more I enjoyed his company. He was very easy to talk to and was a brilliant lateral thinker, which meant our conversations could go leap-frogging off in all directions. But he wasn't Jeff. Still missing Jeff enormously, I took a long time to get used to a new face at the other desk.

Then, one evening in June, I came home to find a thick envelope on the floor with my other mail. Sheila's handwriting was immediately recognizable. Astonished, I ripped the envelope open. There were thirteen sheets of notebook paper inside. The first one was a very brief letter to me:

Dear Torey
I've been wanting to write you, but after my last letter I didn't know how to start. I'm sorry. Anyway I'm still here.

I've sent you these. I wanted to send them to my own mom, but I don't know where she is, so I've sent them to you. I hope you don't mind.

Love, Sheila

Lifting off the letter, I looked at the pages underneath. Each one contained a single, short letter addressed to Sheila's mother.

Dear Mom,
I wish I could see you. I wish I knew what you look like. I tried to get a picture of you, but Dad doesn't have any and nobody else seems to either. I want to know you. Do you have blond hair like I do? Is it straight? Do you have blue eyes? Every time I go out, I look at the women who go by me. I keep looking for someone who might know me. What do you look like? I think if I could find out, I'd feel better.

Dear Mom,
Why did you go? That's something that's always bugged me. I mean, how come you wouldn't take me? Was I that bad a kid? Was I, like, mouthy to you all the time or something? Did I fight with Jimmie? Or did you just get fed up with having two kids?

Dear Mom,
Did you go because of Dad? I know about him now, how he can't stay off the stuff. It makes me angry too. It makes me want to run away. Is that what happened to you? Could you just not stand it?

Folding the letters and putting them back into their envelope, I regarded my name on the front. Up in the corner was the name of the same group home her earlier letter had come from. Going into the kitchen, I picked up the telephone and dialed Information.

Chapter 27

Mr. Renstad's abrupt departure was, as Jeff had suggested, debt-related. What we didn't know at the time was that, contrary to his word, he was still using drugs regularly, and it was with some unsavory underworld characters that he had run up his debts. He and Sheila had escaped just ahead of trouble, as they had apparently done so many times before.

Trouble caught up with him a few months later, though, in the form of the law. He was convicted of a minor drug offense and sent to the state hospital detox center yet again, which is where I had caught up with him. Sheila, meanwhile, had been placed in a children's group home in the community where he had been arrested.

Unhappy with this new situation, Sheila had run away. This prompted her placement in a foster home, and when she ran from there, she was transferred to a children's home in a rural location about an hour's drive east of the city. This sort of place was known colloquially as a "children's ranch," a euphemism for a locked facility. It was from there Sheila's suicide note to me had come the previous summer and it was from there I had received this most recent group of letters.

Having located Sheila at last, I rang immediately and spoke with the director of the ranch, a woman named Jane Timmons.

"From the Sandry Clinic, you say?" she asked in amazement. "Sheila Renstad was treated at the Sandry? Who paid the bills?"

Annoyed with what seemed an unusually rude question, especially as I was a complete stranger, I explained that my relationship with Sheila went back a good deal further, but I did not elaborate on the fact that it was no longer a professional but a personal one. Thirty seconds on the phone and I could tell here was a lady for whom money and status meant much. That I was from the Sandry, a well-known and expensive private clinic, probably opened more doors than all my professional qualifications put together. If I had said I was only a friend, I would have been lumped with Sheila's father and probably not given the time of day.

Jane Timmons told me that Sheila had been at the ranch for just over a year and that for the most part she had been a difficult, uncooperative girl, who mixed poorly and seemed to have few, if any, friends. They had thwarted three different runaway attempts, including one where Sheila had gotten as far as the river and they'd needed to call the police.

I questioned her about the general philosophy of the ranch, and she confirmed for me what I'd already anticipated, that theirs was a program that relied heavily on behavior modification, with the children needing to earn all privileges through a point system. I also asked about Sheila's prospects for being released from the ranch. Jane explained that Mr. Renstad was due for parole near Christmas, and if social services felt it was appropriate, Sheila would go back to him then.

Because Jane Timmons assumed I was seeing Sheila in a professional capacity, our meeting was not subject to Sheila's earning sufficient points. Mercifully. As emotionally and intellectually complex as Sheila was, behavior modification was a system doomed to failure with her.

I arrived at the ranch on the Saturday following Sheila's sixteenth birthday. It was a bright, hot day, following a long dry spell, when I came out. The ranch, a collection of low, modern buildings, squatted along the banks of a dry riverbed. There was not a tree on the property, and the grass had all burned yellow-brown in the summer heat. Only the barbed wire glinted in the sun.

As it was a weekend, Jane Timmons wasn't there, but I was greeted pleasantly by the young man in charge and then transferred to Holly, one of the counselors, who was responsible for the group of children that included Sheila. She took me back to the girls' wing, where Sheila was waiting in her room.

It was a genuine secure unit, with an endless number of heavy locked doors and windows sporting that thick glass with the chicken wire embedded in it that never gave you an undistorted image. Sheila's room was the third to the last on the left. The door, made of pale-colored oak with a small square window and a mortise lock, stood open. Sheila was sitting cross-legged on her bed.

"Hi," I said.

"Hi." There was a long moment's hesitation and then, abruptly, Sheila threw herself into my arms and clung to me tightly. I wrapped my arms around her and held her close.

In the doorway, Holly regarded us. Over Sheila's head, I looked at her. "Could you leave us for a little while?"

She paused, then nodded. "Yeah. Okay."

Sheila had changed enormously in the interceding two years. She had grown taller, but had lost weight. Too much weight. She looked frail. The wacky clothes had been replaced with nothing more exotic than a pair of jeans and a blue T-shirt. The brilliant hair was gone too, as was most of the permanent, and she had grown her bangs out—or mostly out. The result was not a style at all, but an untidy mixture of dark-blond roots, frizzy colored ends, and stray, sticking-out bits, all left to grow far too long without attention.

Sheila examined me as closely as I was examining her. "You're getting old, you know that?" she said. "You got wrinkles."

"Gee, thanks."

"It's just that I never thought about you with wrinkles."

"It happens to the best of us," I said and sat down on her roommate's bed.

The room was small and Spartan. It was no more than a cubicle, really, about eight by ten feet. There was a window at the far end, two iron beds with rather violent pink bedspreads, and a single desk at the foot of Sheila's bed. Her roommate, a girl named Angel, had posters of rock stars plastered on the wall above her bed and an assortment of stuffed animals against her pillow. Sheila had nothing.

I gazed around and then back at Sheila, who had settled again, cross-legged, on her bed. She was an immensely attractive girl, in spite of her thinness and her uncared-for appearance, but there was a melancholy about her I had never previously detected.

"So, are you married yet?" she asked.

"Married? Me?" I replied in surprise. "No. Why? Did you think I would be?"

"Yeah. You and Jeff."

"*Jeff* and me? Jeff and I were ... I mean, not in that way. I was never involved with Jeff. We were just friends. Colleagues, really. Nothing more."

She tipped her head, her expression skeptical.

"What about you?" I asked. "Do you have any boyfriends?"

She didn't reply. There was a moment's pause, just a beat, and she looked back. "So, where's Jeff at? Is he coming out to see me too?"

"No," I said, and Sheila's face fell.

"Oh, I'd hoped he would," she said sorrowfully. This caught me off-guard, as I had never thought she'd felt anything but antipathy for him.

"He's in California now," I said and pondered briefly on whether or not to tell Sheila the whole story about what had happened to him. I decided I should, to make it clear that his departure had been forced upon him.

Sheila listened to the story with rapt attention, her brow furrowing. When I finished, she shook her head slightly. "Gone? He's gone for good?"

"I'm afraid so."

"Oh, Jeff," she murmured softly, shaking her head. "The breaking of so great a thing should make a greater crack. The round world should have shook lions into civil streets, and citizens to their dens."

Hearing those words, I realized they were a quotation, but I didn't know from where.

"You don't recognize that?" Sheila asked. Leaning over the side of her bed, she pulled out a flat under-bed box and tipped up the lid. Reaching in, she lifted out the copy of Shakespeare's *Antony and Cleopatra* that Jeff had given her for her fourteenth birthday. The cover was dog-eared and taped back together in places. I could see several pages were loose.

An enormous silence suddenly loomed up out of nowhere. Sheila held the book in her lap and regarded the worn cover. I just sat, all the words drained from my mind.

At last she began to speak softly. "I wondered why he gave it to me. I thought, what a stupid gift. I mean, who would want to read *Shakespeare*? For fun? Some dorky old woman in sturdy black shoes and support hose. Not me, that's for sure.

"Then I was stuck waiting at the police station one night. I didn't have anything to pass the time, so I started reading it. It was hard to get into, hard to get used to the language—which is weird to me now, because now when I read it, it seems so easy—but that first night I struggled. And I thought, why on earth did he give this to me?

"Then I got here, and it was, like, being in a desert. If you don't earn your points, don't play the game their way, you just sit. It's the boredom factor, you see, that they control you with." The smile was more enigmatic this time. "So I started reading it again. And this time I read it right through. And when I finished, I read it again. And again. I bet you I read it ten times straight through in about two days. And I thought, this is so beautiful. This woman is so wonderful. So *magnificent*. And this man gives everything for her. He gives away the world—quite literally. And yet ... like, they don't even talk nicely to each other about half the time. They're in love in their minds, but in reality, they're always disagreeing, arguing, teasing.

"God ... When I read this, it makes me ... how does one describe it? Expand? No. No, that's not it." She paused, pensive. "It's like I'm in this little attic room—that's my normal life—and there's this skylight above me that I can see, but I can never reach. Then, when I read this, something inside me grows. Pushes me up, and for just a moment, I can lift the skylight and see out. Just glimpse the world beyond, know what I mean? But I can glimpse it. For just a moment I can tell there's something bigger than myself."

Listening to Sheila, I was deeply moved.

She went on talking, her words tumbling out ever more quickly, as if she feared I'd stop her. All this thought, all these insights struggling to light in a vacuum. I could sense her intellectual desperation.

"The story's all true, you know," she was saying. "I went and checked the facts. The whole course of the Western world was affected by what this couple did. Did you know that? Cleopatra was, like, this really incredible woman. She was very strong. A very powerful queen. And yet she is so human. So silly. So funny. God, Torey, in places this is the funniest thing I have ever read."

All I could think was what the hell were we doing with this girl locked up in a secure unit? Why was she here and not in some summer-school literature course at a college or studying the ancient history that obviously intrigued her so much? Where were the mentors who should have spotted this girl along the way? My talents didn't lie here. My knowledge of Shakespeare, like my knowledge of the writings of Julius Caesar, was pedestrian. Where were the English teachers whose hearts should have gladdened at the very idea of a sixteen-year-old besotted with the poetry of *Antony and Cleopatra*?

Her expression slowly growing sorrowful, Sheila regarded the book in her hands. With one finger, she gently smoothed the Scotch tape back over a ragged edge. "You know, that's really sad about Jeff. I'd wanted to see him. I'd wanted him to know I liked the book."

"Maybe I can give you his address, if you'd like to write him," I suggested.

"I think I'd sort of fallen in love with him," she said. "I couldn't tell him that then. Fortunately, I hadn't read this, because I could never have told him I liked it. I wanted him to think I hated him." She looked up. "Isn't that weird? I didn't. I never did. But I was scared he'd hate me if I didn't hate him first." A pause. "Now I wish I'd told the truth."

We continued to talk for more than two hours that Saturday afternoon. Most of the other children, Sheila's roommate included, had earned enough points for a trip into town, and after a noisy clatter of activity while they got ready, we were left in peace. This suited both of us.

Sheila, for once, was very open and talkative. I suspect this was the result of so much time spent on her own. Alone and lonely, she was susceptible to my familiar face. Depression played a part in it too. My overall impression of Sheila that afternoon was that she was quite seriously depressed. All the spark had gone right out of her, and with the exception of her relationship with *Antony and Cleopatra*, she showed interest in very little. As a consequence, I think she was too dispirited to disguise her thoughts as elaborately as in the past.

Feeling concern for her as a continued suicide risk, I felt obliged to bring up the letter she had sent me the previous autumn. "I'm sorry about last fall," I said, "about not answering your letter."

"Ah, yes," Sheila said and looked away. "That letter." She grimaced. "I'm sorry if I upset you. I feel stupid now that I wrote it."

"No, you shouldn't feel stupid. Those were very real feelings. It's my fault. I was gone then. I was in Wales and didn't even know about it until I got back, which was weeks later. I felt so terrible, Sheil, that you'd written and I couldn't answer."

"Let's just not talk about it, okay?"

I regarded her. She had her head down and was examining something on her fingernail. Sheila had always been a curious mixture of tiger and lamb, fierce and spirited on one hand, frightened and vulnerable on the other. I'd often felt utter exasperation with her when she was being tigerish, but it was also what had attracted me to her. Studying her rounded shoulders, her disheveled hair, I sought the tiger hiding there.

"I get to thinking a lot about my mom," she said softly. A pause. "That's your fault, too. Remember that last conversation we had? In the car? When for all that time I had you and her mixed up?"

I nodded.

"Well, I've been thinking and thinking ... trying to pull the two of you apart, I guess. I don't know where I got the thing with you. *You* didn't abandon me. You were just my teacher. Only doing what teachers do. I was just being stupid, I think. Trying to survive."

"How do you mean?" I asked.

Sheila shrugged. "I dunno. By not thinking about those years. By forgetting them. 'Cause that's what I did. I forgot everything. I mean, I *remember* forgetting. It was a conscious thing. I'd move on to somewhere new, like to a new foster home, or like back with my dad, and I'd think to myself, 'I'm going to start all over now.' And then I'd, like, go into my new school and stuff and people would ask me about my life before and I'd just say, 'I don't remember about it.' And really quickly, that'd be true. It's like I'd get reborn each time and all that went before was in some former life. Almost like it wasn't me."

"Did that help you not think of your mother?" I asked.

"Yeah. And not think of you. And not think of Miss McGuire, 'cause I was really happy in her class too. Because I didn't want to remember being too happy. I didn't want to think about those times, because I'd cry. Remembering bad things never bothers me. I think, 'Well, that's shit.' And that's all. But remembering being happy just guts me. So every time I'd do it, I'd just say, '*No*, don't do that.' And pretty soon it was gone."

I looked at her. She raised her head, glanced at me and then looked back at her hands. "Then you came mucking about. You really aren't one to leave things well enough alone, you know that?" she said. The tone was affectionate and she allowed a faint grin, but I knew there was truth in the words.

"You wish I'd left well enough alone?" I asked.

A long, pensive pause followed, with Sheila picking intently at her thumbnail, then finally she gave a slow shrug. "I dunno. I think my life would have been a lot easier if you had. One way or another, you've given me a lot of grief over the years, but ..." She looked over at me. "The fact is, my life would have been a lot easier if practically everybody I've ever known had stayed out of it—my mother, my father, this place, the foster homes, Social Services. So you're no exception."

I smiled. This caused Sheila to smile back. "You don't mind me saying that about you?" she asked.

"No. It's probably true."

A silence came then. Sheila lay back on her bed and folded her hands behind her head. Staring upward, she regarded the ceiling for several moments. I turned to study Angel's rock posters. Most of them were of artists I'd never heard of.

"I think so much about my mom now," Sheila said softly. "I mean, about where she is and things. What she's doing. I don't even know her, Torey."

"Putting it down on paper was a good idea, I think," I said.

"I try to figure out why she did what she did when she left me on that highway. Maybe she didn't mean to. Maybe it was some sort of accident, like, perhaps the door handle came undone.

Maybe I fell out of the car." Still regarding the ceiling, Sheila's expression had grown inward. "Maybe if she knew I was all right, that I wanted to see her ..."

Not quite sure how to respond, I remained silent. Sheila finally looked over. "I'm not sending you those letters because I think *you're* my mom."

"No, I know that."

"I'm done thinking that. I just sent them 'cause ... well, they're *letters*. They only mean something if they're sent."

"I understand and I'm glad to get them."

"Keep them for me, would you?" she asked. "Because someday, I'm going to find her and I'm going to give them to her. I want her to know me, to know how I've been feeling all these years. That's what I've decided. When I get out of here, I'm going to find my mother."

Chapter 28

Dear Mom,
Do you know how unhappy I've been? Do
you know what kind of life I've had? Why
did you do this to me? I lay at night thinking
about it, trying to figure out why I wasn't
good enough for you, but do you know what
it was like, being left behind?

Sheila concerned me greatly. Finding her isolated and depressed, I worried that suicide might easily loom up again as a possible solution. Moreover, her needs didn't seem to be well recognized by the group-home personnel. Like most such institutions, they were understaffed and overstretched. The staff turnover rate, in particular, was atrocious. Most of the care workers were poorly trained part-timers on minimum wage, who came and went on an almost weekly basis, which disallowed relationships of any depth to develop with the children. Among the resident staff, only Jane Timmons and her two deputies were specifically trained to work with disturbed children, and of them, only one had worked at the ranch for more than two years. Jane herself had been there only a little longer than Sheila.

This alone would have been cause for concern in Sheila's case, because none of the adults had been around her long enough to develop a meaningful relationship with her, but the strict Skinnerian approach used to control the children and bring about changed behavior seemed particularly inappropriate for Sheila. To begin with, it encouraged detached, impersonal contact between staff and children. Moreover, Sheila had the sort of personality that did not find it easy to accept coercion, which was how she interpreted the point system, and she was quick to dig herself in. This led, ipso facto, to prolonged isolation.

Unfortunately, I was not in a good position to do much, as I was not seeing her in a professional capacity. Jane Timmons did not know this and it seemed judicious not to enlighten her, which I didn't; however, I knew I'd better not overstep too much. Thus I confined myself to announcing my visits to Jane rather than requesting them, so as to ensure I could see Sheila when I wanted. That, and occasionally "conferencing" with Jane. I knew she would expect me, as a professional, to want to hear about Sheila's life at the ranch, and as I did, I took advantage of the opportunity.

When possible, I came out to see Sheila each Saturday afternoon. It was a fair drive from the city, but quite a pleasant one, and often Hugh and I would make it together. He'd bring his fishing gear along and would disappear off down the river for an hour or two while I talked to Sheila. Thus passed much of the rest of the summer.

Jane Timmons painted a rather bleak picture of Sheila's social behavior. I think I had already surmised that Sheila was no social butterfly. This had occurred to me clear back during the summer when she was working with Jeff and me, because there was never, ever any mention of friends, either male or female. I had never pressured Sheila on this issue, partly because I was not in a good position to do anything constructive about it, and partly because I felt her IQ interfered to some degree with normal peer relationships. This would be a difficult area to deal with, particularly in Sheila's circumstances, and I had ended up feeling that time and maturity would probably be the best solutions.

"Say what?" Jane asked. "What was that? Superior IQ?"

"Yes, you know."

"No, I don't know. What IQ?" she asked.

Shock hit me. All that effort my colleagues and I had gone through the year Sheila was six to confirm her extraordinary giftedness, and it wasn't in her records? "Sheila has an IQ over a hundred eighty," I said.

"Say *what*?" Jane's eyes widened. "One hundred eighty? You must be joking."

"You have no record of it?"

"*One hundred eighty*? Sheila Renstad? *Our* Sheila Renstad? You're kidding, aren't you? Who told you?"

"I was there myself," I said. "I know. I was working with her then, when the testing was done."

Jane fell back in her chair. "Boy, nobody ever said anything about this to me."

Filled with resentment at a system that treated lives with such appalling offhandedness, I went on down the hall with Holly, who unlocked the doors for me. Sheila, as always, was alone in her room.

"We've got to get you out of here," I said.

"You're telling me."

"No, I mean it, Sheila. This is no place for you. Why are you even here? You haven't committed any offenses. Why are *you* locked up? It's your dad who's supposed to be in prison."

Sitting cross-legged on her bed, she looked up at me. "Yeah, well, welcome to my world."

I pulled out the chair from the desk and sat down. A silence came then, sapping my sudden spurt of anger.

"What you get used to after a while, Torey, is that this is just the way it is. There's no use fighting it."

"I can't accept that," I said.

"I can. I've had to."

Dear Mom,
What's Jimmie doing now? He's probably
taller than me these days. I was figuring it out
and he'd be at least fourteen. I can't remem-
ber exactly any more if he was two years
younger than me, or was it even less? Was it
like eighteen months? I keep thinking about
that, trying to remember. It's weird, knowing
you've forgotten about your own brother.

Jane Timmons had wanted me to take up the issue of Sheila's asocial behavior with her, and it was an issue that no doubt wanted exploring, but not that afternoon. For these few hours at least, I wanted Sheila to feel she had control, so we tended to go as she led.

Gloom hung over her that afternoon, as it had on so many others. She lay back on her bed and stared up at the ceiling. I suggested perhaps we could go for a walk, but Sheila vetoed that. She wasn't allowed off the grounds and she could see no point in making a circuit of the barbed-wire fence.

"What would you *like* to do?" I asked at last, when the silence had grown so heavy it threatened to squash me.

"Nothing, really."

There was a quiet pause. She was still lying on the bed, but she brought one hand up to her forehead.

"Well ..." She paused again, her fingers probing along her hairline. "Remember back when I was in your class?"

"Yes."

"Remember how you always did my hair? I used to love that so much, the way you used to brush it and put it in styles." She glanced over. "Do you … I mean, if I gave you … Well, it sounds stupid, but would you fix my hair for me?"

"Yeah, I suppose."

Sheila rose up from the bed and went to the dresser to get her hairbrush. Pausing in front of the small mirror, she gave her hair a few yanks with it and grimaced at her image. "If we got scissors, could you cut it for me?"

"Oh, I don't know about that," I said. "I'm not much of a hairdresser."

She held out the brush to me. "I want to cut off these ends. Please, Torey? I'm fed up like I am."

Gently, I started to work the brush, then the comb, through her hair. It was quite a mess, what with all the bleaching and dying done over the years. Borrowing scissors from Jane's desk, I endeavored to do what Sheila asked of me. I trimmed away the last of the permanent and tried to do in as much of the dyed area as well. This brought her hair almost up to her shoulders in a not very professional blunt cut. Then I just brushed.

Sheila clearly enjoyed my activities very much and it occurred to me as I worked that, given her isolation at the ranch, it had probably been a fair length of time since anyone had touched her. This thought surprised me, but the more I considered it, the more I realized it was most likely true. Indeed, the thought crossed my mind that Sheila had probably spent most of her young life with little positive physical contact.

"Do you have a boyfriend?" I asked.

"Me? Here? No way."

"Have you ever had a boyfriend?"

She didn't respond right away. She had her back to me, because I was still brushing her hair, so I couldn't see her expression, but there was a sense of hesitancy. "No," she finally said.

"Do you want one?" I asked. "Do you like boys?"

"Do you mean, am I a lez?" she asked, pulling away from me and turning. She made a face. "Just because I don't have a boyfriend, you don't have to think that of me." She jerked right back from me. "You're probably thinking now that's why I wanted you to brush my hair. Shit. Give it here. Gimme my brush back."

"Whoa, that's not what I said. And so what, anyhow? I wouldn't care. If I didn't care about Jeff and his preferences, I wouldn't care about you and yours. That's a personal thing, Sheila. I was just asking."

"Yeah, why? What business is it of yours, if I've got boyfriends or not? I don't go asking you about what you're up to, do I?" she responded tetchily.

"Okay, okay. Sorry," I said.

"Hmmph," Sheila snorted and climbed back onto her bed. "Jane put you up to it, didn't she? Jane is so nosy."

"Okay. Sorry."

Silence. Sheila stared at the hairbrush in her hand. Bringing it up, she brushed through her hair on one side, feeling the ends I'd cut. The silence lingered, growing sad as it lengthened. I thought for a moment she was going to cry.

"No, I don't have a boyfriend," she said softly. "And no, I've never had one. I like boys. I liked Jeff. I thought he was a real dude and …" A pause. "But all it ever comes down to is fucking, Torey. And I've seen too many dicks already."

"It can be a little more than that, Sheil."

"I can't have children. Did you know that? After what my uncle did that time. You remember? It was when I was in your class. I can't have babies. So, what other reason would there be?" she asked.

Uncertain what to say, I just sat.

"What I'd like is someone just to cuddle me. Know what I mean? Someone who'd put his arms around me without expecting anything more in return, but I don't think I'll get that. So, I've just decided I'll have nothing at all."

Dear Mom,
I read in the papers this week where they found someone who'd got murdered 25 years ago and no one had ever known she was missing. Everyone just said she went away and nobody ever bothered looking for her. They thought she didn't want to come back. I get so worried that something like this has happened to you. I want to find you. I want

*to talk to you and know you're okay. I want
to make sure that isn't why you never came
back.*

When I came the following Saturday, I brought
Sheila hair-care items I'd picked up at the drugstore. They were nothing much: a jar of deep conditioner, some styling mousse and a blue headband
to keep her half-grown-out bangs out of her eyes.
She greeted these gifts with delight.

"Wow! This is great!" She ripped apart the bag
rather than opening it and lifted up the headband,
shoving it into her hair. "I always wanted to wear
one of these. Because I had bangs, it never made
sense for me to have one, so I never got one. But
this is great. Why'd you do it?"

I shrugged. "Thought you'd like it."

"Yeah, I do. Thanks."

A minute or two passed while Sheila inspected
the items more carefully. She unscrewed the lid to
the conditioner, fingered it, put the lid back on and
then read the directions. "They're probably never
going to let me use this stuff here. They make you
turn in everything. I reckon they think you're going
to smoke it or something. God knows."

I sat down on Angel's bed. She had at least two
dozen small stuffed toys lined up against the pillow
and my weight on the bed dislodged several. I
leaned over and tried to rearrange them.

"I found out when my dad's getting parole. On
October twenty-eighth," Sheila said.

"What do you think of that?"

She shrugged. Turning the mousse container over, she sprayed some out onto her hand, lifted it up and smelled it, then squished the foam between her two palms.

"Where's he going? Will he have a job?" I asked.

"He's going back to Broadview. He's got friends in Broadview. See, that's where he grew up. That's where Grandma used to live when she was alive." She rubbed the mousse into her hair.

This was the first I'd heard Sheila mention any other family members. I knew there were others, including her father's brother, Jerry, who had so viciously molested Sheila when she was six. However, Sheila rarely ever spoke of anyone outside her very immediate family.

"Well, that's good news anyway," I said. "It means you can leave here."

Curling her lip, Sheila conveyed a feeling of disgruntled uncertainty. "I dunno. I'm not sure I want to go back with my dad. I mean, it's been about a million times now that he's said he's going to stop taking the stuff and he doesn't do it. I doubt he will this time either and I'm so fed up with getting stuck in these shitholes."

I didn't say anything.

She looked over briefly. "Know what I'm thinking of doing? Going to find my mom. Seeing if I can live with her."

"How would you do that?"

"Well, don't tell anybody"—Sheila glanced around furtively, as if expecting to be overheard—"but I've been saving up my money, 'cause my dad sends me some every once in a while. And last time when I was in town, I went in the library and I got the address of a newspaper in California. I sent them some money to take out an ad. An ad saying who I was and that I was looking for my mother."

"California's a pretty big place. One newspaper won't cover much of it."

"Well, yeah, I know. But as I get more money, I'll take out more ads," Sheila said. "She'll see one of them, I'm sure."

I regarded her. "And then what?"

"Well, I can talk to her then, can't I? And maybe I can go live with her."

"Sheil, I don't think ..."

She grimaced at me. "You're going to say fuck it, aren't you? I knew you would."

"No, I'm not. I'm just saying go kind of slow on this."

"I know what I'm doing," she replied. "She's probably going to be really grateful I've tried to find her. You hear about this all the time with kids who've been adopted and how their real parents are always so glad when they contact them."

"*Almost* always."

"And she'll be settled and my brother will be there and ..."

"Don't get your hopes up too high, Sheil."

Her shoulders dropped in an expression of exasperation. "I shouldn't have told you. I *knew* I shouldn't have told you. You *are* going to say fuck it."

"I'm not, Sheila. I'm just saying—"

"I do know, Torey, but it's not going to be like you think. Shit, I don't want to stay with my father. And I sure as hell don't want to stay here. I want to be with her. She probably will be grateful I've gone to the trouble to find her. That was a long time ago. It might even have been an accident. I might just have fallen out of the car. Maybe she didn't notice until it was too late. She's probably going to be happy to know I'm okay."

Chapter 29

Dear Mom,
I want to live with you. I'm fed up living with
Dad. It's not that anything bad's happened,
because nothing bad's happened for a long
time, it's just I get so sick of his ways. Of
worrying about him and worrying about the
booze and worrying about the stuff and wor-
rying what's going to happen to our money
and worrying about if he's going to get in
trouble again and worrying what's going to
happen to me, if he does. I want to be with
you and Jimmie. Please, couldn't it be that
way for a while?

"Can you get me out of here?" Sheila asked
when I arrived for my usual Saturday visit. "I'm
going nuts in this place."

"You mean find you another group home?" I asked.

"No. God, no. Just get me out. Take me out. I haven't been off the grounds in, like, about three months," she replied. "I want to go to your house. Will you take me?"

"I'm not sure if Jane will let me. You haven't got a very good track record."

"Hah!" she said with delight. "I've got a *very* good track record. I can run faster than any of them." She snickered at the pun.

"Yes, well, I'm afraid that's just what I mean. And Jane won't be conned into giving you another opportunity."

Sheila gave a low, exasperated moan. "I wouldn't run away from *you*, Torey. You know that."

I didn't know that, to be honest. Not that I thought Sheila was lying. Of all the tricks I knew Sheila to be capable of, she had always been remarkably truthful with me. I had no reason to doubt her honesty now; however, she was a born opportunist. Whether or not she could resist the temptation of running away when the chance presented itself, I wouldn't like to judge.

"Come on. Please? Won't you just try?" she pleaded. "I'm so sick of it in here." A brief pause and she brightened. "I could cook for you. Remember? Like I did the last time? You liked that, didn't you? Please?"

"If I do ask, you know what it's going to mean?" I replied.

"What?"

"The point system. You're going to have to earn points."

With a dramatic swing of her arm over her eyes, Sheila fell back on her bed. "Oh, shit, not you too. *God*, Torey."

"You've got to cooperate, Sheila. You could have probably been out of here months ago, if you'd done what you were supposed to."

"God. Played their stupid game? Collected shitty little—what are they? Fucking golf tees or something? You think I'm going to let someone regulate my life with *golf tees*, for God's sake?"

I eyed her. "You will if you want to come home with me."

"Shit, Torey. I thought there was more to you than that." An angry frown on her face, she fell back on the bed again.

The tiger was stirring. Quite abruptly, I realized Sheila was fighting back. Delighted, I egged her on. "We'll get Jane in here. We can set up a point program and as soon as you've completed it, we'll arrange a weekend at my place. How does that sound?"

"Shitty."

"Very well. Have it your way."

Sheila sat up. "I didn't mean *that*. God, you're in a mood today. What's the matter? You on the rag or something?"

I smiled blandly.

She bared her teeth at me in an expression of irritation before crawling to the end of the bed to snag a piece of paper. "Okay, so get Jane then. Let's get this fucking thing out of the way."

Her mind applied to the project, Sheila earned her points swiftly. Jane was stunned, which, I suspect, was just the reaction Sheila was hoping to elicit. Indeed, as her depression lifted and Sheila increasingly became a force to be reckoned with around the group home, Jane appeared a little bit alarmed by what had been awakened.

Two Saturdays later found me in the car with Sheila, tooling back to the city. "God, this is great," Sheila kept saying. "Trees. Look at all these trees. That's what I miss so much out there. It's like a desert there."

Back in my apartment, Sheila went through it room by room. "Geez, it's weird being back here. Know when I was last here? That night with that little boy. Alejo. Geez, like déjà vu. No, no, that wasn't the last night, was it? I came over and cooked for you. That was afterward. God, Torey, it feels like a lifetime ago." She paused and looked back at me. "Remember how I was telling you the other week how I could sort of shut off parts of my life? Make them feel like they happened to someone else?"

I nodded.

"That's what happened here. I didn't mean to. I didn't try to forget this, but now that I'm back, that's how it feels. Like *really* déjà vu. Like I'm visiting some former incarnation, because ... like I don't think I've ever gone back to a place where everyone else is still carrying on their life, just the way I left them."

Wandering into the kitchen, Sheila caught sight of a group of photographs stuck up on my refrigerator with magnets. Pausing in front of them, she examined them carefully. "Those are pictures from my camping trip," I said. "Look. I caught the largest trout."

"Who's this guy you're with?"

"Hugh. You'll meet him later on, because he's taking us out to dinner tonight."

"So, he's the current fuck, is he?"

"Not quite the way I'd put it," I replied.

"You *do* fuck him, I trust." She was still studying the pictures.

"That's one of those questions, Sheila, that falls into the 'personal' category."

She turned. "We're friends, aren't we?"

"Well, yes …"

"So, there's nothing wrong with telling me that, is there? You do fuck him, don't you?"

"Fuck, no. Make love, yes. There's a difference."

She shrugged. "It's all fucking to me."

I had planned to take Sheila out to the shopping mall for the afternoon. Shut away for so many months, she was keen to enjoy the sights and sounds of crowded places and there weren't many more crowded than a mall on Saturday afternoon. We ate a quick lunch, then I popped into the bathroom to brush my teeth before we left.

Still brushing my teeth, I wandered out of the bathroom to hear a soft tappy sound. Rounding the corner into the living room, I saw Sheila with the telephone in her hand. "Who are you calling?" I asked in surprise.

"No one."

This seemed highly unlikely to me and I must have looked it.

Sheila got a silly look on her face. "Sorry. I was playing. Just messing around. I'm sorry. But, see, you can play tunes with these pushbutton phones. And I just wanted to try it ..."

I still regarded her skeptically.

"Yeah, come here. I'll play 'Twinkle, Twinkle, Little Star' for you."

I was slightly unsettled by the phone incident. Perhaps she was doing no more than playing with the push buttons and I was being needlessly wary, but intuition told me otherwise. Throughout the afternoon I was gnawed by the questions it brought up. Whom had she been calling? Why? And why didn't she want me to know?

The afternoon was a fairly tense one for me generally. With Sheila's history of running away, I knew the mall was a chancy place to take her. I had wanted to give her a happy, carefree time reminiscent of our old times together. Equally, I felt it was important for her to believe I trusted her, but the hard, cold truth was, I didn't really. I had been in business with these kids too long to be anything other than incredulous, and the secret phone call had only served to sharpen my wariness.

As it turned out, I had nothing to worry about. Sheila was delighted with the trip to the shopping center. She went into each and every shop, handled most of what she could get her hands on, tried on endless clothes and hats and jewelry and consumed a nightmarish assortment of doughnuts, caramel corn, cookies, pizza slices and ice cream, all washed down with gallons of Orange Julius. She fell in love with a funky little number made from what appeared to be someone's ready-for-the-trash-can jeans. The top was pretorn and came with its own supply of safety pins conveniently attached. The skirt barely covered her bottom. She had already bought a very rude T-shirt with her own money, so I offered to get her the dress. For a glimpse again of her wacky fashion sense, it seemed a reasonable price to pay.

By the time we got home, Hugh was already there. This startled Sheila. She had taken the key to my apartment from me to open the door and clearly had not expected to find someone on the other side. She screamed in surprise and ran back into the hall where I was.

Hugh, the eternal joker, waited until Sheila and I came through the door. Then he took one look at her, threw his arms up and gave an identical startled scream and ran off into the bedroom.

Sheila's jaw dropped. "God, who's he?"

"I'm a burglar. Go away," came a little voice from the bedroom.

"Is this for real?" she asked.

"That's Hugh," I said with enough exasperation in my voice to let him know we'd just about had enough.

Hugh appeared around the corner with a little floral hat I'd worn to a wedding the previous week perched on his head, but his expression funereal. "Yes," he said, bringing his voice way down into a deep double bass, "I'm Torey's friend, Hugh."

Sheila's eyes had widened to the very edges of her face. "And I thought Jeff was bad," she murmured. "God, Torey, where do you find them?"

The evening was delightful. Sheila spent hours in the bathroom getting ready. She kitted herself out in her new clothes, rude T-shirt and all, and then helped herself liberally to my makeup. Afterward Hugh took us out to a Japanese restaurant where the chef, wielding his knife with artistic precision, prepared our meal right at the table. Sheila, who had never used chopsticks, fumbled and laughed and fumbled again, repeatedly dropping food into her lap. In normal circumstances, Sheila was not inclined toward humor. Her dignity, her sense of self were still too fragile to stand up to hearty laughter. However, on this particular evening she was able to see the funny side of her clumsy efforts and, more crucially, able to tolerate and even join in with Hugh's silly remarks. Indeed, Hugh's comments were so absurd that soon all three of us were convulsed with hilarity to the point that Sheila was not the only one unable to work chopsticks.

Afterward we took in a science-fiction movie. Hugh bought us a humongous container of popcorn and then sat between Sheila and me so we could share it. While waiting for the film to begin, the two of them amused themselves throwing popcorn into the air and trying to catch it in their mouths. I was starting to feel just a little uncomfortable with all this merriment, because I could sense we were getting on other people's nerves and I was worried that someone might complain. Yes, we better settle down, Hugh acknowledged. In a rare display of affection, Sheila clutched hold of Hugh's arm and pressed against him in a half-hug.

That evening after Hugh had left, Sheila and I sorted out our sleeping arrangements in my apartment. She was getting the couch in the living room and I pulled the back cushions off to make it roomier.

"Was he high on something?" Sheila asked, as we worked.

"Who? Hugh? No, he's always like that."

"Wow." She paused to straighten the sheet over the cushions. "You're sure he's not high? He doesn't, like, take something and you don't know about it?"

"No. That's just Hugh," I replied. "I think it's one of the things that attracts me to him so much. I love a good laugh."

She nodded. "I guess I never knew people could be like that if they weren't high. Or drunk or something. I didn't know you could make yourself so happy."

Once Sheila was settled on the couch, I got ready for bed myself. I cleaned up, said good night and then disappeared into my bedroom. It was quite late and I was tired, so within moments of turning out the light, I was asleep.

I awoke with a start. The room was dark. Turning to see my bedside clock, I noticed it was only about an hour and a half after I'd gone to bed and I had that hair-raising sensation of no longer being alone in the room. Rolling over in the bed, I raised myself up. "Sheila?" I whispered into the darkness.

For a moment or two there was no response, then she stepped out of the shadows by the door. "I'm sorry. I didn't mean to wake you."

"What are you doing?"

She didn't answer immediately, so I reached to turn on the light. "Don't!" she pleaded, so I didn't.

I leaned over the side of the bed to see that her blanket from the couch was on the floor. She came forward and lay her pillow down on top of it.

"What are you doing?" I asked again.

"I can't sleep." Her voice was small and child-like. "It's strange out there. I'm not much used to sleeping all on my own. Angel, like, snores and I'm used to her noise. Do you mind if I'm in here?"

"I don't think I snore."

She giggled. "That's all right."

Sheila lay down on the floor and pulled the blanket up over her. Silence descended then. Sleepy, I dozed.

"I liked tonight," Sheila said softly into the darkness. "I like Hugh. You're lucky."

"Yes."

"I had a really good time. That's about the most I can remember laughing in a long, long time," she said.

"Hmmm."

"I hope I get a boyfriend like Hugh someday."

Dozing, I'm not sure I responded.

"Tor?"

I roused myself. "Yes?"

"Do you really fuck him?"

"It seems I've heard this question before," I murmured. "You seem unusually interested in my love life."

"It's just I can't picture you doing it."

I smiled into the darkness.

"Actually," she said, "I'm not sure I want to. It seems so awful to me. I'm not kidding, I'm never going to do it of my own free will."

"You might feel very differently when the right boy comes along."

"No, I don't think so."

A quiet interlude followed, a deep, pensive silence, heightened by the darkness. Then at last her voice, "Tor?"

"Hm?"

"Do you think I'm ever going to get a boyfriend? I mean, if I won't do sex with him, will any boy ever want me?"

"A real boyfriend will love you for much more than sex. And who knows? You *might* feel differently. It's a natural part of loving a man—wanting to touch him, wanting him to touch you."

315

She didn't respond.

"You've had bad experiences, Sheil. Hideous experiences, that a kid just should never have to go through. You've been fucked up in the real sense of the word and that's tragic. But this isn't fucking, not this natural feeling. It *is* love; it's part of love, and you can tell that, because when it happens, it makes you feel happy."

The conversation drifted away then. I had the sense of a thinking silence again, and then, just silence. Settling back into my covers, I closed my eyes.

"I hope he's like Hugh. Funny like him," she said.

"Yes, I hope so too. Hugh's good." A pause. "Now, I hate to be a party pooper, but it's very late. We'll feel like sheep vomit tomorrow morning if we don't go to sleep."

A chuckle from down on the floor. Then silence.

Then her voice again, soft in the darkness. "You know what this reminded me of, this tonight?"

"What's that?"

"Remember that time with your other boyfriend? What was his name? Chad? Remember when he took you and me out for pizza? This tonight was like then. Fun, like that time was."

"You remember that?" I asked, because I distinctly recalled her saying she hadn't remembered it when she was fourteen.

"Yeah. Sort of. Well, not every little detail, but what I remember was the feeling. Feeling really happy. Being with you and him and feeling so good. I remember thinking, this is what it must feel like, if you got a real mom and dad."

I smiled into the darkness. "Yes; I remember feeling good that night."

"It was that way tonight, kind of, too. You know. Kind of a family feeling. Like ... well, a belonging feeling."

"Yes."

"It's nice to feel that way. It's nice to think that the people you're with aren't looking for the first opportunity to open a door and shove you out."

Chapter 30

Dear Mom,
I was a lot of trouble in those days. That's
probably why you had to do what you did. I
think I can understand it, because it was prob-
ably the only thing you could do. But I'm a lot
better now. Here are my good points:

1) I can cook
2) I can do housework really well
3) I will get a job when I get out of here and
   earn money
4) I get mostly A's at school and so am on the
   Honor Roll (well, I was on the Honor Roll
   at my old school. There isn't one here, but
   I will be on one, if I go to another school).
5) I will do what you want now, because I'm
   old enough to know.

October came. Knowing I was her only visitor, I continued to see Sheila on a near weekly basis, and her improvement was remarkable over the early part of the fall. She was keen now to earn points in hopes of a Saturday afternoon spent out away from the ranch and Jane reported much improved cooperation during the week. Sheila still eschewed the company of the other youngsters, but this didn't bother me too much.

With her father's parole coming up at the end of the month, plans were afoot for Sheila's release as well. Jane intended to keep her at the ranch until the middle of November to give Mr. Renstad a chance to get settled. After our last unpleasant parting, I had not talked to Mr. Renstad again and I didn't know if he realized that I was involved with Sheila yet again. As a consequence, all my information came from Jane. She had already told me that Social Services had made his evidencing some sort of stable lifestyle a prerogative of getting Sheila back; however, in October, Jane said that employment in Broadview had been arranged for him through a prison rehabilitation program and all that was left was finding him a place to live.

Sheila took all this news and activity fairly calmly. She'd been through it all on at least three previous occasions, and so maintained an "I'll believe it when I see it" sort of skepticism. And of course, there was another matter.

"Torey! Torey! Come here." She motioned excitedly, when I arrived on the Saturday before Columbus Day. Quickly shutting the door to her room behind me when I came in, she bounced over her bed. "Sit down. I want to show you something."

I sat.

Leaning over her bed, Sheila pulled out the under-bed box where she stored all her treasured possessions. She lifted the cardboard lid and extracted a letter. This she pressed to her chest and grinned at me. "Guess what! Guess what this is." But before I could guess, she thrust it into my hands. "It's from my mother."

I took the letter from her.

"Remember that ad I put in? You know, in the paper? Well, it worked! She saw it and she's written me this whole long letter."

The letter *was* long. There must have been ten or twelve pages written on both sides of the paper in a small, scrawled handwriting. I unfolded it, pressing it flat on my knees, and began to read.

Within the first few paragraphs, my heart sank. There was a strange, desperate note to the writer's prose. She said she had given up a daughter for adoption and then went on for several pages telling a very convoluted story of emotional problems and abusive marriages.

"Sheil, I hate to say this, but ... I'm not sure this is your mother."

"It *is*. She says the girl was four. *I* was four," Sheila replied. "I mean, how many four-year-old girls could this have happened to?"

"Well, not very many in your exact circumstances, but she doesn't mention the exact circumstances. And besides, she says 'give up for adoption.' What your mother did was not quite what I'd call 'give up for adoption.'"

"Yeah, I know, but she was upset," Sheila countered. "Look how she keeps saying how upset she was. God, it's, like, wrecked her whole life. And I knew that's what it would be like. I knew my mom would be so sorry it happened, and she'd want me back, if she only knew where to find me."

Lifting my head, I regarded Sheila. I had seen that look so often in her eyes. She could have been six again, for all the poignant vulnerability in her expression. So desperately, she wanted this to be true. I reached my hand out to touch her shoulder, but she pulled back.

"She *says* my name is Sheila. She knows that," she insisted.

"Lovey ..."

"But she *says*."

"You told her that. Your name was in the advert, wasn't it?"

"But she *says*. Why would somebody lie about something like a name? Why would she want to contact me, if I wasn't her daughter?"

"Because sometimes there are people with very bad problems who can't tell what's real from what isn't real," I replied.

Anger suddenly flared in her eyes. "That's me, huh? That's what you think I am. Crazy. Go ahead, say it, Torey, 'cause that's what you're trying to say."

"That's *not* what I'm trying to say. I'm referring to her, this woman who's written this, not you. I think she wants you to be her daughter. I think she may even believe you are, but you aren't."

"*I am*! That's my mom. I know it is. Read the whole letter. You've just read a few pages. She talks about Jimmie in there. She talks about him and about my having four more brothers too. Younger brothers, 'cause she got married again."

My shoulders dropped. "But you gave Jimmie's name in the advert, Sheila. She's going to know your brother's name is Jimmie before she even wrote the letter, because you *told* her yourself."

Tears came to her eyes. "You're just being spiteful. You don't *want* me to find my mom."

Again, I reached my arms out to her. "Sheila, come on."

Struggling to keep her composure, she turned away from me.

"Sheil, I do want you to find your mom. Nothing would make me happier, simply because I know how happy it would make you; but I don't want you to get hurt even worse than you have been. And I'm so afraid that's what's going to happen here."

"Go away."

"Sheil …"

"Go away. Go *on*. I don't want to see you this weekend. Just go away."

No little "Dear Mom" notes came to me during that week, and when I came the following weekend, Sheila said no more about the letter. She wasn't her usual friendly self, so I could tell I had wounded her badly in the disagreement and she was still keeping her distance. I felt it would be unwise to introduce the issue myself, and felt I would get further by simply being warm and supportive and waiting for her to make the next move. We chatted pleasantly enough. Most of the conversation centered around her preparations for leaving the ranch. Sheila was going to be changing from the small, self-contained school room at the ranch to a large Broadview high school, and she was curious about what kind of curriculum would be offered. We discussed the merits of various courses of study and I mentioned the advantages of selecting a curriculum that would enhance her college placement.

This was the first time the subject of Sheila's life after graduation had been raised. She was now a senior and such decisions should have been looming large, but I had thus far never been included in many conversations regarding her academic future. This was partly because school was the one area where Sheila seemed to be managing well on her own, and partly because Sheila's present was so chaotic that it was hard to divert any attention to considering her future. To my shock, Sheila stated that she had no intention whatsoever of going to college after she graduated.

"You're joking."

"No," she replied. "I don't want to go."

"Of course you do," I said.

"No. I'm fed up with school. I just want to be out on my own. Have a place to live where I can be the boss. I'm not going back into school the minute I get out."

This stunned me. With Sheila's IQ, with her interest in ancient history, her facility for learning Latin and reading old texts, I couldn't imagine that she wouldn't be longing for higher education. I tried to explain to her how much different university life was to high school, how easy she would find the lifestyle. She had long since developed the ability to study on her own, as her environment had never been particularly nurturing educationally, and I pointed out how this would set her ahead in the university community, how she was already likely to succeed.

All my words were of no avail. Unlike the week before, Sheila didn't become angry. I don't think she had that much invested in the discussion. This wasn't an important area to her and she wasn't bothered about defending it; however, she remained adamant. When school was finished, she was going to find a job, her own apartment and get on with life. College could wait.

In our office the following Wednesday, Jules and I were enjoying a leisurely chat over coffee when the telephone rang. The phone sat on a chair between our two desks, and consequently we both moved to answer it, but Jules was closer. He picked it up, then grimaced. "Wouldn't you know? If I answer it, it's always for you." He handed it over.

Jane Timmons was on the other end. "We've got a problem here," she said. "Sheila's disappeared."

"Where? When?"

"She had a supervised visit into the city this morning to get clothes and Annie had taken her into MacGregor's department store. I mean, honestly, Torey, we didn't think she was much of a security risk at this point. She's less than three weeks from being released anyway. She went to use the ladies' and Annie was standing right outside, and she just never came out."

"What happened? Is there a window or something?" I asked.

"Yup. But it's on the second floor. God knows how she did it or where she went from there. It's a flat roof, but ..."

In this brief conversation, Sheila was once more transformed from the pleasant, lively girl I knew into a stranger, familiar with worlds I could hardly imagine.

"The obvious question," Jane continued, "is: she hasn't turned up over there, I assume?"

"No."

"Well ..."

"Is there anything I can do?" I asked.

"Not really. We've contacted the police. Contacted the prison in Marysville where her father is, although I should like to think she's not going to get that far afield." A pause. "Do you have any ideas where she might turn up? Know any friends or anything?"

The first thing to come to mind, of course, was her mother.

"There was a letter ..." I started and then briefly explained Sheila's efforts in that direction.

"Yes, we know about all that," Jane said.

"Oh?" This surprised me, because Sheila had given no indication of having shared this with the staff.

"Routine precautions. We go through all the kids' stuff regularly. We'd known she was writing to newspapers down in California, and I'd not given her any hassle about it. I mean, it seemed harmless enough, and God knows, if the kid could turn up another relative who'd take her, that'd be a blessing. Her father's not exactly made of gold, is he?"

"But did you know about this letter?" I asked. "From this woman in northern California?"

"Yeah, I saw it. Holly brought it in last week for me to take a look at," Jane replied. "Sad, wasn't it?"

The offhandedness, both with which Sheila's things were searched and with which her actions were dismissed, annoyed me deeply, making me unwilling to discuss in any detail my feelings on the importance of this material in relation to Sheila's disappearance. I had never especially liked Jane throughout the period I had dealt with her, but now I felt contempt.

That single telephone call was the last I heard on the matter. Jane didn't call me again. I phoned out to the ranch myself on both Thursday and Friday, but Jane was unavailable and the deputy director told me that they had, as yet, had no success in locating Sheila.

In the first few days after Sheila ran away, I expected to hear from her, or, like the time with Alejo, I thought she might turn up on my doorstep. I was uneasy, because I feared for her physical safety, but I still felt confident that everything would soon resolve itself. After all, how long could she simply disappear?

Quite a long time, I was to discover. Days turned into a week. One week, two weeks went by. Mr. Renstad was released from prison and moved back to Broadview and Sheila was still missing.

I couldn't believe this. I simply could not believe that the girl could just disappear without a trace, and for the first time I came up against the nightmarish reality of how police and other Social Service agencies dealt with the issue of runaway children. And not for the first time, I was forced to confront how different Sheila's world was from mine.

It was impossible not to worry about her. I could imagine all sorts of things, not the least of them that she had actually found this demented woman in California. Or her mother. In a best-case scenario, I pictured her reunited with her mother and Jimmie, living the kind of life she'd always wanted, and I tried to convince myself that's what had happened and that was why she hadn't contacted me. Unfortunately, several variants of worst-case scenarios kept intruding on my thoughts.

November came and I was having to come to terms with the fact that Sheila had yet again dropped abruptly out of my life. As with all such experiences, time finally started to heal my sense of frustration and even the gnawing worry. One evening, I came across the sheaf of "Dear Mom" letters that I had kept in the front of the filing drawer. Instead of leaving them there, I took them out and put them in a box in the attic with all the other mementos of past children. The next morning, I moved the copy of *One Child* I usually kept on my desk to a place where my eye wouldn't fall on it casually.

I was in the midst of a play therapy session with a small, nonverbal four-year-old named Bobby. He was a difficult case, referred to me by one of the other psychiatrists for evaluation, because no one could discern why he didn't talk; and I did not anticipate being disturbed, as everyone knew I was videotaping the session. Nonetheless, just as I was eliciting some excited babbling from Bobby by blowing soap bubbles, my beeper went off. I tried to ignore it, but when I didn't respond, it went off again.

Irritated, I rose and went to the phone on the wall in the therapy room and dialed the front office with one hand, while trying to turn off the video camera with the other. Bemused by my antics, Bobby threw his security blanket over the camera to produce a woolly ending to our taping.

"Well, it's just me who's beeping you," said Rosalie, who worked in the front office. "We've just gotten a fax in for you and I think you ought to come down and have a look at it."

"Right now? I'm in therapy," I said.

"Yeah, Torey, I think you should come right now."

Bringing Bobby with me, I went down to the office at the front of the building and took the fax from my mail hatch. I read it.

Come away, O human child!
To the waters and the wild
With a faery, hand in hand,
For the world's more full of weeping than you
    can understand.

The world's not made for some of us, Torey. The little prince found this out. So did Cleopatra and I think I have too. There's nothing here for me. I'm from some other place. I don't belong here. The world's more full of weeping than I can understand.

Thanks for trying. And don't try to fax me back. I'm doing this from a store and I don't want an answer.

Love, Sheila

"Oh, Jesus," I said, when I'd read it.

"Yeah," Rosalie replied. "When I saw it, I thought you'd better have this quick."

"I've got to get ahold of her." Scanning the paper, I noticed up at the very top in tiny type the fax-sender information. Grabbing the telephone on Rosalie's desk, I rang information. The fax number was identified as coming from northern California, and within moments, I had the telephone number of the store from which Sheila had sent the fax. I phoned immediately.

"Hello, yes, you've just sent a fax to me. It would have been sent by a young girl. Sixteen. Is she still there? This is very important. I must talk to her."

The person who had answered put the telephone on hold and what felt like a hundred years passed, while I waited. Then a click and human sounds followed.

"Hullo?" It was Sheila's voice.

Chapter 31

"Sheila? Sheila, it's me. It's Torcy."

There was no response. She was still there. I could hear the soft sound of her breathing carrying across the miles between us.

"Sheil? Are you okay?"

"How did you find me?"

"Listen to me. Are you okay?" I asked again. "Where are you? What is this place I'm calling?"

"It's the Copyprint store," she answered. There was a numb quality to her voice. I think I had genuinely startled her by tracing the fax so quickly and she didn't know quite how to respond.

"Are you okay?"

"I don't want to talk to you."

"No, Sheila, don't put the phone down. Please? Please?"

"Just leave me alone, okay?" There were tears in her voice. I could hear them in the faint abruptness of her breathing, but she was struggling to keep them subdued.

"No, Sheila. Talk to me. Come on. Stay on the line a bit. Tell me what you've been doing."

Silence.

"What's been happening?"

A sharp intake of air.

"Sheil, don't hang up on me."

"I'm not going to," came the very small voice at the other end.

"Things not been going very well?"

"No."

"What's happened?" I asked. "Can you tell me?"

"I can't talk here. Everybody's listening."

"Well, I want to talk to you. I do. Can you find another phone? No ... wait, don't hang up. Wait. Let me think of something."

"I can't find my mom, Torey," she said. "I've been looking for her and looking for her and I can't find her."

"Oh, lovey."

"Oh fuck, I'm going to cry. Oh, no. I don't want to cry here. Oh, no."

"Sheil, I'm going to come and get you."

"Huh?"

"Don't do anything, okay? All right? And I'll come and get you. I'll bring you home. Can you tell me where you are? Where are you staying?"

Tears thickened her voice again. "I'm not staying anywhere. I'm all by myself."

"Okay, well, listen, stay where you are. I've got the fax number. Let me make some arrangements and I'll fax them back to you there. But stay there and wait for me. And *don't do anything*. All right? Promise me?"

She was crying. Whether from anguish or relief, I couldn't tell, but through her tears she promised she'd stay at the Copyprint place until I faxed back.

The next hour was frantic. She was in a relatively small town in northern California, which wasn't served by a commercial airport. In fact, it was a good two hours' drive away from San Francisco, which was the nearest place to have more than one daily flight from my city. And the flight from here to there was two hours. That made four hours from departure the very least I could expect. Then came disaster. We were approaching the Thanksgiving Day weekend; so when I rang the airport to book a seat, I discovered all the economy seats were booked, not only on the next flight out, but also on the one after that. This meant I wouldn't be able to leave until the middle of the following day at the earliest. This was awful. I felt it was critical that I did go get her, rather than rely on her in her unstable state to make her way back here by herself, especially as she had never flown before and was unfamiliar with the general procedures surrounding air travel. I didn't trust how she might react if I tried to call in outside help, such as the police or Social Services, from the California community she was in.

Then, right in the midst of my panic, my beeper went off again. "Curse this thing," I muttered at Jules. Whipping it off, I threw it across the desk-top.

Jules regarded it, still beeping, then me. "Don't you think you should answer it?" he asked.

Wearily, I phoned down to Rosalie, who trans-ferred the caller. "Help, help! I'm dying! Save me, Doctor! Quick! An infusion of cabernet sauvignon and T-bone steak!" the caller cried in a weak voice. "Tonight at six?"

"*Hugh!* Honestly. You *know* you're not sup-posed to do this."

He was totally unrepentant, as he always was, but it sounded so good to hear his voice that I couldn't be angry. I told him the whole horrible story with Sheila and how I felt it was critical that I got to her as soon as possible, but how impossible that was turning out to be.

Hugh listened thoughtfully. "Book a first-class seat out," he replied. "They won't be full."

I snorted. "I can hardly afford economy, much less first class, Hugh. And I certainly couldn't bring her back that way. Even if I can find seats, and I can't. It's even worse coming back. It's the run up to Thanksgiving that's doing it. There's just noth-ing there."

"I'll pay for it," he said. "I'll get you a ticket. Then maybe you can rent a car. You'll need to rent a car anyway, to get up to her. Then you can just drive home from there. Don't worry. I'll take care of it, okay?"

Stunned by the generosity of his offer, I didn't know quite what to say.

"Well, she's an okay kid," he replied to my silence. "And after all, what's a few bucks in life?"

I told Sheila to meet me in the local McDonald's, as it was about the only place I could think of that would be open late at night, relatively safe for her to wait in and a location I could easily find in a strange town. Hugh financed a first-class ticket to San Francisco for me and I made arrangements to rent a car from there, drive up the coast and pick Sheila up before driving home, a journey of over eight hundred miles.

It never crossed my mind not to do this for Sheila. Always a bit impulsive, I was inclined to get myself into what Hugh termed "grand acts," but I don't think I could have comfortably done otherwise. I always felt a sort of intuitive certainty about my part in a given situation, which, although it made me tend to act first and think later, seldom put me on a course of action that I later regretted. Going personally to get Sheila felt right in this instance, so right, in fact, that I never contemplated any alternatives.

It was ten-fifteen when I pulled under the bright-yellow glow of the McDonald's arches. I could see Sheila through the window, a lone figure hunched over a table. Turning off the ignition, I got out.

She didn't rise when I came through the door, simply lifted her head and watched me. There was a faint smile on her face, an expression of what I took to be relief. Coming to the table, I bent down and hugged her to me. She came willingly, clutching the folds of my wool jacket.

Slipping down on the bench opposite, I regarded her. She was filthy, filthy in the old sense of the word, as she had been when she had first come into my class. Her uncombed hair hung in long greasy strands. The dirt was worn in around her fingernails and up the creases of her skin. Her clothes were rumpled and stained. And just as in the old days, she stank.

"Are you hungry?" I asked.

"Well, I've had some French fries. I thought I better eat something or they'd kick me out."

I myself wasn't hungry. I'd eaten on the plane in a manner quite unlike what I'd been accustomed to and Big Macs were rather an anticlimax, but I went over to the counter and bought one for each of us, along with a large order of fries. I'd had the foresight to bring a thermos flask for coffee to fortify me on the long drive ahead, so I had the girl behind the counter fill that for me, while I got Sheila a milk shake.

Sheila devoured her hamburger and quickly laid into mine, when I said I wasn't hungry for it. Again I was drawn back across the years to see her as she had been, a desperately hungry six-year-old, using both hands to stuff her school lunch into her mouth. There wasn't much more finesse tonight and I guessed she hadn't seen much food in the past few days.

"So, where have you been living?" I asked.

She shrugged. "Wherever I could."

"What kind of money have you got?"

"At the moment? Eighty-five cents. I started out with twenty-three fifty, after I bought my bus ticket, and I've been trying to be careful with it, but ..." She smiled apologetically.

And so we chatted, while she ate, as if nothing at all had happened. I found out from her that she had used my telephone that Saturday she was over to get bus schedules and prices. She described how she had managed to scrimp out the money she needed from the allowances given the children at the ranch. It was fascinating hearing all this, because it showed such intricate planning, and even I had not suspected anything. What we didn't talk about, however, was why she'd done it and what had come of it. Pulling myself back to observe objectively as we spoke, I looked for the signs of suicidal desperation, which I reckoned were still there.

When she had finished, I glanced at my watch. "Well, I suppose we had better be on our way."

Sheila just sat.

I regarded her.

"I don't want to go back to the ranch, Torey. If you've come all this way to take me back there, you might as well have stayed home, because I'm not going. It's a dead zone there and I'm finished with it."

"No. We'll work something out. Your dad's got a place in Broadview. He's settled ..."

Sheila still sat.

"Come on, lovey, let's go."

She let out a great, long sigh and let her shoulders drop. Then, wearily, she hoisted herself up from the seat and came with me.

Pulling the car out of the McDonald's, I sped off down the main road and out onto the highway. I love driving, particularly long-distance driving, for the sense of relaxed autonomy it gives me. When I really get going, it's almost a transcendent experience, giving me the feeling of expanding into a state of unhindered freedom. Having managed to accomplish the most important part of my mission—getting Sheila into the car to come home with me—I was in a superb mood.

Beside me, Sheila sat slumped in her seat. She didn't say anything for several miles. Initially I thought she was going to go to sleep, because it was obvious she was very tired, but she didn't. She just sat, elbow on the car door, hand bracing her cheek, eyes on the road ahead.

The road was absolutely empty. Having chosen the most direct route home, I wasn't on the freeway, but on a minor highway heading due east. At that hour, there was simply no one else driving. In fact, for long stretches there were no lights anywhere, not even from farm buildings.

In the confined space of the car I could perceive Sheila's pain much more clearly than I'd been able to in the plastic cheerfulness of McDonald's. It was almost a physical thing. I would have expected to touch it, had I reached out my hand, and for many miles, I didn't know what would be the best thing to do. Sit in silence? Encourage her to talk? Or maybe just carry on, as if this were all a perfectly ordinary thing to be speeding through the night eight hundred miles from home, and wait for it all to come out in its natural course.

Sheila took down the hand bracing her cheek and folded her arms across her chest. Blowing the hair out of her face, she turned her head and looked over at me. "How come you did this? Came all this way out and got me?"

"Because I love you. Simple as that."

She turned from me, looked out the window at the deep darkness and remained so for a long time. When finally she turned back, I could see tears on her cheeks. They glimmered wanly in the pale green glow of the dashboard lights.

"Want to talk about it?" I asked.

She shook her head. Bringing a hand up, she wiped away the tears, but they came again. And again. She grew visibly upset, a sorrowful anger erupting when she couldn't stanch the tears.

"There are tissues in my handbag," I said and pointed into the backseat.

"I don't want this to happen. I don't *want* to cry."

"It's okay, lovey. I don't mind."

"I *do* mind," she retorted. "I don't *want* to cry. If I let myself start, I'm never going to stop."

"That's been the fear for a long time, hasn't it?"

She nodded and the tears came harder, but she still fought against them. "I'm so fucking angry! I don't want to give in. I don't want to cry. It just makes me weak."

"No, not weak."

"It's not fair! Not right. *You* shouldn't be here. It should have been my mom saying all this to me. Not some teacher." Lifting her head, she looked over at me. "Excuse the term, Torey, but that's all you are. Where are the people who are *supposed* to love me?"

I regarded her.

"Where the fuck *are* they? Where's my mom? Where's my dad, for that matter? Why's it always got to be people like you who do these things for me? Why have my parents never taken care of me? Am I that bad?" And the tears overwhelmed her. Falling into noisy, inelegant sobs, she slumped against the shoulder strap of her seat belt and wept.

I didn't say anything. There come those times when words would seem as if they were a good idea, but in reality they are too paltry for the job.

I remembered another time like this. Drawn back across the years, I was no longer in the nighttime darkness of the car, but in the daytime darkness of the small book closet at school with Sheila, who was weeping in my arms. She'd been a fierce little tiger for so long that they had been the first tears I'd seen her shed, although the school year was almost over. She'd always feared the abyss beneath her tears.

Sheila cried for a very long time. Pulling her legs up and pressing her arms against them, she buried her face and sobbed into the tattered fabric of her jacket. I said nothing, did nothing other than speed us onward through the dark. We were in the mountains by then, the trees coming right down to the road on either side. It had begun to snow, the large, downy flakes falling mesmerizingly before the headlights of the car. The late hour, the darkness, the trees, the snow all combined to create a weird, otherworldly aura. Things no longer felt quite real to me.

At last, the end. She snuffled, hiccuped and struggled to draw breath, but the crying had ceased. Silence followed, a long, deep silence, so crowded with thoughts as to make them nearly palpable.

"I remember that boy," she said, her voice very, very soft and still faintly embroidered with the aftermath of her tears, "that boy I took into the woods."

Watching out through the wipers at the snow, I kept very still. Sheila had never spoken of the abduction that had brought her into my class, which had nearly sentenced her to a childhood spent in a mental institution. Of all the things Sheila had told about over the years, that incident had never once even been alluded to.

"I used to watch him in his yard. He had a swing and his mom would take him out and push him in it. I used to watch. He had a plastic riding car shaped like an elephant. He used to get on it and his daddy would push him. I used to watch him. And then ... He was out there one day by himself and I said, 'You want to come along?' Or something like that. I don't remember exactly now.

But I undid the latch on the gate to his yard and let him out. And I took him in the woods.

"I don't think I ever intended to hurt him. I had this piece of rope with me, but it was just something I had found down by the railroad tracks. I didn't bring it specially or anything; I just had it. And I don't remember *wanting* to hurt him, not in the beginning anyway. I remember walking, taking him into the woods … I made him pull down his pants. I wanted to see his penis. I remember that. I remember thinking, he's just like Jimmie. He *was* just like Jimmie. And I hated him. Torey, I had some thoughts in my mind then that … I mean, I still remember them just like they were yesterday. I remember *exactly* how I felt looking at that little boy. I just hated him so bad and I thought … You're going to hate me, when I say this to you, but … I thought, I want to kill him."

There was a long pause. Sheila lowered her head and regarded her hands in her lap. "I *was* a wicked little girl. Just like my pa said."

I didn't speak.

Sheila looked over. "Do *you* hate me now?"

"No."

"Why not? I would have. If it hadn't been that boy's lucky day, I would have killed him."

I had my eyes on the road, but I could see her in my peripheral vision. She continued to regard me. Finally, she looked away. "I'm a murderer."

"He didn't die, Sheila."

"He would have died. It was just luck he didn't." She drew in a long breath. "I can never forget this. I've never told anybody. I haven't dared tell anybody, but it just sits in my mind. Every good thing that ever happens gets eaten up by this thing, sitting there. I think: I am so wicked. No wonder things keep happening to me. I deserve them. I'm so bad even my own mother couldn't stand me."

"Your mother had nothing to do with it. She left you long before you took that little boy. In fact, if I had to venture any explanation, it's that it was the other way around. She didn't leave you because you did such things. You did such things because she left you."

"So why did she leave me then?"

"Most likely, because she had problems of her own. Because she was a very young girl. She was only fourteen when you were born. Did you know that? *Fourteen*."

No reply.

"So, she would have only been eighteen on that night she left. About a year and a half older than you are now. And she had two kids to worry about and a husband in jail."

Pulling her bottom lip between her teeth, Sheila chewed it.

"I don't think your mother planned to abandon you, any more than you planned to hurt that little boy. I think she was simply overwhelmed. She was pushed to her limits and could cope with not one thing more, not even a small girl acting up in the backseat. And like most of us when we can fight no longer, she ran away."

Sheila made a small, derisive sound. "Well, I sure got her blood, huh? Always running away from my problems."

"Oh, no," I said. "You're not like her. You're much stronger. Much better."

"How can you say that?"

"You might run away when the going gets tough, but the difference is, you come back."

Sheila considered, then slowly nodded. "Yeah, I suppose so."

Chapter 32

During the adrenaline phase of this adventure, I'd had visions of driving all the way back home without stopping, but the folly of that idea began to make itself known by about one in the morning. As we came down out of the mountains and started across the wide expanse of Nevada flatlands, I kept an eye out for motels showing signs of life at the front desk so late at night and finally found one on the outskirts of a small town.

Too tired for anything more than a quick wash, I settled into bed soon after we got in the room; but Sheila, who hadn't been in contact with hot water for weeks, judging from the appearance of her, raided my overnight bag for shampoo and conditioner and disappeared into the bathroom for longer than I could keep my eyes open.

The noise of her rummaging through her things when she came out of the bathroom woke me again, and I lay watching her get ready for bed. "I wish I had something clean to wear," she muttered. "Everything's so grotty." Then she slipped into her bed and put the light out.

An ancient radiator beside my bed heaved and sighed in the darkness. I pulled the blankets up close to ward off the November night.

Sheila turned in her bed. "I don't feel sleepy," she murmured. "I keep thinking about all the things we've been talking about tonight."

The radiator belched, wheezed and settled down again.

"And you know? In a way, I feel really angry with my parents. I *was* just a little kid. I feel so cheated. They should have protected me from all of this."

"Yes, I think you're right."

"It's occurring to me now that maybe ... well ... maybe I couldn't help how I was. I was an awful little kid; I know I was, but ... maybe I didn't deserve what my parents did to me."

Good, I was thinking.

Sheila would have quite happily slept around the clock, I think, and no doubt she needed to, because I think it was probably the first real bed she'd had in some time. However, the weather was deteriorating and I wanted to be on my way, so I prized her out at nine-thirty.

Exhaustion was taking its toll with Sheila. Her mood seemed lighter than the night before, but she was by no means chatty. A remark or two would pass between us and then ten or fifteen minutes' silence before the next comment. I amused myself trying to keep the radio tuned.

"I went to see that lady that answered my ad. And, like you probably already guessed, she wasn't my mother. Thank God." A second small smile. "She was just nuts. Like you said."

I grinned over at her. She shrugged.

"What else did you do?" I asked.

"Nothing, really. For a long time I thought, well … I mean, I just kept hoping I still might find her. I was in California and she was in California. Someplace. I just kept hoping …" Sheila turned her head and looked out the window. "It was pretty awful. I didn't have anyplace to go. I didn't have very much money. I had to sleep rough, mostly. In doorways and stuff. And try to keep away from the weirdos. And I was so fucking cold. And hungry …"

"Why didn't you call me?" I asked.

She shrugged. "I dunno. At first I wasn't going to tell you. I hate you when you're right. You don't exactly rub it in, but you sort of … emanate it. Besides, I didn't want to go back. I still don't, really."

A pause.

"What do you think I should do now?" Sheila asked. "Go back to my dad?"

"Yes, probably. And if you want to know what I think you should really do, it's knuckle down to your schoolwork, so you can get yourself a

347

scholarship. There's still time, and with your kind of talents, there'll be a lot of universities who'd be eager to accept you. I know what you said about not going to university right after high school, Sheil, but believe me, I think it would be the ideal setting for you. You'd love it. You'd have all the freedom you need, and still it's a protected environment. You can study just what you want and really go. Really let your mind race. I think that'd be so good for you."

She sighed. "Yeah, probably."

After that, Sheila slept. We were within the last hundred and fifty miles and I filled the time trying to figure out the logistics of returning her anywhere. Her father wouldn't be expecting her and I certainly didn't want to let Jane or any of the Social Services get ahold of her at that point. The best idea seemed to take her back to my apartment and then contact her father. The following day was Thanksgiving, so I toyed with the idea of inviting Mr. Renstad over and making a big meal for everyone. Somehow, that seemed appropriate.

Sheila roused as I reached the traffic-light stop-and-go driving of the city. She sat up, stretched and rubbed her face. "God, I'm back," she said, looking out the window. From her tone, I couldn't discern whether she was glad or not. I explained to her my general game plan.

"No," she said.

"No?"

"No. Take me home to my dad." She glanced over at me. "For about the last hour, I've been just laying here with my eyes closed, but I haven't been fully asleep. I've been thinking. Thinking over and over and over what we've been talking about, and I've decided I want to go home."

Surprised, I nodded. "All right."

"Do you remember that summer when I was working with you and Jeff in the summer school?"

"Yes."

"Well, remember that one time I asked you if you thought things were ever going to get better for me, if my life was ever going to be normal? And remember what you said?"

I hesitated, trying to recall.

"*I* remember it, because I took very close note of it. You said I had to come to terms with things. I had to accept that my mom had left me. Accept that maybe it was just something that had to happen and it wasn't my fault. And then you said I had to forgive and let go."

I nodded.

"Well, I think I've come to the first point. I was just sitting here, thinking it through, and you know, I don't feel like it was my fault anymore. It still hurts me like hell. I still wish it didn't happen, but it did, and I can see now that maybe my mom just had her own problems, that it was just my bad luck to have been part of them."

She pondered a moment. "And maybe that's true for my dad too. Whatever. Anyway, I'm thinking, like, I can't go over it, I can't go under it, I

349

can't go around it. I've been trying all of them. So, I better go through it."

A small silence.

"I think I'm seeing things differently now," she said. "I think I can accept it."

"Good."

Coming up to the junction turnoff for my road, I held the car at the intersection a long moment, but when Sheila didn't say anything further, I stepped on the accelerator and went on through to join the freeway to Broadview.

"You know," Sheila said, "what I've been thinking most about is what you said about letting go. Accepting, forgiving and then letting go. I think I can accept. I think I can even forgive, but I've been wondering and wondering about letting go. Trying to figure out what 'letting go' entails, and all I can think of is that it means living your life forward. Starting to think of the future more than the past."

"Yes, I think that probably puts it very well."

A small, pensive silence. "You know, I don't think I've ever lived my life forward before," she said. "Even when I wasn't remembering things, I was always wanting to go back."

I nodded.

"If my mom was fourteen when I was born," she said, "if my dad was the same butthead he's always been with me, then there probably never was a golden age. It's weird to realize now that most likely there never really was a 'back.'"

Sheila returned to her father. I didn't make them the all-American Thanksgiving dinner the next day, which would have made for such a storybook ending. In fact, after dropping Sheila off there, I didn't see her again for three weeks.

That journey back from California through the snowy darkness proved to be one of more than physical dimensions, however. Sheila ventured out of other darknesses as well. When we next met in the days just before Christmas, I found quite a different girl. Relaxed and cheerful, she treated me to lunch downtown and spent the entire time relating anecdotes from school.

She wasn't particularly impressed with her new school or her course work, but she was doing well—remarkably well for a girl who had had the disrupted education she'd experienced over the previous year. I was particularly pleased to hear that she had joined the Latin club. More extraordinarily, she very nearly admitted to liking it.

We never spoke of our journey that night, nor of her mother, nor of anything of her past. Instead, we ate croissants, went Christmas shopping together and watched the skaters on the rink in the park. I bought her a copy of Aeschylus's *Oresteia* trilogy, which deals with the family of Agamemnon, as a Christmas gift, knowing that ancient story of matricide and forgiveness would speak profoundly to her. She bought me an Arden edition of *Antony and Cleopatra* and then teasingly included the Cliffs Notes for me.

My own life was taking an unexpected turn over that period. I'd opened the Sunday newspaper a couple of weekends earlier and had seen an advertisement for a midyear vacancy in a special education class for emotionally disturbed children. It was in a small community in an adjacent state. The strange fact was that I hadn't been looking for a new job at the time. I'd thought I was perfectly happy at the Sandry. However, the moment I saw the advert, I'd felt a terrible longing to be back in the classroom again.

I told Sheila that I had applied, although at that point I didn't know whether or not I would get the position. She took my news with the same equanimity that I had taken hers about school and the Latin club. She was bemused by my choice to abandon a well-paying job at a private clinic to return to the classroom. Money was becoming an important issue to Sheila and she had a hard time understanding the rationale behind my actions, but she seemed pleased to think I would be a teacher again.

I did get the job and early January found me almost two hundred miles away from the city in a small town called Pecking. I heard from Sheila occasionally. She never was much of a letter writer, so it wasn't often, and then, as usual, they were seldom letters in the traditional sense. Consequently, I didn't always know what was going on. From what I did hear, she continued to be well settled at her school and with her father. He was making another effort at keeping himself out of trouble. I heard a lot about AA. Sheila joined Alateen, and this was where she met Claire. Claire, who was eighteen and also a senior at Sheila's school, had not come from the same deprived background as Sheila. Indeed, hers was a privileged upbringing of tennis lessons and summer camps. Yet, disguised behind all this was a world of parental drunkenness and abuse. Claire and Sheila found in one another the understanding other peers couldn't give them and their friendship grew.

In March we had a two-day break from school and I came up to the city. Stopping by Sheila's house, I had the opportunity to meet Claire myself. She was a solemn girl with very long black hair and glasses that gave her an owlish look. She had about her that terrible seriousness of adolescence that lends itself naturally to discussions of Sartre or ecology, and Sheila kept agreeing with her when she made dark, profound statements to me. For the first time I saw Sheila as she was, an intelligent, articulate teenager creating her own identity.

I didn't see her again until May, when we met for lunch at a pizzeria in the city. I almost didn't recognize her when I saw her. Her bangs, so long in the process of growing out, had finally reached the length of the rest of her hair and were incorporated in a smooth, blunt cut that swept back from her face and down over her shoulders. She had high-lighted it slightly, which brought up the natural blond and drew attention to its glossiness. The punky clothes were gone, but not her natural sense of style. Layered one over the other were two T-shirts, a cotton dress and a denim jacket, teamed with chunky clay jewelry. Her appearance had the modern sophistication of the catwalk.

"Gosh, you're looking good," I said.

"Yeah, thanks." She pulled out the chair across from me and sat down. "I think it's the freedom showing. Six more days of school."

I regarded her. She had been cagey about her plans after graduation. I'd asked her a couple of times in letters, but she had never responded at all, even to tell me which scholarships she was applying for. This left me intrigued and anticipating a surprise. Secretly, I suspected she'd been accepted to a particularly excellent university and was going to use this lunch to tell me.

We chatted amiably, ordered our pizzas, and chatted some more. Sheila told me that Claire had been accepted at Stanford, her first choice.

"And you?" I asked, unable to contain my curiosity any longer. "What are your plans?"

She had been leaning forward, arms folded on the table, as she'd talked with me, and now she lowered her head. There was a smile on her face, but she stayed like that for a long moment. "How am I going to tell you this, Torey?"

I waited.

Finally, she looked up. "I'm not going to college. I got a job three weeks ago working in McDonald's and when I'm done with school, I start full-time."

"McDonald's?" I said in surprise. "Jesus, Sheila, *McDonald's*?"

"Shhhh." She reached a hand across the table and touched my lips. "Don't let the whole place know."

"You're kidding. Yeah? You're pulling my leg."

She shook her head. "No, Torey. I'm not."

"A brain like yours and you're going to be serving hamburgers for a living? Oh, Sheila, you've got to be kidding."

"I like hamburgers."

"But *Sheila* ..." I protested.

She still had the slight smile on her face. "Look, Mom, I got to do this my way."

"I'm not your mom. No kid of mine would be getting away with this."

"You are my mom. If anybody is, it's been you, 'cause I love you just like one. And I know you love me too." She smiled warmly. "And now, Mom, it's time for you to let me grow up. University later. Maybe. Who knows? But for now, it's going to be hamburgers."

"Oh, Sheila, come on. Not really?"

"Don't criticize. Okay?" she said. "Make it like the old days. Say, 'Sheila, whatever you want to do, that's good. I'm here if you need me. I'm behind you.' Say that to me."

I regarded her. For a long moment I met her eyes, gray-blue in the dim light of the pizzeria. Then a sigh and I grinned. "Very well. You do what you think is right. I trust you."

"Thanks, Mom."

Epilogue

Almost ten years have passed since that afternoon in the pizzeria and Sheila is now older than I was the year I had her in my classroom. She still works in the fast-food industry; however, she doesn't serve hamburgers anymore. Possessed of an unexpectedly astute business mind, she is now manager of her branch and is expected shortly to become one of the youngest franchise holders in her part of the country.

I must admit that, successful as she is, this probably still would not have been what I would have chosen for her, and it is still a little hard for me to come to terms with all that talent being given over to hamburgers. Sheila, when she's in the mood for awful puns, says she relishes her work. She relishes my discomfiture too, I suspect, which is probably the best sign of all. She's her own person now,

comfortable with whom she's become. Her decisions, her plans, her self-worth are not dependent
on my or anyone else's approval.

Sheila does, of course, still have occasional difficulties. Hers was an enormously deprived and abusive childhood, and it would be unrealistic to
expect those experiences not to resurface sporadi-
cally. This happens most notably in her interpersonal relationships. She appears to do well in the
clearly delineated relationships of the workplace,
particularly in managerial situations where there is
no question of the personal intruding on the professional. However, she continues to be challenged
in her private life and finds it particularly difficult
to form close relationships with men. But on the
whole, she has developed into a remarkably stable
and competent young woman.

Perhaps the best way to end is with the last
"Dear Mom" letter I received from Sheila. She'd
kept a diary during the middle years of her teens
and had copied into it the same "Dear Mom" letters that she'd been sending to me. A few years
ago, she came across her old diary and after reading through those letters, she wrote to me telling
me about it. Fixed to the back of her letter was
this:

Dear Mom,
Things have turned out pretty good for me.
I've got a great job and my own apartment
and a dog named Mike. I'm sorry, I don't
think about you much anymore. I mean to,

but I just don't get time. It's too bad you never got to know me. I think you would have liked me. I think you would have been proud.

Love, Sheila

Twilight Children

Torey Hayden

Three voices no one heard – until someone listened

The international bestselling author tells a harrowing yet inspirational true story of heartbreaking victimization and recovery …

When special-education teacher Torey Hayden left the classroom to work in a psychiatric ward, a diverse trio entered her life. Abused nine-year-old Cassandra lashed out at anyone who tried to get close. Four-year-old Drake refused to speak to anyone but his mother. And elderly Gerda was trapped in crippling depression and a self-imposed silence after a stroke.

Though Hayden had seen many difficult cases, these three were among the most troubling of her career, testing her at every turn. From interfering family and caregivers to the challenge of building trust, Hayden recounts her experiences and the small, startling breakthroughs that offered hope. *Twilight Children* is the story of one determined woman and three lost souls who battled against overwhelming odds. Told with compassion, sensitivity, and humour, it is a powerful, unforgettable book that reminds us of the strength of the human spirit.

Make
www.thorsonselement.com
your online sanctuary